W9-BZE-756

An Illustrated History of
LATE MEDIEVAL ENGLAND

An Illustrated History of
LATE MEDIEVAL ENGLAND

Edited by
CHRIS GIVEN-WILSON

Manchester University Press
Manchester and New York
distributed exclusively in the USA
and Canada by St. Martin's Press

Published by Manchester University Press
Oxford Road, Manchester M13 9NR, UK
and Room 400, 175 Fifth Avenue,
New York, NY 10010, USA

Distributed exclusively in the USA and Canada
by St. Martin's Press, Inc.,
175 Fifth Avenue, New York, NY 10010, USA

British Library Cataloguing-in-Publication Data
A catalogue record for this book is available from the British Library

Library of Congress Cataloging-in-Publication Data
Given–Wilson, Chris.
    The illustrated history of late medieval England / edited by Chris
Given–Wilson
        p.   cm.
    ISBN 0–7190–4152-X.
    1. Great Britain—History—Lancaster and York, 1399–1485.
    2. Great Britain—History—Plantagenets, 1154–1399.   I. Title.
DA175.G58   1996
942.04—dc20   95–41311
                                                               CIP

ISBN 0 7190 4152 X **hardback**

First published in 1996
00 99 98 97 96   10 9 8 7 6 5 4 3 2 1

Printed in Great Britain
by Redwood Books, Trowbridge

CONTENTS

List of illustrations   page vi
List of contributors   ix
Preface   xi

Introduction: The Late Middle Ages in England   1
Chris Given-Wilson

THE LAND AND THE PEOPLE

The English landscape   21
Mark Bailey
Population and economic resources   41
Mark Bailey
Family and inheritance, women and children   58
Paul Brand
Health, diet, medicine and the plague   82
Simone Macdougall

FORMS OF EXPRESSION

Religious sensibility   103
Richard Davies
Language and literary expression   127
Ian Johnson
Forms of artistic expression   152
Nigel Ramsay

POLITICS AND THE NATION

The political institutions of the realm   181
Ralph Griffiths
Lawmakers and lawbreakers   206
Michael Hicks
Civil war and rebellion   229
Simon Walker
England and its neighbours   248
Chris Given-Wilson

Picture credits   271
Further reading   275
Notes   279
Index   287

ILLUSTRATIONS

COLOUR PLATES

Entry for *anulus* in the encyclopaedia of James le Palmer	page 69
Seating at meals	70
Entry for *adulterium* in the encyclopaedia of James le Palmer	71
Propitious times for operations and medication	72
Bloodletting	105
The toothpuller	106
The crucifixion and other scenes from the life of Christ	123
Dreamer and Pearl-Maiden	124
Initial by William de Brailes	173
Ramsey Abbey censer and boat	174
The Court of King's Bench	191
The Court of Chancery in session	192
Harlech castle from the south	225
Edward I creating his son Prince of Wales	226
The Wilton Diptych	227
Henry VI crowned king of France	228

BLACK AND WHITE ILLUSTRATIONS

East Witton (Yorkshire)	23
Laxton (Nottinghamshire)	25
Brassington (Derbyshire)	27
How Moor (Cambridgeshire)	31
Orford (Suffolk)	33
Ermine Street	34
Bridge at Moulton (Suffolk)	35
Herstmonceux castle (Sussex)	37
Fountains abbey (Yorkshire)	38
Possible long-term flow of English population, 1086–1540	43
Hockwold (Norfolk)	45
A medieval coalmine (Hartington, Derbyshire)	53
Hammer-lake at Mannings Heath (Sussex)	55
Medieval quarrying at Collyweston (Northamptonshire)	56
The heirs of Conan fitz Ellis	59
Claimants to the throne of Scotland	60
The descendants of the kings of England	61
The south porch of Aylesham church (Norfolk)	62
Marriage ceremony	64
Husband bashing	64

Securing annulment	68
Child maintenance	74
Arbor consanguinitatis	76
The ape physician	84
Laxatives and astrology	85
John of Arderne's clyster pipe	88
Armour-bearer after spasm	89
John of Arderne probes a fistulous hole	94
Procedures and instruments for *fistula in ano*	95
The aggressive owl or *bubo*	98
Wooden funeral effigy of Anne of Bohemia	113
Botiller's tomb, Warrington	114
Archdeacon Sponne's skeleton-tomb	115
Thame church (Oxfordshire)	116
Rycote chapel (Oxfordshire)	117
Roger Cheyne's brass	118
Wall-painting of St Christopher	120
Relic hand	121
John Schorne	122
Ely misericord	125
Dialect map of Middle English	128
Vomiting glutton	134
Abraham worshipping the Trinity	135
The Hoccleve portrait of Chaucer	139
Frontispiece to *Troilus and Criseyde*	141
Canterbury pilgrims	142
Fornicating lovers and cuckolded husband	143
Illuminated initial with Archbishop Arundel and monks of Christ Church, Canterbury	144
Opening of Nicholas Love's *Mirror*	146
Scenes from the Life of Christ	148
St Katherine and her wheels	149
St Agatha and her tormentors	149
John Gower firing satirical arrows at the world	150
Terracotta aquamanile	153
The Middleham Jewel	154
The death of Harold, from the Bayeux Tapestry	155
Building St Alban's church, in the style of Matthew Paris	157
Trinity Chapel, Canterbury Cathedral	159
Detail from the Luttrell Psalter	160
The Pienza Cope (detail)	165
The Ascension (alabaster panel)	166
The interrelationship of designs. A tile from Tring and illustrations of the same scenes from an Anglo-Norman text	169
Neck of a gittern	170
Illuminated initial from the Grandisson Psalter	171
Ivory triptych	172

Drawings from the Pepysian sketch-book	175
The Coronation of Edward III	182
The king and his Court	188
The painted chamber of the Palace of Westminster	193
The Exchequer in the Palace of Westminster	194
The Great Seal of Edward I	197
Plan of the Palace of Westminster	199
Edward I in Parliament	201
Henry VI in Parliament	204
The lion door-knocker of Durham Cathedral	208
Henry VI and two justices	210
Sir William Husy, Chief Justice of King's Bench	211
Brass of Chief Baron Sir John Cassy and his wife	213
A judge presiding over a debate between two serjeants at law	213
The Old Hall of Lincoln's Inn	214
William Catesby	216
Map of lands of the Beauchamp family	218
Badges of the Dukes of Norfolk and Suffolk	220
Monument of Sir Robert Harcourt	221
Boar badge of Richard III	222
The Battle of Sandwich, 1217	232
Rebels in London in 1381	233
Peasants as descendants of Cain	235
Magna Carta (1297 exemplification)	236
The capture of Richard II	238
The siege of Bedford castle, 1225	239
Thomas of Lancaster as a saint	240
The death and mutilation of Simon de Montfort	247
France after the Treaty of Bretigny, 1360	249
Wales following Edward I's conquest	252
The Coronation Chair, Westminster Abbey	254
The Anglo-Scottish border	255
Edward I confronting Philip IV of France	256
The French Succession in 1328	258
The Irish Exchequer in action	261
Late medieval Ireland	262
Portrait of Henry V	266

LIST OF CONTRIBUTORS

Mark Bailey is Fellow of Gonville and Caius College, and Staff Tutor in Local History at the Board of Continuing Education, University of Cambridge.

Paul Brand is Research Fellow at the Institute of Historical Research, London.

Richard G. Davies is Senior Lecturer in History, and Joint Director of Postgraduate Studies, University of Manchester.

Chris Given-Wilson is Senior Lecturer in Medieval History, University of St Andrews.

Ralph Griffiths is Professor of Medieval History, University College of Swansea.

Michael Hicks is Professor of Medieval History, King Alfred's College, Winchester.

Ian Johnson is Lecturer in English, University of St Andrews.

Simone Macdougall is Lecturer in Medieval History, University of St Andrews.

Nigel Ramsay is Keeper of Manuscripts at the British Library, London.

Simon Walker is Senior Lecturer in Medieval History, University of Sheffield.

PREFACE

One of the many pleasures of completing a book is the opportunity it affords to thank those who helped to make it. This is, for obvious reasons, especially so in the case of a multi-authored book such as this one. I should start, therefore, by expressing my gratitude to Jane Thorniley-Walker and Vanessa Graham, the successive History Editors at Manchester University Press responsible for this volume, and to Michelle O'Connell, the Assistant Editor, who undertook the picture research for it, with splendid results.

When Jane Thorniley-Walker first asked me if I might be interested in a project of this kind, my only real cause for hesitation was the fear that I might find it difficult to persuade enough high-calibre historians of the English Late Middle Ages to participate in it. Fortunately, as the roll-call of contributors demonstrates, my fears proved groundless.

The approach adopted is necessarily thematic, with the introduction providing an outline chronology of the period as well as a number of signposts to the later chapters. No attempt has been made to present a conveniently unified approach to the period. The aim, rather, is to cover the ground in fairly systematic fashion, and to reflect and synthesise the best of current scholarship on late medieval England. On occasions, therefore (though not that often) differences of emphasis and opinion between contributors will be apparent – but that, after all, is what the writing of history is about. I am most grateful to each of them, not only for the fact of their participation, but also for the quality of their contributions.

Chris Given-Wilson
St Andrews, April 1995

THE LATE MIDDLE AGES IN ENGLAND

Chris Given-Wilson

Labels are convenient, but apt to confuse. The Oxford English Dictionary defines the Middle Ages as 'the period intermediate between "ancient" and "modern" times, in earlier use commonly taken as extending from *c*. 500 to *c*. 1500, now used without precise definition, but most frequently with reference to the four centuries after AD 1000.' According to Collins English Dictionary, they are '1 (broadly) the period from the end of classical antiquity (or the deposition of the last Western Roman emperor in 476 AD) to the Italian Renaissance (or the fall of Constantinople in 1453); 2 (narrowly) the period from about 1000 AD to the end of the fifteenth century.' Broad or narrow, precise or imprecise, such designations beg a number of questions about how to define the Late Middle Ages. The fourteenth century would appear to be unproblematical, but is the thirteenth century late enough to be Late, and is the fifteenth century really medieval at all, or is it 'Renaissance', 'Early Modern' even?

It is one of the salient points of what we call the Late Middle Ages that people began to think in different ways about historical divisions of time. The common medieval view, popularised by St Augustine around 400 AD, was that the history of the world was divided into six ages, corresponding to the six ages of man: from Adam to Noah (infancy); from Noah to Abraham (childhood); from Abraham to David (youth); from David to the Babylonian Captivity (manhood); from the Babylonian Captivity to the first coming of Christ (middle age); and from the first to the Second Coming of Christ (senility), which would mark the end of the world. After this would come the seventh age, the transition to eternity. Thus people whom we describe as living in the *Middle* Ages in fact believed that they were living in the sixth (decrepit, and final) age of the world, which would climax with the Last Judgement. This overtly Christian and progressive scheme was not the only periodisation of historical time adopted by medieval writers, but it was the most influential, at least until the fourteenth century. During the fourteenth and fifteenth centuries, however, firstly in Italy and later more widely, it became increasingly common to advocate a different approach. Initially this had much to do with self-advertisement; Italian artists and men of letters – 'Renaissance humanists' as they are often called – argued that true art and letters had died with the fall of the Roman Empire in the fifth century, and were only now being revived: 'Of letters and liberal studies at large it were best to be silent altogether,' wrote the fifteenth-century Florentine Matteo Palmieri, 'for these, the real guides to distinction in all the arts, the solid foundation of all civilisation, have been lost to mankind for 800 years or more.'[1] Writers such as Palmieri believed that it was their age which had revived classical civilisation, and it was through such reasoning that the idea of rebirth ('Renaissance') gained ground, and with it the concomitant idea of an intermediate age (*medium aevum*) stretching from the fall of the Roman Empire to their own times. 'In this way,' as Professor Hay put it, 'the *Middle* Ages were born . . . From this point onwards Italians and Europeans in general came to accept a Gothic period of the arts associated with a "medieval" period of history, followed by "modern" art and history.'[2]

Such contrasting views about the Late Middle Ages – one Christian, linear and implicitly pessimistic, the other secular, cyclical and more confident – have proved remarkably enduring. The landmarks of the age are common currency – the Renaissance itself, the Black Death, the Hundred Years War, the Avignon papacy and the Great Schism, the advance of the Ottoman Turks into mainland Europe. But which are the directions that deserve emphasis; the ebb of social and political structures (Catholic hegemony, feudalism) which for centuries had provided European society with its cement, or the rise of new ideas and institutions (religious heterodoxy, the nation-state) which heralded the expanding but fragmented Europe of the sixteenth century? When did the significant transitions occur: with Petrarch, Wyclif and the Black Death in the mid-fourteenth century, with the Wars of the Roses and the fall of Constantinople in the fifteenth, or with Luther and Henry VIII in the early sixteenth? As will be seen, definitions of the Late Middle Ages depend largely upon the angle from which one approaches the subject; cultural historians might argue that by about 1400, medieval forms and attitudes had already in large part given way to those of the Renaissance, while religious historians would perhaps claim that it is only the Reformation of the early sixteenth century which marks the end of the medieval period. Political historians can offer a whole range of dates, usually depending on the area which they are discussing. Historians of late medieval England have traditionally adopted as their starting-point some convenient date in the thirteenth century such as 1204 (the loss of Normandy), 1215 (Magna Carta), or 1272 (the accession of Edward I), but have been reluctant to venture further than 1485 (the accession of the first Tudor king). Broadly speaking, the chronological parameters of this book are from 1200 to 1500, but within that general framework there is plenty of room for variation.

What, then, is distinctive about these centuries? What, if anything, gives them unity? On a European scale, papal authority was by and large on the decline. The period from the late eleventh century to the early thirteenth was the apogee of papal monarchy, when it seemed at times that popes really were the arbiters not only of international quarrels but even of disputes within European nations. Papal power reached its zenith under Innocent III (1198–1215), as his contemporary King John of England found to his cost. By the mid-thirteenth century, however, papal influence was clearly on the wane. Increasingly embroiled in political conflicts within Italy, and increasingly willing, so it seemed, to employ its spiritual weapons in the pursuit of unashamedly political ends, it became the target of growing criticism from within its own ranks, and successive popes did little to help their own cause. Boniface VIII (1294–1303) tried to browbeat both Edward I of England and Philip IV of France into submission, but was eventually kidnapped by agents of the French king from his summer residence at Anagni; Clement V (1305–14) moved the papacy to Avignon, where it remained for seventy years, reviled by the English among others as a puppet of the French monarchy; and when Urban VI (1378–89) attempted to restore it to Rome, he provoked a mutiny among his cardinals which resulted in the creation of an anti-papacy at Avignon. This was the start of the forty-year Great Schism, during which Europe was divided between the 'Roman' and the 'Avignonese' allegiance, and, despite the restoration of a unified papacy at Rome in 1417, it was an ignominy from which the medieval papacy never recovered.

This does not mean that religious sensibility and belief declined during this period, but for growing numbers of European people, disillusion with the institutional hierarchy of the Catholic Church seems to have led to religious expression becoming a more personal matter. It also led, in many countries, to the creation of a less 'universal' Church, and more 'national' Churches, the precursors of the Protestant establishments of the sixteenth century such as Henry VIII's England, where, having broken with Rome, the king proclaimed himself as head of the Church.

Behind the establishment of these more national Churches lay another development sometimes seen as characteristic of late medieval Europe – the decline of feudal monarchy and the rise of nation-states. The appropriateness of 'feudal society' as a term for describing eleventh- and twelfth-century Europe is a question upon which the jury is still out (and is likely to remain so), but it would hardly be disputed that, whatever its validity for the twelfth century, this was greatly diminished by the fifteenth. The 'feudal army' was by now a distant memory (1385 was the last occasion on which a royal army was raised by feudal summons in England, and even then it was a desperate and anachronistic expedient); feudal aids had given way to national taxation, feudal justice to (broadly defined) royal justice; and although landholders continued to describe their tenurial relations with each other in 'feudal' terms (fief, vassal, homage and fealty, and so forth), in reality the feudal structure of landholding society had long since been breached. The old 'land for service, and service for land' nexus had given way to a more varied set of relationships, in which money, for one thing, played an increasingly important part at all levels of society. But what really underlay the national monarchies of late medieval Europe was the administrative transformation of the twelfth and thirteenth centuries. It was, above all, through the creation of powerful royal bureaucracies that, for example, the kings of England (in the twelfth century) and of France (in the thirteenth) were able to rise above the *primus inter pares* notion of kingship, and to assert their higher role as the guardians of national destiny. It is against this background that we need to view royalist assertions of, for example, the right to national taxation, or the development of representative institutions such as the English Parliament, a political, legislative and fiscal forum on a national scale.

The Late Middle Ages in England are sometimes pigeon-holed as the age of Bastard Feudalism. At one level, Bastard Feudalism is little more than a term of convenience for a society which used feudal terminology but paid little heed to its meaning, but numerous other connotations have come to be associated with it: the breakdown of effective justice, the 'private army', the ubiquity of unstable allegiances. Civil war – the 'Wars of the Roses' – was, historians sometimes argue, the inevitable culmination of the increasingly lawless Late Middle Ages in England. The pendulum has swung, however, and nowadays many historians are more inclined to see bastard feudal structures as a force for co-operation and peace-keeping. This raises age-old debates, still pertinent today: does the fact that more criminal activity is recorded mean that more crimes are being committed, or that expectations are rising, that greater efforts are being made to bring criminals to book? Does it represent more beneficial, or more oppressive government? Medieval England – along with the rest of Europe – was certainly a violent place by modern standards, but to pillory the Late Middle Ages as peculiarly lawless is surely to misread the evidence. Long before Bastard Feudalism, there was no shortage of civil war, rebellion, and criminal activity.

Religious historians of the Late Middle Ages still ponder the roots of the Reformation, and political historians debate the real significance of Bastard Feudalism; economic historians, however, display virtual unanimity in ascribing pride of place in determining the nature of the late medieval economy to the Black Death. The Black Death – or bubonic plague – of 1347–50 was the most catastrophic natural disaster in the recorded history of Europe: in the space of about three years, it wiped out between a third and a half of the continent's entire population. Moreover, it became endemic in Europe for the next three centuries, returning every few years with grim predictability to act as a bludgeon on population growth; only with the Great Plague of 1665 did it reap its last great harvest and retreat to its accustomed enclaves – although even now, as recent events have reminded us, it remains a threat. The reaction to the Indian plague of 1994 (and to AIDS in the 1980s) gives some idea of the terror, panic and frenzied search for scapegoats that accompanied the first onslaught of 1347–50. Many believed that the end of the world was at hand; John Clynn, a Franciscan friar from Kilkenny in Ireland, concluded his account of the plague with the words, 'I leave parchment for continuing the work, in case anyone should still be alive in the future and any son of Adam can escape this pestilence and continue the work thus begun' – following which he evidently died.[3]

Yet life did go on, and the irony is that for most of those who survived, the result of the plague was that, in strictly material terms, it got better. This indeed is the real long-term significance of the Black Death. During the twelfth and thirteenth centuries, the population of Europe had been relentlessly increasing: in England, for example, recent estimates suggest a population of about 2.5 million in 1100, 4 million in 1200, and 6 million in 1300. This made for a dynamic economy in the sense that trade expanded, the margins of cultivation were continually pushed back, numerous towns were founded, and so forth, but it also meant that the ratio between land and people – the single most important determinant of standards of living in an agrarian society –

became increasingly precarious. During the last century or so before the plague, much of Europe was becoming over-populated. Land and employment became scarcer; rents and prices rose, real wages fell; vulnerability to bad harvests increased, as did unemployment and under-employment. The Black Death reversed these trends; not universally, and not always immediately, but by creating a labour shortage instead of a labour surplus, and by making more land available to those who survived, its end result was bound to be an improvement in the standard of living of much of the population. At the same time, the successive outbreaks of plague meant a continued fall in population – in England, it had probably fallen back to about 2.5 million by 1400 – and this in turn meant a prolonged period of economic contraction, or at least stagnation. But whatever facet of the late medieval economy historians have chosen to emphasise, the pattern is fairly clear: in the thirteenth century, rising population and an expanding economy, accompanied by growing poverty; in the fifteenth century, stagnant population and an economic depression, accompanied by improved living standards for the majority; the fourteenth century, which witnessed the most catastrophic demographic decline in the recorded history of Europe, was the watershed.

What 'sorts and conditions' of people inhabited England in the Late Middle Ages, and what sort of land did they inhabit? It is a sobering thought to realise that the 4 million or so persons alive in England in 1200 had an average life expectancy at birth of about 25 years, and that even if they reached that age, the majority of them would still not expect to live beyond their forties. This, moreover, is based on an analysis of pre-plague data; after 1348, these figures would have been lower. The great majority of these 4 million – 80 per cent or more – were tenant farmers or labourers and their dependants, who worked the soil, tended their animals, and lived in small, scattered villages amidst their fields. Interspersed among these villages were the towns, monasteries and castles which accommodated the remainder of the population; it was here, for the most part, that the wealthier sort lived, those who owned the land, and who possessed both the judicial and financial rights to perpetuate their ownership and the spending power to drive the nation's economy. New towns were a feature of the times: it has been estimated that about 140 new towns were founded in England between 1100 and 1300. Most were quite small, their populations numbered in hundreds rather than thousands. Only a dozen or so exceeded 10,000, and even London at its greatest medieval extent – in the century or so before the Black Death – never exceeded 100,000. Yet despite their relative lack of size by modern standards, the confined, restless streets and lanes of most medieval towns accentuated the division between rich and poor and threw up an urban proletariat which was to become an increasingly vociferous element in the life of the nation – as their political masters discovered to their cost in 1381.

The number of monasteries in England around 1200 was between 700 and 800. The twelfth century was the great age of monastic foundations in England, with new orders such as the Cistercians, Augustinians and, towards the end of the century, the Carthusians, attracting more and wealthier endowments than the long-established Benedictines, although by and large it was the Benedictines who remained the wealthiest and most populous of the religious orders. In the first years of the thirteenth century they would be joined by the Franciscan (grey) and Dominican (black) friars, who, unlike the new monastic orders, generally established themselves in or near towns. The secular clergy (to which the parish priests, stipendiary vicars and chaplains, and most of the cathedral canons and prebendaries belonged) were also numerous – indeed the ubiquity of the clergy was a feature of medieval society; probably about 2 per cent of the population had taken religious orders of some kind. Few of these were women, leaving perhaps one in fifteen adult males as members of the clergy in the Middle Ages. The sheer proportions of the buildings which they have left – be they the neck-jarring Gothic cathedrals which still rear above urban landscapes in Durham, Lincoln or York, or the eerie, roofless relics of rural Fountains or Tintern ('bare, ruined choirs, where once the sweet birds sang') – are moving testimony to the religiosity of the age.

As well as centres of worship, monasteries and cathedrals were also symbols of lordship – though not to the same degree as castles, which by the later twelfth century were usually being built in stone. Castles were the residential, military and administrative power-centres of the aristocracy; there were between 250 and 300 active castles in England in 1200, about one third of which were royally controlled, the rest in the hands of the barons.[4] The term 'baron' was an elastic one, but could probably have been applied to about 250 men in the early thirteenth century. These men, who included a dozen or so earls, were the greatest members of the landholding class, greater than their fellows by reason not only of their birth and wealth, but also of their political authority and personal access to the king. Beneath them, but shading into their ranks, came a few thousand landholders commonly described as the 'knightly class', not all of whom were knights, and some of whom were scarcely wealthier than well-to-do peasants, but who may justifiably be regarded as sharing the militaristic and social assumptions of the barons, and who included a handful of men whose lands and connections would have been the envy of many a baron. During the later Middle Ages, the English nobility became more precisely stratified; by the late fourteenth century, new ranks such as duke and marquis had been introduced into its upper ranks, and the peerage came to be defined as those families who were entitled to receive a personal summons to meetings of Parliament. The heads of about sixty families enjoyed this privilege in the fifteenth century, and they were at pains to emphasise its hereditary nature, in order to exclude those below them. Beneath the peerage, fifteenth-century landed society may be broadly divided into two groups: the 'county gentry', numbering perhaps 2,000–2,500 families, embracing the knights and the greater esquires; and the 'parish gentry', consisting of the lesser esquires and gentlemen (a term which came into common usage around 1400), and numbering perhaps 10,000 families. Demarcation lines between these groups were never rigid, however, and social mobility was constant; of the families which made up the peerage, for example, about 50 per cent became extinct in the male line each century, necessitating replenishment from below. This was not a caste society.[5]

Nevertheless, late medieval England was decidedly hierarchical – a deferential society, in which status was openly acknowledged and unashamedly displayed. Merchant oligarchies dominated the towns; ecclesiastical dignitaries such as bishops and abbots dominated the Church; and the landholding aristocracy dominated the political life of the nation. Over them all towered the king. Medieval kingship was not an easy task, and of the thirteen kings who ruled England between 1200 and 1500, only four or five (Edward I, Edward III, Henry V, Henry VII, and arguably Edward IV) managed it with any real degree of success. A further four were deposed (Edward II, Richard II, Henry VI, and the boy-king of two months, Edward V); Richard III was killed at the battle of Bosworth, and the remaining three – John, Henry III, and Henry IV – barely survived. Not without reason, therefore, has Shakespeare's portrayal of late medieval England as a bloodstained battleground of noble faction and self-destructive strife gained a hold in the popular imagination.

What was expected of a medieval king? First, he must do justice, and it must be equitable justice. At one level, this meant that he was responsible for the maintenance of law and order – no easy task in a society which was still many centuries away from the idea of either a standing army or a permanent police force. At another level, the king played a vital role as peace-keeper between the great men of his kingdom. This was an essentially personal matter, for the king was, in a very real sense, the personification of justice. A striking example of this comes from the year 1346, when Edward III, called upon by the earl of Arundel to reconsider his decision to proclaim himself the heir to the lands of the earl of Surrey, declared that 'now, on revolving the matter in the court of his conscience', he had decided to reverse his previous decision and allow Arundel the lands.[6] The idea of the king's own conscience as a court of law goes to the heart of the medieval conception of royal justice – and, it might be pointed out, Edward III's willingness to forgo his own claim goes some of the way towards explaining his success as a king. Other kings gained quite different reputations; Edward II and Richard II caused consternation among the landholding class by their blatantly unjust seizures of land, and this in turn goes much of the way towards explaining their failure. Not that these decisions were easy: the king's role as the arbiter of disputes between the magnates of his kingdom imposed continuous demands upon his common sense, and carried with it the constant danger of alienation of the great and powerful. The real problem came when the king ceased (or was perceived as having ceased) to act the part of independent overlord and instead aligned himself with one or other faction, as Edward II and Richard II both did in their later years, and as Henry VI did in the messy years leading up to the outbreak of the Wars of the Roses.

A king must also dispense his patronage equitably. Royal patronage was extensive, much sought after, and came in many different forms: lands and titles, wardships and marriages, offices and commissions and straightforward cash annuities were all available for distribution, and no one denied that it was both the king's right and his duty to distribute them. It was also, of course, both personally satisfying and politically advantageous to him to do so; it was the way he rewarded his friends and supporters for their past service, and hoped to ensure their future service. The dangers, however, were equally apparent: most obviously, the dissipation of resources and the resentment of those who were not favoured – for offence was easily taken. For example, when Richard II concluded his grant of Queenborough castle in 1385 to his favourite Robert de Vere, earl of Oxford, with the words, 'the curse of God and St Edward and the king on any who do or attempt aught against this grant!',[7] it was clear that something was seriously wrong. Yet Richard failed to heed the warning, going on to create his favourite marquis of Dublin, and then duke of Ireland in 1386. In the following year de Vere was appealed of treason and driven into exile, where he died in 1392. Other royal favourites suffered worse fates, such as Piers Gaveston under Edward II or the duke of Suffolk under Henry VI (murdered in 1312 and 1450 respectively). Every king had favourites, of course, not just the incompetent ones, but it was important that they should be seen to earn their rewards, and that those rewards should not be immoderate; far better to gain a reputation for parsimony, like Edward I and Henry V, than for improvidence.

Even more enviable were Edward I's and Henry V's reputations as soldiers, for with success in war other cares rested more lightly on a king's shoulders. Leadership of the realm in war was an obligation which few of England's medieval kings could avoid even had they wanted to – and not many did – for warfare was ever-present in the Middle Ages. The prestige and relative domestic harmony which Edward I, Edward III and Henry V enjoyed was due in considerable measure to their international status as warrior-kings, whereas John, Edward II and Henry VI, all of whom suffered humiliating reverses abroad, also paid a heavy price at home for their defeats. Yet even for successful kings like Edward I and Edward III, warfare brought its problems, for it was an expensive business, and increasingly so as time went on. By the early fourteenth century, the unpaid feudal host was for practical purposes a thing of the past: English armies were now 'contract armies', raised by personal indenture between the king and his war-captains, and paid from the royal purse. Even three or four years of continuous warfare could make unconscionable demands on the exchequer; between 1294 and 1297, for example, Edward I spent some £750,000 on his wars with France and Scotland, and Edward III's military costs during the opening years (1337–40) of the Hundred Years War were not much less. There was only one way in which sums like this could be found, and that was through regular taxation at high rates, which was invariably unpopular, even when accompanied by victory. The political crises of 1297 and 1340–41 were both largely due to the king's financial demands. Henry V died before the complaints against his fiscal exactions became too persistent, but the danger signals were already there in his last parliament, and it is interesting to speculate as to how much longer he could have continued to bleed England for his wars. Warfare, then, was a gamble: an unavoidable gamble, up to a point, but a gamble nevertheless. Whether it was better to have tried and failed (as Edward II did, most notably at Bannockburn), or not to have tried at all (as Richard II was accused of doing) is a moot point, but worst of all was not to try and still to fail, like Henry VI, who did his utmost to compromise with France but still lost practically all his father's lands there.

Thus fair justice, even-handed patronage and the avoidance of military disgrace were important to any king's chances of survival. Naturally there was much else that was expected of a king: the maintenance of the Church; protection of the needy (such as widows and orphans, too often the targets of the greedy, including greedy kings); moderation in his personal habits and lifestyle (complaints about the extravagance of the royal household were commonplace during this period); and the ability to run an efficient, but not oppressive, royal administration – which, more than anything, meant a firm hand in controlling local officials, who seem always to have had an inclination to overstep the mark in the king's name. How well did the men who ruled England during these centuries measure up to the demands made of them?

England in 1200 was ruled by King John (1199–1216), and was an independent, sovereign kingdom in its own right. However, it was also part of a larger agglomeration of territories centred in north-western France. For most of the period between the Norman Conquest of 1066 and the accession of Henry II in 1154, England and Normandy were ruled jointly, and when Henry became king, he added Anjou, Maine and Touraine (his father's inheritance), and the great duchy of Aquitaine (his wife Eleanor of Aquitaine's inheritance), thus creating what is often called the 'Angevin Empire', a vast swathe of lands stretching from the Cheviots to the Pyrenees and encompassing most of the Atlantic seaboard of France (see the illustration on p. 249). Throughout the twelfth century, therefore, English and French society were closely linked. Territorial and political concerns meant that English kings and barons often spent more time on the Continent than they did in England, that the great offices in the English Church and state were as likely to be filled by Frenchmen as by Englishmen, and that French influence pervaded every aspect of English life – linguistic, literary and architectural, as well as political and administrative. However, when Philip Augustus of France (1180–1223) conquered Normandy, Anjou, Maine and Touraine in 1204–06, these cultural and political bonds began to dissolve. The most obvious and immediate consequence of John's loss of most of his Angevin Empire was that he now spent most of his time in England, as did many of the English barons, and relations between them soon became strained. His relentless extortion of payments for his foreign campaigns antagonised his subjects beyond endurance, as did his increasing reliance on foreign 'favourites' – in part a consequence of his inability to trust his own people. Magna Carta, the great charter of liberties which John was obliged to concede to his opponents in June 1215, was meant to patch up their quarrels, but it failed utterly to do so, and by the time John died of dysentery in October 1216, a sizeable group of English barons had risen in revolt against him and invited Prince Louis of France, son of Philip Augustus, to come to England to claim the throne – although he soon abandoned the attempt, returning to France in 1217.

John had committed several of the cardinal sins of kingship: his justice and patronage were inequitable, he was seen as an enemy rather than a friend to the Church, and his cruelty shocked even his contemporaries, accustomed as they were to harshness. Above all, he had failed in war, and failed to win the respect and friendship of those who mattered in the kingdom. His son Henry III (1216–72) was to do little better. Since Henry was only 9 years old at John's death, it was not until 1227 that he entered upon his personal rule, but once he did so he showed himself to be no more of a statesman than his father. Despite a series of campaigns in the 1230s and 1240s, he failed to regain the continental lands which John had lost, and eventually agreed, by the Treaty of Paris in 1259, to acknowledge their permanent loss to the French monarchy. Like John, he was dogged by financial problems and by an apparent inability to establish good personal relations with his barons. His relationship with the papacy was certainly much better than his father's, and, despite his weak and wilful nature, there was no doubting his personal piety: his lasting memorial is Westminster Abbey, most of which he rebuilt between 1245 and 1269, and which is heavily influenced by French Gothic designs of the period. On the whole, however, Henry's fondness for things foreign did little to endear him to his subjects. During the 1240s and 1250s there was mounting criticism of the favour shown to Poitevin and Savoyard favourites at his court, and when, in the mid-1250s, he became involved in an ambitious scheme with the papacy to finance the conquest of Sicily (in return for which his son Edmund was promised the Sicilian crown), matters came to a head. The scheme collapsed in ruins, leaving Henry humiliated and burdened with debts. At a parliament held at Oxford in 1258, a group of disaffected barons forced the king to accept the 'Provisions of Oxford', by which power was handed over to a committee of fifteen. Ironically, the leader of the baronial opposition to the king was himself a Frenchman, Simon de Montfort, who was married to Henry's sister and had been granted the earldom of Leicester. For the next seven years – the period of the 'baronial reform programme' – power oscillated between the king and his opponents, while the country slid towards civil war. It was a situation which was only likely to be resolved by the death of either Henry or Simon, and in the end – almost inevitably, perhaps – it was Simon who died, cut down by royalist troops under the command of Henry's son, the Lord Edward, at the battle of Evesham on 4 August 1265.

Within another seven years, the victor of Evesham had become king. The reign of Edward I (1272–1307) was a watershed in English (and British) history, with the king's rigorous and implacable character setting its mark upon his age. Apart from a brief interlude during the middle years, warfare dominated the reign. By 1284, the conquest of Wales was virtually complete, while the last thirteen years of Edward's life were spent at war with either France or Scotland, and frequently both. This constant campaigning presented the king with financial, organisational and political problems of a new kind, and it is in the king's attempts to find solutions to these problems that the real interest of the reign lies, for they raised issues that were to recur time and again during the later Middle Ages. Edward's warfare demanded frequent taxation. Taxation was not a new idea in the late thirteenth century – the first real tax in England was raised by King John in 1207, and taxes had occasionally been granted to Henry III – but the scale upon which Edward was demanding it during his later years placed an intolerable burden on his subjects. There was also the question of how consent should be obtained to taxation. On one occasion, in July 1297, it was alleged that Edward just asked 'people standing round in his chamber'.[8] In fact, it was becoming increasingly clear that the place for consent to be obtained was in Parliament, and it was during the last years of Edward's reign that Parliament began to take on its late medieval shape – as an institution with accepted (if not yet defined) fiscal and legislative as well as judicial powers.

Despite his undoubted achievements, Edward's reign ended with a decade of glowering stand-off between him and his barons, and lingering mistrust of the ever-increasing demands of royal government. Within a year or so of his death, however, there can have been few who did not regret his passing, for his son Edward II's reign (1307–27) was to prove one of the most deplorable in English history. The first five years of the reign were dominated by the king's increasingly desperate attempts to save his favourite, Piers Gaveston, from the wrath of his opponents, in order to achieve which Edward was prepared to concede almost anything that was asked of him – at least until he could wriggle out of it. It was not enough, however, and in June 1312 Gaveston was murdered by a group of nobles led by Edward's own cousin and unrelenting foe, Thomas earl of Lancaster. Two years later, in June 1314, the English army under Edward suffered its most humiliating defeat of the Middle Ages at the hands of Robert Bruce at Bannockburn, and for the next decade the Scots raided the northern counties with impunity, while at home Edward staggered from crisis to crisis. In 1322, following the brief 'Despenser war' – so called because it was provoked by the king's connivance at the acquisitive thuggery of his latest favourites, the elder and younger Hugh Despenser – he defeated and executed his most persistent enemies (including Lancaster), whereupon he and the Despensers embarked upon a reign of terror, crushing all opposition and amassing vast private fortunes. Edward was far from the persecuted homosexual that some have tried to portray him as – indeed it has recently been argued that he was not homosexual at all, although that is a question upon which there is never likely to be unanimity.[9] He was a weak, foolish and cruel man, utterly devoid of kingly qualities or any kind of statesmanship. It was his own wife, the French princess Isabella, who, together with her lover Roger Mortimer, eventually led the revolution which toppled him in the winter of 1326–27. The deposed Edward was incarcerated in Berkeley castle, where, on the night of 21 September 1327, he was murdered – according to tradition, in peculiarly horrible fashion.

Edward II's deposition, the first in English history, was shocking to many, but was such a personal affair that it had little effect on the institution of English monarchy, which within twenty years, largely thanks to his son Edward III (1327–77), was enjoying almost unprecedented prestige. Edward III seems to have had all the qualities which his father had lacked: a firm but approachable nature, personal leadership, determination, and common sense. He was also stunningly successful in war, which was fortunate for him, because warfare with France and Scotland dominated the reign. The early years were largely taken up with restoring and extending English authority in Scotland, but once the Hundred Years War began in 1337 the focus switched to France. The sums required to maintain this almost continuous warfare were immense, and yet, despite the inevitable opposition which this engendered – and which did on occasions (as in 1340–41) assume serious proportions – Edward displayed a remarkable ability to maintain good relations with both his magnates and the commons (who granted the taxes). His victories helped enormously, of course: Sluys in 1340, Crecy in 1346, Neville's Cross (at which the Scottish King David II was captured) in the same year, and Poitiers in 1356 (where the French King John II was captured) are the most famous. The Treaty of Bretigny in 1360, by which Edward gained the whole of Aquitaine in full sovereignty and various territories, including Calais, in northern France, set the seal on Edward's victories, and ushered in a decade of peace and triumphalism in England. King John was ransomed for half a million pounds, over half of which had been paid before war broke out again; the rebuilding of Windsor castle, paid for with French ransoms and intended by Edward to be 'the Versailles of the age',[10] grandiloquently proclaimed England's new-found status as the foremost power in northern Europe.

It was not to last, however. Within five years of the renewal of war in 1369, France under Charles V had regained most of what had been lost at Bretigny, and England entered a new period of violent domestic upheaval. The twilight of Edward's reign was a miserable epilogue to what had gone before. The king himself was ill and ageing, while his son and heir the Black Prince (the victor of Poitiers) was wasting to a premature death through dropsy. Taxation during the 1370s was at record levels, the government was insolvent, and rumours of corruption abounded. The deservedly famous Good Parliament of 1376 – in which the commons, led by their speaker Sir Peter de la Mare, really took the political initiative for the first time – witnessed a bitter and prolonged attack against the courtiers and ministers seen as responsible for the military and financial debacle, and by the time Edward died on 21 June 1377 the golden reputation which he had enjoyed only a decade earlier had been severely tarnished. Worse still, the Black Prince had died in the previous year, so that the new king was no worldly-wise adult but the 10-year-old Richard II, the Black Prince's only surviving son.

Nor was it only political and military woes that afflicted England during the last decades of the fourteenth century, for social and religious unrest also mounted. The reduction in population following the Black Death and repeated attacks of the plague in the 1360s and 1370s had created new markets in labour and land, driving wages up and prices down, raising both the expectations and living standards of the peasantry, but simultaneously encouraging landholders to adopt ever harsher measures in order to prevent their profits from slipping into decline. By 1377, pressures in both town and countryside were already intense: unfree tenants were rumoured to be refusing to perform their customary services, while John Gower, poet and social commentator, foretold disaster. Four years later he was proved right. In June 1381, the years of frustration, ignited by the imposition of a third poll-tax in four years, exploded in the most celebrated popular uprising in medieval England, the so-called 'Peasants' Revolt'. Throughout the Home Counties and East Anglia, and even as far away as Beverley in Yorkshire and Bridgewater in Somerset, peasants and townspeople rose almost in unison. Thousands of Kent and Essex folk marched on London, occupying the city for three days in a fury of looting, burning and lynching. The chancellor and treasurer of England were beheaded on Tower Hill. The Savoy palace (the London residence of Richard II's uncle, John of Gaunt), and the Temple (home of the legal profession) were burned to the ground. At Mile End on 14 June, and again at Smithfield the next day, the rebels' leader Wat Tyler met with the king and presented him with their demands: an end to serfdom, guaranteed cheap rents, a list of 'traitors' (including Gaunt) to be brought to justice. But at Smithfield Tyler overstepped the mark, and, because he 'doffed not his hood before the king nor in anything did reverence to the king's majesty',[11] was cut down and killed by the mayor of London, William Walworth, whereupon the revolt crumbled and the suppression began in earnest (although elsewhere outbreaks of violence continued for many weeks). What the rebels of 1381 achieved is difficult to say: often enough the answer given is 'very little', but at least the hated poll-taxes were abolished, and it is hard to believe that the rapid decline of serfdom during the next twenty years or so did not owe something to their desperate gamble.

Also among the rebels' grievances were demands for the disendowment of the Church and the abolition of bishoprics. Social and religious disaffection are never easy to disentangle (and it was always in the authorities' interests to present them as linked), but there is little doubt that the anti-clericalism expressed by the rebels reflected widely-held contemporary dissatisfaction with the established Church. During the middle decades of the fourteenth century such sentiments had proved quite useful to the Government – helping it, for example, to resist papal encroachments and to impose heavier taxes on the clergy – but by the 1370s anti-clericalism had given way to a far more dangerous beast – heresy. The origins of Lollardy, as this first English heresy for nearly a thousand years was called, were academic, inspired by the preaching and writing of the Oxford theologian John Wyclif, who based his arguments on his belief in predestination and the denial of transubstantiation, moving on from there to question the authority of pope and clergy; but his views struck a popular chord (not least with the secular establishment, at whom they were principally directed), and by 1382, at the 'Earthquake Council', the Church was so concerned about the spread of Lollardy that it enlisted the lay authorities in its search to root it out. It never quite did so. Despite increasingly harsh penalties, Lollardy's anti-establishment and proto-Puritan stance continued to attract powerful support through the reigns of Richard II and Henry IV, and only after the abortive Lollard Rising of 1414 had equated it definitively with treason did it finally go out of vogue among the wealthier classes. Even so, it survived in clandestine cells and obscure bible-readings throughout the fifteenth century, and was still there when the new tide of Protestant reformist ideas began to seep across from the Continent under Henry VIII.

England, then, was a divided nation in the late fourteenth century, and not all the troubles which Richard II (1377–99) faced were of his own making. Nevertheless, he did little to help his own cause. Like his great-grandfather Edward II (for whose canonisation, improbably, he petitioned the pope), he was temperamentally unsuited to kingship: capricious, vengeful, hot-tempered and stubborn, his personality injected a malevolently subjective element into the quarrels of the political community – and quarrels there were, in plenty. Factional squabbling during the 1380s – over foreign policy, fiscal policy, and almost every other sort of policy – culminated in a brief civil war in 1387 and the humiliation of the king and his courtiers in the 'Merciless Parliament' of 1388, which sanctioned the execution of eight of the king's supporters and the banishment or dismissal from court of some forty more. For some years after this, Richard seemed to have learned his lesson: the second phase of the Hundred Years War came to an end in 1389, thus relieving the financial pressure which had dogged his minority, and during these years the king showed himself more prepared to accept the advice of those whom he did not necessarily count as his friends. But events were to prove that Richard had merely been biding his time, and in 1397 he decided that the moment had come to strike back at those who had humbled him a decade earlier. His chief enemies among the magnates – his uncle the duke of Gloucester, and the earls of Arundel and Warwick – were arrested and convicted of treason: Gloucester was murdered in prison, Arundel beheaded, Warwick exiled. But as Richard's ambition began to soar, his increasing reliance on a small coterie of sycophants seems to have blinded him to the gathering opposition to his regime, and when Henry Bolingbroke, duke of Lancaster (whom the king had exiled in 1398) landed at Ravenspur in Yorkshire with a small invading force in July 1399, support for the king crumbled. Three months later, Bolingbroke had deposed Richard, imprisoned him, and secured his own elevation to the throne. Within a further six months Richard was dead, almost certainly murdered in Pontefract castle.

Despite his manifest shortcomings as a ruler, Richard II still enjoys a reputation as a patron of both the visual and literary arts. It is in fact very difficult to know how active the king himself was in patronising the arts, but there is no denying that the late fourteenth century was not only a brilliant age in English poetry, but has also bequeathed to us some of the finest buildings and paintings to survive from the Middle Ages. Among the latter, pride of place goes to the Wilton Diptych, a small portable altarpiece, painted on both sides, almost certainly intended for Richard II's private religious devotions. As such, it is both a religious and a political work, as well as being technically the finest painting to survive from the English Middle Ages. Whether it was the work of an Englishman is another matter (recent opinion – stimulated by the special exhibition centred on the diptych at the National Gallery in 1993 – tends to the contrary),[12] but it is hardly a matter of great importance; continental influences had enriched English art and letters for many centuries before this, helping to give them that astonishing diversity of composition and form which is their unmistakable hallmark, and would continue to do so for many more. Geoffrey Chaucer (*c.* 1340–1400), the greatest English poet of the Middle Ages, may have written in the English language, but his early models were French and Italian works such as the *Roman de la Rose* and the poems of Dante and Boccaccio. The three major works of his contemporary John Gower were written, one in French, one in Latin, and one in English. Medieval England was a multi-lingual nation; everybody, it can be assumed, spoke English, but Anglo-Norman (much closer to French than to English) and Latin were also in common usage, the former by the upper classes (the descendants of William of Normandy and his followers), the latter as the language of government and scholarship. Nevertheless, English was clearly in the ascendant by the late fourteenth century. Parliament in 1362 declared that it was to be the official language of the lawcourts in future, and twenty years later John Trevisa claimed that by now 'in all the grammar schools of England, children leaveth French and construeth and learneth in English'.[13] Within sixty years of Chaucer's and Richard II's deaths, Anglo-Norman had virtually disappeared from England.

Those same sixty years also witnessed the rise and fall of the Lancastrian dynasty and the final collapse of the Anglo-French empire around which England's foreign ambitions had centred ever since the Norman Conquest. The usurpation of Henry IV in 1399 raised questions about the succession which would not ultimately (as it turned out) be resolved for nearly a century, for, even allowing for Richard's childlessness, Henry was not the primogenitary heir to the throne. That right belonged to the 8-year-old Edmund Mortimer, the earl of March. Although the Mortimer claim was adroitly sidestepped in 1399, and although, while the new dynasty gradually established itself, it lay dormant for many years, yet it never quite disappeared from the political consciousness of fifteenth-century England; and when, half a century on, mounting troubles at home and abroad began to raise doubts about Henry VI's fitness to rule, it was the Mortimer claim, now embodied by the house of York, that was looked for as an alternative. All this was in the future, however. Henry IV (1399–1413) had plenty of other things to worry about for the moment. It is sometimes said that, as a usurper, Henry's principal achievement was simply to have survived; that he barely managed to do so was, of course, in large part a consequence of his usurpation. The first nine years of his reign saw four major rebellions, a series of exceptionally difficult parliamentary confrontations, and a prolonged revolt in Wales under Owen Glendower which came close to destroying English rule in the principality. Henry's last years were more peaceful, but it was only with the succession of his son Henry V (1413–22) that the Lancastrian dynasty really came into its own, and once again, as with Edward III, it was foreign conquest which laid the foundation for the restoration of monarchical authority. The battle of Agincourt (October 1415), the conquest of Normandy (1417–19), and the

Treaty of Troyes of May 1420 (whereby Henry stole a march even on Edward III, and, in alliance with the duke of Burgundy, secured recognition from Charles VI of France of his claim to the French throne) have made of Henry V the archetypal English hero-king. Some of this, it has to be admitted, was due to good fortune – for Charles VI was insane, and France, racked by civil war, was ripe for the taking – but even so it is hard to deny Henry's qualities of leadership and statesmanship. What he might have achieved had he lived longer is unknowable; it was the tragedy of the Lancastrian dynasty that in August 1422 he died of dysentery, aged just 35, leaving a 9-month-old infant as his heir.

It is one of history's neater ironies that Henry VI (1422–61), who was the only medieval English king actually to be crowned king of France, was also the king who ultimately lost virtually all the English lands in France – and indeed, his English throne as well. Yet in fairness to Henry, by the time that he assumed his personal rule in 1437 the tide of war had already turned against England. Encouraged by Joan of Arc, Charles VII of France (1422–61) had repulsed the English advance at Orleans; the Anglo-Burgundian alliance collapsed in 1435; and in 1436 the French recaptured Paris. Henry, torn between war and peace, made concessions to the French which fatally weakened the English position in Normandy and caused a storm of protest at home. After a decade of vacillation and fumbling, the end was quick and relatively bloodless: between 1449 and 1451 the English were driven out of both Normandy, which they had held for thirty years, and Gascony, which they had held for three hundred. The Hundred Years War had ended in defeat for England, and now the political consequences must be faced at home. Henry's government, plagued by debt and scandal, was further shaken in 1450 by the most serious popular uprising since 1381 ('Jack Cade's Revolt'), and in 1453 the king lost his mind and fell into a depressive stupor which lasted seventeen months. Richard duke of York, the heir to the Mortimer claim to the throne, became Protector; Henry recovered, but fell ill again, and once again York was appointed as Protector. In an atmosphere of such uncertainty, it became increasingly difficult for people who mattered not to throw in their lot with one side or the other, and in 1455 occurred the first skirmish of what came to be known as the Wars of the Roses. By October 1460, York felt strong enough to bid openly for the throne, and although he was killed at the battle of Wakefield in December, three months later his 18-year-old son Edward avenged his father's death at Towton in Yorkshire and proclaimed himself King Edward IV.

Apart from a brief interlude in 1470–71, Yorkist kings ruled England for the next twenty-four years. Edward IV (1461–83) showed himself to be of much sterner stuff than Henry VI. The early years of his reign were full of danger, for Henry, his obdurate wife Margaret of Anjou, and their son Edward, the Prince of Wales, had fled from Towton and taken refuge in the north, where they busied themselves stirring up revolt against the usurper. Nor, at times, did Edward IV help his own cause during these years: his secret marriage to Elizabeth Woodville in 1464, for example, was a major political error and lost him the support of the man who had done most to help him gain the throne, Richard Neville earl of Warwick ('Warwick the Kingmaker'). The capture and imprisonment of Henry VI in 1465 eased the situation somewhat, but in 1469 Warwick allied with Edward's own brother, George duke of Clarence, and in the following year drove Edward from the throne and restored Henry VI. Edward was soon back, however; after five months of exile in the Netherlands he returned in March 1471 (landing, like Henry Bolingbroke in 1399, at Ravenspur on the Humber), defeated and killed Warwick at Barnet on 14 April, and three weeks later routed the Lancastrian army at Tewkesbury. On 21 May, it was announced that Henry VI had died in the Tower 'of pure displeasure and melancholy'; he had, of course, been murdered.

After 1471, Edward showed that he was capable of learning from his mistakes, and his 'second reign' proved generally much more peaceful than his first. It is doubtful whether at any time he really felt secure on the throne – as late as 1478 he was faced with another rebellion by his brother Clarence, who this time paid for it with his life – but his financial prudence, his generally sensitive handling of his magnates, and his easy, open manner did much to restore confidence in the monarchy after the traumas of the 1450s and 1460s. Unfortunately for the house of York, he did not live long enough to allow his sons to grow to adulthood. Edward was just 41 when he died in April 1483, his sons 12 and 9. The elder, the Prince of Wales, now by right became Edward V, but his reign lasted a mere two months, for Edward IV's only surviving brother, Richard duke of Gloucester, incarcerated the boys in the Tower and seized the throne for himself, declaring the princes to be illegitimate. Barely a month passed, and the 'Princes in the Tower' were heard of no more. Despite ceaseless speculation, there can be little doubt that it was Richard who was behind their murder. Yet Richard III only enjoyed his bloodstained inheritance for a further two years, being himself defeated and killed by Henry Tudor, the inheritor of the Lancastrian claim to the throne, at the battle of Bosworth on 22 August 1485.

Thus England entered the 'Tudor age'. Yet for several years after Bosworth, it must have seemed to contemporaries that little had changed. Yorkist pretenders – a welcome focus of opposition for disaffected Yorkist supporters – continued to lend an air of instability to Tudor rule, and it required great political skill (which Henry VII possessed) to re-establish the security and prestige of the monarchy. (It is a measure of his success that when he died in 1509, his son Henry VIII succeeded without a whisper of dissent, and that the Tudor dynasty went on to survive the religious and political convulsions of the 1530s and 1540s.) Nevertheless, the accession of the first Tudor king in 1485 has always been regarded as a turning-point in English history, and there is still much to commend that view (not least the fact that it corresponds invitingly to what are often seen as turning-points in European history, such as the voyages of Columbus to the New World, Charles VIII of France's first invasion of Italy in 1494, the rise of German Lutheranism in the 1520s, and, following the invention of printing, the replacement of the manuscript by the book). However, there is less to commend the traditional 'tyranny of 1485' as a full stop to the English Middle Ages. Its usefulness, rather, is that it occupies a middle point between a series of dates, or events, which might in one sense or another be regarded as bringing down the curtain on a panorama which we have come to regard as typically medieval: the Black Death of 1347–50, which decisively and catastrophically brought to a close the demographic and economic expansion of the previous three centuries or more; the end of the Hundred Years War in 1453, severing the Anglo-French territorial links which had largely determined the course of English foreign relations since the Norman Conquest; and the break with Rome, followed by the dissolution of the monasteries, in the 1530s – to name only the most obvious. Compared with the England of *c.* 1200, much else had changed too by the end of the fifteenth century: serfdom had almost entirely disappeared, and 'feudalism' was by now in many ways an anachronism; the English language had triumphed, the distribution of wealth in England had shifted decisively southwards, and Parliament had established itself as the political forum of the nation. These are among the themes discussed in this book. Whatever arguments can be made – and they are perfectly valid – for, say, the Cromwellian revolution of the mid-seventeenth century, or the Industrial Revolution, being equally decisive turning-points in English history, there is no doubting the fact that English society had undergone a fundamental transformation during what we like to call the Late Middle Ages.

THE LAND AND
THE PEOPLE

THE ENGLISH LANDSCAPE

Mark Bailey

Our understanding of the late medieval landscape has improved significantly since W. G. Hoskins's pioneering research, although there remains much to be discovered. The development of more sophisticated tools of analysis and inter-disciplinary approaches involving archaeologists, botanists, and landscape and documentary historians have enabled us to comprehend better the ways in which medieval society adapted to its natural environment. From this research, it is clear that the medieval landscape was neither wild, 'natural' nor unplanned. The Normans conquered an old-settled land where many property boundaries, settlements, fields and trackways dated back centuries. This was especially true of lowland England, although even the uplands bore the marks of human activity. Thus medieval communities were merely modifying earlier landscape forms.

The physical differences between highland and lowland provided an obvious contrast in the landscape of late medieval England, although strong regional distinctions were apparent to contemporaries even within these broad areas. By the twelfth century the area of undulating boulder clay to the east of the Nene valley on the borders of Northamptonshire, Bedfordshire and Huntingdonshire was known locally as Bromswold, and the northern Fenland was known as 'Mersheland'. For all the subtlety of its regional and local variations, the medieval English countryside can be regarded as belonging to one of two basic categories: writing in 1573 Thomas Tusser drew his readers' attention to the differences between 'champion' and 'several' countryside, the former an open landscape dominated by arable farming and the latter an enclosed and wooded landscape characterised by pastoral pursuits.[1] Much of the champion country lay in a wedge which stretched north-eastwards from Wiltshire, through the central and east Midlands to Durham and Northumberland. This was the countryside of vast arable fields and nucleated villages. Several countryside – which was more diverse, intimate and complex – lay to the east (the Home Counties and East Anglia) and west (the north-west, west Midlands and the south west) of this wedge. Although this broad division of England provides a useful distinction of landscape forms, in reality the boundaries between champion and several countryside were not clearly drawn and therefore we must be wary of applying the division too crudely.

A variety of factors combined to shape these local and regional differences in the late medieval landscape. Local variations in geology, topography, the inheritance of earlier centuries, population pressure, commercial opportunities, the rights of communities to exploit natural resources and the executive and regulative power of feudal lordship were all important influences on the development of the landscape. In order to re-create that landscape, we must understand the ways in which medieval communities exploited and managed their resources. Thus the aim of this brief overview is to describe how the English landscape looked and how it was managed in the later Middle Ages, and it necessarily concentrates on the essential fabric of everyday material life rather than the 'gold baubles' of surviving castles and cathedrals. The impact of industry will be considered in the next chapter.

The thirteenth century marked the latter stages of a medieval 'warm epoch' in north-western Europe, when average summer temperatures were perhaps one degree centigrade warmer than today. Warmer and drier summers encouraged the spread of vineyards in southern England and enabled farmers to cultivate grain at higher altitudes: there is evidence of thirteenth-century cultivation at 1,300 feet above sea level on Dartmoor and at 1,000 feet in the Northumberland hills. However, there is growing evidence of climatic change towards the end of the century, as summer rainfall rose consistently on the western hills and ferocious storms ravaged the North Sea. Coastal communities on marginal sites were especially vulnerable, and the sizeable towns of Ravenserodd (Yorkshire), Dunwich (Suffolk) and Old Winchelsea (Sussex) suffered catastrophic marine inundations in the century after 1250.

The growing instability of weather patterns in the late thirteenth and early fourteenth centuries is apparent in the contrast between, on the one hand, the series of bumper harvests in the 1330s and, on the other hand, the terrible crop failures and cattle murrains of 1315–22. Such striking variability in the weather is a likely indicator of a changing climate, and by the fifteenth century summers appear to have become consistently wetter and colder. Mean summer temperature was perhaps a degree centigrade lower than in the thirteenth century, and presaged the onset of the little Ice Age between 1500 and 1700. For most English farmers, long-term climatic change made little difference to their standards of living. Its impact was felt mainly by communities at the upper and lower altitudinal limits of late medieval England, on low-lying coasts or upland moors, where cultivation and sometimes settlement was forced to retreat from earlier sites.[2]

The thirteenth century marked the high point of a long process of colonisation and settlement in the English countryside. Domesday Book (1086) had recorded more than 13,000 places of varying status in England, and by 1300 many settlements had expanded and some new ones been established, although a few had disappeared. At the height of the Middle Ages England

The planned layout of a nucleated village with its ordered house plots and spacious green is clearly evident in this photograph of East Witton (Yorkshire). Located on a main road into Coverdale (top), and less than a mile from the gates of Jervaulx Abbey, the settlement was probably created in this form as a market in the early fourteenth century. The earlier village and church was situated away down the curving lane (bottom left). The present church (bottom) dates from the nineteenth century.

was smothered with settlements, especially in the densely populated south-east, many of which were small by modern standards, but some of which housed more residents than in any period before or since. Although the names of most of these places are easily recognisable today, it is not yet entirely clear how they looked in the landscape. The classic 'Midland village' – where settlement was confined to one nucleated centre nestling around the parish church and surrounded by its open arable fields – was not as commonplace as historians once thought. It is now believed that most Anglo-Saxon settlements took the form of dispersed hamlets and farmsteads, and that nucleation was a relatively new form of settlement which had emerged between the tenth and thirteenth centuries. Nucleated villages could be found in many areas of England by 1300, but were especially characteristic of the grain-producing districts of 'champion' England.

The explanations for this revolution in settlement morphology are complex and still uncertain, mainly because the process was largely complete by the time documentary evidence becomes more plentiful in the thirteenth century. The regular layout of many nucleated villages indicates a planned origin, and it is often assumed that local lords took the initiative in this process. In one well-documented case from the early fourteenth century, Jervaulx Abbey was responsible for the transformation of East Witton (Yorkshire) from a small and straggling row into a nucleated formation planned around a market green (see the illustration above). The acquisition of a royal licence to hold a weekly market, a common occurrence in the thirteenth century, was often an occasion when the layout of a village was reorganised: for example, Melchbourne (Bedfordshire) was almost certainly relaid around a market-place soon after its acquisition by the Knights Hospitallers in the late twelfth century. Other historians have justifiably pointed out that the reorganisation of settlement into a nucleated village could equally have derived from initiatives taken by villagers themselves. In either case, the creation of a nucleated village and the abandonment of surrounding farmsteads was a deliberate act of settlement relocation. Yet some nucleated villages emerged by less formal means. Nucleation at Whittlesford (Cambridgeshire) appears to have been the product of a complex process, whereby two separate foci became fused by the early fourteenth century through a combination of planning, settlement shift and piecemeal expansion. A similar process of piecemeal growth and fusion is evident at Sutton (Norfolk).[3] Medieval settlement was fluid and mobile, and the involvement of peasant communities, the power of lordship and the pressure of population were all important influences in its morphology.

As nucleated villages were late, but not universal, additions to the medieval landscape, many people must have continued to dwell in dispersed settlements of varying forms and antiquity. The hamlets of late medieval Devon had been established long before the Norman Conquest, as had the complex assortment of hamlets and isolated farmsteads which characterised north-east Hertfordshire. Nucleated villages were not common in such places, where the medieval settlement pattern represents continuity with the mid-Anglo-Saxon period and probably earlier. Occasionally, there is evidence that some dispersed settlement was created by deliberate planning in the later Middle Ages. Thus the dispersed and interrupted rows of Pendock (Worcestershire) were created in the twelfth or thirteenth century, and greens were inserted into parts of the Suffolk landscape in the early Middle Ages and their borders colonised during the thirteenth century.[4] For all its varied forms and origins, dispersed settlement was strongly associated with several countryside. By *c.* 1300 hamlets and farmsteads abounded in the wood–pasture region of the forest of Arden (Warwickshire), while villages in the nearby Feldon area were predominantly nucleated and practising sheep and corn husbandry often found in 'champion' countryside.

The mobility of settlement and the readiness to shift or reorganise sites sometimes resulted in the isolation of the parish church. The sites of many parish churches had been established in the late Saxon period or earlier, and were not moved in response to subsequent shifts in settlement. This is a much more likely explanation for isolated churches in the landscape than local folklore about a 'plague village', although the general contraction and shrinkage of settlements in the fourteenth and fifteenth centuries sometimes had a similar effect.

The fluidity of settlement also implies that many houses were rather flimsy constructions. This was probably true of housing belonging to the poorer sections of medieval society in the thirteenth century. Unfortunately, this has left little archaeological record, although documentary sources imply that poorer housing dilapidated very quickly: one house in Walsham-le-Willows (Suffolk) was taken down by its occupant for fear of thieves and rebuilt in a safer location nearby, and its building materials were valued at eighteen pence.[5] However, the quality of housing improved in the later Middle Ages for most people, who became accustomed to sturdy and expensive constructions built partly by professionals. These varied from simple open-hall houses, measuring perhaps twelve metres by four, to more sophisticated buildings with wings and first storeys. Most were built of timber on stone foundations, with plastered and lime-washed walls and roofs thatched with straw. Dwellings were situated inside 'tofts', or – for families of higher status on heavy soils – moats. The toft was essentially a small, often rectangular, farmyard surrounded by ditching and banking sufficiently high to obscure the house from the roadway; such measures offered security from thieves and an effective barrier to grazing animals. Inside the toft were agricultural out-houses for implements and animals, and perhaps smaller homes occupied by members of the extended family (such as younger sons and grandparents); after the thirteenth century, few peasants would have physically shared their houses with animals. The toft was often adjoined to the rear by a 'croft', a small enclosed space which could be used as pasture, garden, orchard or cattle pen. The outlines of tofts and crofts are still clearly visible at some village sites, such as Hockwold (Norfolk: see the illustration on p. 45). Most settle-ments possessed at least one water- or windmill after the twelfth century, employed principally in grinding corn but adaptable to a number of other industrial uses such as fulling cloth.

As arable land comprised, at the highest estimate, around 45 per cent of England's land surface in 1300, its physical appearance was the single most important feature of the medieval landscape. There was considerable variety in the organisation and layout of arable fields. The classic two- and three-field system was strongly associated with the 'champion' country which stretched through southern-central, midland and north-east England. These great arable fields were open, in the sense that the small strips of individual cultiva-tors were not separated from one another by any hedging or fencing, and communal in the sense that individual cultivators were obliged to abide by rules and regulations for collective fallowing, pasturing and perhaps crop

The open landscape and patchwork of the open field-system, created by the pattern of furlongs and strips, are still preserved in the arable fields of Laxton (Nottinghamshire). Although the fields of Laxton have suffered some recent enclosure and engrossment, the road system in places still follows the gentle curves formed by the method of medieval ploughing. The web of grassy pathways which provided access to individual strips is easily traced.

rotations on the land. Each great field was subdivided into smaller furlongs, which were delimited by grassy headlands and baulks and reached by myriad paths and trackways. Individual strips of arable – often no larger than half an acre – were delimited by stone markers laid on the ground, and created a patchwork effect which is still visible in the fields of Laxton (Nottinghamshire; see the illustration on p. 25). Each furlong was ploughed in a manner that created the parallel 'ridge and furrow' pattern, which is still preserved in pasture on heavy soils throughout Midland England (see the illustration opposite). Medieval ridge and furrow was normally curved into a reverse 'S' shape, and varied in width depending upon soil type and date; in the east Midlands, the most common width between surviving medieval ridges is seven to nine metres. Ridge and furrow is most associated with communal, regular, open-field systems.

The classic two- and three-field system created a largely open landscape, mainly because its communal basis removed the need for extensive hedging. Temporary fencing could sometimes be found within the fields, and the fields themselves may have been bordered in places by hedges, but overall this was an unbroken landscape. By the thirteenth century these open fields had consumed much of the cultivable land within a parish, pressing hard upon small survivals of woodland, pasture and meadow. Woodland was uncommon in these areas, and hedgerow trees were mainly confined to black and white poplar, ash, elm, willow and oak; exotic trees were very rare. The two- and three-field system is well documented in England, mainly because it survived until Parliamentary enclosure in the late eighteenth and early nineteenth centuries. Consequently, it has achieved a prominence in historical literature which is perhaps disproportionate to its importance in the Middle Ages. It is now known that it was a relative newcomer to the medieval landscape, and that field systems in many parts of England conformed to older and more varied forms. The classic open-field system emerged between the tenth and thirteenth centuries, broadly in the same regions as nucleated villages. Of course, the pace, extent and nature of this change varied from place to place: by the early fourteenth century villages in the Feldon area of Warwickshire possessed an assortment of two-, three- and four-field systems.

The two- and three-field system represents a particular attempt by medieval communities to ration and regulate their better arable land more effectively in the face of population pressure and the growing power of local lordship. But many areas of England did not respond to these forces in this manner, and as a result the landscape was much less open. In many places, arable land lay open in small strips but was not organised into regular fields nor subject to strict communal control of fallowing and cropping regimes. Such loose and irregular open-field systems could be found in eastern Norfolk, eastern Devon and west Suffolk. The arable land at Brandon (Suffolk) was organised into at least twelve open 'fields', which also contained a number of small enclosed parcels of arable.[6] In contrast to these irregular open field-systems, the medieval arable in central and northern Devon and central East Anglia was enclosed in many small hedged fields and cultivated in severalty, a field system and landscape feature of considerable antiquity. Medieval colonisers in the uplands of Cumberland held single farmsteads surrounded by their enclosed arable land, while lowland communities worked open fields with some communal regulations.[7] Such complexity and variety is apparent throughout 'several' and upland England.

This stunning photograph reveals the ridge and furrow pattern of medieval arable land, now preserved in pasture and highlighted by snowfall. The arable of Brassington (Derbyshire) was organised in open fields in the twelfth and thirteenth centuries, but was then converted to pasture and enclosed in piecemeal fashion during the course of the later Middle Ages. The pattern of hedged enclosures has ossified the layout of individual strips in the former open fields.

In common with rural settlements, field systems were not static but liable to undergo changes in the later Middle Ages. Indeed, the fifteenth century was – if anything – a period in which enclosures became more widespread. The irregular open fields which dominated some parts of thirteenth-century East Anglia had largely disappeared by the sixteenth century, to be replaced by small 'manifold enclosures, severed with so many deep ditches'.[8] In eastern Norfolk these small piecemeal enclosures provided farmers with greater individuality and flexibility in arable farming, but in west Suffolk they were the basis for a conversion from arable to pasture ground. Similar enclosures of arable land for pasture at Brassington (Derbyshire) preserved the earlier ridge and furrow and the tenurial strips of the former open fields (see the illustration above). In all three cases, enclosure was a gradual and piecemeal process, undertaken by dozens of individual cultivators over more than a century to produce a landscape of small hedged fields. In the changed economic circumstances after the Black Death, the commitment to maintaining the open fields was weak among the local community and local lords in such places. In other places, most notably areas of Leicestershire and Warwickshire, the enclosure of open fields and conversion to pasture occurred on a grander scale through the aggressive engrossment of land by certain lords and individuals in the fifteenth and early sixteenth centuries. While the potential for rapid or piecemeal change in some villages should not be underestimated, it must be emphasised that most field-systems changed little in the later Middle Ages.

Late medieval England was not a thickly-wooded country, consisting of 'farmland with islands of wood'.[9] Woodland comprised perhaps 10 per cent of the land surface *c.* 1300, although it was unevenly distributed. Some regions – such as the East Anglian Fenland and Breckland – were entirely shorn of woodland, yet the Weald and parts of Staffordshire and the Home Counties possessed considerable reserves. But few medieval communities had inherited much woodland from their forebears, and any 'wildwood' had long since disappeared. The remaining woodland in 1300 owed its survival either to intensive management policies or to the forest laws.

The forest was a legal construct designed to preserve the king's supply of deer and increase royal revenues. It had been developed by the earliest Norman kings, who introduced special laws and empowered a judiciary to regulate the exploitation of resources on behalf of the Crown over designated areas of land.[10] The forest, therefore, was a place of deer, not woodland, and incorporated various forms of land use including woodland, heath, moor and even arable land. The areas of countryside which were placed under forest law were determined partly by environmental factors, but also by the proximity of royal estates and palaces; hence forests were concentrated in the north-west and in an arc between Berkshire and Somerset, but were absent from Kent and Sussex. By 1300 forests were run by professional officials with the aim of producing a steady flow of income, and some venison, for the Crown. Yet forest law did have the effect of preserving woodland, because in order to protect the habitat of deer it carefully regulated land use and restricted the spread of arable land. Epping in Essex was situated in a densely-populated county where arable land was scarce, but the preservation of its extensive woodland owed much to its position within the much larger area covered by the forest of Essex. The area covered by forest law was greatest in the mid-twelfth century, when around 150 royal forests covered perhaps a third of England's land surface. Thereafter, successive monarchs gradually withdrew large areas of England from forest jurisdiction, as when Edward III disafforested the whole of Surrey in 1327. By 1350 only 15 per cent of England lay under forest laws, after which the system slowly decayed.

The social status of venison, and to some extent hunting, generated a demand among the nobility for hunting franchises within forests (known as chases), and the introduction by the Normans of the fallow deer encouraged the fashion for private deer parks; fallow deer were easier to keep in small confined areas than the native red or roe deer. Monarchs were prepared to grant such licences for a fee, and the number of parks increased dramatically during the thirteenth century until by *c.* 1340 there were around 3,200 parks spread widely across England, but with particular concentrations in the west Midlands and the south-east. Not all survived the Middle Ages, but they were a powerful imprint of social status upon the landscape. Bounded by enormous pale fences, parks varied in size from a few acres to a few hundred, and contained as many deer. Hunting was not really viable in most parks, and they represent an early example of 'farmed' meat. Like forests, they contained different forms of land use, notably open areas of pasture in which the deer roamed, known as launds, and some arable land. But there was a particularly strong association between parks and woodland, and medieval scribes often used the terms interchangeably. Parks were segregated internally to protect the woods from grazing deer, divisions which are still apparent in Bradgate Park (Leicestershire).[11] Indeed, as deer had no commercial value, the running costs of parks were often offset by controlled stock-fattening in the park or the sale of its woodland. Cropley park (Suffolk) contained mature timber with a capital value of over £1,200 in 1391.[12]

Woodland was patently of considerable value in the Middle Ages, and was normally exploited in one of two ways. Where large areas of woodland lay interspersed with pasture, and where the commercial potential for woodland products was limited, management techniques were relatively extensive. These areas were dubbed 'wood-pasture', and comprised a largely unenclosed landscape dominated by species such as oak, beech and hornbeam. The right to take the timber of mature trees belonged to the local lord or (in forests) to the king, but the 'open' nature of wood-pasture indicates that local communities exercised a range of common rights which were regulated either by the manorial lord or by forest officials. Common rights for local communities varied in their extent, but often involved grazing and animal stints; the right to take wood for the repair of houses, fences and ploughs, and dead wood for fuel; and to lop young branches for winter fodder. Such practices were often damaging to young trees, and largely inimical to tightly controlled and 'improved' woodland management; nevertheless, wood-pasture was still a 'managed' landscape.

More intensive management strategies prevailed in some deer parks and in densely-populated regions of England where individual woods tended to be smaller and where commercial opportunities were greater. These woods were often bounded by banks, ditches and fences, which implies that strict control was exercised over grazing and that common rights had been extinguished. This allowed greater protection of the woodland and permitted a regular and controlled renewal of resources. Oaks were most common in this type of woodland, although ash, lime (pry) and maple woods were not unknown, and were nurtured to varying stages of maturity. After many years of growth, mature trees were felled for timber and employed in substantial building projects. Pollarded oaks, holly and hazel coppices were cut annually or on a rotational system (often of four to eight years) to produce rods, poles and undergrowth, which were used for fencing, fuel and fodder. Hence the management of many woods in north Kent moved away from an extensive wood-pasture system during the twelfth and thirteenth centuries towards enclosed woods employing intensive coppicing methods, a change stimulated by the growing opportunities to supply fuel to the London market before the Black Death. Woodland in Cumberland comprised open wood-pasture for much of the Middle Ages, until rising demand for charcoal in the late fifteenth century encouraged a widespread change to enclosed coppice management.[13]

Between 10 and 15 per cent of England may have been moorland and heathland in 1300. The upland landscape of medieval England contained open tracts of mossland, marshland and moor similar in appearance to today's peat moorland. Its soggy and leached soils were largely uncultivable, although during the thirteenth century a few hardy colonists succeeded in grubbing some arable land from the valley sides in places such as Weardale. In many Lake District and Pennine villages these wastes constituted around two-thirds of the total land surface.

Yet it would be wrong to dismiss this soggy and rough pasture as an empty and otiose landscape. Red deer roamed freely, and thus many moors fell under the jurisdiction of a royal forest; at one stage there were thirty-nine forests spread across the Lake District and Pennines. The exploitation of all medieval upland was regulated either by the forest laws or by a local manorial administration, and from the thirteenth century the growing competition for rough grazing land encouraged closer definition of rights and territory. Most medieval moors acquired stone boundary markers, and stone walls of many miles were constructed across Fountains Fell in Malham (Yorkshire) after a famous boundary dispute among three local lords.

Although access to the resources of moorland was controlled by lords, local tenants were invariably permitted valuable common rights. Grazing stints on moors were much coveted by valley communities, and many peasants possessed rights to collect bracken and cut peat. Such links between lowland villages and upland pastures were long established and vital to the local economy. Farmers could also hire extra pasture for their cattle, horses and sheep, a practice which spawned temporary settlements (or shielings) high on the moors during the summer months in places such as Derwent and Loweswater.[14]

The area covered by lowland heaths in the Middle Ages was substantially greater than today, especially on the acidic and sandy soils of Dorset, Surrey and East Anglia. The famous heaths of Thomas Hardy's Dorset were probably as extensive as those in the Middle Ages, which indicates that much heathland has been lost in the last century. Medieval Breckland was a wild and treeless landscape, where small villages clung to islands of arable land in a sea of heath. Medieval heaths had less bracken and grass – and more furze and ling – than modern heathland, creating a colourful landscape of forlorn beauty and savage dignity. Although these vast tracts were largely uncultivable, they were not regarded as useless waste. Heath will quickly revert to scrub and woodland if not closely grazed and regularly disturbed, and so the survival of heathland as a resource and a landscape feature depended upon heavy exploitation and proper management.

Once again, access to most heaths was regulated either by forest law or by a manorial lord. Sheep flocks and rabbit warrens were maintained by lords, and their close grazing disturbed the light soils and thus helped to maintain the distinctive heathland habitat. Indeed, rabbits were rare animals in medieval England; they thrived only on heathland, and were introduced by the Norman aristocracy for their tender meat and valuable fur. But heathland yielded other useful resources, which further justified its protection and survival. By controlling and reducing the intensity of grazing on Kennett heath (Cambridgeshire), it was possible to produce an annual crop of ling, which was then sold on local markets. Ling, bracken and furze provided excellent fuel and useful thatch or fodder, and care was taken to protect these plants against damage from fire and implements (such as mattocks) likely to damage their roots. Local communities valued their grazing and litter rights, and were also permitted to dig flint- and chalk-pits for building material. Heathland was a widespread landscape feature, simply because it was regarded as a valuable resource both by lords and by local communities. The prejudice which dismisses heathland as wasteland is modern, and is inappropriate to the Middle Ages.

Rough pasture, such as that found on moorland and heathland, was more abundant than meadowland, i.e. waterside pastures which produced a mowable hay crop. Meadows comprised less than 1 per cent of England in

The slow, meandering creeks and streams of the medieval fenland are apparent in these remarkable cropmarks at How Moor (Cambridgeshire). The 'moor' (meaning wetland) was unreclaimed peat fen during the Middle Ages, where myriad creeks wound their way around clumps of reeds and sedge. The cropmarks of a larger water channel are evident in the centre of the photograph, to the left of which runs Vermuden's Drain of 1651.

1300, and were often highly rated at more than twice the value of arable land.

Marshland was more widespread in medieval England than it is today, especially around the Yorkshire Ouse, the Somerset Levels, the East Anglian Fens and many low-lying coastal areas. Marshland sustained some settlement on islands of higher ground, but for the most part comprised meandering creeks, stagnant pools, reedbeds, bog-myrtle thickets, grassland and outcrops of woodland (see the illustration above). Although abounding in natural resources, this was a mysterious landscape inaccessible in places except by boat and popularly assumed to be infested with demons. Yet summer grazing rights in Romney Marsh were greatly prized by communities on the surrounding upland, and marshes teemed with freshwater fish, wildfowl, peat, reeds and sedge.

The variety and value of marshland products and the persistent threat of flooding did not discourage some communities from reclaiming marsh for arable land, especially in the twelfth and thirteenth centuries. Canterbury Cathedral Priory funded substantial drainage projects around the fringes of Romney Marsh; there was extensive reclamation around the silt ridge in the northern Fenland; and there were piecemeal intakes in the Somerset Levels around the river Parrott between Athelney and Muchelney.[15] In many places, medieval reclamations were merely developments of earlier (often Romano-British) efforts, and dykes, sea-banks, sluices, weirs and linear drainage channels – familiar features in the modern landscape – became more common before *c.* 1300. Yet the history of marshland is a history of inundation as much as reclamation, and disastrous flooding of the Kent and Sussex marshes in the early fifteenth century made significant inroads into earlier gains. One surge around Wisbech (Cambridgeshire) in 1439 flooded over 10,000 acres. These losses partly reflect a rising sea level but also a lessened commitment to maintaining drains and sea-banks in the long period of agricultural depression after the Black Death.

Towns grew in size and number during the twelfth and thirteenth centuries, and by *c.* 1300 around 10–15 per cent of England's population lived in an urban environment. Many of the 500 or so places which exhibited urban characteristics were small, and would be regarded as little more than large villages today. Few late medieval towns possessed a population in excess of 3,000 people at their peak, and only a dozen exceeded 10,000. The largest regional centres, Bristol, Norwich and York, may have housed around 20,000 each, but London dominated the urban hierarchy with a population of perhaps 70,000–100,000 in *c.* 1300. Other leading towns included Coventry, Lincoln, Salisbury, Lynn, Newcastle, Canterbury, Bury St Edmunds, Exeter, Great Yarmouth and Colchester. Most towns were established on converging routeways, and many of the largest were located on navigable rivers.

Most medieval towns contain some evidence of a regular (often rectilinear) street pattern, reflecting a phase or phases of deliberate planning or reorganisation at some stage in their history. Even an old-established town could be laid out anew on an impressive grid pattern, such as Bury St Edmunds (Suffolk). But planning was especially apparent in the many 'new towns' which emerged during the twelfth and thirteenth centuries, either as garrisons in northern England and the Welsh Marches or as speculative trading centres established on favourable routeways. Many of the latter possessed no fortifications but were ordered around a large and commodious market-place and its approaches, on to which fronted regular burgage plots which were long and narrow in shape: Marshfield (Gloucestershire) provides an excellent example of the genre.[16] To implant towns on the landscape, either as extensive redevelopments of earlier and smaller settlements or as new ventures planted on virgin sites, required initiative from a powerful lord and perhaps encouragement from local peasants. However, as the power of feudal lordship declined in the fourteenth and fifteenth centuries, so their imprint on urban landscapes diminished. It is not coincidental that towns which first prospered in this later period, such as Puckeridge (Hertfordshire), have a more 'organic' layout.

If lordship was one factor influencing urban landscapes, then the fortunes of an individual town was obviously another. Urban foundation was sometimes speculative and carried no guarantee of success as a trading centre. Towns which were created under the aegis of garrisons often failed when the fortress was subsequently abandoned; a single farmstead marks the site of the fortified medieval borough of Caus (Shropshire) and a straggling village that of Lidgate (Suffolk). Many English towns suffered stagnation or decay after the fourteenth century as they struggled to cope with declining trade and population in the wake of the Black Death. Consequently, places such as Orford (Suffolk) and New Radnor (Herefordshire) still retain the regular and 'rural' features of their planned medieval origins, while other speculative centres, such as Newton (Dorset), have disappeared entirely.

The aerial photograph of Orford (see the illustration opposite) creates the impression that the urban landscape of medieval England was ordered and spacious. This is true to a certain extent. All medieval towns were surrounded by their own arable fields and pastures, and even Westminster possessed commodious meadows to the north of the abbey behind the built-up waterfront of the river Thames. There was agricultural land within the town walls of Kingston-upon-Hull (Yorkshire), and urban properties in the south-east corner of Durham City were well spaced and interspersed among the borough's fields, where many townsmen kept cattle. Similarly, demographic

The layout of the planted town of Orford (Suffolk) has changed little since the Middle Ages, from the port on the river Alde (right) to the spacious market-place and Henry II's castle with its fine octagonal keep. Seventy-two burgess plots were recorded here in the early fourteenth century, and the rectilinear pattern of the original town is still discernible. The arable lands next to the river (top) were salt marshes in the Middle Ages, although some attempt was made to reclaim them for pasture in the thirteenth century.

contraction after the Black Death resulted in the dilapidation of properties and the creation of open spaces in former built-up areas, a process identifiable at Winchester.

Although a sense of space was evident in all medieval towns, the best sites in the larger towns were densely settled. The older towns were often hemmed in behind defensive walls, and prime locations in the vicinity of market-places, bridgeheads and gateways were much sought after. Cheapside (London) was crammed with subdivided tenements before the Black Death, and property frontages were significantly smaller around the market-place in Alnwick (Northumberland). Buildings became so densely packed together that market-places in larger towns suffered from infilling as temporary stalls gradually transformed into permanent shops, and serious encroachment of this kind is recorded in 1279 at Hertford market.[17] In an attempt to maximise narrow but coveted frontages, timber houses were built either with a high, short wing adjoining the street and a deep development to the rear, or with a subdivided range of small commercial outlets adjoining the street, individually let, with access provided through a courtyard to a rear tenement.

Town walls were perforce maintained throughout the Middle Ages at active garrisons and ports liable to attack, but even in places where fortifications had become unnecessary the walls were sometimes maintained as a symbol of civic pride and independence. Expansion at such places could only be sustained through suburban areas. Some suburbs were planned to accommodate wealthier sections of urban society, such as Redcliffe (Bristol), but more often they were piecemeal developments of poorer immigrants stretching outside the larger towns 'in an untidy ribbon along the lines of the principal approach roads'.[18] Attempts to regulate road maintenance in towns and enforce com-

The Roman Ermine Street formed one of late medieval England's major lines of communication between London and the north. In the foreground it approaches the edge of the chalk uplands of north-east Hertfordshire, and then cuts away northwards through the valley of the Ashwell Cam (top left). Like many Anglo-Saxon settlements, the village of Reed (right) avoids the Roman road; indeed, the road forms the parish's western boundary. Reed's distinctive grid pattern, dispersed layout and woodland (bottom right) were all evident in the Middle Ages, and probably much earlier. In the middle ground, the medieval urban foundation of Royston sits boldly astride the busy intersection of Ermine Street and the prehistoric Icknield Way, another important medieval routeway.

munal responsibility for street repaving were only partially successful. Many urban streets suffered encroachment by buildings and obstruction by waste matter, and those of Southampton were described as 'full perilous and jepardouce to ride or goo theryn'.

The development of towns on trade routes of national and regional importance underlines the importance of inland trade and travel in many facets of medieval life. The spread and growing efficiency of royal justice, estate management and commercial activity all depended on an effective road system. Yet the English were not great road-builders in the Middle Ages, partly because they were able to adapt and resuscitate a comprehensive network of major roadways inherited from Roman and prehistoric times, many of which were ridgeways. The main roads of medieval England were broadly similar to the trunk roads of the twentieth century, although their earlier routeways were less standardised: the Great North Road, for example, comprised a number of alternative routes snaking northwards through Hertfordshire and the east Midlands (see the illustration above). Surfaces were not maintained to the standards of Roman military roads, although contemporaries made few specific complaints about the state of major roads. Journey times were reasonably fast given favourable conditions, and Gloucester could be reached from London in four days. Recent research has identified an impressive growth in horse-drawn transport during the thirteenth century, a development which was especially pronounced among peasants in south-eastern England, for whom commercial opportunities were greatest. Horses were twice as fast as the traditional oxen, and their growing importance implies a substantial growth in the volume of road traffic and the regularity with which journeys were made.[19]

The density of local roadways, tracks and lanes was much greater than today: open fields, wood-pasture, moorland and heathland all permitted rights of way. The densely-settled parish of Wimbish (Essex) had at least twenty-five medieval roadways known by name. All roads were subject to sporadic upkeep and piecemeal improvement, and concern for the safety of travellers in 1285 resulted in an order to reduce roadside cover on main routes 'where a man may lurk to do evil'. Stone bridges were commonplace, especially after the thirteenth century, and maintained either by landlords, religious guilds or public alms. Two parallel roads on the Suffolk/Cambridgeshire border formed the main east–west route from the Midlands into central East Anglia, and in the fifteenth century both spawned substantial stone bridges over the river Kennett (see the illustration below). The construction of two contemporary bridges at Kentford and Moulton implies a competitive element to bridge-building by local communities, a factor which is also apparent along a seven-mile stretch of the Cornwall–Devon border at Greyston, Gunnislake and Horsebridge. Indeed, fifteenth-century stone bridges, often built by the same mason, are not uncommon in Cornwall.[20] Other improvements in roadways included the construction of causeways over low-lying areas liable to floods; the erection of thousands of stone crosses to mark prominent pilgrimage routes; and regular bequests from testators for the upkeep of local roads.

Water transportation was especially important in marketing bulky goods of low value such as grain, fodder and fuel. Some historians have championed

Modern irrigation and water extraction techniques have largely drained the river Kennett, but this fine fifteenth-century bridge at Moulton (Suffolk) still proudly marks one of the main east–west routes between Suffolk and Cambridgeshire. As the route through Kentford, three miles to the north, became the preferred road in later centuries, there was no necessity to replace this bridge with a larger construction capable of carrying a greater volume of traffic; hence Moulton's bridge has survived and Kentford's has not.

medieval improvements in inland waterways, arguing that few villages in England were farther than fifteen miles from a navigable stretch of water.[21] Certainly, the profusion of small ports along the coastline of southern and eastern England attests the particular importance of coastal traffic and the strength of the London and foreign markets. However, river transportation was more expensive than coastal, and often prone to disruption by low water levels and obstructions such as weirs and bridges. Artificial cuts and canals seldom covered substantial distances, although they were not uncommon and were locally important: one fenland lode terminated in a small dock basin at Isleham (Cambridgeshire), around which the village was probably replanned in the thirteenth century.[22] There were certainly improvements in the system of inland waterways in the later Middle Ages, especially on east-flowing rivers in south-east England, but the constraints imposed by a lack of investible capital funds and inconsistent demand suggests that their overall significance should not be overstated.

Imagining the medieval landscape viewed from the sea, the modern observer would be struck by the absence of man-made landmarks: no pylons, no concrete sea defences, no piers or sprawling seafront developments. The only obvious human landmarks, employed by medieval seafarers, were castles and churches which until the Industrial Revolution rated among England's largest buildings. Stone castles were common throughout England in the thirteenth century, but especially in the politically marginal zones of the north and the Marches. Most comprised a keep, which served as a residence and fortress for the lord, and a surrounding bailey: Orford provides a good example, dating from the late twelfth century. The next generation of castles, built in the golden age of English military architecture (1250–1350), placed less emphasis on the keep and more on the curtain walls which bristled with flanking towers. Castles built before the mid-fourteenth century, with their massive keeps or concentric walls of scientific complexity, were an awesome expression of feudal authority.

They were also expensive to maintain. After *c.* 1350 fashion, political circumstances, the economic climate and forms of warfare all changed, and as a result many older castles fell into partial or utter decay, or – like Kenilworth (Warwickshire) and Windsor (Berkshire) – were redeveloped along new lines. Later castles were based on regular plans, often constructed around the four sides of a courtyard, and greater emphasis was placed on airy, comfortable and commodious domestic accommodation. The brute strength which had characterised the great Edwardian castle had been supplanted by 'show castles' of comfort, decoration and display. These were essentially fortified manor-houses which flaunted the wealth and taste of their owners, surrounded by water and guarded by large and impressive gatehouses bristling with heraldic arms. Herstmonceux castle (Sussex) was a brick construction of the 1440s with comfortable residential and lodging quarters and large glass windows (see the illustration opposite). Yet the threat of French raids demanded some attention to defence, and its heavily machicolated gatehouse, walled towers and gunports provided a practical deterrent. Deterrent is the keyword, for recent research has shown that the late fourteenth-century castle at Bodiam (Sussex) was – in reality – indefensible.

Castles belonged only to the wealthiest sections of society, but – as the focal point of an extended household and estate administration – they

Herstmonceux (Sussex) is a commodious and elegant 'show castle' built of brick in the 1440s, where emphasis was placed on display and comfortable accommodation rather than defensive prowess. The walled towers and machicolated gatehouse offered some deterrent to attackers, but in military terms it was less effective than the more overtly defensive keep, dating from the twelfth century, at Orford (see p. 33).

served as important centres of consumption. The same was manifestly true of the 800 or so houses of the monastic and mendicant orders in medieval England. The wealthiest Benedictine houses occupied large, enclosed sites in the centre of England's major towns, incorporating a range of domestic and administrative buildings. Many possessed impressively defended gatehouses which – as the experience of abbeys such as St Albans and Bury St Edmunds illustrates – were not entirely for show. The centrepiece of the monastic site was, of course, the conventual church, which could dominate the surrounding countryside. The cathedral church at Ely (Cambridgeshire) could be seen from five counties. The vast majority of English monastic sites were established by the end of the thirteenth century, and few underwent any substantial changes thereafter. The great period of monastic expansion in England had ceased by the mid-thirteenth century, and few new building projects of note were attempted after the mid-fourteenth century: not one English house wholly rebuilt its conventual church in the perpendicular style of the late fourteenth and fifteenth centuries. The economic tide had turned against English monasticism nearly two centuries before the Dissolution.

It would be wrong, however, to imply that the physically imposing conventual churches formed the main imprint of monastic houses upon the medieval landscape. Monasteries and episcopal sees were major landlords, whose managerial policies on their estates contributed enormously to the general trends thus far described: they developed properties in towns, established village markets, drained marshland, built bridges, managed woodland, created deer parks and so on. Of course, in many parts of England their management and

One of England's largest and earliest (1132) Cistercian houses, Fountains abbey (Yorkshire) provides a fine example of the layout and grandeur of a leading monastic house. Its most striking feature – the bell-tower on the north transept – is sixteenth-century, but much of the site was developed in the thirteenth century. To the south of the conventual church and cloisters is an extensive range of domestic buildings, dominated in the foreground by the separate refectories of the lay brothers and the monks. The course of the river Skell (right) has been cleverly integrated into the domestic range to provide a ready supply of running water.

development of the landscape has to be considered alongside the efforts of hundreds of other lords and thousands of peasant farmers. Yet in parts of northern England the Cistercian houses were especially prominent and influential in reorganising settlement and developing vast tracts of moorland for agricultural purposes (see the illustration above). The development of agriculture and settlement in Ryedale (Yorkshire) was largely shaped by the efforts of Rievaulx abbey.

In stark contrast to the history of conventual churches, around 6,000 parish churches were wholly or mainly rebuilt in the Perpendicular style between *c.* 1370 and the Reformation. This was a striking achievement in a period of economic contraction, and implies that patronage of religion by the laity was shifting away from monasticism towards the locality. As one landscape historian has commented, this achievement is 'more inspiring than any other human contribution to the landscape, because [parish churches] express the highest aspirations of local people and symbolise the lives of whole communities'.[23]

Some of the parish churches which were rebuilt towards the end of the Middle Ages remained rather plain and small, but others evoked the grandeur and scale of conventual churches. They featured decorative stonework, large stained-glass windows with parallel tracery, porches, aisles, clerestories, raised nave roofs and enhanced spires and bell-towers. Internally, they incorporated ornately decorated pews, pulpits, rood screens, monuments, side chapels and wall-paintings. The internal refitting of parish churches in the fourteenth and fifteenth centuries and the explosion of Perpendicular architecture undoubtedly reflect the vitality of parish life in the later Middle Ages, its enhanced sense of communal identity and a general concern for the spiritual health of the parishioners' souls. The rebuilding of the parish church was both a commemorative and a charitable act, although it is axiomatic that it also required considerable financial support: as Richard Morris has wryly observed, 'churches of quality did not come cheaply'.[24] Indeed, parishes with a poor or seriously diminished population would have lacked the resources to undertake any reconstruction, and the parish church of the severely shrunken village of Dunsthorpe (Lincolnshire) dilapidated and fell into disuse in the fifteenth century. Yet a parish blessed with a wealthy patron or devoted inhabitants could profoundly influence the development and appearance of its church. St Mary Redcliffe (Bristol), a suburban parish in a prosperous city, was rebuilt in sumptuous style by its confident and wealthy mercantile elite for both their religious and civic ritual. Such churches reflect parochial wealth, but also its morale and organisation.

In sketching the broadest and most constant features of the late medieval landscape, it would be imprudent to understate or overlook changes which occurred *within* the period. The mounting pressure of population and the growing power of local lordship before *c.* 1300 affected parts of England differently, but everywhere it induced an expansion and infilling of settlement and a shift towards grain production. Consequently, territorial rights were defined more carefully, different forms of land use became more closely integrated, and the differences between predominantly pastoral and predominantly arable regions were partially eroded: regional distinctions began to converge. After the Black Death, the collapse in population initiated a swing away from arable farming and a move towards more extensive farming methods. There was a widespread abandonment of arable land, a subtle shift towards enclosures, some re-establishment of marshland over earlier intakes, and a thinning out of settlements (see the next chapter). Similarly, differences between regional landscapes became more accentuated, to the extent that one historian has identified 'a divergence in regional fortunes . . . and there emerged some of those distinguishing characteristics which were to mark out the [Leicestershire] wolds in all subsequent centuries'.[25] Thus the English landscape became regionally more distinctive and perhaps a little 'wilder' – in the sense of less intensively managed – in the later Middle Ages.

The medieval landscape would not be wholly unrecognisable to a modern observer transported back in time. It is, perhaps, surprising to discover that arable fields occupy approximately the same area in modern England as they did in the Middle Ages, although their geography and physical appearance have obviously changed. Developments in the later Middle Ages – especially urban growth, the rebuilding of parish churches, and the reorganisation of villages – have left deep imprints upon the English landscape which even the 'progressive' achievements of modern society have, as yet, failed to eradicate entirely. Discounting the immense impact of industrialisation and the sprawl of settlement in the past forty years, the main differences between the modern and medieval landscapes are the reduction and destruction of wood-pasture and wetlands, and the vast plantations of conifers on former heath-land and moorland.

Throughout medieval England, we are struck by the integration of different resources and the dependence of communities upon delicate ecosystems. Arable farmers depended upon woodland for their fuel, marshland for their fish, and pasture for their livestock. It seems impossible to write of 'waste-land' in medieval England. Scrawny heaths were preserved because they were vital to the lords and local communities whose responsibility it was to maintain them, and even moorland was integrated into the economy of villages situated on lower ground. The technical limitations of medieval agriculture and the perennial need to nurture and replenish all natural resources meant that communities bought stability and sustainability at the cost of low agricultural productivity. To medieval society, 'conservation' – the sensitive and integrated management of resources – was a matter of survival.

POPULATION AND ECONOMIC RESOURCES

Mark Bailey

Although the medieval English economy was more sophisticated than is sometimes portrayed, there is no disputing that its main resources were land and the labour of the people who worked it. Its main products were grain, wool and a small range of basic manufactured products employed primarily in the home and on the farm. This narrow range of available goods and services is explicable by the low level of average income earned by the mass of the populace, structural limitations in the system of marketing and a lack of technical knowledge. There was no systematic investment in the infrastructure of the economy by centralised authorities and the flow of credit and capital funds was limited, both of which created further constraints to economic development. It would be wrong to think in terms of an integrated national economy in late medieval England.

Another factor influencing economic development in medieval England was its social and institutional structure, which in turn affected both the distribution and control of resources. Control of land was firmly vested in the ruling elite; it has been calculated that in the mid-fifteenth century the peerage held one-fifth of England, the Church and Crown held one-third, the gentry held one-quarter, and the peasantry held the remaining one-fifth. In addition, the produce of all land was subject to tithe payments to the Church and taxation and purveyancing by the Crown. Wealth, as measured through the acquisition of land, was concentrated among a numerically small group. The nobility and the upper ranks of the peasantry held their land in freehold tenure, whose title could be defended in the common law courts. Most peasants held land in customary or copyhold tenures which could only be defended in manorial courts, although in practice the occupier enjoyed some rights and a degree of security. A land market did exist in the Middle Ages, which provided some opportunity for peasants to acquire more land, but it was closely regulated by landlords.

Similarly, lordship implied some control over labour. The feudal system was cemented by a bewildering range of personal obligations which tied individuals to a superior lord. These bodily ties ranged from, for example, the requirement that a knight perform military duties at a royal castle, to an unfree peasant performing weekly labour services on the lord's manorial farm. Personal unfreedom (commonly known as villeinage or serfdom) was the condition of over half the population in some areas in the thirteenth century, and placed particular restrictions on the freedom and mobility of labour. Theoretically, a villein owed specified labour services on the lord's demesne, was not permitted to leave the manor or marry without the lord's permission, and could not seek legal redress in the common law courts. The free peasantry were burdened with some feudal obligations, but generally enjoyed greater freedom of time and action in the disposal of their land and the employment of their own labour. Although a minority in England as a whole, free peasants were not evenly distributed; they were concentrated in the northern counties, Kent, East Anglia and Lincolnshire, while villeins were most prominent in the Midlands. Once individual peasants – free and unfree – had discharged all their personal obligations, they were able to participate in a labour market based on negotiated contracts. Yet even this was not entirely free from seigneurial interference, particularly after the Black Death when the Statute of Labourers endeavoured to control the level of wages, the method of hiring and the length of employment. Women and children contributed significantly to the domestic economy, and were increasingly employed for wages when labour was scarce.

Long-term flows of population are assumed to have a significant effect on the utilisation of economic resources in pre-industrial economies, where the potential for technical change is limited. A sustained growth in the number of people is associated with expanding and new settlement, the extension of arable cultivation, a growth in the provision of basic goods and services, and an increasing volume of trade; a sustained decline in numbers will have the opposite effect. The Middle Ages provide a special fascination for the historian because they offer extreme examples of *both* experiences. The graph on p. 43 illustrates the extraordinary contrast between the rapid and sustained demographic growth of the twelfth and thirteenth centuries and the sudden, and then sustained, decline after the mid-fourteenth century.

Attempts to calculate the size of medieval England's population are beset by severe difficulties, because the documentary evidence at both the national and local level is so poor and scanty; there were no censuses and no parish registers to record baptisms, marriages and deaths. Consequently, historians must rely upon educated guesswork and a variety of indirect indicators to establish flows of population, although the fruits of such ingenuity are the subject of dispute and controversy. Yet we can reasonably speculate that the listings of landholders in Domesday Book and of taxpayers in the 1377 Poll Tax and the 1523/24 Lay Subsidy can be massaged to produce a national population of approximately 2.5 million in 1086, 2.7 million in 1377 and around 2.4 million in 1523/24.

Establishing the trends of population between these isolated benchmarks is more problematic than the graph suggests. There was sustained and rapid demographic growth between *c.* 1100 and *c.* 1300, although there is less agreement over the size of the population at its peak or its timing; on balance, we

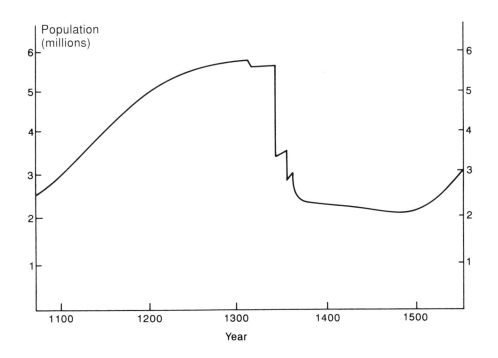

might speculate that there were close to 6 million people in *c.* 1300, after which the population ceased to grow. The Black Death of 1348/49 killed around 40 per cent of England's population, and successive epidemics in 1361, 1369 and 1375 sapped any immediate demographic recovery. Thereafter the population stabilised or fell slightly before symptoms of sustained recovery first became apparent in the early sixteenth century.

A demographic peak of 6 million people may appear unimpressive by modern standards, but this level was not again achieved until the eighteenth century. England in 1300 must have appeared a densely-populated country to contemporaries, where available resources were stretched to fulfil the basic requirements of many people. However, the population was not evenly distributed throughout England. The area north-west of an imaginary line drawn between the rivers Severn and Humber was the most sparsely populated; the most populous parts of England were the coastal areas of East Anglia, Kent and Sussex, and parts of Lincolnshire, the east Midlands and south Devon, where many villages were larger in 1300 than in 1900. The least populous areas were regions of upland, heathland and extensive woodland, such as the Weald. It is important to emphasise that over 80 per cent of the population lived in rural communities.

Lack of evidence undermines most attempts to establish the causes of demographic change in the Late Middle Ages, and controversy among historians is rife. The rapid growth in population during the twelfth and thirteenth centuries was the result of a surplus of births over deaths; birth rates probably rose as economic opportunities expanded, and the absence of epidemic disease on a significant scale kept death rates relatively low. However, population was growing at a slower rate, and then stagnating, by the late thirteenth and early fourteenth centuries. Birth rates probably began to fall as land and employment became scarcer, and a succession of harvest failures raised death rates. The arrival of plague in 1348/49 heralded two centuries of persistent

43

epidemic and perhaps endemic disease, which is assumed to explain the failure of the English population to recover before the early sixteenth century. However, recent research has speculated that a fall in birth rates also contributed to the demographic recession; if plague killed the younger generation disproportionately, if young women responded to labour short-ages by seeking employment and delaying marriage, and if fewer widows chose to remarry, then birth rates must have declined in the fifteenth century.

The single most important product in the medieval economy was grain. The range of field crops available to medieval farmers was limited to wheat, rye, barley, peas, beans, vetches and oats; root crops and ley grasses were unknown, and any vegetables or industrial crops were only grown on a small scale in gardens. The performance of agriculture varied regionally, because differences in soil quality, market opportunities and cropping practices all influenced the intensity with which the land was exploited. In some areas, such as the north-east and parts of the west Midlands, at least half of the arable land lay as fallow each year, yields were low, and most farmers tended to be self-sufficient. Yet in other areas, such as coastal Kent and Sussex, fallows could be eliminated when necessary, yields were high by contemporary standards, and farmers looked to the market to dispose of their crops.

Although some regions were more successful than others in responding to the demographic and commercial challenges of the Middle Ages, in general we are struck by the low efficiency of medieval grain farming; yields per acre were around one-tenth of modern yields. Technical advances in agriculture were restricted to a few progressive regions, and capital investment was limited even on the estates of wealthy landowners. It is not surprising that medieval agrarian productivity was low, given that animal manure was the main source of soil fertilisation, the soil was infested with weeds, storage facilities for grain were poor, irrigation and drainage were nominal, average farm size was very small and many farmers perforce shared both tools and beasts of burden. Cumulatively, these technical and structural limitations increased the susceptibility of grain farming to disruption by bad weather and poor harvests, and grain prices in medieval England fluctuated significantly from year to year. As imports of grain were negligible and seed corn had to be provided from the previous crop, a succession of poor harvests could have disastrous medium-term consequences for the economy.

The constant need for manure and traction necessitated that even pre-dominantly 'arable' areas of England possessed animals. Horses and oxen were the main source of traction, the former more common in the south and east and the latter in the north and west. Cattle provided milk and hides, but – like horses – they were poor grazers and thus required winter fodder to sustain them, which limited the numbers that most farmers could keep. Only a few areas, such as the Stour valley (Essex), developed any specialism in dairy farming. In contrast, pigs were popular everywhere among the lower orders of society because of their ability to convert the most unpromising food into meat. Likewise, sheep could survive on the poorest pastures and were highly versatile, providing wool, milk and – when old – meat; few animals were slaughtered young. In 1300 there were at least two sheep in England to every human, and they could be found almost everywhere. There were approxi-mately 100,000 sheep in Sussex in the 1340s, concentrated mainly on the Downs but also in grain-growing areas. Wool was the chief cash crop of medieval agriculture, and was much sought after throughout Europe for its high quality. The very best wool was produced on the uplands of the Welsh borders, in Lincolnshire and the Pennines.

In a predominantly agrarian economy, it is reasonable to suppose that the overall level of economic activity was largely determined by the expansion and contraction of agricultural output. The population rise of the twelfth and thirteenth centuries corresponded with a general period of agrarian prosperity, during which the production of grain and wool expanded perhaps twofold. The area under cultivation was extended, especially where reserves of wood, fen and waste were abundant. Older-settled land was exploited more intensively, rent levels rose, commercial opportunities expanded and the price of most basic commodities increased more rapidly than did costs. Yet this long period of economic expansion had slowed in some places and ceased in others by the third and fourth decades of the fourteenth century. By the 1330s there were marked signs of contracting agricultural activity in some regions: in northern England, for example, arable land fell out of cultivation and sheep flocks contracted on the estates of Cistercian houses.[1]

By the end of the fourteenth century there are unequivocal signs of agrarian retrenchment throughout England. Prices for many agricultural products fell, and profit margins were squeezed further by a persistent rise in wages. An over-supply of grain, coupled with higher production costs, was the major consequence of sustained demographic decline in the late fourteenth and fifteenth centuries as land became abundant relative to labour. Farming became less intensive, some arable land was abandoned entirely, rents fell and tenants were hard to find. Many villages bore the scars of agrarian retrenchment and depopulation, and the sites of house plots abandoned in this period are clearly evident at Hockwold (Norfolk; see the illustration below). Pastoral activities

Neither the straight hedges and ordered fields of Parliamentary enclosure nor recent housing development have managed to eradicate medieval earthworks at Hockwold (Norfolk). This small inland port was favourably located on the edge of the medieval fenland, but demographic and economic decline resulted in the abandonment of many house plots, crofts and pathways. It provides a very good example of the physical contraction of settlement which afflicted most places in England during the century or so after the Black Death.

fared better than did grain farming, mainly because they were less labour-intensive and because demand for meat, wool and hides displayed greater resilience, but even pastoral farming was depressed by the mid-fifteenth century. Nevertheless, the swing to pasture was discernible everywhere, and in some areas large tracts of arable land were enclosed and converted to pasture during the fifteenth century. This development was particularly evident in central and southern counties, where previously the area under pasture had been limited. If a village was already small and poorly located, and if a local landlord was sufficiently determined and aggressive, enclosure could result in the extinction of the community.[2]

The ebb and flow of agrarian fortunes carried different consequences for different sections of medieval society. The benefits of agrarian prosperity in the twelfth and thirteenth centuries accrued mainly to the landlords, whose income from land rents and the sale of produce increased appreciably; by such means, the annual income of the Bishopric of Worcester rose from £330 in 1185–86 to £1,307 in 1312–13. The rising income of many seigneurial households during this period was matched – and sometimes exceeded – by a rise in expenditure. The household accounts of the medieval nobility provide fascinating reading, and reveal major expenditure on food, travel, retinues, plate, fine textiles and the building or maintenance of a number of residences. The rebuilding of many English cathedrals in the thirteenth and early fourteenth centuries was founded upon this period of agrarian prosperity.

Wealthier peasants who possessed enough land to produce a sizeable surplus for the market – over fifteen acres – also prospered. But the growing pressure of population resulted in a reduction in holding size for the majority of peasants, to the extent that nearly half of England's population in *c.* 1300 may have had insufficient land to sustain themselves. In such circumstances, the availability of alternative employment off the holding was vital to their survival, and in good years most smallholders managed to scrape together sufficient income to subsist. But the purchasing power of a day's wage diminished significantly during the course of the thirteenth century, and a large pool of underemployed people competed for any available work, which implies that the mass of English people endured lives that were increasingly hard and uncertain. The poorest sections of society were least able to cope in years when bad harvests struck; hence the successive harvest failures and cattle murrains between 1315 and 1322 resulted in widespread famine and the death of perhaps one-tenth of the population.

Landlords' income declined during the late fourteenth and fifteenth centuries as the value of land fell significantly, wage bills rose and markets for agricultural produce became over-supplied. The Bishopric of Worcester's income fell from over £1,300 in the early fourteenth century to £947 in 1453–54. This was scarcely a catastrophic decline, but it dictated that landlords reduce their household expenditure and manage their estates with greater care and flexibility; few undertook extensive building programmes. Many major landlords gradually withdrew from the direct exploitation of their manorial demesnes and turned towards the relative security of *rentier* farming.

In contrast, this period could be regarded as a golden age for the lower orders of society. Land was easily acquired at attractive rents, average holding-size increased, employment was abundant and well paid, and the purchasing power of a day's wage rose. Their improving standards of living were apparent in the construction of more robust and larger houses, incorporating more (although still rather basic) furnishings; better and more fashionable clothing; a more varied diet, including consumption of more meat and ale; and a greater participation in leisure pursuits. The increased bargaining power of the peasantry and their willingness to take collective action to redress grievances forced landlords to make substantial concessions in terms of land tenure and social status. By the end of the fifteenth century, villeinage had effectively disappeared from England. Yet for all these general advances, village society may have become more polarised during this period. On the one hand, smallholders lived comfortably by supplementing their produce with craftwork and wage-labour where employment opportunities were plentiful. On the other hand, a small but ambitious class of yeoman farmers was able to construct larger farms and take over the leases of manorial demesnes.

The English economy became substantially more responsive to commercial forces in the twelfth and thirteenth centuries as population and trading opportunities grew, and the division of labour became more pronounced. The extent to which commercialisation came to influence economic life is impossible to measure, largely because of the inadequacies of the source material, but there can be no doubting its growing importance. For example, there were significantly more towns and village markets in England in 1350 than in 1100. Domesday Book (1086) records around 120 boroughs in England, and casually mentions a few other market centres, yet by the mid-fourteenth century there were perhaps 500 'towns' in England, and around 2,000 weekly village markets had been licensed by the Crown. Even small towns had certain streets or sections of the market-place given over to specialist sales, such as livestock, or trades, such as fishmongers. As towns grew in size and number, their trading privileges and the legal rights of their leading inhabitants became more clearly defined and extended.

By *c.* 1300 England had acquired a dense network of weekly markets, often sited a few miles apart and held on different days of the week. But it is important to stress that most transactions in these markets were confined to small quantities of very basic goods, mainly grain, destined for local consumption: 'a great deal of trading remained a matter between neighbours, between lords and tenants, or between villagers and pedlars'.[3] Weekly markets were supplemented by a growing number of licensed fairs held on nominated days during the summer months. Small village fairs provided opportunities for itinerant marketing, especially in livestock, and for enjoying conviviality; in 1284 one manorial official was fined for staying too long at Highworth fair (Wiltshire). A number of fairs established a regional reputation, attracting buyers of wholesale goods for noble households. The fair at Ely (Cambridgeshire) was regularly attended in the late fifteenth century by representatives from Thetford priory.[4] A small number of fairs in eastern England attracted an international clientele in the twelfth and thirteenth centuries, such as Boston (Lincolnshire), Bury St Edmunds (Suffolk), Northampton, Stamford (Lincolnshire) and St Ives (Huntingdonshire).

Although the growth of markets and fairs was a function of expanding trade, it also reflected the increasing sophistication of the institutional structures which supported and governed it. The transformation of the English legal system and the development of the common law between *c.* 1160 and 1220 created an appropriate and reliable mechanism for seeking redress, and thus a firm base upon which to conduct trade. The Crown took an active role in replacing local weights and measures with a standardised national system, and in providing a strong and centralised currency. The growing volume of coinage in circulation, and the introduction of smaller coins such as half-pennies and farthings, is another indicator of growing commercial activity; in 1311 the amount of coin in circulation in England exceeded 1 million pounds, compared with a maximum of £50,000 in 1000.

Trade in domestic markets constituted the bulk of commercial activity in late medieval England, but the opportunities presented by foreign markets were not insignificant. Ports in the south and south-west had well-established links with southern France and the Mediterranean, while those along the east coast looked to the Low Countries and the Baltic. At various times in the later Middle Ages England was highly regarded as an exporter of raw materials such as wool, tin, lead and hides; foodstuffs such as grain and herrings; and manufactured goods such as medium-quality woollen textiles and pewter. In return, it looked to the Baltic for timber, tar, rope, furs and oil; to the Iberian peninsula for oil, iron, leather, wax and fruit; to France for wine, salt and woad; to the Low Countries for luxury woollen cloths; and to the Mediterranean for silk and spices. For most of the Middle Ages this trade was dominated by foreign merchants, mainly Italian or those affiliated to the Hanseatic League. However, during the later fourteenth and fifteenth centuries a greater proportion of this trade fell into the hands of English merchants operating predominantly from London; as a consequence, however, the foreign trade of ports such as Boston, Lynn (Norfolk) and Great Yarmouth (Norfolk) suffered.

Commercialisation left a discernible imprint upon both the product and the intensity of medieval agriculture. Livestock husbandry on most aristocratic estates was organised along commercial lines, rearing cattle for fattening or milk, and integrated sheep farms producing wool for export. Most of the wool produced in medieval England was sold as a cash crop, the best of which was exported to the Continent. Millions of fleeces passed each year through the main wool ports of Kingston-upon-Hull (Yorkshire), Boston, Lynn, London and Southampton. Such commercialism undermines the traditional assumption that agriculture in medieval England was overwhelmingly subsistence-based. The broad distinctions in the landscape noted in my previous chapter – the differences between arable-dominated 'champion areas' and pastoral-dominated 'several countryside' – indicate some regional specialisation of production, and by implication some trade between regions. Furthermore, the growth of towns in the twelfth and thirteenth centuries was only possible through the production of grain surpluses by rural areas, and the recent suggestion that London housed as many as 70,000 to 100,000 people in 1300 can only indicate that grain and cattle farming in its hinterland was highly commercialised.[5] By one reckoning, a third of all grain produced in medieval England was sold.[6] In certain favoured areas, historians have identified strong traits of specialisation and commercialisation combined with relatively high levels of output. Thus eastern Norfolk concentrated on the production of barley for the London market, and some grain from the Nene valley was exported through the fenland rivers to Lynn and possibly the Continent. However, it is important to stress the regional nature of these developments, and other regions of late medieval England were more resilient to commercial change. Regions which were poorly located and politically marginal, such as Shropshire and areas of northern England, were characterised by subsistence farming and a lack of specialisation in grain production.

For all our attempts to destroy the old 'myth' that medieval England was a backward economy inhabited by subsistence farmers, there were distinct limits to the influence of commerce on the economy. The impressive increase in urban and market foundations is an imperfect indicator of commercialisation, because not all were successful. Some towns and village markets were little more than speculative ventures by landlords, whose desire to channel, control and profit from local trade had little chance of success. This was especially true of markets established after the mid-thirteenth century, when many of the best sites had been occupied and most areas were already well provided with marketing outlets. The market at Corneybury (Hertfordshire) was poorly located in a highly competitive locality, and foundered soon after it was licensed in 1253.[7] Similarly, the role of the major fairs was undermined by competition from the larger towns, which could offer a continuous supply of luxury goods and a more permanent base for foreign merchants; hence St Ives's fair declined in the late thirteenth century, and was badly depleted by 1340. Put simply, there was insufficient domestic or foreign trade to sustain all of England's speculative marketing institutions, even at the peak of economic activity around 1300. Furthermore, historians must beware the facile assumption that commercialisation *per se* is a 'good thing'. We must not overlook the probability that many poor producers sold their produce, not to raise profits, but simply to raise the cash to pay their rent, with adverse consequences for their standards of living.

It is also clear that marketing opportunities ceased to expand during the fourteenth century, after which they declined sharply. The sustained demographic decline and agricultural recession of the late fourteenth and fifteenth centuries reduced both the number of people living in towns and the volume of goods traded in the economy. Admittedly, the growing prosperity of the lower ranks of society meant that the contraction in trade was not commensurate with the decline in population, and there was some sectoral growth in manufacturing industries. A few towns prospered, notably those which – for a variety of reasons – managed to capture a growing share of local trade, such as Buntingford (Hertfordshire), or which diversified into the production of industrial goods, such as Castle Combe (Wiltshire) and Lavenham (Suffolk). As a consequence, a greater proportion of England's wealth may have become concentrated in the towns during the period after the Black Death. Yet even a highly successful textile-manufacturing centre such as Colchester (Essex), which grew rapidly between *c.* 1340 and 1420, suffered declining fortunes in the later fifteenth century.[8] After the 1420s there are few indications of commercial vitality anywhere in the economy.

The contraction in the volume of trade – both domestic and overseas – was caused by widespread problems of over-supply; by shortages of bullion throughout Europe, which contributed to a fall in the amount of coin in circulation in England by approximately one-third between 1311 and 1417; and by the disruption to overseas markets through persistent warfare. As a consequence, many small towns suffered depopulation and a reduction in market income in the fifteenth century. Some towns suffered greatly, and in 1405 the inhabitants of Lyme Regis (Dorset) complained of severe economic difficulties caused 'by the buffetings of the sea and the assaults of enemies, as by great and frequent pestilences'.[9] In places such as Caus (Shropshire), the economic problems were insurmountable and the town was reduced to little more than a small village by the early sixteenth century.[10] Another indication of contracting commercial activity during the fourteenth and fifteenth centuries is the disappearance of perhaps two-thirds of all licensed village markets and many of the village fairs. Of twenty-one licensed markets and towns in medieval Bedfordshire, only eleven were functional in the sixteenth century. Yet this weeding out of weaker and unviable markets had one substantial benefit: it meant that England's marketing system in 1500 was a leaner and more rational structure, and less dominated by feudal lordship, than it had been in 1300.

A clear distinction between 'industrial' activities and other forms of non-agricultural employment in the later Middle Ages is difficult to draw. To write of medieval 'industry' is – by modern standards – something of a misnomer. First, none of the extractive industries operated on a large scale, and most 'manufacturing' industries involved little more than the processing of basic agrarian products such as grain, leather and wool. The amount of capital equipment employed in production was limited, and hence the units of production were small and often located in domestic surroundings. Secondly, many goods were essentially 'handicrafts', which could be manufactured by a work-force which did not require a wide range of skills or sophisticated technical knowledge. Of course, there were those workers who exhibited a high level of skill in a particular craft, and certain urban crafts required their workers to complete training as apprentices. But workers who had acquired some expertise with a particular raw material could turn their hands to a variety of trades; at various times carpenters could construct houses, make bows, build ships, and fashion household utensils. Thus it is invidious to categorise their work in shipbuilding as an industrial activity and their other pursuits as craftwork.

If most non-agricultural employment did not require a highly trained work-force, then it follows that employment patterns were often flexible. Few workers concentrated on one task or skill throughout the year, and most turned their hands to a variety of different tasks as the opportunity presented. Similarly, the same workers were often engaged in many, if not all, the stages of production, from provision of the raw material to the retailing of the finished good. As shipbuilders, our carpenters might be employed solely as skilled labourers in the dockyards. As utensil-makers, they might be involved in all stages of production, from felling the timber, scappling the wood, and selling the finished product from their workshops.

Given these difficulties of definition, it is more helpful to distinguish between the scale and quality of production rather than the types of work. The majority of workers were engaged in the production of small quantities of basic goods. Craftsmen of various kinds could be found in all peasant communities, where they provided the local community with essential agricultural goods and services. Every town and almost every village possessed some victuallers, selling food, ale and fodder, and some craftworkers, producing basic leather goods, metalwork and utensils. However, local demand was not sufficiently strong to sustain full employment in these tasks, and it is not uncommon to find that most of these workers also sought other tasks and maintained small arable holdings. Although the seasonal and discontinuous nature of most handicraft and industrial work should not be understated, the volume of people involved sporadically is impressive. If nearly half of England's population did not possess viable arable holdings in *c.* 1300, many families must have cobbled together a living from various by-employments. The range of available employment varied according to local conditions, but was greatest in regions with a diverse resource base. Residents of marshland communities found work in stock rearing, fishing, fowling, basket-making, reed and turf cutting, so that by 1300 the reclaimed siltlands of the northern Fenland had become one of England's most densely populated regions.

In contrast to these village craftsmen, some producers looked to markets beyond their immediate locality, which necessitated the manufacture of goods of higher quality and/or their production on a larger scale. In either case, there were advantages in producers congregating together. This trend is clearly observable in the larger towns, where a wide range of luxury goods and professional services were available to a large number of consumers. The records of thirteenth-century Coventry (Warwickshire) mention over 300 different occupations, such as vintners, parchment-makers, goldsmiths, spicers, scriveners, lawyers and doctors, and there were around sixty recorded trades in a moderate-sized town such as Durham.[11]

Regional specialisation in production was also apparent in those handicrafts or industries which required large quantities of raw materials or fuel: hence pottery- and glass-making in the Middle Ages was located in areas of extensive woodland which possessed the requisite fuel to fire the furnaces. In other industries, regional specialisation evolved through a growing division of labour in the production process, with workers concentrating on particular tasks. The most obvious example is commercial textile manufacture, where various specialists (spinners, weavers, fullers, dyers, shearmen, drapers, etc.) found it advantageous to live in close geographical proximity. Thus certain regions or places became renowned in late medieval England for the production of a particular product: hence the Forest of Dean acquired a reputation for its ironware, and Colchester for its russet cloth. It is to these 'industrial' specialisms that we must now turn.

England was transformed during the Middle Ages from a net importer of woollen cloth to Europe's major producer and exporter. As the manufacture and export of the finished product increased, so exports of raw wool declined. In the 1340s, England exported around 30,000 sacks of raw wool and only 5,000 cloths to the Continent annually; by the 1540s, 120,000 cloths were exported, but only 5,000 sacks of wool. This extraordinary growth in woollen textile manufacture corresponded with a radical shift in the location of production. In the twelfth and thirteenth centuries, when English manufacturers produced small quantities of higher quality cloths, production was concentrated in a few, old-established, urban centres, such as Leicester, Northampton, Stamford, Winchester and York. Yet by the mid-fourteenth century cloth production in many of these older textile towns was declining at precisely the time when English exports of cloth were expanding. New and specialised centres of manufacture emerged in other towns and certain *rural* regions, whose leading villages gave their name to particular styles of cloth, such as Kersey (Suffolk) and Worstead (Norfolk). Parts of the Cotswolds, the Kennet valley, and the Mendips became renowned for their production of good quality woollens; parts of Devon, north Essex and south Suffolk for medium quality woollens; and parts of the Pennines between Leeds and Manchester, and the area north of Norwich, for coarse cloths. Industrial villages such as Lavenham and Castle Combe were pockets of growth and prosperity in the general economic conditions of contraction and decline in the later fourteenth and fifteenth centuries. Towns which acted as distribution centres for these rural areas, and engaged in some manufacture themselves, such as York, Norwich and Colchester, also enjoyed relative prosperity.

This startling success demands an explanation. After the Black Death, the growing prosperity of the lower orders of society throughout north-west Europe created a larger market for coarse and medium-quality woollens. English manufacturers were able to capture a growing share of this market, for a variety of reasons. After the 1330s, the export of raw wool from England was subject to excise duty by the English Crown, while cloth exports were liable to a much less punitive tax. European textile manufacturers continued to buy English wool because they lacked a viable alternative supply of high-grade wool, and consequently their English counterparts could acquire the raw material more cheaply. But it is one thing to possess a cost advantage over competitors, and another to exploit the opportunity. Only a few areas of England developed a commercial textile industry, and it is traditionally argued that only those regions with the requisite geographical advantages – fast-flowing water for fulling mills, and local supplies of wool and fuller's earth – prospered. The old textile towns, it is argued, had neither the space nor the head of water for fulling mills, and their trade guilds (which regulated trading and employment practices) were restrictive and inimical to new work practices. Yet this interpretation is not strictly correct: for example, the construction of mill-races permitted the operation of fulling mills on most lowland rivers, and they were common enough on the slow-moving waters of East Anglia. Furthermore, the regulative practices of trade guilds – which enforced a rigorous quality-control of the labour force and the finished product – were well-suited to the production of luxury textiles, but largely irrelevant once the emphasis had shifted to a product of lower quality. The new ingredients for commercial success in cloth production were good-quality wool and workers who could perform competent but uncomplicated spinning, weaving and dyeing. For this, manufacturers sought a flexible but cheap labour force with a broad background in craft production. The emerging centres of England's rapidly expanding textile industry were located in predominantly pastoral districts, characterised by weak manorialism and loose social structure, where reserves of underemployed and semi-skilled labour abounded.[12]

Some shipbuilding was undertaken in many of England's small coastal ports, but invariably on a small scale with only local significance. Salt production was located at certain inland brines, such as Droitwich, and mainly at salterns on coastal marshes in Lincolnshire. The industry declined after the fourteenth century as costs rose and cheaper imports were available from the Bay of Biscay. The most important coastal and marshland industry was undoubtedly fishing, although as an activity it has left little documentary evidence. Freshwater marshes teemed with eels, dace, perch and wildfowl which were trapped in weirs, nets, wicker baskets and from small boats. The shallow draught and adaptability of many medieval boats meant that they could be launched from almost any foreshore, and residents of most coastal communities fished casually for crab, ling, plaice, flounders, mackerel, hake, dabs and cod. Some communities supplemented this part-time, opportunist, fishing by working the vast shoals of herrings and sprats which migrated down the North Sea each year during the late summer and autumn. England was famous throughout north-west Europe for its herrings, which were salted or smoked and widely distributed. After a number of violent and piratical clashes with the Cinque Ports, Great Yarmouth emerged as the centre of the English herring trade, although Scarborough (Yorkshire) was also important in the north. In the early fifteenth century Scarborough possessed a fleet of around 100 small boats (deckless vessels of *c.* 20–30 tons) engaged in the herring season, which was swelled by crews from villages along the coasts of Durham, Yorkshire and Lincolnshire; even a small village with no haven, such as Sizewell (Suffolk), committed between six and twelve boats to the autumn herring season.[13]

Few skippers owned their own fishing boats; they relied upon employment by boat-owning merchants or wealthy farmers for the duration of the herring and sprat seasons. Opportunities for work were greatest in the late thirteenth and fourteenth centuries when the scarcity of food heightened the importance of herring, and to a lesser extent sprats, as a cheap and nutritious source of food; at this time around 100 large boats were operating from Yarmouth, each of which expected to land over 100,000 herrings each season. However, demand for herring had declined by the fifteenth century, as population fell and standards of living rose. Recession in the herring trade contributed to the pioneering of new fishing grounds by boats from Scarborough and East Anglia, seeking deep-sea cod and ling in Icelandic waters. Demand for larger fish such as cod remained high in the late fourteenth and fifteenth centuries, which explains the emergence of fishing communities such as Polperro (first documented in 1303) and Mevagissey (1410) along the Cornish coast.[14]

The reduction in English woodland during the twelfth and thirteenth centuries encouraged the exploitation of other forms of fuel, most notably peat turves and coal. Coal production expanded discernibly after *c.* 1250, and some

In the Middle Ages coal was often extracted from small vertical shafts, at the entrance to which was piled debris from the underground workings. Consequently, many medieval coalmines take the form of 'bell-pits', similar to those visible at Hartington (Derbyshire). The intriguing gridmarks around these bell-pits may be associated with later workings.

activity is recorded on all English coalfields by the close of the Middle Ages; output peaked during the fourteenth century, after which demand fell as the price of other fuels became cheaper once again. Most mines were small (see the illustration on p. 53), and the coal was extracted through open-cast mining or bell-pits (vertical shafts used rather like a well). Coal was expensive to transport, which restricted its market beyond the immediate vicinity of the mine, although small parcels of coal did reach wider markets, principally London and blacksmiths' forges in the south-east. The main coal-producing (and exporting) region was the north-east, especially in the vicinity of Whickham, Newcastle, Bishop Auckland, and Durham City. But it would be inaccurate and misleading to write of a 'coal industry' in the Middle Ages. Production in many places was limited and discontinuous, and even north-east England produced only *c*. 50,000 tons of coal each year. As Hatcher writes, 'the vast majority of medieval mines ranged only from the intermittent scratchings of peasant farmers . . . to modest partnerships or undertakings employing at most a handful of labourers'.[15] In all the extractive industries, many miners continued to maintain a smallholding at least.

Deposits of iron ore could be found throughout medieval England, and were worked locally by numerous village blacksmiths; iron was an indispensable component of agrarian life. Yet the quality of English ore was variable, and certain high-quality products – such as decorative iron and military hardware – were made with purer ore imported from Spain and, to a lesser extent, Sweden. In some years during the fifteenth century, England imported around 3,000 tons of iron ore. Overall output of iron is difficult to establish, but from a base of around 1,000 tons in 1300 it probably grew fivefold over the next two centuries.[16]

Production of iron on a large scale depended upon the local availability of fuel, rather than the location of the ore itself. Iron ore must be smelted in furnaces to render it workable, a process requiring abundant supplies of fuel, preferably wood or charcoal. Indeed, a burgeoning centre of iron production in Craven (Yorkshire) failed because of insufficient quantities of local fuel. Considerable reserves of woodland were required to sustain production on a large scale, and consequently the industry became concentrated in the Forest of Dean and the Weald. Even here, evidence of the medieval iron industry is difficult to trace on the ground and in documents, because the ore was smelted at small and temporary bloomeries which were abandoned as local supplies of wood became exhausted. Towards the end of the Middle Ages, however, the availability of water became an important factor determining the location of iron production. Water had always been needed to wash the ore and to quench the final product, but by the fifteenth century it was also harnessed to drive water-mills which powered the bellows and hammers in the furnace. The growing use of water power, and the introduction of blast furnaces, greatly increased the size and output of plant, and tended to reduce the peripatetic nature of ironworking. These innovations were mainly adopted in the Weald, which by the end of the fifteenth century had supplanted the Forest of Dean as England's main iron-producing area (see the illustration opposite).

English tin was esteemed throughout Europe as the purest available, and was exported in growing quantities from the twelfth to the mid-fifteenth century. Tin-miners enjoyed considerable freedom from local manorial control, and were permitted to prospect anywhere, with the exception of

Stimulated by demand from the London market and royal armaments, the Weald emerged at the centre of England's expanding iron industry in the later Middle Ages. Large-scale iron production required fuel for the furnaces and water power to drive the bellows and hammers. As plant size increased in the fifteenth century, narrow river valleys were dammed to provide a suitable head of water. Appropriately, this hammer-lake at Mannings Heath (Sussex) is still surrounded by dense woodland.

gardens, orchards, churchyards and highways. Deposits of tin abounded in alluvial soils in Devon and Cornwall, and were extracted by streaming the soil with vast quantities of water. As these alluvial deposits were not exhausted until the end of the Middle Ages, there was little open-cast or shaft mining before 1500. Most miners concentrated solely upon the extraction of the ore, which they then sold to merchants for smelting. Both miners and smelters were subject to regulation by the stannaries, which served both as a regulative body for the industry and as the Crown's medium of taxation. Cornwall was divided into four stannaries, one of which corresponded approximately to the area covered by Bodmin moor.[17]

Lead was another metal which abounded in medieval England, especially in Derbyshire, the Mendip hills and parts of the northern Pennines, and was exported to many areas of north-west Europe. Most miners either worked on their own, paying an agreed percentage to owners of mineral rights, or as hired labourers. Extraction of lead was restricted to places where veins of the ore approached the surface, and so the mines were either open-cast or simple bell-pits. Prior to *c.* 1300 the latter were drained by bailing, although some deeper mines were rendered workable in the fifteenth century through the use of simple drainage tunnels. The output of lead was limited and highly variable; the main area of production, Derbyshire, produced only 370 tons in 1300, and estimated English output in 1500 was 625 tons.[18]

The physical evidence contained in most of England's parish churches testifies to the importance of stone quarrying in medieval England, but – once again – the industry is difficult to identify in the documentary sources. This

Medieval quarrying has left little record in documentary sources, although it was undoubtedly significant in villages situated along the outcrop of Great Oolite stone which stretched from south Lincolnshire to Somerset. At Collyweston (Northamptonshire) the ground disturbance caused by medieval workings is still apparent.

indicates that extraction of stone was casual in many parts of England, and not subject to systematic regulation by manorial authorities. Material for most building projects was simply picked up from local fields or open pits in the East Anglian Breckland, where flints and chalk clunch abounded. However, cornerstones and external stones were often imported from the east Midlands; indeed, England's best building material came from the deposits of oolite stone found in a long crescent stretching from south Lincolnshire to the Cotswolds (see the illustration above). The quarries at Barnack (Northamptonshire) and Taynton (Oxfordshire) achieved particular fame, as did marble from Corfe (Dorset). The output of this industry is impossible to measure, but it is perhaps significant that neither Barnack nor Corfe were especially large or wealthy places in the Middle Ages.

The broad economic and demographic changes of the later Middle Ages are reflected in the changing distribution of assessed taxable wealth. Information culled from the Lay Subsidy of 1334 indicates that the greatest density of wealth in England was concentrated in the arable heartlands south and east of a line between the rivers Severn and Humber, and in particular the prime grain-producing areas of coastal East Anglia and Kent. The dating of the 1334 subsidy is fortuitous, because it provides us with a snapshot of the regional distribution of wealth in England at the end of the long period of economic and agrarian expansion. It reveals that the ability to grow grain and support a dense population were the main determinants of taxable wealth at that time. Yet when the basis of taxation was reassessed in 1524, the distribution of wealth had shifted significantly. The arable heartlands of Midland England had suffered most, and wealth had become concentrated to the south and east of London and in south-west England. Areas of industrial specialism such as the Weald, the Stour valley, Devon and the Forest of Dean had made the greatest gains in wealth, reflecting the shift towards manufactured goods in the century after the Black Death.

Although England was as populous in 1500 as in 1100, the changes in economic life and social structure were substantial. Serfdom had effectively disappeared by 1500, and with it the rather arbitrary jurisdiction over land and labour exerted by feudal landlords, to be replaced by a stronger and more centralised state. Of course, considerable imbalances remained in the distribution of power and resources in English society, and the legal position of many tenants was not entirely secure. But the mass of the populace now exercised greater control over their time and actions, and could seek employment in a wider range of non-agricultural occupations. At the end of the Middle Ages England possessed a more flexible and skilled work-force, who enjoyed a higher standard of living, although conditions were to worsen once again for the lower orders of society in the sixteenth century.

The forces which brought about the dissolution of feudalism in England are complex and hotly debated, but demographic change and the tensions within feudal society were undoubtedly the primary influences. Yet the growing importance of domestic and overseas trade acted as a major catalyst to change. The extent of commercial activity in late medieval England was not startling by modern standards, but production for the market increased during the later Middle Ages and brought with it a greater diversity of employment, regional specialisation and more sophisticated marketing institutions. Towns became more important, especially London, and urban culture more sophisticated. These were important developments, because they resulted in a more efficient use of resources: in very general terms land productivity probably rose in the twelfth and thirteenth centuries, and labour productivity probably rose in the fourteenth and fifteenth centuries. And, crucially, although a severe contraction in the volume of commercial activity occurred towards the end of our period, the advances that had been achieved in the infrastructure of commerce were retained. England in 1500 possessed a manufacturing and consumer base which provided a portent for changes to come.

FAMILY AND INHERITANCE, WOMEN AND CHILDREN

Paul Brand

Shortly before 1299 Mariota, the aged and feeble widow of Richard Stoyle, was entrusted to the custody of her daughter Isabel who lived in Lincoln with her husband Peter. Another relative, William Stoyle, subsequently complained that Mariota was being kept against her will and procured her release by the city authorities. From subsequent litigation we learn that the arrangements for Mariota's custody had been made not by those authorities nor by any other kind of external agency but by William Stoyle and her other relatives.[1] Nor is this the only evidence for collective action by a group of kinsmen. In 1285, for example, Alice, the wife of Andrew of Braham, was rescued by a group of her kinsmen from the husband who was maltreating her and brought back from Suffolk to her home village of Roade in Northamptonshire.[2] It was also common for a group of kinsmen to participate in the negotiations which preceded a marriage, ensuring that satisfactory property arrangements were made before the marriage went ahead.

What our evidence does not prove, however, is that kinsmen acted together with any real frequency. This is hardly surprising. The system used for reckoning kinship was bilateral; paternal and maternal relatives were equally members of any individual's kin group. This meant that only brothers and sisters ever possessed exactly the same kin. The Church's rules forbade marriage between quite distant kin. Even after the rules were relaxed in 1215, marriage was prohibited between individuals who shared a great-great-great-grandfather. This prevented the reinforcement of existing family links through marriages between kinsmen. Property ownership was individual, not shared between members of a larger kin group. Nor did the kin group share responsibility for the crimes and misdeeds of fellow-kinsmen or have the right to share in compensation paid to their fellow-kinsmen, as they had once done.

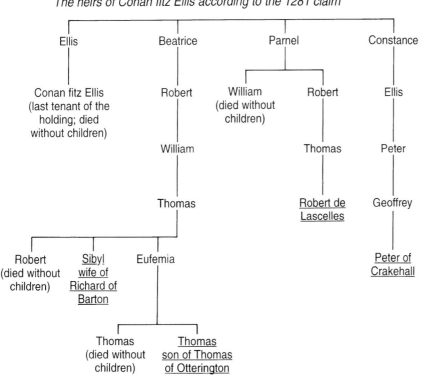

The heirs of Conan fitz Ellis according to the 1281 claim

Note: The 1281 claimants are those whose names are underlined

Property claims indicate that some individuals were able to trace quite distant relationships. In 1281 an extensive holding at Holbeach in Lincolnshire was claimed jointly by four descendants of the three aunts of Conan fitz Ellis. He had possessed the holding and died without children during Henry III's reign (see the illustration above). The claimants were the great-grandson, great-great-granddaughter, great-great-grandson and great-great-great-grandson of the three aunts. Their claim required them not just to know of their relationship to Conan but also to trace all the intervening steps between the aunts and themselves.[3] But it is likely that only a relatively small landowning elite possessed this kind of detailed knowledge. Their memory of their family's ancestors may often have been assisted by the compilation and preservation of family trees of the kind shown in the illustrations on pp. 60, 61. Lesser mortals were probably much less aware of their blood ties with more distant kin. It has even been suggested that the relative scarcity of marriages annulled on grounds of consanguinity (blood relationship) may reflect not so much an absence of marriages between kin as a lack of knowledge of, or inability to prove, the more distant relationships. Their relative unimportance may also be demonstrated by the absence of any distinctive terms for them. The single term 'cousin' had to cover a multitude of more distant kinsmen and women.

While it would clearly be wrong to suggest that wider family and kinship ties had no place in later medieval English society, their role seems to have been limited. Of much greater everyday significance were the relationships

Part of a family tree showing the descent of the main claimants to the throne of Scotland. The three stern-looking ladies are the three daughters of David earl of Huntingdon, a younger son of David I king of Scotland (d. 1153): Margaret, the wife of Alan of Galloway; Isabella, the wife of Robert Bruce; and Ada, the wife of Henry Hastings. The tree accompanies a text of the French verse chronicle of Peter of Langtoft written in the early fourteenth century.

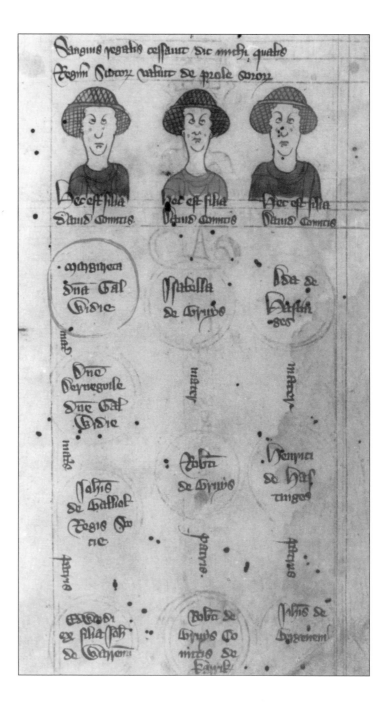

between members of the nuclear family: between husband and wife and between parents and children.

Under canon law, all that was required for a valid marriage was the agreement of a man and a woman to take each other as husband and wife. No priest had to be present, no ceremony was required, no particular form of words had to be used, no witnesses were needed. Nor was it necessary for either party to obtain the consent of parents or kin or lords. Some couples certainly did get married in private and informally. Analysis of the marriage cases heard at Ely

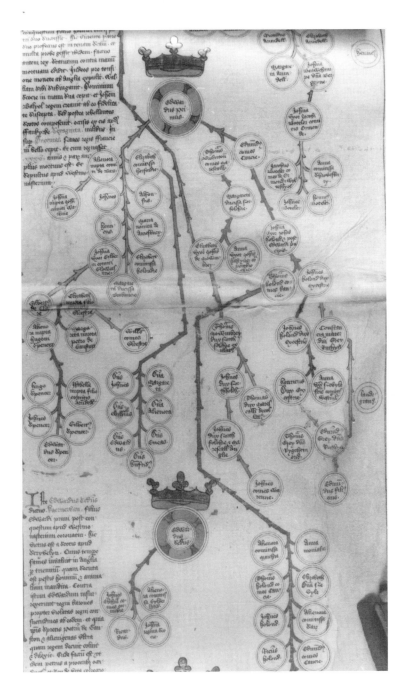

Part of a family tree showing the descendants of the kings of England. The part illustrated shows Edward I and his descendants and Edward II and his descendants. On the left-hand side is a list of popes; on the right-hand side a discontinuous listing of emperors. Each king also has a short entry relating to the main events of his reign. The manuscript dates from the reign of Edward IV.

between 1374 and 1382 has shown that over two-thirds involved 'clandestine' marriages of this sort, contracted in a bed or in a field or elsewhere. It was much more common, however, for couples to get married in public before witnesses and with the participation of a priest. The public ceremony was indeed so much the norm that couples who cohabited after a clandestine marriage were subject to ecclesiastical punishment for their failure to celebrate their marriage through the proper public ceremony, and might even be required to remarry publicly. A public marriage was normally preceded by the private betrothal of the parties. This was followed by the publication of the

The elaborate church porches of English churches of the later Middle Ages performed a variety of functions. The upper rooms that many contain were used for teaching and also for parish and guild meetings. Among the purposes the ground floor served was as a covered space where the main part of the formal marriage ceremony might take place. It was only after the most important part of the marriage ceremony was over that the newly married couple entered the church for a nuptial mass. The porch shown here is the late fifteenth-century south porch of the church of Aylesham in Norfolk.

banns by the local priest announcing the forthcoming marriage and asking if there were any reasons why it should not take place. Most of the formal cere- mony took place not inside the church but immediately outside the church door, generally inside the porch (see the illustration above). It was here that the couple repeated their words of consent, that the bride was given to the groom and the groom gave a ring to the bride as a token of his readiness to fulfil the terms of the marriage contract. The priest was a participant in this ceremony but it was the couple themselves who were the celebrants in the 'sacrament' of marriage (see the colour plate on p. 69 and the illustration on p. 64). The wedding proper might then be followed by a nuptial mass inside the church. Eating and drinking followed elsewhere.

Although the Church insisted that only the consent of the couple con- cerned was necessary for a valid marriage, secular law and social practice both insisted that marriage was too important a matter for the couple alone to decide. This was particularly so where either partner had inherited or would inherit a property holding but had not yet come of age. If the father was still alive, he would arrange the marriage and could expect to receive payment from the partner or his or her family for doing so. Although he had no direct sanctions in the case of disobedience he could in effect disinherit the heir or heiress, and most seem to have done their father's bidding. If the father was dead, the right to arrange a marriage belonged in law to their guardian; who he was and what sanction he possessed in the case of disobedience are discussed below (see pp. 79–80). An adult getting married was under fewer constraints. In 1215 Magna Carta had confirmed that all lords had a right to consent to the remarriage of widows who were their tenants. By the end of the thirteenth century, however, only the king still exercised any degree of control over the remarriage of the widows of his tenants. In theory, lords also had a right to consent to the marriage of the daughters, and sometimes also the sons, of their villeins. In practice, lords simply received a payment for their permission without being able to exercise any real control over the choice of partner. Even this seems largely to have disappeared during the course of the fifteenth century.

Marriages were commonly preceded by bargaining about property between the families of the bride and groom or between bride and groom themselves. This seems to have gone on at all social levels. At the higher levels it might lead to elaborate written agreements. The normal expectation was that a bride would be accompanied by a dowry in money or goods, provided by the father of the bride or other relative. Alternatively, a dowry might take the form of land. More commonly, it was the groom who was expected to bring land to the marriage. A standard part of the ceremony was for the husband to 'endow' his wife: to promise that she would get one-third (or sometimes more) of his lands as her dower for the rest of her life if she survived him. Even at the peasant level it was not always necessary for a couple to wait until the groom's parents were dead before marrying. A son might take over a holding at marriage and agree to support his aged parents. He would either provide them with a separate cottage or allocate them their own room in the main house. At higher social levels a son might be given some of his father's lands at marriage or before to allow him to establish his own separate household. It was even possible for a son to marry without lands if proper assurances were given that he would inherit in due course and that his wife would get a life interest to support herself if she survived him.

On marriage, a husband acquired a position of authority over his wife and her property, what chief justice Mettingham at the end of the thirteenth century called 'primacy and mastery at the table and everywhere else' (see the colour plate on p. 70).[4] Husbands did not try to keep their wives at home. They were, however, expected to exercise some degree of control over their movements. Lawyers sometimes talked of wives being under the 'rod' of their husbands. 'Rod' may be meant literally, but more probably it stands as a symbol of authority. Although there was no civil remedy for wives who were maltreated, they were not entirely helpless (see the illustration on p. 64). Wives could and did leave brutal husbands, turning to their kin or others for support (see p. 58). They could also secure from Church courts a promise of better behaviour or even a judicial separation (technically described as a 'divorce from bed and board', though it left neither partner free to remarry) on the grounds of the husband's cruelty.

Even in the Middle Ages it was not always the wife who was subject to physical assault by her husband. This illustration reminds us that husbands were also sometimes subject to violence at the hands of their wives. Such violence was much more commonly taken as a subject for illustration than the reverse phenomenon, probably precisely because it reversed the normal expectations. Another marginal illustration from the Luttrell Psalter, showing the wife beating her husband with a spindle.

An illustration of the most important part of the marriage ceremony, the exchange of promises between groom and bride in the presence of a priest and a man and woman, presumably parents of the couple. Here they stand for the much larger group of relatives and friends normally present at weddings. The illustration comes from a fourteenth-century manuscript of the *Liber Sextus*, an official collection of canon law texts promulgated by Pope Boniface VIII in 1298 and copied into this manuscript from the official text sent to the University of Oxford. The illustration comes from the beginning of the section on marriage (*De sponsalibus et matrimoniis*).

More significant in bolstering the husband's authority may have been the control which marriage gave the husband over his wife's property. Any money or other movables the wife possessed became in law wholly the property of her husband and at his sole disposal; indeed, one lawyer stated starkly in 1299 that a wife 'can have no property except in her dress'.[5] The position with respect to any land the wife held at marriage or which she inherited afterwards was more complex. A husband could lease, sell or even give away any of her land without consulting her. Provided she survived him, however, she was entitled to revoke the lease or grant through a legal action which explained that during their marriage she had been 'unable' to oppose his wishes. The same action allowed her to revoke leases and sales even when she had joined with her husband in making them. The only way an irrevocable grant of the wife's land could be made was for the couple to grant the land by means of a final concord registered in a royal court or by analogous conveyance registered in a town or manorial court. Before such a conveyance was accepted the wife had to be examined on her own to see if she really did consent. We do not know how often wives refused, but it is clear that the procedure was not just a meaningless formality. A husband could not proceed with litigation relating to his wife's land on his own. A statute of 1285 did, however, allow a wife to defend her title to her own land even in the absence of her husband. The husband's property remained under his own sole control.

The husband's power over his wife's property was power without enforceable responsibility. The general assumption was that the husband would manage his wife's property and his own in such a way as to keep them both in food, clothing and accommodation of a kind appropriate to their rank. There was, however, no legal mechanism to ensure that a wife received such maintenance from her husband, and in a number of late thirteenth- and early fourteenth-century cases where widows were alleged to have lived apart from their husbands in adultery during their late husbands' lifetimes, we are told by the widows that the real reason they had been living apart from their husbands was that he had sold all or most of his lands and that they had been forced to go elsewhere (generally to kinsfolk) to be provided with the necessities of life.

The law also favoured the husband as against his wife on the question of sexual fidelity within marriage (see the colour plate on p. 71). Although it was no longer the case that a husband could kill his wife and her lover even if he surprised them together in bed, it was apparently acceptable for a husband in these circumstances to castrate the lover. From the last decade of the thirteenth century it also became possible for husbands to bring a civil action for damages alleging the 'seizure' of a wife and the carrying off of the husband's goods, even where the wife had left home voluntarily with what she may have thought of as 'her' goods in the company of her lover. In 1308, for example, Stephen of Upton sued his former apprentice Robert of Hedon for the 'seizure' of his wife Sibyl at London and the taking of his goods and chattels. A jury found that this was no forcible abduction but the final episode in a long affair. She had taken jewels, gold, silver, linen and wool worth £60 to her father's house. These were probably the goods Sibyl had brought to the marriage, and the couple had then supported themselves from their sale. The court awarded Stephen £60 damages for the goods and chattels and a further 100 marks for the 'malice and trespass' involved. As he was unable to pay, Robert was imprisoned. He seems only to have been released five years later.[6] In this case the adulterer was not directly punished for adultery but for taking the husband's chattels. No similar action was available to a wife deserted by her husband. From 1285 onwards, any wife who left her husband to live in adultery forfeited her right to dower unless she was reconciled with her husband prior to his death. Between 1287 and 1307 'adultery' was pleaded against widows claiming dower in well over 100 cases. No similar rule applied where a husband left his wife to live with his mistress.

It was generally the case under the rules both of the common law and of local manorial custom which applied to villein tenants that a husband whose wife had held property in her own right could expect to retain control of that property for the remainder of his life as 'tenant by the curtesy'. The only requirement was that the marriage have produced at least one child who had lived long enough to have been heard crying. Under the rules of the common law a widow was entitled to only one-third of her husband's property. Her entitlement was, however, not just to one-third of the land he held at the time of his death, but also of any land he had given away or sold at any time since marriage. Nor was she required to have borne a child to her late husband. All that was necessary was that she have reached the age at which she could 'earn' her dower through sexual intercourse. She was entitled to hold these lands for the remainder of her life. Local custom sometimes allowed widows to claim one-half rather than one-third of their husband's lands. This was the general rule for all lands not held by knight service in Kent, but Kentish custom allowed the widow to retain the land only until she remarried or forfeited her entitlement by bearing a child. Manorial custom varied but also commonly allowed a widow as her 'free bench' one-third or one-half and sometimes all of her late husband's holding, for life or until she forfeited that entitlement through remarriage or child-bearing.

Husbands could arrange for their widows to get more or less than the common law or local custom assigned them. For much of the thirteenth century a man could assign specific lands at the time of marriage as dower. These might be less than one-third but not more. By 1300, however, a widow could waive such an assignment and claim her common law one-third instead. During the second half of the thirteenth century some husbands began to arrange on acquiring land for it to be granted jointly to themselves and their wives and used third parties to resettle land they already held in the same way. Chief justice Thomas Weyland made both kinds of arrangement for the benefit of his second wife Margery during the decade and more that preceded his disgrace in 1289. His intention was to ensure that she got more than one-third of his lands when he died. The unintended effect was to leave her in control of extensive lands that would otherwise have been forfeited when he went into exile in France in 1290. By 1300 unfree peasants had also begun to make similar arrangements, though here a rather different mechanism had to be used to provide the widow with her 'jointure'. The holding was surrendered to the lord in the manorial court and he then re-granted it to the couple.

It was only after the Black Death that free landowners began to gain still more flexibility in controlling what happened to their lands after their deaths with the development of the 'use'. Lands were granted to 'feoffees to uses', generally a group of friends, servants and confidants. The feoffees became, for most legal purposes, the owners of the land, but the previous owner continued to receive its income. The original owner (the *cestui que use*) could also determine who got the land after his death, normally through a last will and testament. Initially, the arrangement depended solely on the good faith of the feoffees, but gradually the newly emerging court of Chancery came to provide a full range of remedies to ensure that they carried out the wishes of the *cestui que use*, both during his lifetime and after his death. If a husband had granted his lands to feoffees to uses before marrying, he could now determine by his will just how much or how little went to his widow and on what terms, and thus might, for example, impose conditions that prevented her remarrying.

A widow could also expect to receive one-third of her husband's movable goods after his death, one-half of them if there were no surviving children. This share was only payable after all outstanding liabilities, such as funeral expenses and debts, had been met. Contemporaries were unsure whether widows derived this entitlement from Magna Carta, the 'general custom of the kingdom', or the custom of a particular county or locality. During the course of the fifteenth century, however, husbands gained the freedom to bequeath all of their movables as they wished.

The wife who died first had, under common law, no chattels to leave by her will. Canon law, however, took a different view, and some pressure was placed on husbands to allow wives to dispose of part of their husband's goods in their wills. Prior to *c.* 1350 husbands frequently gave their wives permission to make wills, allowing them to bequeath that share of their husband's goods to which they would have been entitled had the husband died first. Thereafter the practice seems to have declined and by the mid-fifteenth century such wills had become rare. There was also some doubt as to whether unfree peasants could properly make wills, since in law all their property belonged to their lords. This was also an area where Church and State took different views. In practice villeins commonly made wills leaving their chattels, though some lords insisted that these be proved only in the manorial court.

A relatively small number of marriages were ended by annulment (technically a divorce 'from the bond of marriage') granted by an ecclesiastical court. Under canon law there were various reasons for granting such an annulment. The couple might be within the prohibited degrees of kinship or might be too closely connected through the 'spiritual kinship' created by standing as godparent to a child at baptism or confirmation. One of the partners might have been coerced into marriage through 'force and fear'. This was interpreted quite restrictively. In 1362/63 a young woman said she had been threatened with being taken by the ears and thrown into a pool if she did not consent, but she did not succeed in her divorce suit. A husband might be incapable of sexual intercourse with his wife. A peculiarity of English Church court practice was for a group of 'honest women' to be deputed by the court to test whether or not the husband was capable of responding to sexual stimulation before granting the annulment. By far the most common reason, however, was that one of the partners had previously contracted a valid marriage with a third party. A suit was brought by the third party claiming the partner as husband or wife and seeking annulment of the existing marriage. It did not matter that the first marriage had been a clandestine one and the second one publicly celebrated, or that the second had gone for years without challenge and that there were children. Under canon law the prior marriage always prevailed over any subsequent marriage (see the illustration on p. 68). We need not believe in all of these alleged 'precontracts'. Some at least were the product of a partner's wish to discard their current spouse and marry another. A little perjury was all that was needed.

Once a marriage had been annulled the former wife could secure the

The late medieval 'divorce' or annulment of marriage was a formal process conducted in the Church courts which culminated in a formal 'celebration' of the annulment, a judgment dissolving the tie of marriage between the couple. This illustration is from an early fourteenth-century manuscript of the *Decretum* of Gratian, the basic textbook of canon law which was compiled *c.* 1140, with commentary provided by the standard gloss of Johannes Teutonicus (*c.* 1215) plus the marginal apparatus of Bartholomew of Brescia (*c.* 1245). This manuscript once belonged to the abbey of St Alban's. It shows the crucial moment in the process of securing an annulment. The scene is not atypical in showing that the couple have a child born before the annulment; it is atypical in not showing the third party who was most commonly declared married to one of the 'divorced' partners at the same time as the other marriage was dissolved.

Facing page Entry for *anulus* (ring) in the encyclopaedia of James le Palmer, d. 1375. Part of the marriage ceremony was for the groom to give a ring to his wife as a symbolic token or 'wed' of his willingness to perform the terms of the marriage contract between them. This picture comes from a fourteenth-century illustrated encyclopaedia of canon law, theology and general information known as *Omne Bonum*, compiled by one James the Englishman (Jacobus Anglicanus). He has recently been identified as James le Palmer, an Exchequer clerk who died in 1373.

immediate revocation of all grants and leases made by her ex-husband and from the second quarter of the thirteenth century there was a special form of legal action available for this. Greater problems arose when land had been granted jointly to the couple. In some instances the courts awarded half the land to each. In others the courts took some account of the circumstances of the annulment and a partner who had failed to disclose his or her own prior marital contract lost the whole of the land to the 'innocent' party. The church courts normally dealt with any claims to movable property granted at marriage. Just occasionally such cases reached the secular courts. In 1290 Agnes the daughter of Richard de Brok recovered livestock, grain, clothing and money to the value of £66 given by her father to Edmund of Navestock, her ex-husband, as her 'dowry'. Edmund had secured an annulment on the grounds of a precontract shortly after the wedding but was still attempting to keep the whole of her dowry.[7]

Any child born after the marriage of its parents became a full member of the family and able to inherit land from either parent. The marriage had, however, to have been a full public ceremony performed at the church door. When John del Heith fell sick some time in the late thirteenth century and thought he was dying, he married Katherine, the mistress who had already borne him two children. John was too sick to rise from his bed, but the local vicar was present and the couple went through the full formal ceremony with the giving of a ring and the form of words used in the church-door ceremony. When John recovered the couple had another child, William. In a judgment of 1306 the courts held that under English law William was just as illegitimate as his elder brother and sister.[8] Canon law allowed children born before the marriage of their parents to be 'legitimised' by the marriage, and there was even a special part of the ceremony where the couple and their children were covered by a

Seating at meals. It is often difficult to reconstruct the day-to-day patterns and social practices of the past. There is little to give us information about where and how people sat when they took meals together. What chief justice Mettingham says about the husband's primacy at the 'table' appears to be borne out by this illustration (one of the marginal illustrations from the Luttrell Psalter, made for Sir Geoffrey Luttrell, Irnham in Lincolnshire, c. 1325–40), showing the man of the house clearly in control at this particular meal.

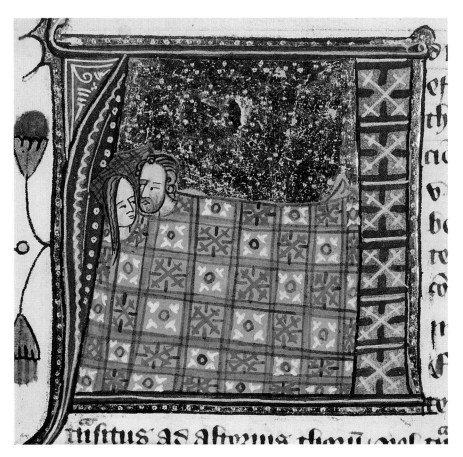

Entry for *adulterium* in the encyclopaedia of James le Palmer. The wider social significance of adultery arose from the fact that it was a relationship which involved at least three people: husband, wife and lover or mistress. Only husband and mistress (or is it wife and lover?) appear in this illustration of the entry 'adultery' (*adulterium*), which also comes from the encyclopaedic *Omne Bonum* of James le Palmer. But perhaps the artist seeing the couple in bed is the third person involved.

mantle and the children 'legitimised'. English secular law did not, however, consider 'mantle-children' legitimate. An attempt by the Church to have English law brought into line with canon law was rejected at the council of Merton in 1236 after a heated discussion in which the lay magnates refused to change the law of England on this point. English law did not, however, require that children have been conceived after marriage for them to be legitimate. Eldest children may often have been conceived before a full ceremonious marriage had taken place but born after it.

There was a very strong presumption in late medieval English law that a husband was the father of his wife's children. This was best expressed in the pithy English tag quoted by chief justice Hengham in a case of 1307: 'Wo so boleyth myn kyn, ewere is the calf myn' ('whosoever bulls my cow, the calf is always mine'). The presumption could only be rebutted by proving that the husband was impotent, or that he had been out of the country when the child was conceived, or that the couple had been formally separated by a Church court. It was not enough to prove that husband and wife were not living together, or even that the wife was living with another man when the child was conceived. Posthumous children were also considered legitimate, provided they were born within a limited period after their father's death. In 1287 a jury found that Beatrice the widow of Robert of Radwell had given birth to a son named Henry forty weeks and eleven days after her late husband's death. The justices held that this was not her late husband's child since it had been born twelve days after the maximum permissible term.[9]

Children born outside wedlock were 'nobody's child' (*filius nullius*) for most legal purposes. They were not capable of inheriting property from either of their parents. If they themselves acquired property, it could only be inherited by their children. If they died without any it returned (escheated) to the lord of whom it was held. Only in one context was an illegitimate child regarded as having even a mother. This was where a lord alleged that the child was his villein. It was a well-established principle of villeinage law that although legitimate children inherited their father's condition, illegitimate children took that of their mother. In a number of thirteenth-century cases we have the curious spectacle of men or women insisting on their own illegitimacy in order to benefit from their mother's free status, while their lord insisted that they were the legitimate children of one of his villein tenants who was their father. Not all illegitimate children were born outside wedlock. By the later fifteenth century the English secular courts seem to have taken the view that any children born to a couple whose marriage had subsequently been annulled were rendered retrospectively illegitimate. Earlier they had taken a more nuanced view, and the good faith and knowledge of the parties in entering into the marriage had then been considered important factors when deciding whether or not the children should remain legitimate.

The normal assumption was that, during childhood at least, parents, and more specifically the father, would provide maintenance for his children in the form of food, clothing and shelter within the family household (see the illustration on p. 74). It does not seem to have been common in later medieval England, except at the higher social levels, for parents to send their children to other families to be fostered. Even adolescent children, who were capable of making a significant contribution to the household economy, were not regularly hired out to other households as servants. It is less clear how long adult children could expect to go on living at home. There is some evidence

Facing page A working instrument to indicate propitious times for operations and medication by means of movable indexes of the sun and moon, set on any given day at the degree and sign of the zodiac, and illustrating the importance of astrological calculations in medicine.

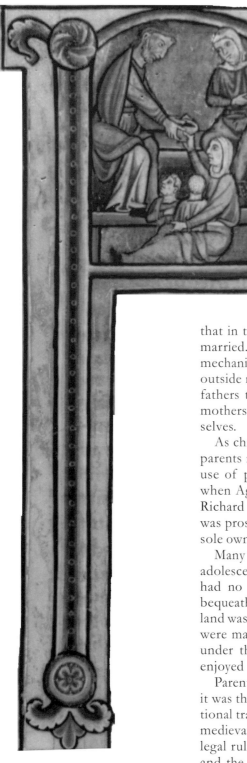

The father's responsibility for maintaining his children with the necessary food, clothing and shelter was only rarely the subject of any kind of graphic representation in the later Middle Ages. This vignette illustrates a passage from the Book of Samuel (here called the Book of Kings) and shows Elkanah giving food to his wife Penninah, apparently for her to feed her two sons. The other woman is his second wife Anna. It comes from a thirteenth-century manuscript of the Bible.

that in the more prosperous families children stayed at home until they got married. The majority of parents were happy to support their children. A legal mechanism was needed, however, to ensure the support of children born outside marriage. This was provided by the Church courts which could order fathers to make a regular payment (most commonly, two pence a week) to mothers to support their offspring until they came of an age to support themselves.

As children grew older, more mobile and more useful for household tasks parents might need and were expected to reinforce their control through the use of physical punishment. A jury in 1289 was, however, clearly shocked when Agnes the widow of Thomas of Sculthorpe beat her 10-year-old son Richard and trampled on him simply to get him out of the house, when she was prospecting for a second husband and wished to misrepresent herself as sole owner of property she held jointly with her son.[10]

Many children died before their parents: some during infancy, others during adolescence or young adulthood, still others as mature adults. Such children had no claim on their parents' movable property. They could thus only bequeath property they had themselves acquired. The position with regard to land was somewhat different. Children who died before their parents, but who were married with children of their own, passed on to those grandchildren under the principle of 'representation' the rights which they would have enjoyed had they survived.

Parents were commonly survived by some, if not all, of their offspring and it was the death of parents which most commonly triggered the inter-generational transfer of property within the family. The basic starting-point of later medieval English law was that such transfers should be governed by general legal rules, but that different rules applied to the transmission of movables and the transmission of land. However, a number of developments which took place during the later Middle Ages allowed parents to circumvent these rules and gave them the power to determine themselves what should happen to their property.

The general rule was that a man's surviving children had a right to a specific share of his movable goods (including any cash) when he died. They were entitled to one-third of these assets after the payment of debts and funeral expenses, and each son and daughter was entitled to an equal share of this third. This right seems to have derived from canon law, which in turn derived it from post-classical Roman law, though it was commonly described as being due by reason of the 'general custom of the realm' or attributed to local custom. After *c.* 1400, and for reasons still not wholly clear, this automatic entitlement seems largely to have disappeared, and a property-owner gained full power to leave his property as he saw fit. It only survived as a general entitlement in the north of England (within the ecclesiastical province of York) and in certain specific places in the south of England including the city of London.

When a property-owner died in possession of land or other real property the common law had detailed and complicated rules for ascertaining who was entitled to succeed (see the illustration on p. 76), though the right to take actual possession of the property concerned was often postponed because of the life interest of a surviving spouse in part or all of that property (see above, p. 66). The initial preference of the inheritance rules was for descendants of the dead property-owner. Within this group, the first preference was for eldest sons. If the eldest son was still living, he took all of the property. If he had died, his children inherited his claim to all of the property by virtue of the 'representative' principle. Thus even if there were younger sons still living and the eldest son had left only daughters, those granddaughters inherited rather than one of the sons. If the eldest son had died without children, the right to inherit passed to the second son, if still living, or to his descendants, if there were any. If there were no sons or their descendants, the right to inherit passed to the daughters, and the property was divided equally between all of them. If any daughter had died, her descendants (whatever their number) took jointly a share equivalent to that which would have gone to their mother if she had still been alive. When it was grandchildren or even great-grandchildren who took part or all of an inheritance as 'representing' their father or mother or grandfather or grandmother, the question of entitlement as between siblings was settled by applying similar rules. If there were any males, the eldest male took all of the share; if only females, the land was divided equally between all of them.

Only if there were no surviving descendants could the land be inherited by collaterals. Here, the first preference was for the eldest brother or his descendants. If there were no brothers but there were sisters or their descendants, the land passed to them in equal shares. If there were neither brothers nor sisters nor their descendants but there were uncles (or cousins descended from them), the land went to the eldest uncle or his descendants. If there were no uncles or their descendants, it was divided equally between aunts and their descendants. If there were no uncles or aunts or their descendants, the collateral kin of the next generation back inherited (and so on).

These general rules might in practice be modified by the workings of local custom. The most common variation preserved the general preference for males but removed the preference for the eldest (primogeniture) and required equal division between all surviving sons and their descendants. This applied generally to all land not held by knight service in Kent (gavelkind) and also in a number of other areas. Local manorial custom followed the same general

The textbooks on English law written in the later Middle Ages would have benefited from the inclusion of simple diagrams to illustrate the basic rules of inheritance law. The compiler of *Britton*, a textbook written in the last decade of the thirteenth century but drawing heavily on the earlier work known as *Bracton*, seems to have intended to include just such a diagram but did not get round to doing so. Many of the manuscripts of *Britton* have a blank where the diagram was supposed to be; others, quite inappropriately, borrowed an *Arbor Consanguinitatis* ('tree of relationship') from older canon law works, giving the Latin names of various relatives and kinsmen and the degree of their relationship to 'Ego'. This was of great value in working out the prohibited degrees for the canonical rules on marriage, but quite useless for the English inheritance rules. This *Arbor Consanguinitatis* comes from a copy of *Britton* which belonged to St Augustine's abbey at Canterbury and is now in the British Library.

lines of preference for sons and their descendants over daughters, equal division between daughters and preference for descendants over collaterals. Some manors followed the common law in giving all to the eldest son; others followed Kentish and other local customs in dividing the land equally between all sons; still others gave all the land to the youngest rather than the eldest son (ultimogeniture).

The inheritance rules might also be significantly modified by the terms of the grant under which the land had originally passed to the deceased owner or his ancestor, if that grant had taken the form of an entail. This might take the form of a grant to a particular individual and the 'heirs of his body' or a particular individual and the 'heirs male of his body'. In the first case, the land would only pass to his descendants; in the second it would only pass to and through his male descendants. Alternatively, an entail might take the form of a grant to a particular individual and a named wife or husband and the 'heirs of their bodies' or the 'heirs male of their bodies'. This would mean that the land stayed in the hands of the original grantee and spouse for their lifetimes and then passed to their children and their descendants, or in the second case passed only to and through their joint male descendants. Other yet more complicated arrangements were possible. When Thomas Weyland acquired lands in Campsey Ash and five other Suffolk villages in 1280, it was on terms that gave him, his second wife Margery and their son Richard a joint life estate in these lands. After their deaths the lands were to pass to the heirs of Richard's body.[11]

When property was entailed in this way, the property would 'revert' or return to the grantor or his heir if there were no descendants of the required kind, unless the grantor had made provision for the land to 'remain' out for a second beneficiary and similarly restricted groups of his or her descendants. The second beneficiary (the 'remainderman') would commonly be a brother or sister of the first grantee. There might then be provision for other remainders in favour of other children or more distant relatives if the first remainder failed. Under the 1280 settlement of Campsey Ash and other Suffolk lands, for example, there were successive remainders over to Richard's half-brother John (Thomas Weyland's eldest son by his first wife), and the heirs of his body, and then to Thomas's son Thomas (a second son by Margery) and the heirs of his body. There were similar multiple remainders over in many of Thomas Weyland's other acquisitions of the 1280s. These ensured that if any of his children died their lands would pass to their surviving brothers and sisters or half-brother and half-sisters.

Entails did exist even at the beginning of the thirteenth century, but they were comparatively uncommon. They came to be used more and more over the course of that century. Their popularity was enhanced when, *c.* 1260, the courts began to provide remedies which protected the interests of the remainderman as well as the heir under the entail. In 1285 c.1 of the statute of Westminster II, known as *De Donis*, ensured that land granted in this way had to remain in the family of the grantee and could not (like other land) be granted away by its owner. Initially this 'protection' lasted only for the first three generations, but judicial interpretation turned it into a permanent bar to alienation some time in the second half of the fourteenth century. This was only destroyed *c.* 1470 with the invention of the collusive 'common recovery'. The extending bar on the alienating of entailed land made granting land through entails attractive to grantors, both because it helped to safeguard the ultimate reversion which they commonly retained, and because it assisted them in accomplishing the goal of keeping the land within the family of the donees (often a junior branch of their own family, but sometimes the senior branch).

Heirs only inherited those lands which the owner still held at the time of his death. Since prospective heirs possessed no power to control what an owner did with land during his own lifetime, he could effectively disinherit his heirs by grants made prior to his death. An owner might have various reasons for doing this. Financial necessity was one; family sentiment might be another. For a father or mother with illegitimate children a lifetime grant was the only way of ensuring his land passed on to them. In 1258, for example, Edward of Westminster, Henry III's chief artistic adviser, settled extensive properties in Westminster, Southwark, Enfield, Stepney and Bengeo on his mistress, Katherine of Ely, for her life, with successive remainders over in favour of their sons Odo, Nicholas and Thomas. At the same time Katherine settled a messuage in Westminster which had once belonged to Edward's father, Odo of Westminster, on Edward for life with successive remainders over to the same three children.[12] No other arrangement could have ensured that these lands came to the children after their parents' death or ensured that each of the children could inherit from their brothers if they died without children. Since neither Edward nor Katherine had any legitimate children, the heirs they disinherited were not in this case their own descendants. Other parents made lifetime grants to younger children who would not otherwise have inherited any of their parents' lands. Such an 'advancement' might be a mark of affection for a favoured child; it might also be the result of a specific prior agreement. In a 1292 case we hear of a husband, Adam of Blackburn, promising his second wife Alesia at the time of their marriage that if they had children he would give them part of his land or £40 to purchase land, and then granting land to Robert, a child of this second marriage.[13] Some lifetime grants did not disinherit the future heir or heirs, but merely advanced the time at which part, or less commonly all, of the inheritance was transferred to them. Such anticipatory grants were commonly made in order to allow the future heir to set up his own household on marriage. In 1287, for example, Thomas Weyland gave his eldest son John all his Irish lands plus his Suffolk manor of Middleton, evidently in anticipation of his marriage to Mary, the daughter of Richard and Alice de Braose. Richard and Alice shortly thereafter made a matching grant of the Suffolk manor of Clopton to the new couple.[14]

There were two main drawbacks for grantors in making such grants. Although it was possible to ensure that the grantor retained the land for the remainder of his life, it was always necessary that it pass temporarily into the possession of the grantees or of a trusted third party for some period of time before the land could come back to him. It was easy to slip up on the details and, if this happened, the whole transaction might be rendered null and void. It was also possible for the grantees or the third party, once the land was in their hands, to fail to honour the agreement to return the land to its original owner. The other was that once such a transfer had taken place, it was impossible for the grantor to change his mind and decide that, after all, he wished to favour another of his children rather than the one to whom he had granted the land.

Parents came to exercise a much greater degree of control over the inter-generational transfer of property with the development of the 'use' (see also above, pp. 66–7). The working of the use also depended on a pre-mortem grant of property. The great advantage of the use over these older types of arrangement was that it left the owner in effective control of the property and able to continue enjoying its income and living on it. Nor was he bound by whatever intentions he might have had for the property at the moment of putting the land into use, for he could go on changing his mind right up to the time of the making of his last will. The bulk of lands probably continued to pass to the owner's heir, but it was now possible to postpone this until after the lands had paid off the debts of the *cestui que use* or after the death of his widow. It also now became possible to wait until death to 'advance' younger sons and non-inheriting daughters by granting them part or all of the property.

Special arrangements were necessary when property came to children who were not yet of an age to manage it. The basic rules governing the 'wardship' of lands inherited by children were already in place by 1200. For lands held by knight service, the lord of whom the land was held was entitled to hold the land and receive its income until the child concerned had come of age (21 in the case of male heirs; until marriage or the age of 16 in the case of female heiresses). The lord could assign or sell or lease this right to third parties. For land held in socage, wardship went to the closest kinsman or kinswoman on the opposite side of the family to that from which the land had come. Thus, in the commonest case, where land had been inherited from the father, the wardship belonged to the mother. Socage wardship lasted only until the heir came of age at 15, and under legislation of 1259 the guardian was liable to pay over the net profits of the lands to the heir once he or she had come of age.

These rules only applied, however, to 'inherited' land. As more and more land came to be held in use and to be transferred from one generation to the next by will, they gradually lost importance. The rules which applied when land was left by will were similar to those which had previously applied when land was granted to a child. The grantor or testator appointed a temporary custodian to manage the land, and that custodian was answerable for the net income of the land once the child had come of age. It was also the child's guardian who in law had control of any movables or money the child owned during his or her minority, and all guardians (including guardians in knight service) were under an obligation to manage this property for the benefit of the heir and restore it to him or her when he or she came of age.

The rules relating to the wardship or custody of the child who inherited or acquired property while under the age of majority were still more complex. If any of the land which the heir or heiress had inherited was held by military tenure, the child's wardship belonged to the lord of whom the land was held or, if there were several such holdings held of different lords, that lord whose ancestor had been the first to grant land to the heir's ancestor. If all the land which the heir or heiress had inherited was held in socage, the wardship of the heir went to the kinsman or kinswoman who had custody of their land. The right of wardship over the person of the heir was not, of course, in itself profitable; indeed, it represented a potential charge to the guardian, since he was responsible for the maintenance of the child while in his wardship. What was profitable was the closely connected right to arrange a marriage for the heir or heiress if he or she had not already been married during the lifetime of his or her parents. The right of wardship over an heir and the right to arrange his or her marriage could be given or sold to third parties, though in the case of the heir or heiress holding only socage land, any profit from a sale or from arranging a marriage came back to the heir. Neither kind of guardian was able to compel his ward to accept the marriage partner he or she had chosen, but the heirs or heiresses who refused the partners chosen for them by their lord without good reason were liable to pay the full value of their marriage and, if they went further and chose their own partners, they became liable to pay double that value. Children who acquired property while under age but whose fathers were still alive seem to have remained in the custody of their fathers. By the late thirteenth century it had become established that this was also the rule if such children inherited lands from or through their mothers during their fathers' lifetime. It is less clear what happened to children who only acquired property after the death of their fathers. When this was through the death-bed bequest of lands to them by their father as *cestui que use*, the father seems normally to have also arranged in the will who was to have their wardship.

The family was the basic building-block of late medieval English society. At its heart lay the relationship between husband and wife. That relationship was in theory created simply by the mutual consent of the parties, though this was normally given in a public ceremony, reflecting the importance of marriage to the wider society, and the parties were often guided in their choice of partners by external social and legal constraints. At the moment of marriage the partners looked equal, but that initial equality was soon replaced by an unequal relationship in which the husband was the dominant partner. He possessed exclusive control in law over all the couple's movable property, and during his own lifetime control over his wife's lands as well as his own. From the late thirteenth century onwards the law also helped to establish and maintain a double standard in sexual morality that favoured husbands. Wives who had lived apart from their husbands, with lovers, were penalised by the forfeiture of their dower, and the courts allowed husbands to bring actions for the abduction of their wives. There were no similar measures to penalise errant husbands or to allow the prosecution of their mistresses. Although marriages could be terminated by annulment, most came to an end only with the death of one of the partners. At the beginning of our period, it was the wider society, through general legal norms, which then determined what happened to the property which the couple had held. These assured the wife an automatic fixed share both of her late husband's movables and of his lands. By the end of our period legal and social change had brought the husband the same kind of control over the couple's property after his death as he had possessed during his lifetime. He was now able to determine what proportion, if any, of his movables his widow would receive, and also to decide what proportion of his lands would pass to his widow, and on what terms.

The main purpose of marriage was the procreation of children. All children born to a wife after marriage became at birth full members of the conjugal family unit, unless circumstances rendered it impossible that the husband was the father. Birth was the only mechanism for recruitment to the conjugal family. There was no adoption in late medieval England, and late medieval English law did not allow the retrospective 'legitimisation' of children born to a couple before marriage. Children were from birth subordinate members of the family unit and subject to their father's authority. They possessed no rights, even as adults, to any of the family property. Typically, rights in the family property passed to them only on the death of their father. Here too a significant change took place during the later Middle Ages. At the beginning of our period, the inter-generational transfer of property within the family was normally governed by general legal rules. These came during the later Middle Ages to be modified or wholly superseded through the creation of entails, the use of other lifetime settlements and, more radically, by the adoption of the use.

Husbands were powerful figures within the family at the beginning of our period, but their power was limited by the existence of legal rules which created automatic property entitlements for their wives and children after their deaths. The overall effect of the main legal and social changes affecting the family which took place during the later Middle Ages was to increase that power still further, giving them discretionary control over what happened to the family property after their death as well as during their lifetime. There was no radical change in the structure of the family or in the distribution of power within it in England in the later Middle Ages. The changes which did take place merely strengthened and enhanced the existing patriarchal authority of the male head of the family.

HEALTH, DIET, MEDICINE AND THE PLAGUE

Simone Macdougall

Shortly after his accession in 1327, the young king of England, Edward III, was presented with a splendidly illustrated copy, made by a clerk, Walter de Milemete, of an ancient text called the *Secretum Secretorum*.[1] This work on statecraft, purporting to be a letter from Aristotle to Alexander the Great, was a suitable gift for the new king, likening him as it did, by implication, to the young Alexander himself. However, integral to the text was a long section which constituted a regimen for the king and afforded advice as to health, the importance of correct diet and how the operations of the universe might affect its microcosm, man. Such knowledge was considered as important as statecraft to a ruler, and reflected the medical views of the time.

It was believed that the body, like the universe, was composed of four elements: fire, air, earth and water, embodying the four qualities of hot, cold, dry and wet. Food and drink consisted of these elements and qualities, and formed in the process of digestion the four bodily humours: blood, yellow bile, phlegm and black bile. Fire corresponded to yellow bile, which was hot and dry; air to blood, which was hot and wet; earth to black bile, which was cold and dry; and water to phlegm, which was cold and wet. The humours nourished the body and its vital organs, maintaining its innate heat and vital spirit. A person's individual temperament, whether sanguine, choleric, phlegmatic or melancholic, arose from a preponderance of one of the four constituent elements and its corresponding qualities and humour. Providing all elements were in harmony, a healthy humoral balance would be maintained; but any upset, lack or excess of a particular humour would create bodily imbalance and dysfunction, resulting in sickness and ill health. Six factors, known as the six 'non-naturals', while not innate to humans, were inescapable influences on their bodily well-being. These were the surrounding air, motion and rest, sleeping and waking, food and drink, secretion and excretion and passions of the soul. Hence the correlation of what in modern parlance would be called environmental factors and lifestyle with health, together with factors such as sex, age and occupation, were well understood in the Middle Ages, but their understanding and consideration were underpinned by the humoral pathology which underlay all medical theory and practice and was embodied in Galenism,[2] the essence of which has been outlined above.

The physician had three main diagnostic tools to determine people's bodily state: uroscopy, pulse and astrology. Uroscopy was linked to the process of digestion and the operation of the liver. With due regard to texture, smell and even taste of urine, and twenty-one possible colour distinctions that were thought to be detectable, the patient's state of health, process of disease and its possible outcome could be deduced. The observable colour distinctions were often illustrated in diagrammatic charts which reveal that often medical illustration was not an ancillary textual embellishment but a practical aid to the practising physician.

Pulse, which was meant to be taken with the four fingers of the hand on the radial artery at the patient's wrist and measured over a duration of 100 beats, was related to the heart, although there was no conception of the heart as pump. Twenty-seven distinctions of heartbeat, named according to their rhythm by terms like 'ant-like' or 'sluggish', were thought detectable.

Uroscopy and pulse, in the hands of a practised physician, could reach a high level of competence and sophistication, but in popular literature and manuscript illustration they became a source of humour and objects of satire. The ape physician in his ermine trim gown and cap (usually reserved for academic physicians), enthroned and judiciously inspecting the urine flask symbol of the medical profession, while taking the pulse (wrongly for an ape!) of the unfortunate patient on crutches with distended stomach, suggesting dropsy, is an amusing example (see the illustration on p. 84). Rationality was not a trait accorded the ape, who was associated with passion and appetite. The sly and deceitful fox was another animal used to poke fun at the physician, while in Langland's fourteenth-century work, *Piers Plowman*, the doctors send an urgent letter to Liar, 'asking him to join them, and help them analyse urine'.[3]

While uroscopy and pulse related to internal bodily function, the operations of the universe affected man both internally and externally. The zodiac was believed to govern his outward anatomy, each sign having a particular correspondence to a part of the body, while the planets, especially the moon, affected his humoral disposition. Hence astrology proved an important diagnostic and prognostic tool. A favourable conjunction of the planets in relation to the patient's sign in the zodiac was a vital indicator of the most propitious time for the administration of drugs or conducting surgical operations. In an illustration in Walter de Milemete's work, the moon's benevolent expression indicates its favourable position in Scorpio, Libra or Pisces for the administration of the laxative herb which one physician holds and the other has compounded in a vessel for administering to the king (see the illustration on p. 85). Had the moon been in Saturn an adverse effect would have resulted, according to the text. The importance of astrological influence was long accepted. In 1424 one William Forest had received an injury to the muscles of the thumb of his right hand when the moon had been 'dark and in a bloody sign' of Aquarius. Three barber-surgeons were exonerated from charges of negligence in their procedures to stop the bleeding and save William's hand, on account of the 'malevolent constellation' at the time of the injury.

As with uroscopy, so astrological computations became perfected and rendered in practical form. A sophisticated example is the volvelle in the Book of the Barber-Surgeons of York, which as a working instrument would enable complex calculations to determine propitious times for operations (see the colour plate on p. 72). Cruder forms of volvelles, zodiac-men and uroscopy charts found wide circulation in England in the early fifteenth century, often in folded form in girdle books attached to a belt worn round the physician's waist, and constituted on-the-spot ready-reckoners for bedside prognosis.

The fundamental therapy both in preventive medicine and in the treatment of sickness was dietary and medicative – to direct an individual's regimen according to the six 'non-naturals' and to prescribe those foods, drinks and medications according to the allopathic principle of contraries, namely to counter the effects of foods that have hot and dry qualities, which would exacerbate a man of choleric disposition, with foods of the opposing quality, thereby redressing humoral harmony and restoring good health. All drug preparations based on herbal simples and compounds had known effects, being, for example, purgative, laxative or restorative, and administered in the right degree of potency (a matter of mathematical computation by the fourteenth century, based on the degree of heat in any potion), would have the desired effect. However, the key to healthy living was diet, and moderation in all things; but unlike today, medieval diet was hardly a matter of conscious choice involving nutritional factors, being rather determined by availability of foodstuffs and purchasing power.

Aping the physician and his diagnostic procedures of uroscopy and pulse. The ape was associated with passion and appetite and not rationality, which the doctors claimed informed their diagnostic judgements. Representing the physician as an ape or sly fox was a popular way of poking fun at the medical profession.

Doctors present a laxative herb to the king when the moon is favourable. Laxatives in varying forms and strengths were often advocated in regimens for the healthy and sick alike in order to purge and cleanse the body of harmful or excess humours. The time of their administration was all-important; if the moon was in Saturn an adverse effect could occur. The focus of the King's physicians is on the benevolent disposition of the moon.

The aristocratic diet of the period, as revealed in household accounts of the crown and higher nobility, was characterised by the consumption of large quantities of meat and fish. Beef, pork and mutton, both salted for storage and preservation, and fresh meat purchased in urban markets, were common. Poultry was consumed to a lesser degree, while game was considered a luxury. Among fish, pike, bream and fresh salmon and eels were considered luxuries, while salted, white and red herring and salted or dried white fish, such as cod or ling, were more common. A well-stocked fish-pond was a feature of most manors, while proximity to ports determined the amount and variety of fresh fish available. Froissart observed that 'the English live on mild-flavoured food and good, heavy ales which keep their bodies humid',[4] but evidence suggests that increasingly the aristocracy sought to flavour both their meat and fish in spicy sauces, the ingredients for which were mainly imported as dried fruits such as figs, dates, prunes and raisins, and became increasingly exotic and expensive by the fifteenth century, when sugar, cinnamon, mace and ginger, almonds and rice became more widely available. While ale brewed from barley-malt was the staple drink of aristocratic households, with allowances amounting to a gallon per head per day, the mark of high aristocratic living was the consumption of wine, imported mainly from Gascony from the 1290s; however, Rhenish, Castilian and even Greek wine also figured, and by the fifteenth century, sweet Mediterranean wines such as malmsey, which is reputed to have permanently drowned the sorrows of George, duke of Clarence, in 1478.

Cereals were consumed not only in the form of ale, but also bread; wheat bread for the upper nobility, as opposed to a rye and wheat mixture for the lower echelons of the household, white bread (wastel) being the most admired. Dairy produce, fresh fruit and vegetables appeared less important in the aristocratic diet. Eggs were often used in fish sauces or in luxurious confections. The main vegetables cited are leeks and onions, while apples, pears, strawberries, cherries and plums present the seasonal variety in fresh fruit. The late fourteenth and fifteenth centuries would appear to be periods of increasingly conspicuous, if not elaborate consumption, with three or four courses, involving numerous dishes in each, being a feature, an indication that food was not just a matter of nourishment but also a status symbol and manifestation of wealth.

Peasant diet is distinguished from the aristocratic by its very plainness and the comparative modesty of amounts consumed. Chaucer in the *Nun's Priest's Tale* serves to point this contrast very well when he refers to the poor widow who had no *sauce piquante* to spice her veal, nor wine to drink, but lived on milk, bread, boiled bacon and the occasional egg.[5] Before the Black Death, a cereal-based diet of bread and pottage characterised peasant diet, with ale as the main drink. Garden produce – onions, leeks, cabbages and garlic together with apples and pears – gave some nutritional intake, while animal protein was provided by bacon and modest dairy produce. A diet that was at best scarce could mean that in a bad year people could starve, and while all diet was at the mercy of the changing seasons and constrained by problems of storage and transportation, the susceptibility of the peasant to periodic emergencies was all the greater. Times of temporary indulgence could be followed by real deprivation. However, after the Black Death, peasant diet changed in three respects, as those who had survived had greater bargaining power with regard to their jobs and wages in a time of labour shortage. Peasant wheat consumption increased as they baked it for bread rather than boiled it for pottage, ale consumption rose and they ate more meat and, if contemporary literature and legislation is to be believed, aspired to aristocratic diet and even dress. Langland, while moralistic and disapproving in tone, illustrates these shifts and aspirations well in the figure of Waster and his companions in *Piers Plowman*:

> Waster would not work any more but set out as a tramp. And the beggars refused the bread that had beans in it, demanding milk loaves and fine white, wheaten bread. And they would not drink cheap beer at any price, but only the best brown ale that is sold in the towns. And the day-labourers, who have no land to live on but their shovels, would not deign to eat yesterday's vegetables. And draught-ale was not good enough for them, nor a hunk of bacon, but they must have fresh meat or fish, fried or baked and *chaud* or *plus chaud* at that, lest they catch a chill on their stomachs![6]

Sumptuary legislation in the fourteenth century reveals attempts to control both the extravagances of the aristocratic diet in 1316 and the aspirations of lower members of society to emulate them in 1363, both in diet and in dress. Both measures proved unenforceable but reveal a desire to reaffirm social distinctions in eating habits, dress and lifestyle.

Aristocratic dress, like food, became more sumptuous in the fourteenth century, and fashions were constantly changing. The long and voluminous 'houppelond', with its sleeves which almost swept the ground, gave way to short, narrow-waisted tunics with two-coloured hose. Chaucer's parson denounced its red and white variant for making men look as though they had hernias and had had half their 'shameful privy members . . . slain'. Silk, furs and jewellery were a feature, as were elaborate head-dresses for ladies, considered health hazards in the view of one observer, as providing haunts for lice and mice! The need to keep clothes sweet-smelling, as they would be infrequently washed, was not lost on the apothecary of Edward IV's household, who was instructed to fumigate the king's doublets, robes, sheets and shirts with sweet-smelling herbs and flowers.

In modern terms, aristocratic diet appears high in fat and low in fibre, and the relatively low consumption of fresh fruit and vegetables would seem to indicate a deficiency in vitamin C. Fatty fish and some eggs made it richer in vitamins A and D, and with meat and fish as the bulk food, it would appear high in protein. Vitamin deficiency, it is now appreciated, can lead to a variety of skin and eye ailments, accentuated among the peasantry who were most vulnerable to seasonal fluctuations in crop yields and their effects on quantity and quality of food.

However, it was problems of over-rich diet and over-indulgence leading to digestive disorders that occupied many regimen texts, which were tailor-made for the aristocracy who could afford them, and which reflect aristocratic habits rather than those of the lower orders of society. Furthermore it was only the aristocracy who, with the widest choices in food, could, it was felt, amend their dietary ways and resist 'Sir Surfeit': '"Never allow Sir Surfeit at your table", said Hunger to Piers the Ploughman, "don't trust him, he's a great gourmand and his guts are always crying out for more dishes."'[7]

Chroniclers suggest that resistance to surfeit on the part of some English kings had been weak: Henry I had died of a surfeit of lampreys, while King John was thought to have succumbed to a surfeit of peaches. It is interesting that regimen texts reflect, as dietary warnings, those very 'deficiencies' noted in aristocratic diet, while advocating the known luxuries.

Following the *Regimen Salernitanum* they advocated avoidance of certain fresh fruits, especially pears and peaches, which were only acceptable if baked or steeped in wine respectively. Onions were not good for the choleric, though acceptable for the phlegmatic. Veal and most poultry were favoured to breed good blood, as were freshwater fish and sea fish. Wines of good quality were advocated, the clearest and reddest being the best, and cheeringly, wine in moderation would fortify the body, nourish, bring happiness and delay the onset of old age!

Laxatives and purgatives to encourage vomiting and excretion to rid the body of noxious humours figure large in regimen texts. Rhubarb was considered particularly efficacious; damsons 'make your entrails soluble and slack'. Hyssop was a purge and cleanser, while wormwood banished intestinal worms. Apothecary lists reveal such medications in demand and use. Constipation was one of the most common conditions, for which clysters or enemas might be the only solution. The master surgeon, John of Arderne, who practised in Newark from 1349 and in London after 1370, wrote a small treatise on clysters.[8] He graphically describes the clyster pipe in action (see the illustration below), designed his own pipe, to which a pig's bladder was to be attached, and advocated his own recipe over the basic salt and water solution; this consisted of green camomile boiled with wheat bran, to which a handful of salt and clear honey or oil would be added. Half a pint would fill the clyster bag. He claims that he gained honour and reward for his clyster preparation, which was better than that of the Lombards in London who administered clysters, which did not always work, to choleric or constipated men.

Recipes against drunkenness and its effects also figure. One part juice of white cabbage and juice of pomegranates, and half a measure of vinegar

Man undergoing a clyster, which was advocated for constipation and other problems of a digestive and intestinal nature. John of Arderne, a fourteenth-century English surgeon, advocated his own clyster pipe and bag made out of a pig's bladder, and his own clyster solutions.

A severe case of spasm after too much carousing following the wedding of Lionel, duke of Clarence, in Milan in 1368. This armour-bearer was so bent up that his body resembled a crossbow (*ad modum baliste*). He was cured with a charm written on parchment which was suspended in a pouch tied round his neck. When committing the charm to writing, Arderne uses Greek letters, so that it does not get into the wrong lay hands.

boiled, an ounce to be taken before drinking wine, would do the trick.[9] The effects on the English of drinking wine in hot or foreign climes, which were noted by Froissart when referring to the campaigns of the Duke of Lancaster in Spain, and which resulted in belly-flux or dysentery,[10] are echoed in the pages of John of Arderne. He refers to the testimony of Lord Reginald de Grey's son, who had attended the marriage of Lionel, duke of Clarence, in Milan, to the daughter of Galeazzo Visconti in 1368. There the English were troubled with spasms due to the strong, hot wines and too much carousing. One armour-bearer had such a severe spasm that his head was drawn backwards nearly to his feet, 'just like a cross bow' (see the illustration above), and he was almost dead from pain and starvation. His cure reveals a 'magical' dimension in English medicine, for a charm written on parchment was suspended in a pouch tied round his neck, and within four to five hours he was cured.[11] The use of a parchment charm did not prove so efficacious nor aid the fortunes of one Roger Clerk of Wandelsworth, who had rolled up an old piece of parchment in gold cloth around the neck of Johanna, wife of Roger atte Hache, promising that it bore a charm that would rid her of her fever. When brought to answer before the mayor of London in 1382, he was found to be an illiterate quack, and his penalty was to be paraded through the streets of London on a horse, the blank parchment and a whetstone round his neck for his lies, and a uroscopy flask hung on his chest and back to symbolise the profession he had sought to usurp.

Bloodletting was another widely recommended evacuation procedure both in the case of illness and as part of preventive medicine. Laymen and religious underwent it at prescribed intervals. The time of bloodletting was important, as were the age, habits and strength of the patient. The phlebotomy-man became another facet of medical illustration (see the colour plate on p. 105).

It was well understood that if incorrectly performed, complications such as haemorrhage or septicaemia could ensue. Edward I underwent bloodletting to a harp accompaniment to take his mind off the process. He advocated it for his second wife Margaret, in response to her physician's request. Cupping, a lesser form of bloodletting, was often performed by women and associated with the bath-house, while leeches were used to draw out impurities in the blood. They were also advocated for a variety of skin blemishes in women, and were to be administered under a physician's supervision. The powers of bloodletting were deemed superlative:

> Phlebotomy clears the mind, strengthens the memory, cleanses the stomach, dries up the brain, warms the marrow, sharpens the hearing, stops tears, encourages discrimination, develops the senses, promotes digestion, produes a musical voice, dispels torpor, drives away anxiety, feeds the blood, rids it of poisonous matter and brings long life.[12]

Similar superlatives were used by John of Mirfield, a fourteenth-century cleric associated with St Bartholomew's, London, to praise the virtue of exercise in his *Florarium Bartholomei*.[13] A complement to phlebotomy, medications and baths, exercise involved 'neither fear, nor distaste, nor expense, but pure recreation of soul and body'. As with food and dress, there was a hierarchy of exercise according to social rank. Walking was free to everyone, and especially good in hilly places where the 'air is pure'. However, riding, according to Mirfield, was 'only for the wealthy', and in this context hunting was seen as the sport and exercise of kings.

Mirfield, appreciative of the more sedentary or enclosed life of religious, advocated alternative exercises for them – rope exercises in their room or weight training with a 30 lb stone, tugging games with a staff, prising a penny out of a clenched fist or breathing exercises. For 'playful youth' he recommended running, wrestling, jumping and stone hurling. By the fifteenth century tennis was popular, while football had made its appearance among the lower classes before 1350, for around that time Edward III issued a decree that people were to stop playing the worthless game of football and start practising their archery instead, so that they could kill more Frenchmen in war. The game was still being played in the fifteenth century, and to devastating effect, judging by the youth who ruptured his intestines in what was referred to as that 'execrable, worthless and dangerous game', and was healed by the miraculous intervention of King Henry VI. In the context of exercise and rank, it is understandable why consternation greeted the 'idling, ditching, digging and other improper occupations' so enjoyed by King Edward II, but which were unworthy pursuits for a king.

To assess the overall health of the aristocracy or any other stratum of medieval society in relation to diet, therapies adopted, or medications they undoubtedly used, is extremely difficult; however, both contemporary testimony and modern researchers agree in pointing the finger at the town as the hotbed of infections. The health hazards of urban life were not lost on medical authors or municipal authorities conscious of crowding, insanitary conditions and problems of 'industrial pollution'. When Aldobrandino of Siena wrote his *Livres dou santé*[14] in 1256 for Beatrice of Savoy, countess of Provence and mother of Queen Eleanor, wife of Henry III of England, to accompany her on her visit to her daughter, he included a section on how to know which towns are best to live in. He referred to matters of location and soil, smell and sounds as important factors. In terms of diet, the better-off urban dweller had the choice of the markets; after all the town was *the* market and supplier, aiming to provide a plentiful supply of foodstuffs at affordable prices to its inhabitants and those outside. Evidence is available to suggest that wheat bread was the staple in the towns, that fresh meat- and fish-sellers multiplied in response to demand, and that the meat of young animals afforded the choicest cuts at high prices that reflected the demand. The abundance of brewers reflected high ale consumption, while the wine trade also developed in this period. Greater fruit consumption and choice would appear to equate with evidence of gardens concentrated in the towns and suburbs, especially of London. Food supplies were always problematic, as they came from outside, and legislative efforts were made to provide greater storage to stock against disasters of famine that could affect supply. Regulations to ensure the quality and freshness of food supplies are evident, but it was often the urban poor who were left the 'remnants', which included butchers' offal and the meat of diseased animals.

The major health hazards of urban life were linked to the problems of effluent disposal and hygiene. Butchers were notorious for dumping the leftovers of their trade in the streets and the Thames. The problems of latrines giving on to open drains and cesspits and the river, endangering water supplies, were constantly stated, but measures to improve conditions in the fourteenth century by piped water systems to houses, refuse collection and draining systems, while adding to the cost of urban living, were gradually made.

Given this environment, it is perhaps no wonder that the urban merchants, clergy and nobility of the court, in the case of London, should constitute the major clientele of the professional physician and surgeon. The evidence for their practice far outweighs that for rural practice, and creates an unfortunate imbalance. However, the medical market-place in the towns was a wide open and highly competitive one, in the absence of controls and licensing, which were much slower to develop in England than on the Continent. By the late thirteenth century, for example, in Paris, licence to practise medicine in the city and suburbs required a degree from the Paris medical faculty or some other recognised medical faculty, such as Salerno, Montpellier or Bologna. Having a university medical education was the mark of professionalism in the eyes of the Paris physicians, who in 1271 legislated to control the practice of surgeons, apothecaries and herbalists in the city. The surgeons formed a guild in defence of their profession, which was viewed by the physicians as a 'mechanical craft'. Only in the Italian universities had surgery long been integral to the teaching of its medical faculties, enjoyed status and made considerable innovative advances. Elsewhere the surgeons sought to distinguish themselves from the more lowly barbers, who combined their traditional activities with minor wound surgery, bloodletting and dentistry. All sought to distinguish themselves from the great array of empirics and quacks who they felt, by virtue of their rashness, caused countless deaths.

The universities of Oxford and Cambridge used Paris as a model, but as regards medicine and its influence, that is where the similarity ends. The first record of a medical faculty at Oxford dates to the early fourteenth century, and it was to remain the smallest faculty. Twenty people have been identified as holding the degree of Doctor of Medicine in the century, while only fifteen, mostly clerics, can be associated with medical practice. Surgery did not figure at all in the English universities, nor can any association be established with surgeons whose own writings, as in the case of John of Arderne, reveal undoubted learning and access to a wide medical library. Indeed, to establish how and where English physicians and surgeons who did not study abroad gained their learning and training is very difficult. The comparative lack of influence of Oxbridge in medical developments in England may be explained by the fact that both universities were provincial; unlike Paris, neither was equated with the court and the wealth, patronage and power it afforded. One of the few known English-educated physicians associated with Merton College, Oxford and the court was John of Gaddesden (*c.* 1280–1349). His work, the *Rosa Medicinae*, composed *c.* 1305–17,[15] was widely disseminated in England and abroad, and while an avowed 'compilation', based on ancient and more contemporary authorities, is infused with his own observations and practice. Gaddesden claimed to have cured the son of Edward II, the future Edward III, of smallpox by enveloping him, and all else round his bed, in red cloth, thereby demonstrating the doctrine of sympathy, that like would attract like.[16]

It is to London one looks for evolution in medical professionalism and controls, and not to the universities *per se*. London had its own structures for medical care, if not for teaching, and these were the guilds and corporations. The barbers' guild, founded *c.* 1307, chartered in 1376 and incorporated in 1463, was one. The apothecaries reveal organisation by 1312; the surgeons by 1368/69. An attempt by the university physicians, sanctioned by the king, in 1423, to break into London and combine with the surgeons to become the ultimate legitimising force in the practice of English medicine and surgery, proved short-lived. By 1435 the seventeen surgeons confirmed their own Fellowship, and by 1493 made an agreement with the barbers, while the College of Physicians was formed in 1518. The London surgeon John Bradmore had no doubt come to royal notice owing to his successful extraction of a barbed arrow from the cheek of the future Henry V at Kenilworth, after the battle of Shrewsbury in 1403. Bradmore tells of his method and the instrument he invented for the operation in the *Philomena*, which he wrote between 1403 and 1412 and which was translated into English in 1446. A payment of 40*s* for medicines for the king and his household in 1403 reveals his court association, as does his appointment as searcher of the port of London in 1408. Life in association with the royal household had its dramatic moments. It was Bradmore who was called in to attend to the king's pavilioner William Wyncelowe, who in a suicide attempt had stabbed himself in the abdomen, rupturing his intestines. Bradmore attended him over an eighty-day period, and he survived.[17] The Agincourt campaign of 1415, among others, provided employ for numerous surgeons in the king's pay.

Association with king and nobility could take the form of a long-term or life annuity, which could carry food allowances, robes and travel expenses in return for priority treatment. Often governmental posts or ecclesiastical benefices went hand in hand with the appointment. The foreigner David de Nigarellis held an 80 mark annuity from the king, which in 1412 was supplemented by his salary of £40 per year as keeper of the royal mint. John Bray, physician to William, earl of Surrey, to John of Gaunt, Edward III and Richard II, enjoyed a rising scale of £5, then £10 and £12 respectively from these clients. Ecclesiastical preferment was sought by Edward I for his physician Nicholas Tyngewick in 1306, in the form of the church of Reculver in Kent. His repayment for the long and faithful service of his surgeon, William of York, in 1303, by providing him with a place of retirement, resulted in poor William (with servant and horse) being shunted to and fro, firstly to Ramsey Abbey, and then to Butley Priory in Suffolk, where excuses for not receiving him were overridden and where he finally ended his days in 1312. Richard II demonstrated similar loyalty and sympathy for his physician, John Leech, who when his eyesight was failing was released from court duties and assigned seven and a half pence as an esquire of the royal body.

The greater abbeys appear to have offered comparable terms in return for medical services. Worcester made an arrangement with John de Bosco in 1329: in return for an annual stipend of 40s, a corrody to provide him with the best quality ale and food, and a horse and groom, he promised to give faithful medical service and patient confidentiality. While such annuities provided security and could prove lucrative, individual payment per treatment became favoured by surgeons and physicians, as this maximised their bargaining power. Evidence of pre-treatment contracts, or even part-payment in advance, becomes increasingly evident in the fourteenth and fifteenth centuries, and contributed to the long-held reputation of physicians as greedy, fraudulent and stingy. John of Mirfield recounts in his *Florarium Bartholomei* an amusing anecdote reflecting the physician's obsession with fees, even unto death: 'There is a story that is told about a certain physician to whom thirteen pounds had been owing for three years; who, when he was at the point of death, and was admonished that he should confess his sins and partake of the Eucharist, could be brought to answer nothing else except, "Thirteen pounds" and "Three years."'[18]

The fee was the practitioners' single bargaining counter, but it determined who could afford the services of physicians and surgeons. The philanthropic ethic of treating the poor free had been promoted by Galen and was echoed by Henri de Mondeville, an influential fourteenth-century French surgeon whose work was translated into English. He advocated an almost Robin Hood mentality, and recommended a form of fiscal diagnosis of all patients prior to treatment. He also believed that those to whom one could not refuse treatment, namely lords, their relatives, chamberlains, justices, bailiffs and lawyers were notoriously bad payers. Mondeville suggested a sliding scale of fees: 'take from the rich a hundred pounds, take fifty from a man of middling fortune and from a pauper a goose, a duck, a chicken, a young hen, a cheese and eggs', but nothing from one who is truly poor.[19] The reputation of the surgeon had to be maintained and his specialist talents rewarded.

The English surgeon John of Arderne echoed this latter sentiment. He considered himself the only 'master surgeon' capable of operating on anal fistula – *fistula in ano*. He had 'gained great honour and praise throughout England' as a result of his successful treatment of this condition in Adam, second baron Everingham of Laxton, Nottinghamshire, who had developed the condition in Gascony, where it had been deemed incurable. Upon Adam's return to England, Arderne had been called in and made a contract with him prior to undertaking his treatment, which proved successful. Adam was completely cured within six months, and was to remain well for a further thirty years or more, a form of long-term advertisement for Arderne's operation, which his text, a *practica* for the operation *fistula in ano*, written in 1376 and intended for the instruction of his fellow master surgeons, and incorporating much of his

The fourteenth-century English master surgeon, John of Arderne, conducts an exploratory probe into a fistulous hole to establish whether it perforates the rectum. The surgeon could opt for operation by ligature or by incision for a perforating fistula. Arderne called the probing instrument the *sequere me*.

own practical experience, illustrates. Step-by-step procedures are given and illustrated for the complex operation, together with the instruments used, which in two cases were Arderne's own inventions (see the illustrations above and opposite). In his text he reveals that he never took on treatment of this condition without a down payment of at least 100 shillings. Arderne also appears to suggest social distinctions in payment for treatment accorded. For the noble and 'great', anything from 100 marks to £40 plus an annuity of 100 shillings for the patient's lifetime, plus robes and fees; for the less well-off, a scale of £40 to 40 marks without any additional fees.[20]

The social rank of his patients was a matter of distinction to Arderne, and his work provides a vivid and colourful insight into his clientele and the surgical treatments he carried out for their conditions. Among his fistula patients were Henry Blackburn, treasurer of the household of the Black Prince, Reynold, fourth baron Grey of Wilton, the mayor of Northampton and the custodian of the Franciscans in York. Swellings, skin growths, wounded limbs, gout, piles, haemorrhoids, urinary stone and other genito-urinary complaints constitute the array of conditions he treated. Analogies drawn from nature vividly describe conditions he saw as a surgeon, for example the case of a man with a bloody pile 'like a mulberry', or the chaplain of Colston's nodule within the skin of the nipple of his right breast that grew from 'the size of a pea' to that of 'a hen's egg in the shape of a spinning top' to the case of the knight in the forces of the Duke of Lancaster at Ageçir, Spain, who had a sudden attack of wrymouth, so that his mouth was drawn back nearly to his ear and his facial expression resembled 'the fish called the flounder'.[21] He gives a treatment for prolapse of the rectum, on which the fifteenth-century copyist comments 'with this medicine was King Henry [IV] of England cured of prolapsed rectum', while his treatment of black soap, vigorously beaten with pitch and placed in a walnut shell over the navel of patients who found

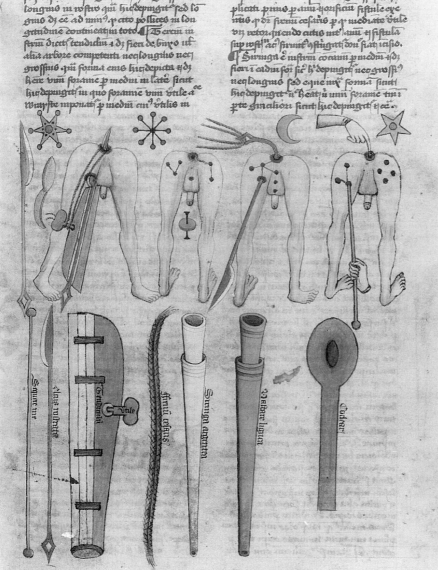

Procedures and instruments to be used for the operation *fistula in ano* for which John of Arderne gained great fame. This dangerous operation involved use of a probe (*sequere me*) and a billed or snouted needle (*acus rostrata*), which was a grooved director along which a razor-like scalpel could be passed for incision and division of the fistula. Arderne invented two further instruments, a wooden board with a peg-hole (*tendiculum*) to tighten a ligature as a peg would in a violin, and a spoon (*coclear*) to be held by the surgeon's assistant to protect the wall of the rectum during incision. Twisted thread (*frenum cesaris*), the ends of which, having been passed through the fistula and rectum, would be tied to the peg of the *tendiculum*, and one silver and one wooden syringe are also shown.

difficulty in passing urine, was tried on John of Gaunt duke of Lancaster.[22] Arderne's text also reveals the competitive world of the fourteenth-century medical market-place characteristic of London and other urban centres. He disparages 'certain ladies', whose treatments consisting of pills, plasters and Antioch potion do their patients no good.[23] He is equally wary of barbers, advocating that certain operational procedures should be hidden from them, as they will usurp them and bring dishonour to the master surgeons' craft; and he points out their own bungling operations, as in the case of the London fishmonger who accidentally injured his arm with a knife.[24] He promotes his own ointments, such as *tapsivalentia*, and reveals a sleeping powder used by rogues in France on pilgrims in order to rob them, but which he advocates as a painkiller.[25] Never slow to reveal his successes over the inadequacies of others, Arderne, in his *Practica* and *Liber Medicinarum*, provides us with one of the most vivid and widely disseminated works of English surgery in the period.

The surgeon deserved his fees. His work, unlike the physician's, was manifest and his reputation always on the line. Matthew Rellesford, a London surgeon, charged George Baylle 40*s* for stone, and John Roper, tailor, 10*s*, with 5*s* in advance, for treating a diseased foot. Both dissatisfied patients sought damages from Matthew in 1443. Where failure resulted or a condition deteriorated, litigation often ensued. The surgeon John le Spicer was accused in 1354 of causing 'a certain enormous and horrible hurt' on the right side of the jaw of Thomas Shene in his effort to heal a wound. Litigation of this sort would appear to have been on the increase in the late fourteenth and fifteenth centuries, indicating that where contracts or down payments had been made, patient expectancy was high. However, patient co-operation was demanded, as in the case of the action brought by the prior of Guisborough and Richard, a canon, against the York physician, Matthew Rutherford, in 1433, whom they accused of negligent treatment of Richard's leg. Matthew in defence stated that his patient, in defiance of his orders, had persisted in eating unwholesome food and had thrown away his medicines.

Evidence of payment in kind and the nature of rural medical and surgical practice is rare. Perhaps the operations of the 'toothdrawer' Matthew Flynt bring one closer. In April 1400, he was allocated 6*d* a day at the Exchequer for treating 'any poor lieges of the King' in London without charge. The illustration in the Encyclopedia of Jacobus the Englishman, now identified as James Palmer, an exchequer clerk who died in 1375,[26] gives a rare glimpse of such an operator at work (see the colour plate on p. 106). He was one who prized the teeth he extracted, as trophies worn round his neck, as the best advertisement for his services, the large pincers being the tool of his trade. Some insight into English rural practice in the fifteenth century is revealed in the book of John Crophill of Wix in Essex.[27] He combined his practice with his function as bailiff of Wix priory and ale tester for the manor in 1461. He lists men and women patients, including a carpenter, shepherd, sexton and cordwainer from whom he had taken urine samples and 'done curys for'. His treatments included two short recipes for gout and warts, and a charge of 1*d* may have been a fairly standard one for his services.

It is in the cost of treatments and their preparation that apothecaries came into the equation. They were meant to operate on the prescription of the physicians, and Chaucer suggests that they were allies in guile. However, by the fourteenth century apothecaries were dispensing directly over the counter those potions that were considered restorative or harmless, such as rosewater. Apothecary controls exercised by the guild, concerning freshness, proper strengths and quality of ingredients, are evident. It was Richard of Montpellier, spicer, who in conjunction with the physician Nicholas Tyngewick supplied drugs for the ailing Edward I, who was taken ill on his expedition to Scotland in 1307. The range of items that were sent to him at Lanercost priory consisted of an electuary made with amber, musk, jacinth, pearls, gold and silver; sugar rosettes; Damascus rosewater; pomegranate wine; herbal baths; a special ointment prepared six times for his legs; and a plaster of rare gums and ambergris for his neck. His painful condition was ultimately complicated by dysentery which took the king's life and left his £134 16s 4d apothecary bill unpaid. The ingredients which were both rare and expensive were considered 'noble' for a king. Social distinctions made in medical recipes were not just to facilitate cheaper or alternative treatments for the less well-to-do, but often to make a correlation between the nobility of a treatment's ingredients and the status of the person to whom it was applied. Similarly the art of coating the pill to make it more palliative was well understood. The panoply of possible treatments available in the physicians' armoury is illustrated in those treatments proposed for another royal patient, King Henry VI, during his bout of madness in March 1454. Electuaries, potions, syrups, confections, laxatives, clysters, gargles, baths, ointments, head purges, poultices and bleedings were recommended.

It was with a similar armoury that physicians and surgeons had faced the plague which hit England in the autumn of 1348. Contemporary English medical texts and chronicles were muted in their descriptions of reactions to the plague and its particular symptoms, unlike their continental counterparts who distinguished it from other epidemics by its speed, severity and widespread nature. Disorientation and despair pervade the social observations made in the *Brut Chronicle*: 'In these days was death without sorrow, wedding without friendship, wilful penance, and dearth without scarcity, and fleeing without refuge or succour.'[28] The chronicler Geoffrey le Baker noted that recovery was more likely if buboes developed than if carbuncles appeared all over the body. The buboes were large swellings in the armpit, groin or on the neck that might blacken, suppurate and emit a vile stench. They appeared within two to three days.

Of the three forms of plague, bubonic, pneumonic and septicaemic, this description would appear to denote bubonic plague. The word *bubo* means 'owl' in Latin, and when the owl is depicted in manuscript marginals it is linked with *pestis* or *pestilencia*, denoted by buboes, but not always associated with what became known as the Black Death. John of Arderne explained that just as owls loved dark, secluded places, so the buboes appeared in those of the body – the armpit or groin. The aggressive owl in the margin of John Bradmore's *Philomena* (see the illustration on p. 98) refers back to an entry on the Black Death. Bradmore's text, written in the fifteenth century, reveals – as do so many others – a heavy reliance on continental authors in relation to causation, prevention and treatment of the Black Death, in particular Guy de Chauliac, surgeon to Pope Clement VI at Avignon, who had witnessed it there in 1348, and John of Burgundy, whose tract on the plague written *c.* 1365 received wide circulation in abridged and translated form in England. By the time of Bradmore, the fact of plague recurrences was well understood; England had experienced such in 1361, 1368–69, 1371, 1375, 1390, 1400 and 1405. The plague pandemic of 1348 had become endemic.

Most learned continental opinion attributed the causes of the plague to a universal air condition brought about by a deadly planetary conjunction of Saturn, Mars and Jupiter in Aquarius. This, in conjunction with corrupted vapours from earth and water, spread the poisonous air or miasma; hence its widespread transmission and contagion, which came about through three forms of contact – via the pores of the skin, via respiration or via the gaze of an infected person associated with the mythical creature, the basilisk. The idea

The aggressive owl or *bubo*, indicating pestilence, as it gave its name to the buboes which appeared in the armpit or groin, and were also signs of bubonic plague.

of humorial susceptibility of some to the plague was noted. Flight was the best course of action, but the authors of plague tracts suggested preventive measures and, to a lesser extent, cures. These were structured, as the regimen for the healthy had been, according to the six 'non-naturals'. Regarding the avoidance of pestilential air, one should have regard to the location of one's home, correcting or purifying the air and avoiding contact with infected persons. The advocacy of sweet-smelling aromatics – marjoram, savory and mint for the poor, wood of aloes, amber and musk for the rich – to counter the stench associated with putrefaction and corruption was not only a matter for individuals in their homes, but was echoed in renewed sanitary legislation issued by many civic authorities in England in the years following the plague and depopulation. Drainage and sanitation were addressed, and measures against the depositing of offal and manure in the streets reiterated. An alternative view held by some was that those associated with stench had an immunity to the plague. Some sought to attain it by spending hours inhaling the stench of latrines.

Diet was to be light; fruits, and food cooked in honey, were to be avoided. Vinegar could be mixed with anything, and garlic was deemed efficacious. Moderate exercise was advocated, but no hot baths, that would open the pores of the skin to contagion. Keeping the body purged and cleansed was all-important, and bloodletting as an evacuative process was recommended. Medications such as Armenian bolus, Lemnian earth (*terra sigillata*) and agaric as simples, and compounds containing theriac, emerald, mithridate, pills of aloes, saffron and myrrh were advocated for their cleansing and invigorating properties or as antidotes to the poison. Ultimately one had to have regard to one's soul and God, whose divine anger had to be appeased, but such medical and social measures as indicated illustrate some form of reaction whereby informed medical opinion was consciously sought to speak for a wider community need, and civic measures may be seen in conjunction with rather than separate from this.

Matters of social and psychological impact are difficult to measure, as is the efficacy of those provisions that were adopted. Many must have felt, as a contemporary English poem stated, that 'against death is worth no medicine'. By the fifteenth century, recurrences of plague were met with the reiteration of measures advocated for 1348 and the 1360s, and plague came to be only one of a 'lethal cocktail' of epidemic diseases that were part of English life and included typhus, smallpox, epidemic dysentery, malaria (in East Anglia) and the mysterious English sweating sickness, probably an acute form of viral infection. However, a heightened awareness of matters of hygiene and sanitation is evident, as is the value of health as a wider social matter in the increasing civic legislation of the period. There was also a proliferation of small treatises advocating simple remedies and instructions for general health and the plague tractates – a new form of medical literature in themselves – which by the fifteenth century circulated in the vernacular.

The translation of the learned medical and surgical treatises into the vernacular in the fourteenth century reveals the selectivity of translators and copyists in subordinating the theoretical aspects of the texts in favour of a clear, step-by-step procedural approach in surgery and practical advice in medical recipes, indicative possibly of a consciousness of wider public demand and need. Many of the general vernacular medical treatises of the period included recipes against the plague, one attributed to King Edward IV himself in response to the dreadful English pestilence of 1471. Another, by the Dominican Thomas Multon, was written in English: 'so that everyman both learned and unlearned may better understand it and act accordingly: be his own physician in time of need against the venom and malice of the pestilence.'[29]

The 'popularisation' of learned medicine in the form of 'self-help' treatises did not diminish the growing status and distinction of the medical profession, whose advice was still sought by the crown and nobility. In 1424 Humphrey, duke of Gloucester, sought a regimen from the physician Gilbert Kymer – its advice echoed that of the *Secretum Secretorum* presented to Edward III nearly a century before. Structured according to the six 'non-naturals', it gave advice which, if followed, promised Humphrey the wisdom of Solomon, the triumph of Alexander the Great and the great age of Methuselah.

FORMS OF EXPRESSION

RELIGIOUS SENSIBILITY

Richard Davies

Only a few years ago it was possible to pass public examinations at a high level and with a high grade by asserting that the later medieval church was 'full of abuses' and that the Reformation was all about the English people finally putting paid to them. Indeed, this was almost the only way to get a high grade, because this was the view not only of the textbooks but of English Reformation scholars generally. In part this was the product of a traditional denominational divide: the Protestant historian looked back to a triumph of good over evil, while the Catholic scholar preferred to draw a line over the medieval antecedent and concentrate on post-Reformation revival and resilience in the Roman faith and Church.[1] Another reason for the shallow roots of Reformation scholarship in England has been the historical divide at 1485. In university terms, this very exact divide led to medieval church historians fading out their courses and writings well before the end of the fifteenth century, while the early modern historians set off at a sharp gallop into the Reformation with little heed or knowledge as to what went before. It suited the great figures in both schools to imply that there was little of importance or attraction in that dark void between. Both then had a nasty shock when the 1485 barrier collapsed as abruptly as the Berlin Wall in constitutional, political, social, economic and cultural history. There has been, to be fair, a recent counter-hypothesis, that even or especially so great an epoch as the Reformation might not necessarily have deep historical roots, rather as the universe cannot be straitjacketed into traditional concepts of time and space.[2] If unconvincing to most late medievalists, at least the case is put constructively; we are not faced with a religious counterpart to Richard III's po-faced thought-police.

Other walls have come tumbling down too. Historians of the European reformations have found it impossible any longer to tolerate the vicarage tea party that passed for so long as study of the English Reformation and twittered over it as a free-standing, God-driven entity with no comparative relationship to occurrences abroad, save for the occasional excruciating reference to some German merchant dropping off a Lutheran tract on an Essex quayside and thereby jerking the English people one step further towards redemption. As important, if as yet of very mixed benefit, the walls between so-called 'ecclesiastical', 'social' and 'political' history have been sorely breached from within. 'Seven whole days, not one in seven; I will praise Thee', bellowed generations of English villagers. They and their medieval forebears seem to have meant it and expected Thee to give them something substantial, material and ideologically persuasive in return.

From without, eager suitors from such fields as anthropology, sociology and semiology have offered marriage and even hope of long-term bliss to later medieval church historians, while fashionable if ephemeral whores such as post-modernism have offered them, like everyone else, a dirty but enjoyable weekend. On the domestic front, the biggest challenge has come from the micro-historians – the historians of localities, the New Antiquarians – to whom every individual, every home, every pig has something different but undeniable to say, undermining every generalisation and perspective and preaching regional and familial cultures to the uttermost atomism. Finally – indispensable but spreading all around them the gloom and misery inherent in men and women doomed by birth to such vocations – there have come the archivists, textualists and palaeographers, questioning every document, its provenance, its typicality, its function, its capacity (usually none) for use. The sound of their collective teeth-sucking has become the ubiquitous dawn chorus from the back rows of every lecture and book-review. All in all, where once a historian could speak grandiloquently of later medieval religion without thinking seriously about anything much at all, nowadays he or she cannot even thank the audience for their invitation before being gunned down from all sides for incorrect clearing of the throat.

However, there is *no* fence to sit on. High marks are *not* awarded for taking a middle, 'moderate', 'sensible' view. The fact is that some recent historians have seen the later middle ages as truly Merry England, where the populus enjoyed themselves hugely and the Church was in charge of the entertainment; and indeed, when a person came to die, the Church organised that too with maximum comfort and least inconvenience to the dying, the bereaved and the community: something perfectly balanced between an opiate of the masses by the ruling elite and a fun park driven by the market forces *of* the masses. Some see this as the best sort of religion, some as a chimera waiting to vanish overnight. Other historians see the later medieval Church as hopelessly at odds with the laity, a powerful but inflexible institution, the perennial heavyweight champion of the world but now carrying, if imperceptibly to most, the flab of too many years of adulation, riches and soft defeats of easy opponents. Finally, all church historians continue to worry about the Black Death and its presumably seminal effects on English society: fear, morbidity, nihilism, hedonism, loss of confidence in traditional religious and social precepts and practices, detachment from the established Church, or even closer huddling to that Church. There has been much speculation, but little clear proof. Among the likelier, or at least more persistent, nominations have been consistent efforts to identify 'the rise of dissent' and 'the growth of individualism' in post-plague England. The

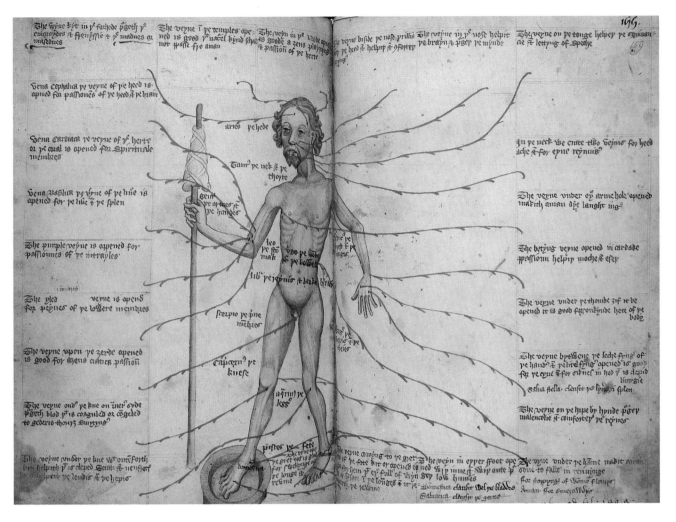

Phlebotomist or bloodletting-man illustrating the veins and points at which blood was to be let, what ailments would be relieved as a result and the signs of the zodiac associated with the parts of the body in question. Tightening or loosening one's grip on the staff illustrated could increase or ease the blood flow.

The toothpuller illustrating the tools of his trade – the pincers –
and the fruits of his work – the extracted teeth.

debate continues. At least it seems agreed now that the effects were subtle rather than spectacular.[3]

One major shift in all historical discussion has been from the institution to the individual. Where once it was assumed that great folk thought, spoke and acted, and little people responded like dogs, many historians have swung round to minimise the role of the director – pope, king, lord, university, bishop, mayor, priest, husband – and maximise that of the directed.[4] In part, this is connected with a deterministic view of history, emphasising the limitations on the great of environment, technology and practicality, and their own awareness of the art of the possible. Thus, where once it was supposed very comfortably that medieval Englishmen despised Jews and women because the Church told them to, the debate now concerns whether men did indeed really dislike one or both and, if they did, whether this did not really originate in their own conceptions which were then forced on to the Church for legitimisation. Either way, taboo subjects remain as to whether medieval Jews and/or women *deserved* to be infuriating to medieval men, in the sense that the only acceptable answer at present is 'no'.

In fact, it is quite possible that the pendulum has now swung much too far away from giving weight to the force of institutional, customary and hierarchical authority. A theme worth considering is whether the importance attached to any medieval individual's perceptions of his or her own life can be squared with a willingness by that individual to conform to the norms suggested or imposed by his or her family, neighbours or authorities. Now, around the year 2000, we have a great concern for the individual as a fulcrum for our existence, whether expressed in the booming personal-counsellor industry of the Western world or in reaction to a well-publicised orphan in Eastern Europe or a dying baby in Africa: societal problems have to be reduced to individual tragedies in order to win an empathetic response from our own selfishness. Death being seen increasingly as final, individuality becomes paramount: what you get here is all you get. In medieval England the individual was not so paramount, and death was not final. These were the given parameters, and each person adjusted his or her own expectations accordingly. They were not deluded recidivists. Uneducated in a modern sense, most were; but as integrated, worldly-wise and capable of significant direct action, they could have taught their modern descendants a lesson. Whatever the current fashionable interest in the literature of personal piety, prayer and devotion, stressing how wide and deep it spread, the fact remains that group identity was the supreme requirement: family, village, craft-guild or religious guild, to name four of the best known. Each demanded discipline while offering security and identity; religious practice and piety were moulded to legitimise and support each unit and its membership.[5]

The assertion that medieval Christian beliefs, rites and festivals were closely related to pre-existent and continuing pagan practices has become almost an article of faith in itself, impervious to the limitations of the available evidence, alongside the still more dubious alternative version that paganism and assorted superstitions and magickings flourished unabashed in their own right in the undergrowth beneath the official panoply of a Christian society.[6] Considering how many current British 'traditions', be they village fetes, morris dancers, kilts, druids, fair play on the cricket field, or the mystique of monarchy have such demonstrably shallow and inauthentic roots, still more the persistent nonsense about satanic worship, ritual child-sacrifice etc., we should be cautious about supposing that the medieval millennium saw a time-less sustenance of ancient beliefs and practices, especially without the media and authority structures to impose and sustain anything which did not strike the actual participants and audience as useful or entertaining. A strong element of pragmatism was present, and what was patently artificial or dis-agreeably didactic got little response. Where the later medieval Catholic Church was so strong was in its accumulated base of popular practices, beliefs and festivals, and its willingness to introduce or respond to fashion. If any-thing, its weakness was its tolerance, not its intolerance. In so far as it ended up with heretics to persecute – not that it had many in England – it was the dissenters' intolerance which forced the issue, not the Church's.

It is more fruitful to consider what later medieval people did, rather than whether their ancestors had been doing it for thousands of years already. Maybe, as with everything, the burgeoning of written records in our period exaggerates the novelty of some of their interests, as most controversially the abrupt rush of Robin Hood into popular identity in the later fourteenth and fifteenth centuries. All that apart, the Christian year was basically geared very congenially into the resources, interests and climate appropriate to each of the later medieval English seasons, and English people were able to carry out each rite with pleasure and a sense of purpose. It is possible to go through each of the familiar festivals and fun days in detail to illustrate this symbiosis, and several good historical and/or anthropological studies have done so.[7] Much of the explanation is very obvious, but none the less valid for it. In this respect, it is quite likely that pre-Christian society followed a very similar round of fun, fast and festival, with 'excuses' for each phase nominated to something particular to each society, often in the cause of subjugating popular practice to social deference and conformity.

The Medieval Church's year – the social year – combined days of dedication and determination in the good times with days of relaxation and refreshment in the bad times. Some historians have said that the medieval Catholic Church simply sold out to its congregation's lowest values. In fact, medieval people constructed their local Church to protect themselves from themselves. Thus, Christian Christmas in England came to the rescue of the deep midwinter stagnation, to re-establish values: the importance of the family network in medieval society, however unappealing in personality; a legitimised respite in meat and drink from that strict winter diet otherwise enjoined by climate and confirmed as from God by the Church – with particular merit urgently attached to eating the family pig, whose health through the bitterest months of January and February could otherwise only be at the expense of the family's own.

From Christmas to July the Church took the village through its active work-year with a zestful do-it-yourself guide. The thrust of its Sunday services reflected what was on the minds of the congregation, so they were glad to come and confident that everyone they wanted to speak to would be there. On Shrove Tuesday the last little scraps of the best winter reserves were served up with a bit of fun, on Ash Wednesday hangovers and food-poisoning were given the placebo of communal dedication to work. The village slogged through Lent, wrestling its recalcitrant land back into production, larders at home bare or stale or at best boring; the parish church went in sympathy into morose, undemanding mode. With Easter came the great symbiosis of

Christian redemption and social optimism, with the obligatory annual confession of all individuals marking their chance to start the new season of activity in harmony with their community as with their God, because medieval confession to one's parish priest required practical amendment of wrong-doings. The medieval priest's checklist of sins prioritised misdeeds of action, i.e. involving a third party, over misdeeds of thought, and therefore required a righting of the action as the precondition of peace with God.[8]

After Easter came a sequence of cheerful festivals, in which the climate allowed for outdoor activities to be included. Accordingly, the secular side of the lay–religious partnership in such celebrations loomed larger. Hoke Day, when young women waylaid and ransomed 'young' men, was a hugely popular occasion of tolerated role-reversal and misrule, to which the Church attached no official rite but had skilfully customised itself as the beneficiary of the ransoms – and lucrative they were, which an anthropologist might find very indicative in respect of the zeal of the women and the anxious generosity of their male victims. Rogation-tide was the most serious of all to the village, when the priests led the way in procession round the parish limits, ostensibly calling down God's blessing on its acres, in practice metaphorically urinating on the boundaries of its territory to warn off encroachment by predatory neighbours. May Day was the feast to which the Church lent least formal meaning and, given the season, was one where people might think to travel outside their village to more spectacular events, with sports, dance, eating and professional entertainments. Edward IV famously took the chance in 1464 to travel against the local rush-hour and effect a quiet wedding with Elizabeth Woodville at her home in Grafton Regis (Northamptonshire). Corpus Christi was the great new fashion of the later medieval period, and much studied recently.[9] Certainly, after its papal promotion in 1317 it spread through towns across Europe, and its focus upon the humanity of Christ was absolutely in line with the sentiments of the time. None the less, what is principally associated with it are the civic plays, organised collectively by the different guilds and highly indicative both of the pecking order among them and of their collective pre-eminence within the conurbation. There was little spontaneity, but an implied admonition to the plebs to watch, admire and take note of their own passivity and non-participatory status.

The Church went into tick-over during summer and autumn, rather like the royal government, law courts and universities, because the laity were too engrossed in the imperatives of life such as harvesting, trading and fun – squirrelling furiously against the bitter winter hibernation ahead – to require spiritual diversion or legitimisation of hardship. It has been protested that this is to ignore such things as the myriad of specific patronal festivals, where each parish acknowledged the saint(s) to whom its own church was dedicated. This objection is of no great weight: there is little evidence that local patron saints tipped the universal order of the heavenly hierarchy very much in people's minds (apart perhaps from the Celtic fringes), and many of the greatest saints had had the prudence to place their principal moments in life outside high summer anyway. Midsummer's Night was full of bonfires and barbecues, replete with nominal references to the purging of the air, and villages certainly held summer fetes, but the Church never bothered to claim the former and only usurped the latter into the rightly famous English village *church* fete in a much later era, when its more obligatory religious occasions had lost their commercial appeal.

The convention is that there are some five major sources from which the religious mentality of the English people might be culled: records of local church administration, last wills and testaments, churchwardens' accounts, artefacts, and creative, personal, literature. To this last category belongs the literature of complaint and criticism, now often despised because of the 'untypicality' of its provenance – humanist, heretic, troublemaker or professional moaner.[10] The current fashion is to exclude them on grounds of 'Well, they would say that, wouldn't they?' Fairly enough, primers, liturgy and saints' lives are much preferred as massively more numerous in surviving copies; the significance attached to contemporary works of mystic piety and private instruction may prove more cyclical.

Not only because the organisation of religion was – significantly – far from uniform, a true list of sources would stretch out far longer, including many fragmentary survivals which can safely be assumed to have been far from unique in their time and sad witnesses to the sheer volume of what we have lost and the imbalance in what survives. There are, of course, the major archives of monasteries, university colleges, the papal curia and cathedrals, all institutions which were formally distanced from the common person, but wherein explicitly and implicitly the voice of that person can be heard. There are the guild and fraternity records, often from towns and cities, and the records of church courts. There are the mighty records of the royal courts, wherein not infrequently some dispute or incident was located in a context involving religious practice – most simply, for example, a fight or murder on the way in or out of a service, or a family burial confirming some local's memory of a birth twenty-one years before, or a dispute involving some long-term responsibility for local church property, practice and custom. Ecclesiastical tax returns to the crown, especially those long, as yet unconsidered, lists of churches exempted on grounds of poverty in the exchequer memoranda rolls (PRO E159), can help set the social and economic context. Just to mention that context is to affirm, too, that as religion is integrated with society in recent studies, it becomes hard to think of any later medieval source that would not be now considered 'relevant' to a study of sensibilities and practice.

Among those overtly religious sources generated by layfolk themselves, last wills and testaments have for long attracted most attention, although at present the pessimism of methodology has closed in, as always in well-worked fields.[11] Where once the testament was taken to be the one certain insight into a medieval layperson's mind, drawn up in the face of God and a final chance to reflect on and settle one's order of priorities among people, places and things in one's life, a welter of objections has now been entered. The simplest include a consideration that many more men than women left wills, for a married woman could not so do without her husband's assent, and few did. Then, too, the very fact of the religious and personal context of the will – death, purgatory, judgement – encourages suspicion that the will testifies what a good Christian *should* think and do, rather than what each particular Christian actually did. The presence of a priest at the death-bed, in both key pastoral role and as local source of scribal literacy and familiarity with testamentary procedures in law, may explicitly or even unintentionally have coloured the content and sense of the testator's document. It was the duty of a priest then, as of a lawyer now, to do his best by the most grisly of clients, and while no medieval priest could hope to con God with the ease with which his modern counterpart can gull judge, jury and parole board with tales of new-found remorse, community work and religious faith, nevertheless he had an essential duty to do his very best to save his parishioner's soul by his rituals, instructions and other services to him or her throughout life, and especially at the end. God would not want a priest to try to deceive God's own self, but would applaud a priest's every effort to present the best case; and, more importantly, would view with great approbation the priest's effort at the death-bed to comfort both the dying and the kin and community left behind.[12]

The Church had developed since around the twelfth century a concept of purgatory, a zone of fear and yet also of hope.[13] This waiting-room to Heaven, finite in individual time and thus a refinement or even antithesis to the older idea of a final, universal Last Judgement, provided for revision of the record of life. Since one could scarcely hope to perform personal acts of merit within purgatory, the Church naturally provided tariffs of posthumous payments and life-acts which could compensate. These could be arranged in advance by a person in life, or by his or her loved ones and well-wishers after the person's death. In the latter case, as with all rites surrounding death, the psychologist and anthropologist have easy pickings regarding guilt, comfort, gap-closing, vicarious compensation, familial and communal continuity, status affirmation and so forth. In fact, St Augustine of Hippo had identified most of this succinctly and with approval eleven centuries earlier. Medieval layfolk had much the same candid awareness and were simply glad of the opportunity.[14] Operating out of a much more inhibited society, a few medieval historians have designed tricksy subliminal and subconscious dimensions to funeral piety. Medieval people would read such ululations with puzzled brows and a sense that, at best, it was all rather a convoluted statement of the obvious. They might not be far wrong.

The role of death in medieval religion's influence over society has been much emphasised, perhaps because the most visible and striking surviving evidence emphasises it so much. Obviously, too, sentiments were expressed in directly religious terms at the time of death, where religion's influence in life was often more subtle and socially implicit. None the less, it is impossible not to lay stress upon the key part religious forms and sensibilities played for the dying and the bereaved. There was, of course, the testament to be finalised, with the Church underwriting the individual's obligation to do right by those to whom he or she was in debt, both literally and in terms of obligation to family, servants and community. It is to be emphasised that there was no line drawn here between settlements and bequests to laity and to church. Although, anecdotally, much is made of the occasional requests for a multiplicity of masses and more commonly for other forms of direct memorial and intercession, the Church had come into line with social opinion to lend religious sanction to the belief that a testator's first thoughts should be for his or her own kin. Indeed, it has been recorded in various circumstances that those who founded the most significant chantries, hospitals and collegiate churches were most often those who had no immediate family to consider, for example Richard Whittington in London, Sir Geoffrey Massey in Eccles, Sir John Fastolf in Caistor, and childless Bristol merchants generally. Current research into religion in southern townships suggests that the leading witnesses to testaments were often those leading inhabitants who filled the roles of churchwarden, bailiff and constable and ran the town.[15] Much has been written about the influence of the priest at the death-bed in the making of wills; more should be written about the influence of such lay governors in settling the dying one's affairs with the community.

The Church had developed a strong concept of individual purgatory since the twelfth century, often portrayed – especially by French historians – as a deliberate extension of ecclesiastical control over the laity at their most vulnerable hour, with a particular view to marketing a range of church services and institutions to the testator and the bereaved, by which the horrors of purgatory could be ameliorated and shortened by paid-for acts of intercession and piety. As has been pointed out, the concept had to offer comfort as well as terror, and it did; there was an attainable afterlife of bliss, and not one requiring a wait until the end of time and the awfulness of God's arbitrary judgement. Good works in life could be supplemented or made up by good works after death, and the bereaved could join in as cathartic release.

Were it indeed the case that the Church had here dreamed up and marketed the most lucrative cosmetic industry of all time out of pure cynicism, it would still have to be acknowledged that it had met a genuine psychological and social need across the whole range of society, and that the comfort and consolation it provided were fair value for the price, as compared to many other proffered commodities, then as now. There is really no doubt that the market was already there, and that the Church only responded to demand. Although the old saw, indeed a true one, is that it was required that a third of an estate should be 'the soul's part', this third did not disappear gross into the Church's own coffers in cash. It is, indeed, difficult to think of any will, even a clerical one, where a really major part of the estate was bequeathed directly to the Church, the vanities of mausoleum-building apart. The Church pointed to the poor in particular, to schools and colleges, almshouses, maidens without dowries and even prisoners as legitimate recipients of piety.[16] The fabric of the local church usually only came to the fore as a legatee when something specific was under construction or repair. The Lollards were quite appalled in the post-Black Death era, when labour was short and employment available to all, that the Church should have lured benefactors into such massive over-provision of ease for the work-shy.[17]

The dying persons required consolation: literally that they had made their peace with their neighbours, symbolically (through the 'housel', the final unction) that they were at peace with God, personally that they had provided for their dependants in family and/or in service as well as they could, socially that they and their family would not be shamed by a poor show during their rites of passage, eschatologically that they had their best chance of eternal life. The rites of funeral must then encompass all these, with the actual process of interment not even necessarily the key moment, still less the sole one, in the pageant. By giving the very poor the easiest chance of salvation and the very rich the hardest, the Church provided for symbiosis between social standing and funeral ritual. Thus the corpse of John of Gaunt must needs be borne in ceremony down the whole backbone of England in 1399, and the houses of York and of Neville bear their slain of Wakefield (1460) to the family vaults in the south of England once the dynastic tide of the civil war had gone in their favour. Lady Margaret Beaufort collected the far-flung bones of her ancestors to Wimborne Minster, requiring local churchwardens to dip into their boxes to pay respectfully for overnight candles wherever the bones rested *en route*.[18] The Capetian kings of France taught their Plantagenet

The very costly funeral of Richard II's first wife, Anne of Bohemia, in Westminster Abbey on 3 August 1394 reflected her husband's personal grief, as too the use of a death-mask for her effigy, which was highly unusual for women in England. The funeral and tomb effigies of men were now tending to warts-and-all realism, but they still preferred an all-purpose stereotypical beauty for their womenfolk. The archbishop of Canterbury declared at the funeral that 'it was more joie of hir than of any whoman that evere he knewe'. The earl of Arundel arrived late and tried to leave early; the king assaulted him on the spot and had him arrested.

country cousins how a royal burial was an emphatic reassertion of charisma and authority, especially when a lifelike wax effigy of the deceased in his pomp was used as substitute for the deteriorating corpse below. As caution against too much cynicism, the surviving death-mask of Richard II's first queen, Anne of Bohemia, does her no favours but, as intended, bears witness to the king's own grief (see the illustration above). Defying the conventions, he displayed to the world that he was burying the woman he loved, not some bland stereotype of idealised queenship.[19]

Funerals were statements. At the highest level, they stated the importance and goals of the deceased, with armour, heraldry and didactically composed processions of kin, retainers, priests and poor folk. They implied that the deceased's heirs inherited the importance but would also take up the goals. Tombs with their effigies then fixed these values for posterity, with the deceased in full regalia, the men usually in armour, however limited their actual military activity in life, and looking piously comfortable about their prospects. The men did increasingly take on some semblance of individuality and true age in face and physique, although always such as might favour them. By contrast, their wives, by now commonly at their side, retained an unmatronly and unspecific beauty. Those widows who had charge of the tomb-building seem to have been disinclined to claim equality through ugliness by breaking this convention. A few couples took to holding hands into eternity, such as Sir John and Lady Botiller at Warrington (see the illustration on p. 114). Presumably she had not been holding his hand when he was lynched in 1463. A few others – high churchmen especially, like Henry Chichele at

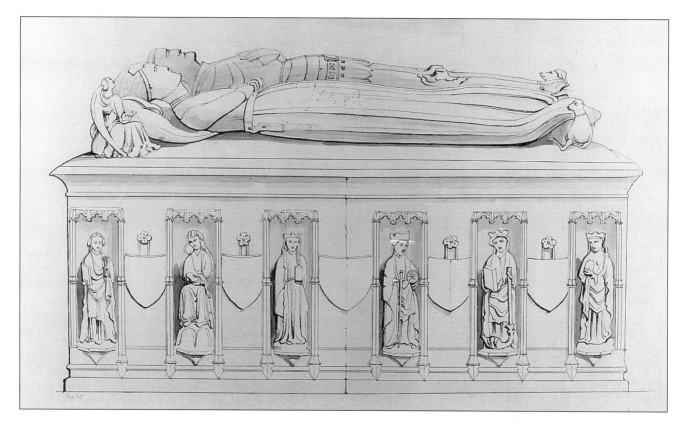

Sir John Botiller (1429–62) became fatherless at 2, was married at 15, knighted at 17, an MP at 20, widowed (see the ring on his middle finger) and remarried by 25, divorced at 29, and married for a third time (to a widow) before his own early death, to which an (unfortunately mythical) violent legend attaches. His first or third wife (both were called Margaret) holds his hand into eternity on their tomb in St Elphin's, Warrington (Cheshire). If the latter, she had also been represented holding her first husband's hand on their tomb too. Whether she held her third husband's as well is not known. Male saints line Sir John's side of the tomb, female saints Dame Margaret's. God the Father has been defaced in the depiction of the Trinity on Sir John's side, either by some sectarian objecting to a physical depiction or by a non-ideological vandal.

Canterbury or Thomas Bekynton at Wells – opted for the double-decker tomb, with emaciated skeleton below, but no less confidence and regalia above (see the illustration opposite). These might even exclaim something in their wills, like Cardinal Beaufort's famous cry, 'I would tremble, did I not know Thy mercies!', but they did know them and so did not tremble much.[20] At gentry level, the funeral affirmed the family's claimed place. The famous 'over the top' funeral of John Paston I declared the arrival of a *nouveau* and controversial family in the first rank of Norfolk society; for once, it seems likely that the Pastons were not untypical.[21] What curiosity exists in their case is in their failure then to provide their patriarch with a commensurately fine tomb. It is a rare will indeed where the testator does not provide for a funeral in keeping with his or her standing, even in those few cases where a caution is entered that the event should be kept within reasonable bounds. It is as though the dying person was not afraid of death but was afraid of making a poor one.

The funeral required visible signs of status, ensconced in piety. The poor, especially the local poor – the testator's poor – provided valuable evidence and intercession by their very presence and receipt of clothing, food and cash in charity. The Church taught that this was so, and, since the poor were an ever-present local problem, bystanders were glad to believe it. The funeral called for a roll-call of kin, an assembly of all those with any blood connection with the deceased and his or her estate, and it did no harm to remind the neighbours of the breadth of the family's network and resources. Finally, the community itself was encouraged to pay heed and to identify itself, sincerely or not, with the bereaved family hereafter. All in all, the immediate family had

The *memento mori* or *transi* tomb is best known in England through the great tombs of Archbishop Henry Chichele at Canterbury and of Bishop Thomas Bekynton at Wells, but is also found, especially in the south Midlands, among middle-ranking gentry of the mid-fifteenth century and often with some connections with royal government or each other. The corruption of the body beneath is contrasted with the dignity in life above. While some have argued that the deceased is showing his awareness that public achievement is ephemeral and worthless as against the ultimate corruptibility of all human flesh, others have argued that status and achievement are actually claimed here as permanent and divorced from that fleshly decay. William Sponne (d. 1447/48) was archdeacon of Norfolk from 1419 and the leading legal administrator for the bishops of Norwich of his time. He lies in St Laurence's, Towcester, of which he was the often-absent but always-mindful rector from 1422.

to thank their kin, friends and the community for their attendance and recognition with a good meal, and a good meal was what they themselves wanted, too, after the elaborate public ritual of burying their patriarch. It was an invaluable opportunity for legitimate reappraisal of relationships, over and above the everyday mugging-along in the fields or random, infrequent long-distance encounters, set in a context calling for perspective and integrity. The 'wake' was well established by the later medieval centuries: refreshment, release, reappraisal, re-encounter. Thus, children's funerals were small and private, within the horizons of their own nuclear familial worlds; patriarchal funerals were large and public. Examples illustrate the rule: when little Ann Mowbray died and threw the dynastic stategy of the House of York into disarray, she was given a major funeral and a tomb in the royal abbey of Westminster as a claim to her inheritance on behalf of her child-fiancé, Prince Richard. Richard III and his queen, Anne Neville, went into private despair over the death of their only child, Edward (if not for the same reasons), but in 1484 any public advertisement of the usurper's lack of a direct heir was so impolitic that we are still not sure where the boy is buried; evidently it was in no royal place. The Pastons and Stonors, more fecund, accepted natural culling of their broods as a fact of life, and mixed various degrees of personal sadness with a common denominator of undemonstrative funeral. It was society, not the Church, which set the requirements for funeral display and the price of salvation.

Posthumous memorial was synonymous with posthumous intercession. Nothing was donated or built without an expectation of reciprocal response from the subsequent beneficiary, user or mere observer. Nothing was idle

The fabric of St Mary's, Thame (Oxfordshire) was maintained by three different parties: the chancel by the absentee rector, a prebendary of Lincoln cathedral; the north side of the nave by New Thame; the south side by Old Thame – the two settlements are still clearly distinct in the town. In 1442–44 the north transept was built at a cost of £28 15s 3d to the New Thame parishioners, of whom well over 100 subscribed. Their Old Thame counterparts duly maintained symmetry with a south transept of the same date. The tithe barn, almshouses and old school on the south side of the church complete an evocative grouping, but are mainly sixteenth-century.

show. It is true that great tombs, hospitals and churches were designed to remind posterity of their founders, but not as mere vicarious eternal being through fame; rather, in the hope of real eternal life, attained by the intercessions of those coming on behind. There is considerable debate whether families did seek to build up displays of lineage through tombs, or whether it was each generation for itself.[22] Old-established Kent gentry do indeed seem to have been content to rest on their ancestry, without flamboyant addition, leaving it to the new families to spend assets on establishing comparable urtombs and chantry chapels of great size.[23] One point to bear in mind is that most families failed to sustain a direct male line anyway beyond three or four generations. Fairly rarely, it would seem, did the beneficial son-in-law want to identify with his wife's ancestors, especially because wealth married wealth in later medieval England, so he usually had his own family church as his spiritual home. In Thame church in Oxfordshire (see the illustrations below and opposite) Richard Fowler chose burial, as godson and designated heir, in the tomb of Richard Quartermain, the last and considerable of a fine name, and his wife. He was admittedly heir to Richard's wife, by blood, and left no sharp lineage of his own, but such a collation none the less remains very rare.[24]

The landed gentry did not depart from their parish churches either in life or in death. The idea, more clever than persuasive, that they 'privatised' their

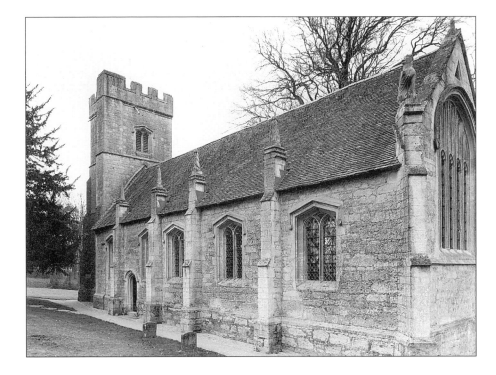

In 1449 Richard Quartermain (1392–1477) and his wife, Sybil Englefield (1400–83) established a chantry at Rycote (Oxfordshire) on her property and their main home for three priests to pray for their good estate and, after death, their souls in perpetuity. The chapel, with its superb fifteenth- and seventeenth-century furnishings, remains in fine order. By 1449 the couple would know they were to be childless, if not how unusually long a life still remained to them, but they did not turn to pious large-scale benefaction as some simple substitute path to perpetual memory as their family line ended, being actually close and affectionate with their collateral heirs on both sides. It has been argued that the gentry were 'privatising' their own religion, withdrawing from the community of the parish church, at the end of the Middle Ages, both mentally and through household chapels. Rycote was certainly not meant as a rival to the mother-church at Thame, where Richard and Sybil Quartermain founded a chantry with alms for six poor men and located their own fine tomb.

religion, retreating to their household chapels, takes no account of their need to affirm by ritual their proactive headship of their manorial estates and tenants through placement at church services and by tombs after death.[25] The later medieval gentry shifted old tombs to the rear of the church and took up their places in the chancel. In a time of complex debate, they never really sorted out the relationship between status and received pious norms. Hence, mainly in the fourteenth century, they were buried in tombs four-square and central, blocking out the view of the altar to the congregation. The trend thereafter was to take up the closest positions south, or, if needs must, north of the altar and leave a clear view. The very greatest often built an entire chapel on to a church or annexed some part of it, an incentive, as it often turned out, for their heirs to develop a mausoleum in time on the spot.

Brasses were an immediately attractive development, especially once literacy developed as an alternative to visual message; cheaper financially, physically easier to accommodate, and convenient to integrate into the overall discourse – overall discourse is the hallmark of the late medieval Perpendicular English church. Brasses reflected the wider spectrum of ambitious society in post-Black Death England. Few rich and great landowners settled for a brass, but it allowed the burgeoning strata below to leave their personal mark within the most elite parts of a church. Crudely, size still came into it as an eternal measure of esteem: while knights and their ladies had life-size brasses, merchants (save the greatest fat cats in East Anglia and the Cotswolds) and yeomen generally settled for half-size or less. And last, and significantly, a few parish priests achieved belated recognition, if mainly through dinky miniatures. To single out the unusual is not always helpful, but Roger Cheyne esquire of Cassington in Oxfordshire (d. 1398) is worth considering. He was never denounced as a heretic, even though all around him his collateral kin and heirs were regarded as Lollards up to their necks. His brass

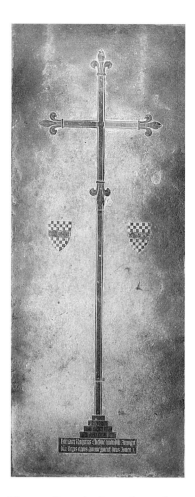

The non-figurative brass chosen for or by Roger Cheyne (d. 1398) in St Peter's, Cassington (Oxfordshire) reminds us that not every *nouveau* and not every childless man of means sought perpetual fame through a striking tomb, as some current fashion contends. Roger, perhaps a bachelor, noted simply that he was 'sometime an esquire of the lord king', an ample account of his life and fortune. Note, however, that the Lollard-supporting Cheynes of Drayton Beauchamp (Buckinghamshire) were the heirs of both Roger and, ultimately, of the infamously unorthodox Sir John Cheyne of Beckford (Gloucestershire). Perhaps Roger quietly shared the family's liking for self-effacement.

(see the illustration at left) is placed centrally at the head of the nave in the small Norman/Early English parish church of which he became lord – a long cross, not a portrait – and designates him simply as 'formerly an esquire of the king'. Over such a simple artefact historical debate is conducted. Does the brass, in context, prove that Roger declared himself in death as being in sympathy with his heretical kin, with their Erastian commitment to the state and avowed contempt for personality, their faith in Christ alone as Redeemer, and yet their inbuilt satisfaction that they themselves had achieved a success in life and empathy with their environment that should be recognised?

It is possible that we look too hard to find individual sensibility in later medieval religion and ignore the pressures and the inclination to conform. This is a natural recent reaction to the time-hallowed belief that a cruelly inhuman late medieval Catholic Church imposed strict uniformity of practice and a prohibition on individual thought and sentiment. Thus, one much-discussed recent study of the imagery and deployment of the Eucharist has suggested modishly that, whatever may be handed down or intended by authority, it is the recipient who sees and interprets for him- or herself.[26] The Eucharist may be deployed for community solidarity, for personal salvation, for status-display, for healing, for discipline, for factional demonstration and much else. The adjacent imagery of the Body of Christ had many expressions, and has very recently been examined in the context of the Peasants' Revolt of 1381.[27] More generally, Eamon Duffy's overview of lay usage of religious rites, ceremonies, artefacts and literature proposed an immensely rich range of individual choice, yet retaining an essential unity within the diversity and commitment to the church building as the fulcrum.[28] Almost inevitably, ecclesiastical historians are now following the political and social historians, coming from such a late start. Between the crude extremes of uniformity and individualism, attention is now on the formative agencies around the individual, with attention to the influence of the family – traced, for example, through similarities in content in the wills of one generation and the next, a methodology in need of considerable further sophistication and sometimes in danger of stating the obvious; it may work better among comfortably orthodox families than among those with a critical mind, still less those with a discreet or committed sympathy for Lollard ideas. The late, great K. B. McFarlane pointed out forty years ago that the group of friends among Richard II's household knights who were keenly interested in John Wyclif's ideas produced wills that were highly idiosyncratic and yet closely akin to each other's: each individual, as it were, stating a preference to reflect the rest.[29] Archbishop Thomas Arundel's famous self-deprecatory introduction to his will follows that of his father forty years earlier. By contrast, three mighty northern prelates, Walter Skirlaw (d. 1406), Thomas Langley of Durham (d. 1437) and Henry Bowet of York (d. 1424) shared the same powerful, lengthy and distinctive introduction to their wills. One can only suggest that Bowet and Langley were mightily moved as they pored over the detail of the late bishop's will for administrative purposes and, together or by serendipity, chose it for their own valedictions.[30] The Grover brothers, prosperous yeomen of early sixteenth-century Chesham, provided long, near-identical wills with idiosyncratic provision for their wives.[31] The younger finalised his will four days after executing that of his brother, perhaps moved by bereavement to arrange his own affairs and perhaps too influenced by the circumstances; but whereas his brother had asked for burial with their parents *inside* the church, next to the south porch, the younger asked for burial by the nave wall adjacent to the porch *outside*. Did he thereby reconcile an exquisite mental struggle between family solidarity and perceived personal standing?

Apart from family, there was godfamily, something which was taken seriously in later medieval England, perhaps partly because godparents were chosen carefully as those likely and capable to advance the general well-being of an infant through life, far from providing mere spiritual and moral support. With luck, one's lord or superior might be persuaded to stand; John Hopton of Suffolk's second wife generated lots of little Christines around their household, the Staffords lots of little Humphries. There is some anecdotal evidence of a father's best friend actually refusing to act as godparent because he hoped to marry his baby to his friend's baby at the earliest legal moment, and wanted to avoid canonical niceties about kinship. The 'gossip', i.e. godsibling, has entered the language as that person or conversation in whom the most trivial, intimate and malicious reflections on the community may be invested.

Apart from the dysfunctionalist historian, who is not sure, there is confidence too that each individual listened to the parish priest and – from a mixture of respect and prudence – was generally ready to agree to the religious agenda he proposed, especially since, in most cases, the priest would conform to the existing customs of the parish.[32] Rather to the irritation of critical historians, most parishes, when asked, said they found no fault in their priest. There is the usual trickle of parish animosities: a few priests living in sin, a few lazy about services, a few often absent, a few not repairing their part of the church, a few who were quarrelsome, one who did not take off his cassock before turning out in village soccer matches.[33] The historian's problem is whether some of these charges are malicious, the product of private feud between incumbent and leading villager (i.e. churchwarden); whether (a greater problem) many more parishes simply did not care; or (greatest of all) whether most priests and parishes had worked out a kind of *Sun* culture, far removed from the standards laid down by the good and the great but extremely comfortable to themselves. There is, for example, the question of sermons. In big towns there was evidently an audience, perhaps an eclectic one rather than a majority, and some debate about their provision and quality. In rural areas it remains an open question whether regular sermons were wanted; or, perhaps more likely, an occasional visiting preacher was a welcome treat because he was occasional. There must be a suspicion that historians are listening here to the demanding, untypical few and to their own congenital propensity to hold forth, rather than to the medieval majority.

The truth is that villagers seem to have asked three things of their priest: first, that he conduct all the required services, and in basically seemly fashion, so that their village was in conformity and good standing with the wider identities of diocese, state and Christendom; second, that he himself live a reasonably good life and thus set a good example – probably as celibate, but his personal arrangements would be set against his performance as a neighbour; third, that he provide social comfort within the parish – support for the dying and distressed, advice (and even literacy) in village administration, arbitration and reconciliation in village rows. The parish could do without their incumbent having several degrees in law or theology;

St Christopher was popular all over Europe, especially from the thirteenth to fifteenth centuries, both as an example of 'salvation through service' and as reflective of the increased amount of both secular and pious travel. Besides numerous woodcuts and other portable representations, the saint appears in wall-paintings in many highway churches, usually very large and opposite the main door, so that travellers would see him and stop to seek his customary protection from sickness and death for one day, no doubt making a small offering to the church in exchange. In St John the Baptist's, Little Missenden (Buckinghamshire), the saint has yet to realise the value of facing the door and of showing some actual progress in his carriage of Christ; this he did as the later Middle Ages wore on.

indeed, they would probably prefer it. Their priest was their symbol of upstanding and one of their most important local arbitrators and social workers; he was not, in practice, the representative of the class-overlord, however much the manuals of instruction urged him to oversee a social status quo. If he were the incumbent, his freehold tenure made him immovable, even if he upset the lord by abetting the peasants in some dispute.

Apart from family and priest, there were the elders of the manor, village or township. These, as recent research has shown, took on the principal offices of the church quite as much as they did those of the secular self-government of the community, perhaps in part for status or as a responsibility of rank, but also as part of their control of the lesser fry of the community, evidenced more starkly in their membership of juries sitting in judgment on local crime, administrative roles in the manor courts, and electoral enfranchisement in 1430.[34] More immediately, it is now being revealed that these greybeards were very frequent among the lead-witnesses to death-bed wills, influencing and integrating the social, religious and communal desiderata of the dying. The lord may have played a lesser part, particularly since so few English manors had a resident squire. Where a landlord indeed has his *caput honoris*, it is very likely that the economic and social structure of the estate was far removed from that of the traditional village, and power and religious organisation likewise. Most castles and major manor-houses included a chapel or even church in their perimeter, wherein the household could be educated daily into their social and religious unity. It seems that most lords wanted to include, not exclude, their servants in their own acts of worship.[35]

There has been recent talk of the 'interiorisation of religion', especially among the landed classes. This, simply put, means that they were finding religion more, not less, important in later medieval England. It argues that inwardly they wanted to work out their own faith, as an aspect of individual existence; while outwardly they needed to provide enhanced symbols and structures which would both satisfy their servants and retainers and bond them in loyalty through rituals of social identity with their lord. All this is very subtle. However, it cannot overlook the fact that, in the end, lords and gentry led the way in building and rebuilding the churches of the land, beautifying them not in idle ways but with references to the most striking and central of religious imageries – as to which, incidentally, they seemed to have agreed with the leaders of independent communal village projects and the humblest of individual designs and bequests – and finally being buried in them. The friars of London piled high in their churches the corpses of the upwardly mobile whose ambitious lives had drawn them in hope to London and Westminster, the centres of economic and government power.[36] Far more, from the real establishment – the great magnates, the civil servants,

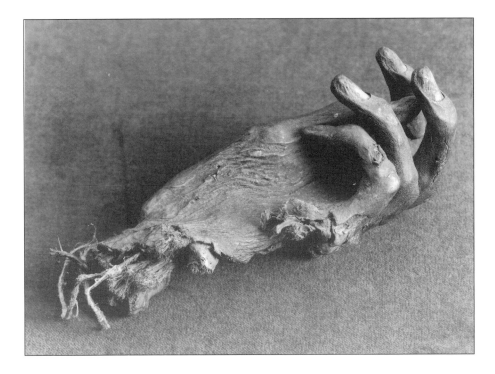

The hand of St James the Apostle was reliably said to be in Torcello cathedral by 640 AD at the latest; it then passed via Archbishop Adelbert of Hamburg-Bremen to Emperor Henry IV in 1072. His widowed daughter-in-law, Matilda, brought it to England and used it to enhance Reading Abbey (Berkshire), the foundation and burial site of her father, King Henry I. Both sides competed for the hand during Matilda's own long contest for the throne with King Stephen, but in 1155 it was re-established at Reading Abbey where, as part of the affirmation of the Angevins' right to the throne, St James's festival was built up with numerous indulgences for pilgrims on 25 July, a fair that day and an early burst of (rather uninspiring) miracles. Becket's shrine at Canterbury and the fame of substantially more of St James's mortal remains at Compostella soon overshadowed Reading, but the hand remained an object of veneration; by dipping it (in a container) in water, its curative powers were made available by post. It is now in St Peter's, Marlow (Buckinghamshire).

'Saint' John Schorne (d. by February 1315) had no contemporary fame but soon enjoyed a minor cult around his grave and the well he had found in a time of drought in his parish of North Marston (Buckinghamshire). In the fifteenth century he soared in popularity and is found depicted in many of the new 'wool churches' from East Anglia to the south-west, always with the Devil, whom he had trapped in his boot. The canons of St George's, Windsor secured North Marston church and moved the saint to their own chapel to fund its lavish building. Schorne continued to be a very successful fund-raiser among pilgrims to both sites until the Reformation, a genuinely 'popular' rather than ideologically-created saint, whose cult was peaceful, not sensationalist.

the lawyers – preferred a country burial in the place where they had their birth or their estate.

Outside of religious sensibility practised through the group structures of life, lie the most famous interconnected religious options of them all: pilgrimages, shrines and relics.[37] To critics then and now they epitomise the Church's hypocrisy and the laity's deception and credulity. This is neither the time nor place to rehearse the familiar story of Jerusalem, Rome, Compostella, Canterbury, Walsingham and Windsor, and their undoubtedly aggressive marketing by their keepers through a well-oiled tourist industry. These were, of course, only the brightest stars amid constellations of lesser holy places, while main-road parish churches, with their St Christopher wall-paintings and statues (see the illustration on p. 120), set out their stalls to the passing trade. Chaucer gave his pilgrims a jaunty air, which Margery Kempe confirmed with her complaint about her treatment by her companions when she tried to keep them serious all along the way. The Lollard William Thorpe and Thomas Arundel, archbishop of Canterbury, differed sharply about the propriety of fun on a long, tiring journey, but the primate's insistence that the frailties of pious laity needed to be accommodated has at least the virtue of charity.[38] To a modern eye, the accretion of miracles around the more successful shrines seems dubious, and there were critics at the time, too, but miracles were and are often in the eye of the beholder, and none the worse for that, where, as in the vast majority of cases, they brought comfort in distress and no harm to anyone else. In so precarious and perilous a world, optimism and hope were as efficacious remedies as any. The worship of actual statues or relics (see the illustration on p. 121), perhaps in hope of magic, was indeed an ever-present danger, but in general people seem to have known the line. To have a favourite relic or statue, and to honour and cherish it, as indeed to have a favourite saint – perhaps one identified with one's trade or guild – is, short of obsession, as harmless and indeed congenial as having a favourite sentimental possession, football team or pop group, providing comfort, identity, vicarious excitement and inspiration – albeit misplaced, no doubt, in many cases. It might be noted that the most popular 'rising saints' in late medieval England – Henry VI, John Schorne (see the illustration above), John of Bridlington and Edmund Lacy of Exeter – all had a gentle humanity to their profile and, although approached for cures and physical relief, were almost untouched by the dubious, even hysterical, expectations attached to earlier cults. Finally, in the last medieval centuries, it does seem that people were closing in upon Christ himself as their aid, with even the Blessed Virgin well behind, and no one else remotely in the frame. To travel and see the holiest of sites remained none the less an inspiration for many, a refreshment of faith and life by experiencing a wider horizon. Shrines and pilgrimages were not oppressive or obsessive to later medieval folk.

Nowadays, confident generalisation about religious sensibility is difficult, because so much fine scholarship is pouring in upon the riches of surviving material. Here, for example, only passing attention has been paid to the buildings and their ornaments (see the illustration on p. 125): the placing of the altar, the transparency or otherwise of the rood screen as the veil or window between the worldly and the sacred, the relationship of gender as between saint and sinner (if only because, as yet, it has proved an elusive and overly subjective debate), the different pieties of each gender (for the same

Previous page The Crucifixion and other scenes from the life of Christ. '"Consummatum est" . . . The lord of lif and of light tho leide hise eighen togidres.' As the pivotal event in human history, the Crucifixion was the most intense focus of artistic and literary representation in medieval culture. In devotional tradition, readers were intended to imagine themselves physically present at these biblical events, looking on with the same horror and compassion as the grief-stricken family (bottom left), while at the same time commemorating the divinely loving purpose of the Passion.

Dreamer and Pearl-Maiden separated by a stream marking the life–death, earth–heaven divide. This rather unskilled picture, possibly copied from a more impressive volume, is taken from the sole manuscript in which *Pearl* and *Sir Gawain and the Green Knight* are to be found. The highly medievalised Celestial Jerusalem, where the maiden lives as a saved soul and Bride of Christ, is out of bounds to the dreamer while he remains on this earth. The dreamer's touching but wrong-headed desire to join his dead daughter indicates, however, a movement of his soul towards heavenly things.

reasons), the guilds, or the place in society of the Lollards.[39] This chapter passes over the contribution of the universities, the religious orders, the fashionable preachers in London and the humanist golden circles; not because I personally doubt their contribution to religious sensibility, but because currently their hallowed roles have come to seem much more marginal. None the less, although these sacred cows are in trouble, they are probably victims of fashion; they will return. They need to find scholars who will bring them back. Nothing has been said here of the manipulation of religious sensibilities in the legitimising of kingship, dynastic change, war (both external and internal) and rebellion in later medieval England. There is a major topic to be explored here, but, if only as a hostage to fortune, one might suggest that it is easier to exaggerate than underestimate it.[40]

Currently it is the view that the later medieval Church in England was vigorous and in rapport with all its lay flock. This was because, amid the considerable social changes of the time, the protagonists – the people of England – could draw what each wanted from the Church's common fund to demonstrate that this was evolution, not revolution. Vigour, not apathy, engenders keen debate and criticism. Thus runs the explanation of the undoubted range of comment and complaint about aspects of contemporary religious practice and provision. Politically, the papacy stood fairly distant; in personal matters, it was kind.[41] Thus, if we accept the current orthodoxy, the English people were more than happy to referee themselves in their use of the Church as a ring for their moral and social sparring. The Church's own Queensberry rules remained adequate and flexible to cater for most people's participation in the sport. Obviously, the Lollards and a few other malcontents from the university and the gutter illustrate that not every contestant was content, but losers always sulk. Much depends on what we make of what came next. From one viewpoint the sixteenth and seventeenth centuries showed up these old rules as totally inadequate when faced with a brutal attempted take-over of the game by rival Mafia *outside* the ring, perhaps in alliance with old malcontents within. On the other hand, most English people – from lords and gentry to townsfolk to peasant family –

Misericords – the undersides of choir-stalls – allowed woodcarvers and their clients to delight themselves and us all over England with their moral, allegorical, historical, mythical and bawdy scenes. Women are usually depicted unflatteringly, save when nursing babies, getting on with some work or (a back-handed compliment?) confessing. In the fifteen surviving domestic brawl scenes, the woman is always attacking the man – perhaps (but maybe only by modern wishful thinking) in conscious role-reversal mode? Male–female tenderness is almost non-existent. Frequently women are seen as gossipers and scandal-mongers, often while they sit spinning, when the Devil can draw up a chair and help them spread the discord. Eve, as the ur-model of women's fatal weaknesses and underminer of mankind, was ever-present in medieval religious words and illustrations. Here, in Ely Cathedral (1340/41), she and Adam flank the serpent entwined in the Tree of Knowledge.

seem to have carried on as they always had: balancing what was best for public harmony with one's self with what was best for private harmony within oneself. Reformation history used to dictate what the late medieval Church was about. Now, late medieval church history tends to dictate the nature of the Reformation.

LANGUAGE AND LITERARY EXPRESSION

Ian Johnson

Until the Battle of Hastings, English enjoyed a substantial role as a written language, with laws, sermons, chronicles, history, secular and religious poetry and prose all being represented in a long, inventive and sophisticatedly voluminous tradition of vernacular writing.[1] As Wessex was the dominant kingdom, a 'classical' West Saxon written standard evolved and even continued to be used for a while after the Norman Conquest, as scanty surviving examples indicate. But with the disempowerment of the native aristocracy and the Normanising of the Church, the language of polite literature overwhelmingly became Anglo-Norman, which differed somewhat from continental French and was the medium of impressive achievements in romance, saints' lives, religious and historical works. From this tradition English substantially gained the practice of rhyming verse. Latin, however, was the sovereign language of learning and authority, also producing considerable imaginative literature throughout the period. Inasmuch as most Middle English literature is translation of one kind or another, the influence of Latin and French language and culture should not be underrated. John Gower, the late fourteenth-century poet, excelled in all three tongues. Linguistic boundaries were being crossed all the time as a matter of routine, so it would be misleading to regard the different languages of England as constituting cultures cut off from each other.

One might be forgiven for thinking, on first glance at its extraordinary variety, that the English language veers off in a number of novel and arbitrary directions after the Norman Conquest.[2] In fact, with the recession of the culture which previously enforced the West Saxon literary standard, dialectal variation, previously masked by West-Saxonisation, becomes visible on a grand scale as texts/scribes spell more as they speak. What is also uncovered is a considerable simplification of grammar, already under way pre-1066, but

Dialect Map of Middle English. Recognisably different dialects tended to merge into each other at borders which were indistinct or even mobile; for during this period London was shifted from the southern to the east Midland area. Surviving written texts, our main evidence for medieval dialects, often reflect intriguing mixes from the different areas and time-periods in which they were recopied. A text composed by a northerner (using earlier west Midland sources) might, for example, get copied and modernised in London for East Anglian patrons by a Westcountryman. This map overlooks the pervasiveness and changing fortunes of French, and the vast cultural authority of Latin.

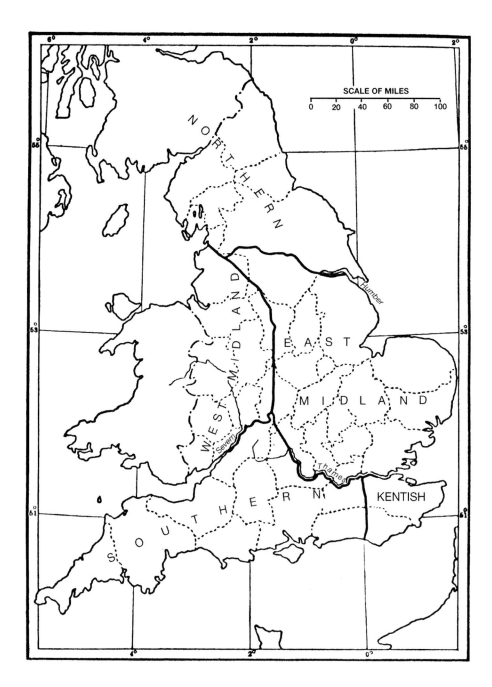

again rather concealed by ossified scribal practice. Old English had a plethora of different grammatical word-endings. Many of these (*-a, -e, -u, -an, -um*), indicating such features as case, gender and number, which exercise today's students, get levelled helpfully to *-e*, and end up in some instances being optional or dropped altogether. This levelling of inflexions characterises the transition from 'Old' to 'Middle' English.

'Ther is so gret diversite / In Englissh, and writynge of oure tonge', as Chaucer put it in *Troilus and Criseyde* V. 1,793–4. Roughly speaking, there were five main dialect areas (see the map above): northern (extending into

Scotland), west Midland, east Midland, southern and Kentish (which takes in eastern Sussex). One does not have to be a linguist to get a very quick impression (even from the few extracts quoted in this chapter) of what looks more northern (like the works of the *Gawain*-poet) and what looks like the east Midland/London language of so many other surviving texts (like Chaucer's). The capital, intriguingly, 'moves' in this period from the southern to the east Midland dialect area, owing to substantial immigration and important business links with that region. This English, being henceforth that of the politically, economically and culturally predominant capital, and comprehensible to southerners and northerners (who might otherwise find understanding each other awkward), became Standard English; and with the advent of printing in the last quarter of the fifteenth century, this standard hardened all the more.

The dialect map illustrated on p. 128 ignores the distribution and usage of Latin and French. When, where and how who used which languages in which proportions, to whom and for what purposes, was a matter of varying social practices and individual circumstances. From the end of the twelfth century the upper classes were using English even though they may have been speaking French to each other. Their dealings with the lower classes, intermarriage with Anglophones and loosening of ties with France, which was now becoming a familiar enemy, all contributed to this. From the mid-thirteenth century, French words (frequently carrying social cachet), mainly concerning law, government, Church, fashion, food, customs and things military and aristocratic, cascaded into English, as those who previously spoke French brought their vocabulary along with them. By 1300 upper-class children were apparently learning French as a foreign language, and by the end of the fourteenth century it was something of an accomplishment. During most of this time the English-speaking middle class were carrying the prestige of English up with them. In 1362 Parliament was opened in English, and the native tongue became the official language of the law courts, as French was so poorly understood. English was common as the language of school education by mid-century, and after 1400 French was a matter of ever more general ignorance. Towards the end of the fourteenth century and in the early years of the fifteenth century English was being used by Chaucer, Gower, Hoccleve, Lydgate and others for polite literature aimed at audiences no lower than the court or even royalty itself, as for instance with Lydgate's monumental *Troy Book*, dedicated to Prince Henry (later Henry V). Meanwhile, Anglo-French was fast losing its place among the upper classes; Chaucer felt able to raise a laugh at the parochially embarrassing use of it by his Prioress, and it seems that Gower, perhaps acknowledging the same trend, continentally Frenchified his Anglo-Norman *Mirour de l'Omme*.[3]

To return, however, to the period of the ascendancy of Anglo-Norman letters, what became of English literary tradition during those unpropitious years? There appears to have been a continuity in religious prose, and Old English heroic alliterative verse tradition did survive, albeit very loosened, most notably in the *Brut* of Laȝamon, a Worcestershire priest who adapted the couplet chronicle of Jerseyman Robert Wace, itself derived from the *History of the Kings of Britain* of Geoffrey of Monmouth. Laȝamon, using archaising diction and a verse-form reminiscent of pre-Conquest poetry, tells, in his national epic, of the nobility of the English ('of Engle þa æþelæn tellen' (line

7)), and brings King Arthur into English literature for the first time.[4] Telling of Britain and its kings from the foundation-myth of the Trojan Brutus through to Cadwallader, the last British king, and the advent of the Anglo-Saxons, the *Brut* charts cycles of dynasties, their noble and brutal heroes, their traitors and cowards, in a history unsoftened by the chivalry, courtesy or love-interest of the Norman overculture. La3amon's diction and intermittent recourse to imagery show affiliations with Old English riddling conceitful-ness, as when the bodies and armour of Arthur's enemies are envisioned as steel fishes lying in the River Avon:

> hu lige i þan stræme   stelene fisces;
> mid sweorde bigeorede   heore sund is awemmed;
> heore scalen wleoteþ   swulc gold-fa3e sceldes;
> þer fleoteþ heore spiten   swulc hit spæren weoren.

> how steel fish lie in the river trammelled with
> swords, their swimming impaired; their scales gleam
> as if they were gilded shields; their fins drift in
> the water like spears floating there (lines 10,640–3).

An inventively grim wit turns the normal order of imagery on its head; these are not men imagined as fish, but fish imagined as men. Internal rhyme ('sweorde bigeorede . . . wleoteþ/fleoteþ'), occasionally present in Old English poetry, but also in French and Latin, is woven into the basic allitera-tive verse-structure. La3amon's Arthur, intriguingly, 'should come again to aid the people of England' ('sculde 3ete cum Anglen to fulste'; line 14,297), a fantasy of restoration, perhaps. However, it should be noted, as Barron and Weinberg point out in the introduction to their edition (pp. liv–lv), that 'British' and 'English' tend to be interchangeable terms in what is more a history of Britain than of a single race. All in all, the *Brut* represents a fasci-nating and complex negotiation of Celtic, Norman and English identities.

Middle English romance used history to various ends, taking its narratives from the matter of Britain (often Arthurian), France (frequently Charlemagne and his knights), Greece and Rome (classical stories). It might not be too irre-sponsible an exaggeration to say that just as there is no such thing as a trivial folk-tale, so, given its frequent folk-tale origins and socio-psychological dynamic, there is no such thing as a trivial romance. Romance confronts the most basic concerns of family, inheritance, marriage, land-ownership, prop-erty, kinship, kingship, political legitimacy, social stability and disruption, the passage of time, enemies within and without, social rites/rights of passage, membership of society, transgression and atonement, fortune and fate. The deep-seated psychic logic of romance requires a world governed by poetic justice, in which the normal laws of cause and effect succumb to ideals and marvels in order to accommodate the deepest human desires and anxieties. Romance finds solutions which reintegrate states of social/personal disloca-tion. Its characters do not just represent parts of human society but also aspects of the self. Whereas in Old English literary tradition the hero was proved by the ultimate test of a valiant and memorable death, the romance hero solves the test and lives to preserve and renew the proper order of life.[5]

Romance-necessities are most visible in adaptations of non-romance. In classical legend, the first poet, Orpheus, is granted his wife's release from the Underworld on condition that he must not look back at her until they are safely in the daylight; but, in the words of John Walton, 'He turned hym and

Erudice he saw. / Allas he lost and left his wyf behynde'.[6] In this aureate alle-gorical early fifteenth-century version of the story, certainly no romance, Orpheus is guilty of looking at the foul hell of earthly wretchedness instead of the divine daylight of the Ultimate Good.[7] The bold and vivacious thir-teenth-century romance, *Sir Orfeo*, however, requires Orpheus to be not just a poet-lover but culturally assimilated, socially significant, and royally chival-rous:

> Orfeo was a king
> In Inglond, an heiʒe lording,
> A stalworþ man and hardi bo [both],
> Large [generous] and curteys he was also.
> (lines 39–42)[8]

Antique Thrace is now Winchester, where 'Sir' Orfeo has political as well as poetic supremacy. His kingly harping, echoing the harmony of the spheres, embodies social, personal, marital harmony and happiness. When Eurydice, Dame Heurodis, is abducted to a Celtic Otherworld by a Faery King, Orfeo, devastated, abandons his kingdom, an 'unnatural act' to the medieval frame of mind. To avoid making the hero a monument of regal dereliction, a beneficial new plot is created, a test of loyalty for Orfeo's viceroy steward which also turns out to be the test to find a successor. After ten years suffering and harping in the wilderness, Orfeo, having pursued a faery hunt through a rock into the Otherworld, wins Heurodis back with his minstrelsy, but, more than strikingly, does not lose her for a second time. A king must have a queen; the logic of the genre requires restoration of the body politic. Orfeo simply takes Heurodis by the hand and within a few couplets they are back in Winchester. Orfeo, now unrecognisable as a hairy beggar, is welcomed back as a minstrel into his palace by his steward, who is keeping good faith with his master by patronising minstrelsy. The harp is familiar to the steward. When Orfeo says he found it by a corpse ripped to shreds, 'totorn smale' (line 538), the steward swoons eloquently with becoming grief. 'King Orfeo knewe wele bi þan / His steward was a trewe man' (lines 553–4), worthy of the succession. At the romance's triumphantly healing end, both king and queen are recrowned, suit-ably enough, 'Wiþ al maner menstraci / Lord, þer was grete melody!' (lines 589–90). Love, poetry, music, kingship and loyalty are all proved by narrative testing. Far from mangling the myth, *Sir Orfeo* rewrites it boldly for its own time with new relevance; that is what myths are for.

The language and preoccupations of romance frequently overlap with other literary forms: lyrics, religious works, saints' lives. Hagiography is full of testing, transgression and atonement, exemplary conduct, love (human and divine), service to ideals, and resistance to the forces which threaten human-ity. Romance took on at times a hagiographical colouring, especially in peni-tential tales of knights whose adventures were mirrors of pilgrimages for individual salvation. *Sir Gowther* is a wonderfully lurid example.[9] A devil's son, baby Gowther, making a bad start in life, sucks nine wet-nurses to death, and snaffles off his mother's nipple. Later, he enjoys killing his mother's retinue and cleaving their horses' backs in two. He rapes maidens and wives, slays hus-bands, and persecutes the clergy with diabolical relish, incinerating a nunnery (having deflowered the inmates). His penchant is to

> . . . make frerus to leype [leap] at kraggus [cliffs]
> And persons for to heng on knaggus [hooks],

> And odur prestys [priests] sloo.
> To bren armettys [burn hermits] was is dyssyre:
> A powre wedow [widow] to seyt on fyre,
>   And werke hom mykyll [much] woo.
>
> (lines 196–201)

When he finally hears that his father was a devil, an image of the original sin in us all, Gowther wakes up to his own wickedness and decides on a life of papally-imposed penitence, redeeming himself by silence, eating only food brought by the mouth of a dog, accepting the identity of 'Hob the Fool', fighting Saracens, and founding an abbey. His holiness, as was proper with saints, is proved by miracles which occur after his death at his tomb.

The edifyingly spectacular, at times sensationalistic, endurance undergone by saints or romance heroes, is transcended by the supreme self-sacrificial lover of each recalcitrant and frail Christian soul, Christ, who in narrative, lyric and prose epitomises the rescuing knight-wooer. The *Ancrene Wisse*, a guide (*c.* 1200) for three upper-class enclosed sisters, advises on dress, washing, becoming conduct, the cultivation of, and rationale for, the life of prayer, meditation, confession, penance, self-denial and holy love. Written, like other texts in the so-called 'Katherine-group', in western 'AB-language', and probably produced in the Lingen area of Herefordshire, quite near to where Laȝamon composed his epic, it seems to draw on a continuing tradition of Old English rhythmical religious prose, alliterating like verse but much looser (a feature shared also with Latin devotional prose). The *Ancrene Wisse* is rhetorically deft, varying tone, pace and address with an intimate but authoritative affective design on its audience. Its parable of a knight wooing a lady beset by her enemies is a case in point:

> Herto falleð a tale, a wrihe forbisne.
>
> A leafdi wes mid hire fan biset al abuten, hire lond al destruet, ant heo al poure inwið an eorðene castel. A mihti kinges luue wes þah biturnd upon hire swa unimete swiðe þet he for wohlech sende hire his sonden, an efter oðer, ofte somet monie; sende hire beawbelez baðe feole ant feire, sucurs of liueneð, helpe of his hehe hird to halden hire castel. Heo underfeng al as on unrecheles, ant swa wes heard-iheortet þet hire luue ne mahte he neauer beo þe neorre. Hwet wult tu mare?

> There is a story linked with this, a hidden allegory.
>
> A lady was completely surrounded by her enemies, her land laid waste, and she herself quite destitute, in a castle of clay. But a powerful king had fallen in love with her so inordinately that to win her love he sent her his messengers, one after another, often many together; he sent her many splendid presents of jewellery, provisions to support her, help from his noble army to hold her castle. She accepted everything as if it meant nothing to her, and was so hard-hearted that he could never come closer to gaining her love. What more do you want?[10]

The rhythmically reinforced completeness of the lady's wretchedness ('biset *al* abuten . . . *al* destruet . . . *al* poure'), is balanced by her equally complete taking for granted of the knight ('underfeng *al* as on unrecheles'), an unnatural misapplication of the courtly convention of ladylike disdain. Though the parable is cast in the third person, second-person direct address breaks through, implying accusingly that 'you' are that ungrateful lady: 'Hwet wult tu mare?'

A later, fourteenth-century, prose guide for beginners in the contemplative life, *The Cloud of Unknowing*, builds on the same tradition of affectively imagining Christ, but it moves beyond this, instructing on the approach to God by the 'Negative Way', the *Via Negativa*, in which metaphoric discourse is used but ultimately transcended.[11] For God, being incorporeal, is inexpressibly beyond corporeal human language, beyond earthly senses and experience, and can better and more intimately be approached 'negatively' by using language to deny language. This produces a tendency to paradoxical expression and a focus on such negative concepts as darkness, nowhereness and absence. Thus what to the Outer Man is 'nouȝt . . . Oure inner man clepiþ [calls] it Al' (p. 122). The contemplative, starting with meditation on the Passion, reduces his mind to an unselfed 'nakid entent', shorn of senses and consciousness, informed not by knowledge but by love of God, and thereby subject not so much to seeing Him but to being touched by His revealing light through the Cloud of Unknowing which is always between Humanity and God:

> Þan wil he sumtyme parauenture seend oute a beme of goostly [spiritual] liȝt, peersyng þis cloude of vnknowing þat is bitwix þee & hym, & schewe þee sum of his priuite [mystery/secrets], þe whiche man may not, ne kan not, speke. Þan schalt þou fele þine affeccioun enflaumid [feeling inflamed] wiþ þe fiire of his loue, fer more þen I kan telle þee, or may, or wile, at þis tyme (p. 62).

Metaphysical intensity is rendered with a colloquial immediacy appropriate to intimate devotion but never overblown or fanatical. A matching temperacy informs the satirising of the antics of would-be mystics:

> Many wonderful contenaunces [gestures] folowen hem [them] þat ben disseyuid [deceived] in þis fals werk . . . Som sette þeire iȝen [eyes] in þeire hedes as þei were sturdy scheep [giddy? brain-diseased sheep] betyn in þe heed, & as þei schulde diȝe anone [die at once]. Som hangen here [their] hedes on syde, as a worme were in þeire eres [ears]. Som pipyn [squeak] when þei schuld speke, as þer were no spirit in þeire bodies: & þis is þe propre condicion of an ypocrite (pp. 97–8).

Such comic disadvantage is, more gravely, spiritual disadvantage, a token 'of þe lackyng of þe werk of þis book' (pp. 99–100).

Probably the most celebrated prose work in the English tradition of devotional imaginings is Julian of Norwich's *Revelations of Divine Love*, or *Showings*. In May 1373 she had visions of Christ and His teaching which were written up in a 'short' text and, a number of years later (probably), in a considerably longer version, which ruminates on her experiences further.[12] Going beyond affective meditation to explore the rationale of key elements of Christian theology like the nature of the Trinity, the function of sin, the Father-/Motherhood of God and their interrelations, Julian writes with the rhythmic ease and lexical and phrasal patterning born of familiarity with the rhetoric and content of devotional prose and with the fertile intertextuality of reading, ingesting and reworking biblical text and commentary-tradition. Sophisticated theological exposition combines with an appreciation of the permeating simplicity of the divine love of which theology is a complication. The compassionately attentive, unsensational yet acutely lingering particularity of her vision of the process of dying in the Passion is characteristically arresting:

> After this Criste shewid a partie of his passion nere his deyeng. I saw his swete face as it was drye and blodeles with pale deyeng; and sithen more pale, dede, langoring, and than turnid more dede into blew, and sithen more brown blew, as the flesh turnyd more depe dede; for his passion shewid to me most propirly in his blissid face. (p. 24).

Vomiting Glutton. 'Is noon so hungry hound in Hertfordshire/Dorste lape of that levynge, so unlovely it smaughte!' Gruesomely amusing though it may be, such 'sick' humour invokes a stern moral tradition. The glutton is never to be sanctioned or let off without repentance.

Christ's own meaning, as told to her through grace, is rendered with prophetic simplicity and incantatory resonance:

> Our lord Iesus oftentymes seyd: 'I it am, I it am; I it am that is heyest; I it am that thou lovist; I it am that thou lykyst; I it am that thou servist; I it am that thou longyst; I it am that thou desyrist; I it am that thou menyst; I it am that is al; I it am that holy church prechyth and techyth the; I it am that schewed me here to thee' (p. 37).

As is common with the cadences of religious prose, this passage moves towards the poetic to make its impact.

Concomitantly, William Langland's religious poem, *Piers Plowman*, ranges from prosaic looseness to traditional metrical discipline, in accordance with its purposes. Composed in the alliterative style more often associated with the north and west, but intended for a London and national audience, which it quickly achieved, the poem was written and rewritten between about 1367 and 1385, surviving in over fifty MSS in (probably) four distinct texts, A, B, C and Z (a subject of intense editorial controversy). The B-text is often held to be the most critically rewarding.[13] Contemporary with Chaucer's works, produced in the same city, yet so different, *Piers Plowman* is a unique concoction of allegory, satire, diatribe, debate, spiritual autobiography, prophecy, prayer, psychic drama, theology, vulgar comedy, philosophy and reworked biblical history. Will, a projection of Langland himself, stumbles (not always with comprehension) through shifting dreamscapes and mysterious allegorical encounters in his search for the elusive Piers Plowman, an evolving and cumulative embodiment of the will of God and of the varying potentials within humanity for the life of Christian spirituality. In dealing with the problems of how to live, how to love, how to find and know the truth and how to be saved, *Piers Plowman* ranges from the gross and ridiculous to the contemplative and sublime.

In the early stages of the poem, a satirical moral allegory of social ills and individual penitence, each member of society, represented partly by the personified Seven Deadly Sins, a lurid gallery of grotesques, must repent before going on a pilgrimage to gain St Truth's pardon. Before coming to contrition, Gloton (Gluttony), for example, gulps down over a gallon of ale; his guts rumble like two greedy sows; he urinates four pints in the time it takes to say the Lord's Prayer (instead of praying he is pissing); he breaks wind so thunderously and so venomously that fellow-revellers wish furze to be applied to the offending orifice; he staggers around like a minstrel's bitch tottering on its hind legs; his eyes go dim (befitting his spiritual blindness); he falls over and Clement the Cobbler, catching him by the middle, lifts him on to his knees, though not to pray (see the illustration above).

> Ac Gloton was a gret cherl and a grym in the liftyng,
> And koughed up a cawdel [mess] in Clementes lappe.
> Is noon so hungry hound in Hertfordshire
> Dorste lape of that levynge [remnant], so unlovely it smaughte [tasted/smelled]!
>
> (V. 354–7)

The morning after the night before, Gloton repents and joins a penitent humanity. But society still needs a guide to St Truth. At this point Piers, a humble and idealised ploughman, pipes up; he knows how to get there, but first needs the help of all to plough his half-acre. Under his direction, society is formally reconstituted and each estate, with some exceptions, fulfils its function.

Abraham worshipping the Trinity, 'That oon dooth, alle dooth'. In the Middle Ages Abraham's meeting with three angels was treated as a recognition of the Trinity. This seemingly bizarre representation, which adopts the common medieval technique of investing more than one meaning in a single image, has affinities with the strange composite and multi-layered phenomena that people the narrative of *Piers Plowman*.

But when the eagerly-awaited pardon is finally delivered, Piers tears it up in anger, for it only repeats the Athanasian Creed's message: do well and go to heaven, do ill and burn in hell; a strange 'pardon' indeed. At this moment of crisis Piers disappears and is thereafter largely elusive, as is, at times, the meaning of the poem. Will subsequently encounters, and debates with, a series of abstractions and faculties of the soul like Clergie, Thought, Wit. This introspective, intellectual phase of the poem eventually collapses into a more affective, faith-driven search, involving patient poverty, humility and love/charity.

Piers re-emerges in a dream within a dream as the guardian of the Tree of Charity, whose fruit (souls) the Devil would bear off, unless Jesus can save them through His Crucifixion. For Christians seeking salvation, as for Old Testament figures, redemption is a matter of faith, the personification of which Will meets. Thus, Faith-as-Abraham appears as a herald, proclaiming Christ abroad through faith. As such he is the appropriate figure to teach the doctrine of the Trinity, the paradox of three in one and one in three, a mystery embodied in Genesis in his meeting with three angels (visually expounded in Abraham's adoration of the Trinity in the illustration on p. 135):[14]

> Thre leodes [persons] in oon lyth [body], noon lenger than oother,
> Of oon muchel and myght in mesure [size] and in lengthe.
> That [that (which)] oon dooth, alle dooth, and ech dooth bi his one [self].
> (XVI. 181–3)

The action of the Son and the Holy Spirit in accordance with the will and justice of the Father comes to fruition on Good Friday. Langland's evocation of the Crucifixion balances the divinity and humanity of Christ with sublime poise (see the colour plate on p. 123):

> '*Consummatum est*', quod Crist, and comsede [began] for to swoune,
> Pitousliche and pale as a prison [prisoner] that deieth;
> The lord of lif and of light tho leide hise eighen [eyes] togidres.
> The day for drede withdrough and derk bicam the sonne.
> The wal waggede [shook] and cleef [split], and al the world quaved [quaked].
> (XVIII. 57–64)

'It is finished', says Christ (John XIX. 30). Ambivalently, He is only 'as' a prisoner dying, for though in His humanity He truly is a dying prisoner, in His undying divinity He is acting a role to defeat Satan. And so Langland expresses His death not as a passive extinction but as a conscious laying-together of eyelids, a paradoxical depiction of death befitting the deathless 'lord of lif and of light', and echoed by the equally impossible darkness of the sun and personification of the terrified day. The wall of the Temple splits, heralding the transfer of holy power from Synagogue to Church, and the whole created world acknowledges its creator, quaking as He departs His created form.

Piers, already bearing deep associations with Christ Himself, now takes on an apostolic function. The true Church is established, but is soon threatened lethally by the Seven Deadly Sins, by Contrition faltering within, and by fraternal corruption undermining the sacraments. Conscience goes off as a pilgrim to find Piers who will destroy the source-sin of Pride, 'And siththe he gradde [cried aloud] after Grace, til I gan awake' (XX. 387), and the poem ends. The whole cycle seems to be starting again. But the ending is not all negative; it is realistic to the plight of all Christians. The search by the individual conscience informed by faith and love for Piers and all he embodies now breaks out into the waking world, not just of the dreamer, but of the reader, too.

An equally distinguished, though sharply different contemporaneous dream-poem, *Pearl*, also concerns itself with the means of salvation and the reconciliation of earthly and divine perspectives.[15] This poem of bereavement and consolation opens with the narrator's loss of a 'pearl', almost certainly his dead baby daughter. Falling asleep, he wakes in a paradisal dreamscape and meets a beautiful pearl-bedecked lady, his daughter, now transformed into a Bride of Christ, who from the other side of a stream symbolising the heaven/earth divide, counsels against grief and allows him a sight of the Celestial Jerusalem where she lives. The dreamer does not take too well to being taught by an ex-infant, resenting her easy passage to salvation when he has suffered on earth. His comically earthbound mentality is repeatedly exposed, as when, assuming with snobbish vainglory that his little girl is the sole Bride of Christ, he ludicrously feminises heroic diction, imagining her doing over and driving out her female rivals amid the celestial carnage of a marital coup:

> Over alle other so hygh thou clambe [have climbed]
> To lede wyth hym so ladyly lyf.
> So mony a comly onunder cambe [comely [lady] under comb]
> For Kryst han lyved in much stryf;
> And thou con alle tho dere out dryf [have driven out]
> And fro that maryag al other depres [driven out],
> Al only thyself so stout and styf,
> A makeles [matchless] may and maskelles [spotless].
>
> (lines 773–80)

Just as knights are, for example, 'hard under helm' elsewhere in battle poetry, she, in a parodic martial formula, is 'comly onunder cambe' ('comely under comb'), and 'makeles' ('matchless') not for her perfection in Christ but for her pugilism. Not for the first time, the Pearl-maiden slaps the dreamer down, lecturing him forcefully about salvation and the ways of heaven. The vision ends when the dreamer rashly leaps into the stream separating him from his daughter and heaven (see the colour plate on p. 124). Breaking the decorum of theology, but manifesting a truly God-ward movement of his soul, he awakes frustrated but consoled, and entrusts his own soul, his own pearl, to God.

Pearl is technically the greatest *tour de force* in English poetry. Abounding in thematically concatenated numerological patterns (e.g. 1,212 lines, twelve-line stanzas, twelve holy gates, 12 × 12 thousand Brides and so on), and imitating the circularity and transformative function of the pearl itself in finishing with a transformation of the first line, it is both alliterative and rhyming and is arranged into stanza-groupings revolving round, and interlinked by, slowly-changing keylines and theme-words whose meanings shift and echo at critical points of the poem's development, often pivoting on earthly versus heavenly values. Thus 'cortaysye' can be earthly courtesy or heavenly grace, and 'clot' is a clod of earth and also the Hill of Sion on which the Heavenly Jerusalem is built.

The finest Middle English romance, *Sir Gawain and the Green Knight*, now generally accepted as having been written by the same poet, also ends, after a painful cycle of learning, where it began.[16] One Christmas, while Camelot is unsuspectingly festive, into the merriment crashes a huge Green Knight with a monstrous axe. He treats the silence of Arthur's court like an adult taunting frightened children:

> . . . runischly [fiercely] his rede yyen [eyes] he reled [rolled] aboute,
> Bende [knitted/raised] his bresed [bristling] browes, blycande [shining] grene,
> Wayved his berde for to wayte quo-so [who] wolde ryse.
> When non wolde kepe hym with carp [speak with him] he coghed ful hyghe,
> Ande rimed hym [cleared his throat] ful richly, and ryght hym [proceeded] to
>   speke:
> 'What, is this Arthures hous,' quoth the hathel [knight] thenne,

'That al the rous [fame] rennes of thurgh ryalmes [realms] so mony?
Where is now your sourquydrye [pride] and your conquestes,
Your grindellayk [fierceness] and your greme [anger] and your grete wordes?
Now is the revel [revelry] and the renoun of the Rounde Table
Overwalt [overthrown] wyth a worde of on wyyes [one man's] speche,
For al dares [cower] for drede withoute dynt [blow] schewed!'
Wyth this he laghes so loude that the lorde greved;
The blod schot for scham [shame] into his schyre [fair] face.

(lines 304–17)

Is Camelot now no more than words? Words silenced not by deeds but by the mere words of one man who, after all, has only come, so he says, to play a Christmas game befitting beardless Camelot? Some game it turns out to be – an exchange of beheading blows. Gawain, representing Camelot, hoping not to have to take the return blow if he does his job properly, slices off the visitor's head. But the Green Knight picks up his head and tells Gawain to report to the Green Chapel a year hence. The following winter Gawain sets out, facing certain death. On his journey he finds Christmas hospitality at a wonderful castle where he gets himself involved in another game, an agreement to exchange daily winnings with his host. Thrice his host goes out hunting and presents his kill to his guest; and thrice Gawain trades in the kisses he gets from the lord's wife, a lavishly beautiful temptress with a suggestive turn of phrase, who enters his bedroom each morning and strains his chastity and courtesy to the limit. Gawain acquits himself with honour, and, in good faith, passes on chaste kisses to the lord of the castle. What he understandably omits to hand over on the third day is a green belt/girdle, which, says the lady, will preserve the life of its wearer.

At the showdown at the Green Chapel, the Green Knight, winding Gawain up wickedly, twice stays his axe-blows at the last moment, and at the third swing, does no more than nick his neck. Gawain leaps to his feet in relief, but it is not over. The Green Knight, revealing himself as Gawain's host, explains his three blows. Gawain, he says, showed his truth in thrice handing over the kisses, but the nick was merited for not handing over the girdle. The Green Knight, now taking on the role of a confessor-figure, not only punishes but absolves Gawain, finding him the best of knights, 'On the fautlest freke that ever on fote yede' (i.e. the most faultless man who ever trod this earth) (line 2,363), who only failed because he loved his life, 'the lasse I yow blame' (line 2,368). Gawain, however, his perfect reputation in tatters, throws an anti-feminist tantrum, comparing himself to worthies like Samson and Solomon who were undone by the wiles of women. Henceforth, he will wear the girdle as a baldric of penance and shame. The endless and perfect continuum of virtues represented in his own personal shield-symbol, the pentangle, is thus superseded by the imperfect broken circle of the girdle, a circle nevertheless made whole again by knotting (an analogue to Gawain's neck healing). The courtiers of Camelot, delighted to see their beloved knight return, laugh at his tale of shame, and ironically, sport the green girdle believing that it enhances the renown of the Round Table. The force and comedy of this text, time and again, are sourced in the tension between the demands of idealising romance and the frailty of fallen human nature.

The career of Geoffrey Chaucer (see the illustration opposite) centres to a significant extent on the diversity of literary forms and strategies he took to

The 'Hoccleve' portrait of Chaucer (1411–12) marks the self-conscious iconographic institutionalisation of Chaucer as the founding figure of a 'national' poetic tradition. 'Perhaps', according to Derek Pearsall ('Hoccleve's *Regement of Princes*'), 'the first nonroyal portrait that claims to be an accurate likeness', it was inserted into Thomas Hoccleve's *Regement of Princes*, a work drawing on the 'advice to princes' tradition, and sanctioning the programme of royal self-representation by which Henry Prince of Wales, later Henry V, sought to legitimise and popularise the Lancastrian regime through promoting English as the medium of administration, political life and poetic culture.

negotiate literary authority.[17] His early dream-poems combine notions of literary authority with an undermining playfulness while exploiting the latitude offered by dreams of a framework for fiction. The problematics of literary-historical truth are parodically non-confronted in the *House of Fame*, in which a reluctant Geoffrey is carried off by a mock-Dantean eagle to learn about love-tidings and the supposed truths of literary/historical fame – all to help his writing. Just as we think we are going to get the message of the tale delivered, it peters out:

> Atte laste y saugh [I saw] a man,
> Which that y nevene nat no kan [I can't name];
> But he seemed for to be
> A man of gret auctorite.
>
> (lines 2,155–8)

This typical evasiveness burdens the reader with interpretation all the more. *The Book of the Duchess*, however, despite its mysteriousness and strange mix of comedy and elegy, does close with an emphatic grasp of meaning. Written about the death of Blanche, wife of John of Gaunt, the poem casts its dreamer as encountering a grieving knight, a projection both of Gaunt and of the lovelorn poet. Teasing out the story of his love, the dreamer finally gets him to acknowledge that she is indeed dead:

> 'Allas, sir, how? What may that be?'
> 'She ys ded!' 'Nay!' 'Yis, be my trouthe!'
> 'Is that youre los? Be God, hyt ys routhe [a pity]!'
> (lines 1,308–10)

The dream has done its work.

Chaucer's most sustained single piece of writing, *Troilus and Criseyde*, is evasive once more. This tragic romance, set in doomed Troy, tells of Troilus' passion for Criseyde (a controversial and ambiguous character), of the ploys used to win her, of how the fortunes of war cause her (inexcusably or not) to desert him for another, and of how, ultimately, Troilus laughs from the heavens at his own death. The narrator of *Troilus* is a suspect conduit of literary authority, for his muse is a Fury, Thesiphone, a figure of unreasoned emotional excess and language unconstrained by rationality. Accordingly, his verses weep, reminiscent of the tearfully misguided measures which signify unenlightenment at the beginning of Boethius' *De Consolatione Philosophiae*. Reworking the papal title, 'Servus servorum dei', the narrator casts himself as 'I, that God of Loves servantz serve' (I. 15), preaching a sermon on love to an audience (see the illustration opposite). But what it finally means, when Troilus laughs from the heavens at his own tragedy and when an anti-pagan Christian voice breaks into the narrative to close the poem, is a rich difficulty, for it does not unmake the emotional force of five books of earthly tragedy.

An overtly comedic Christian structure of pilgrimage, ostensibly ending with repentance and salvation, is the form taken by Chaucer's most celebrated work, *The Canterbury Tales*, an encyclopaedia of human types, experiences and literary discourses (see the illustration on p. 142). Probably written between *c.* 1387 and his death in 1400, they are not finished, but are nevertheless accorded an ending of authority, within sight of Canterbury, with *The Parson's Tale*, a manual of penance. The generic range of the *Tales* is stupendous. *The Knight's Tale* is a philosophical romance of pagan antiquity, *The Miller's Tale* and *The Reeve's Tale* fabliaux, *The Franklin's Tale* a *lai*, *The Pardoner's Tale* a moral *exemplum*, *The Prioress's Tale* a Miracle of the Virgin, *Sir Thopas* a parodied romance, *Melibee* a moral prose allegory, *The Monk's Tale* a collection of tragedies, *The Nun's Priest's Tale* and *The Manciple's Tale* beast fables. Some are in game, others in earnest, some both. They relate to each other with as much complexity as their tellers, if not more. *The Miller's Tale*, for example, undercuts but does not obliterate *The Knight's*. Sword and noble tournament are matched by buttock-burning coulter and low cunning. The Knight's top-to-toe formal *descriptio* of Emelye, the object of the two heroes' love, is answered by the Miller's inventory of the attractions of the young wife Alisoun in domestic and saucy English images. The student Nicholas's initial approach to her is a wicked travesty of courtly love. When her husband is away he just grabs her groin. She playfully threatens to cry out for rescue in suitably high-camp romance

The famous frontispiece to *Troilus and Criseyde*, with the Chaucerian narrator in the pulpit preaching his sermon on love to 'yonge, fresshe folkes' (V. 1,835). The love-tragedy he tells, though, is hardly a conventional sermon, however much the dangers and excesses of (pagan) love may eventually be condemned at the end of the poem.

fashion, but grants her love with indecent haste 'atte laste' once he has spun her a few lines of mock-courtesy:

'Why, lat be!' quod she. 'Lat be, Nicholas,
Or I wol crie "out, harrow" and "allas"!
Do wey youre handes, for your curteisye!'
  This Nicholas gan mercy for to crye,
And spak so faire, and profred him so faste,
That she hir love hym graunted atte laste.
                    (I. (A) 328–90)

Canterbury pilgrims. As with the 'Hoccleve' portrait of Chaucer, this picture of Chaucer's most famous characters comes not from a Chaucer manuscript but from an impressive manuscript of poetry by another Chaucerian imitator enjoying royal patronage, John Lydgate. Like other poets responsible for the fifteenth-century Chaucerian apocrypha of spurious works, Lydgate cashed in on Chaucer's prestige by adding this *Canterbury Tale* of his own, complete with a highly Chaucerian prologue in which he himself mixes with Chaucer's fictional pilgrims.

This tale, involving, as fabliau does, deceit and elaborate ruses to gain sexual (or economic) advantage at the expense of a stock character (often a husband), offends the Reeve who, in his revenge-fabliau, has a miller bested by two students who 'swyve' his wife and his daughter in a bed-hopping farce of breakneck intricacy (see the illustration opposite).

Other tales also contend with or complement each other. The Friar and Summoner tell tales against each other's professions. The Wife of Bath, Merchant, Franklin (and to a lesser extent the Clerk) tell stories dealing with marriage and male–female relations. Chaucer the pilgrim, having been ordered rudely to cease his (deliberately) idiotic romance of *Sir Thopas*, osten-

sibly a tale of mirth, then goes to the other extreme with a long, highly senten-
tious moral allegory, *Melibee*.

A common factor for all the tales is that they are refracted through Chaucer
the pilgrim, a naive reporter who offloads the responsibility for tales on to their
fictional tellers. This provides the occasion for much irony and ambivalence.
The reader has to take up the burden of interpretation where there is no evident
voice of authority in the text. *The Parson's Tale*, however, is to be taken as
straightforwardly authoritative. It marks the end of the tale-telling game,
'knytte[s] up al this feeste', and sets its sights on penance and the Heavenly City,
'Jerusalem celestial' (X. (I) 47–51). The *Retracciouns* which run on from this tale
'retract' tales inasmuch as they conduce to sin, which is surely dependent on the
reader as much as on the writer. Here Chaucer does seem to be acknowledging
some responsibility, perhaps, albeit couched in evasive conditionals.

Fornicating lovers and cuckolded
husband: 'And on this goode wyf
he leith on soore. / So myrie a fit ne
hadde she nat ful yoore; / He
priketh harde and depe as he were
mad' (Chaucer, *Reeve's Tale* I.
4,229–31). An unmistakably familiar
scene in fabliaux, which were,
characteristically, amusing prank-
like tales of sexual and mercenary
trickery.

The self-undermining ironies of Chaucer, the richly questioning ambiguities of the *Gawain*-poet and the radical satire and introspective theological quest-ing of Langland are notably absent from fifteenth-century literary produc-tion, even though Chaucer and Langland MSS were much copied and read throughout the 1400s. In Thomas Hoccleve's *Regement of Princes* (see the illustration on p. 139) and in his other works, and in the works of Walton, Lydgate (who continued *The Canterbury Tales* in his *Siege of Thebes*), in Skelton, in later medieval romance and early Tudor song, the influence of Chaucer continued to be felt and proclaimed. However, the political climate for new literature was profoundly altered. The strictness of Archbishop Arundel's clamp-down on biblical translating and the production of theological writings and the enthusiastic orthodoxy of kings like Henry V account in no little part for the orthodoxy of fifteenth-century literature, which, for all its fascination and affectivity, shows technical accomplishment without the innovativeness and ideological latitude of the fourteenth century.[18]

Ideologically the most powerful orthodox text in Middle English was Nicholas Love's archiepiscopally-sanctioned *Mirror of the Blessed Life of Jesus Christ* (written before 1410), which, reflecting the wording of Arundel's mem-orandum mandating it against dissent, was written 'to confusion of alle fals lollardes & heritykes' (p. 223; see the illustration on p. 144).[19] Love demanded lay obedience and stalwartly defended the orthodox view of the Eucharist in the *Mirror*, whose success is reflected in its survival in more manuscripts than any other medieval English prose work. The Wycliffites whom Love opposed held that their New Testament in the mother tongue was open to the under-standing of simple souls, that everything expressed obscurely in the Old Testament was plain in the New, and that all who had charity had perfect understanding of the Bible anyway. These opinions, all the more dangerous for being appropriated from orthodox sources like St Augustine and standard Bible commentators, threatened the ecclesiastical stranglehold on biblical authority and the governance of the laity. Therefore Love chose to render a work in which the gospel text is protected with layers of meditative and homi-letic material directing the audience in orthodox spirituality at their own level.[20] Thus his text opens (see the illustration on p. 146):

> Quecumque scripta sunt ad nostram doctrinam scripta sunt vt per pacienciam & consolacionem scripturarum spem habeamus, ad Romanos xv⁰ capitulo [For what-ever is written is written for our instruction, that by patience and consolation of the Scriptures we might have hope].
>
> Þese ben þe wordes of þe grete doctour & holy apostle *Powle* consideryng þat the gostly leuyng [spiritual living] of all trewe crysten creatures in þis worlde stant specialy in hope of þe blysse & the lyfe þat is to come in another worlde.
>
> Ande for also mich as tweyne [two] þinges pryncipaly noryschen and strenkþen þis hope in man þat is pacience in herte & ensaumple of vertues & gude liuyng of holy men writen in bokes; Ande souereynly þe wordes & þe dedis [deeds] writen of oure lorde Jesu criste verrei god and man for þe tyme of his bodily liuyng here in erthe; þerfore to strenkeþ [strengthen] vs & confort vs in þis hope spekeþ þe Apostle þe wordes aforseid to this entent seying þat all thynges þat ben written gen-eraly in holi chirche ande specialy of oure lorde Jesu cryste þei bene [they are] wryten to oure lore [for our teaching] þat by pacience & conforte of holi scriptures we haue hope that is to say of the Life & Blysse that is to come in anothere worlde (p. 9).

For Love, the Life of Christ is 'souereynly edifiyng' (p. 10), the highest form of literary expression. His exposition of St Paul reflects his desire to provide a

Facing page Illuminated initial with Archbishop Arundel and monks of Christ Church, Canterbury, from a manuscript of William of Nottingham's commentary on the famous gospel harmony of Clement of Lanthony. It is telling that this arch-opponent of vernacular Scriptures and patron of the 'official' gospel-harmonising Life of Christ in English, Nicholas Love's *Mirror*, should choose such a book in which to be portrayed as sanctioning continued monastic devotion to parabiblical Latin (the utter antithesis to lay vernacular scripturalism).

The opening of Nicholas Love's *Mirror of the Blessed Life of Jesus Christ* (the same passage as quoted in this chapter). The handwriting of this manuscript is reasonably legible to the modern eye. The considerable number of surviving manuscripts of this devotional text is a reminder of the immense success of Love's *Mirror*, which was Arundel's official 'recommended reading' for those of orthodox piety, and a counterblast to the Lollard Scriptures. Some of the success of the work must also, however, be due to Love's undoubted skill as a writer of English prose.

wider audience with a Life of Christ underwritten by Holy Church, offering hope to all, and steering the laity clear of illicit adventures with vernacular Bibles.

Allied to Lives of Christ (of which over twenty in a huge range of forms are extant; see the illustration on p. 148) are Saints' Lives, which had enduring popularity throughout the Middle Ages.[21] We have already noted how hagiography influenced penitential romances like *Sir Gowther*. The sensationalism and violence of romance often attend the heroic feats and martyrdoms of literary saints. In John Capgrave's mid-fifteenth-century *Life of St Katharine of Alexandria* a vicious contraption of flesh-tearing wheels is prepared for the saint.[22] But at the last moment, an angel 'wyth wynde and feere [fire] / Brake alle the wheles':

Thei spryngyn aboute [fly] be pecys [pieces] in the place.
Somme haue harm on legges and on knes [knees],
Somme men arn [are] hurt on handes and on face.
The feer fley ful wundyrly.

(V. 1,359–62)

4,000 pagans are triumphantly scorched to death. According to Osbern Bokenham's version in his *Legendys of Hooly Wummen* (1440s), a mere 1,000 perish as the machine crashes down on to them (see the illustration on p. 141).[23] Bokenham's St Agatha, in the same sensationalist vein, has her breasts mutilated with pincers (see the illustration on p. 141). Her torturers are exhorted by the wicked consul Quyncyan:

'anoon, go to,
O tormentours, & to þis damysel ying [young]
Sumwhat shewyth of youre kunnyng [skill].
Touchyth hyr a lytyl from þe herte
Vp-on hyr pappys & doth hyr smerte [pain],
And let hyre knowyn what ys peyn.'
And þei anoon hyre gunne to streyn [hold/clasp];
Sum wyth pynsouns [pincers] blunt & dulle
Hyr tendyr brestys begunne to pulle.

(lines 8,584–92)

Yet she feels no pain, for her senses, 'Wych to my lord god halwyd [hallowed] haue y', are nursed from within her soul by invulnerable spiritual 'pappys' (lines 8,618–25). Her physical wounds are wondrously cured by her faith. Women saints like Agatha, Christine, Lucy, Margaret and Katherine, for all the voyeurism they suffer in their torments, are far from passive. Defying parental and judicial power, they show daunting intellects, eloquence and abusive humour, self-consciously dictate their fates, and are not mere characters in a story but, according to the culture of the day, real personalities, shedding gracious influence on hagiographical composition itself and on the real lives of people. They aid the penance and very salvation of those who write or read their lives, as the intercessory prayers which punctuate their texts commemorate.

This chapter has sought to give an impression of the interlinked variety of literary forms of the period. To conclude by means of *occupatio* (a favourite medieval rhetorical ploy whereby you tell your audience what you are choosing not to tell them), there is much more literature from the period which should not be overlooked – lyrics ranging from mnemonics and drinking songs to hymns to Christ and the Virgin, love-poems, saucy dialogues, laments and dance-songs; the drama, generally cycles of dramatised biblical history associated with guilds from towns like Chester, York and Wakefield (not forgetting *A Tretise of Miraclis Pleyinge*, the first sustained dramatic criticism in English, albeit anti-theatrical); and fifteenth-century prose romance, particularly Malory's inappropriately-entitled *Morte Darthur*, which chronicles the whole of Arthurian history. *The Owl and the Nightingale*, a wittily abusive debate between two birds, is the first poem seen to master courtly French octosyllabic couplets in English. Further important works include the *Cursor Mundi*, a colossal encyclopaedic historical poem spanning Creation and Last Judgement; Walter Hilton's poised and affective prose treatises on the mixed,

Scenes from the Life of Christ (Sermon, Betrayal, Flagellation, Bearing of the Cross). Each scene of the Life of Christ had potential for devotion, whether in visual art or in written works. A reader of meditative works like Love's *Mirror* and countless others, for example, would be instructed by the writer to 'behold' gospel events, think feelingly on them, derive appropriate moral lessons from them, and move on from this to prayer and perhaps even to a holy meeting with Christ Himself within the reader's own soul.

St Katherine standing amid the wreckage of the flesh-tearing wheels devised for her terror and torment, with heaven-sent angels with swords rescuing her, and her pagan tormentors justly felled: 'An aungel yaf þe engyn swych a swap, / Euene as it had ben a thundyr-clap, / That on a thousend pecys to grounde / It fel' (Bokenham, *Legendys of Hooly Wummen*, lines 7,131–4). This indomitable and popular female saint inspired numerous English versions of her Life and was frequently represented in visual art.

St Agatha with breasts being pulled by tormentors with pincers. 'Touchyth hyr a lytyl from þe herte / Vp-on hyr pappys & doth hyr smerte. / And let hyre knowyn what ys peyn': a common ordeal for women saints. The hideously gleeful exertions of the tormentors and the devoutness of the material mark a complex range of medieval sensibilities, including love of outrageous spectacle, admiration at amazing human endurance, prurience, voyeurism and tender piety: 'gret pyte / How þe blood owt ran yt was to se' (lines 8,597–8).

John Gower firing satirical arrows at the world. Judging by the distance from which he is shooting, and the sheaf of extras in his belt, Gower (dubbed 'Moral Gower' by his friend Chaucer) evidently believed in the potential efficacy of his works for commending virtue and condemning vices. His discourses dealt not only with politics and society but also with the ethical and spiritual life of the individual. Gower wrote with forcefulness and distinction in all three national tongues, Latin, French and English. This illustration is taken from a copy of his Latin *Vox Clamantis*.

active and contemplative lives; and Richard Rolle's self-advertising and influential outpourings of mystical poetry and prose, together with his remarkable commentary-translation of the Psalter, which, like *The Ancrene Wisse*, was seized on by Lollard revisers. The Lollard Bible, polemic, exegesis and sermons are of immense historical significance, as, on the orthodox side, are the impressive devotional products of Carthusian and Brigittine sensibility like *The Mirror of Our Lady* and *The Orcherd of Syon*. The most intellectually ambitious textual arrangement of the period is Reginald Pecock's mid-fifteenth-century interlocking programme of orthodox theology, philosophy and polemic, which aimed to out-argue the Lollards on their own vernacular ground and resystematise the catechism. Unfortunately, Pecock was declared a heretic, and on publicly recanting, saw copies of his works consigned to the flames. The orthodox but turbulently freelance *Book of Margery Kempe*, which still attracts controversy, is an extraordinary spiritual 'autobiography'. Autobiographical too is Hoccleve's most arresting poetry, especially his accounts of himself after mental illness and his dialogue with his friend. Another acquaintance of Chaucer, John Gower, created three major works in the three major national tongues, his French *Mirour de l'Omme*, his Latin *Vox Clamantis*, a satirical disquisition on the condition of England (see the illustration above), and his English *Confessio Amantis*, a collection of stories ostensibly on the theme of love, arranged in a confessional narrative frame of the Seven Deadly Sins.

Though Chaucer's reputation lived on, through Skelton and others, to the Renaissance and beyond, it is salutary to remind ourselves that Chaucer did not produce the most popular poem of the Middle Ages. That honour, witnessed in well over 100 surviving manuscripts, belongs to the long-forgotten *Prick of Conscience*, which discourses at immense length on the ghastliness of life, the fear of God and the Christian way, among other themes. *Pearl* and *Gawain*, at the opposite end of the scale, exist in a single unremarkable manuscript which by chance survived the great Cottonian Library fire of 1731, and, like other manuscripts, might easily have been thrown out or destroyed. In accounting for the forms of literary expression from this period, we simply do not know what we are missing, but there is more than enough left to us to assure us that this was an age of stunningly rich diversity, achievement and innovation.

FORMS OF ARTISTIC EXPRESSION

Nigel Ramsay

All studies of medieval English art are severely hampered by the fact that so little of it survives. The closing down of the English monasteries in the late 1530s was marked by a destructiveness that was not matched by any of the various programmes of dissolution that took place on the Continent, in the sixteenth century or later. The English religious houses were reduced physically to ruins (as their lead roofs were stripped off), or were adapted into serving as residences for the gentry and nobility; their contents were inventoried and then sold or taken away for the Crown's use. When St Thomas Becket's shrine in Canterbury Cathedral was taken to pieces, the king's receiver said that the gold and silver and precious stones and sacred vestments from it filled twenty-six carts.

It is true that gold and silver plate and vessels were always seen, throughout the Middle Ages and in all parts of Europe, as assets that could be converted to other uses if need be, and only the most hallowed of reliquaries were ever seen as meriting preservation on the grounds of antiquity. Nevertheless, it is one distinct distortion of any modern view of English art, that no shrine or other major piece of metalwork survives from any of the monasteries. Leave aside architecture, where the cathedrals and a good many castles (but just a handful of palaces) still stand with little alteration, and illuminated manuscripts, of which a fair number of the best examples are preserved in an almost pristine state (having always been seen as too precious to be produced on any save the most special of occasions); beyond these there is very little that was not preserved by the chance either of removal from this country or of conversion to some other use which hid it from view. The early twelfth-century Gloucester Candlestick (made of an alloy of silver, copper and other metals, with intricate openwork decoration, for St Peter's Abbey, Gloucester, between 1107 and 1113 and now in the Victoria and Albert Museum) and the early fifteenth-century reliquary of the Order of the Holy Spirit (given by Henry IV's wife Joan to her son John, duke of Brittany; now in the Louvre) both survived by being on the Continent throughout the period of English iconoclasm that began in the 1530s and ended only in 1660. The Westminster Abbey 'retable', a superbly painted panelled piece of *c.* 1270 which in many ways resembles metalwork, survives only because it was cut up and its panels served other-side-up as a table-top.

Conversely, some of the finest pieces of English sculpture, mural painting and metalwork have been found in recent years, and there is undoubtedly much more to be discovered. For instance, while it is undeniable that today's cautious methods of conservation enable mural paintings to be preserved – for hundreds of these were merely covered with whitewash in the sixteenth-century – their very preservation probably also prevents the discovery of pieces of sculpture that were buried under the floor or were hidden or incorporated in the wall in the Late Middle Ages or at the Reformation. Victorian church restorations were often destructive of the fabric (as architects altered it to what they believed it had once been or should have been), but they resulted in the recovery of dozens of late medieval carved alabaster figures and panels of religious imagery. The Middleham Jewel (now in the Yorkshire Museum) was found in 1986 in a field near Middleham Castle; it has lost almost all of the enamelling that was once set into its surface, but it is still a very rare example of a late fifteenth-century rich woman's pendant jewel (see the illustration on p.154).

Some impression of what works of art once existed can be gained from

Terracotta aquamanile. Popular art has survived no better than court art. This early fourteenth-century equestrian knight is perhaps of German rather than English making, though it is very similar to badly damaged pottery found in English sites; in any case its design is taken from the copper-alloy aquamaniles that were produced in great numbers on the Continent, serving as water-containers on rich men's tables.

The Middleham Jewel. The front (shown here) is engraved with the Holy Trinity and is set with a sapphire; the back is engraved with the Nativity and certain saints. It was made in England between about 1475 and 1480, and is of gold; it was once set with enamel, of which a fragment survives in the 'E' of Ecce, to the right of the sapphire.

what survives of medieval archives and libraries. The English monarchy's high degree of dynastic continuity and, perhaps even more importantly, its generally strong hold on English government, have resulted in the Crown's archives being, by European standards, astonishingly full of detail on both the private (or privy or domestic) and the public (or state or governmental) expenditure of the monarch. By the same measure, it is harder to discover much about the artistic patronage of the nobility or gentry, or for that matter of the wealthier ecclesiastics, unless they fell out with the Crown so far as to lose both their life and their possessions and have their papers seized.[1] The account rolls of quite a number of religious houses have been preserved, from the thirteenth century onwards; but even the wealthier houses, with good sets of records, such as Westminster Abbey, Durham Cathedral, or Christ Church Cathedral Priory, Canterbury, were rarely patrons of major works of decorative art, and even for their building works tended to rely on gifts from others.

The upshot of these vagaries of fortune must be to risk our overvaluing the importance in terms of patronage of the Crown as compared with its peers, both lay and spiritual. Equally, it would be easy to underestimate the level and the general significance in artistic terms of some of the artistic world's principal supporters. Even the most painstaking efforts to gather together the evidence of lay patronage will inevitably fail to do it justice, simply because the documentary evidence is not there: the non-royal financial records that have survived best are those of the humdrum expenditure on repairs by undying institutions (such as cathedrals, bridge trusts and town corporations).

The twelfth-century chronicler William of Malmesbury was to refer to 14 October 1066, the date of the Battle of Hastings, as 'that fatal day for England'. Its importance for the direction in which English art was to develop

is, however, questionable. Edward the Confessor had already begun the rebuilding of the royal abbey of Westminster in a style and form modelled on that of buildings in Normandy.[2] And Edward had begun the policy that William the Conqueror continued, of appointing men from the Continent as bishops. Certainly the construction of new cathedrals and castles was commenced, and such men as Lanfranc, archbishop of Canterbury from 1070 to 1089, sought to correct the perceived deficiencies of English monastic learning by importing patristic and other Latin theological texts from the Continent. On the other hand, England had long had its own distinctive and vigorous artistic style (termed the Winchester School by modern art historians, although it was actually prevalent in all of south-east England), which had been highly influential in such Norman centres of book-writing and illustration as Jumièges and Mont-Saint-Michel.

An emphasis on the linear, and more particularly on the drawing of the human figure in a slightly nervous or agitated *mouvementé* style, has generally been accepted as a salient characteristic of English art until at least the end of the fourteenth century. From around the 1050s, book-illustration in England shows a movement towards the more solid painted forms that we characterise as Romanesque, but the linear strengths of the native style were far from being driven underground by the Norman invasion. England was celebrated for its skill in the production of embroideries, and these must all have depended on drawings made on the underlying fabric, over which the needlewomen executed their embroidery. Only thanks to its underdrawing did the Bayeux Tapestry (see the illustration above) gain its sense of movement and spontaneity. The Tapestry (as the embroidery is so misleadingly called) was undoubtedly designed by an Englishman, since – quite apart from its overall style – its inscriptions include some English words and uniquely English letter-forms, and it is now generally accepted that it was made for Odo, bishop of Bayeux. Since Odo fell from power in 1082, it must have been made before that date; and since he was earl of Kent, with estates in that county, it is as likely as not that he had it made in Canterbury. It is, however, hard to be confident as to whether it was made for Odo's own dining-hall, as is perhaps sug-

The death of the English king, Harold, at the Battle of Hastings, from the Bayeux Tapestry. He is shown twice, first at the moment that he is struck by an arrow and then (at the right) as he falls to the ground, mortally wounded. The tapestry was embroidered for Bishop Odo of Bayeux, probably in Kent, before 1082.

gested by certain secular touches (scenes from the fables of Aesop in the borders, and the naming of two of Odo's vassals), or for his cathedral of Bayeux, as might be implied by its emphasis on Harold's swearing an oath on relics at Bayeux.[3] This uncertainty of function is, however, a clear reminder of the more general lack of distinction between the sacred and the secular in medieval art. A work of art could easily be created for one setting and then be transferred to another, and, still more confusingly for the art historian, a work of art could easily combine both functions: much private jewellery was decorated with religious symbolism and inscriptions, and biblical stories were as likely as secular epics or fables to be used for large-scale schemes of decoration in a secular context. The Bayeux Tapestry is merely characteristic of its age in its combination of the lay and spiritual worlds.

The 'twelfth-century renaissance' is a phrase that has been coined by historians in the present century to describe the revival of learning throughout Europe; in such centres as Bologna and Paris, a variety of the most important theological and legal texts were elucidated and glossed. Set texts were commented on, and the glosses or commentaries (which rapidly came to be as long as the texts themselves, and to encircle them on the page) themselves became standardised. Fame and fashion drew the ambitious from England as much as from the rest of Europe to go to the 'schools' or nascent universities. In the twelfth century, England was perhaps culturally closer to Continental Europe than at any time since, and it fully participated in the renaissance. Although the revival was not in any direct sense an artistic one, it had in the longer term the effect of making the universities displace monasteries as the leading cultural centres. The universities at first were under the Church's control, for the Church successfully maintained its right to control the whole educational system; but then, little by little, the clerks' training slipped away from the ecclesiastical world. A clerk came to be someone who could write, who was literate to a reasonably high level, and who was not intending to take holy orders more than it was necessary for him to do for his career's sake; he might be a married man, and he might earn his living as a scribe. The university towns thus became centres of the book trade, and book production came to be separated from the other decorative arts. In Oxford and Cambridge, as in Paris and Bologna, it was realised that there was a living to be made in writing, decorating and binding books; scholars were at first the sole clients, but then other clients, lay and ecclesiastical, followed. The arts of the book were cultivated in a highly professional way and to a reasonable standard of production. A book written and sold in thirteenth-century Oxford (see the colour plate on p. 173), be it a canon law text for a student or a much more highly decorated and illuminated Psalter-Book of Hours for a lay patron, will not really bear comparison with the handsome late eleventh-century patristic texts copied in the scriptorium of, say, Christ Church Cathedral Priory, Canterbury, impressive by their height and spacious layout. On the other hand, the purchaser in Oxford was not having to pay for drawings that would have been superfluous to his needs; what he was buying was a text, rather than a work of art.

The twelfth-century renaissance did more than transform the copying of scholarly books into an industry, and England's participation in the cultural life of the Continent was far from being limited to students' attendance at universities. For one thing, in the second half of the twelfth century the Romanesque style of painting was dramatically affected by the Byzantine. It is not clear whether this came from Venice or from Rome or from the Norman kingdom of Sicily, or by some other channel of influence, but it is unquestionable that it had a major impact on English art. In such illustrated books as the Winchester Psalter (British Library, Cotton MS Nero C. iv), there is some very direct Byzantine influence; it has been suggested by some scholars that two of the pictures in the Psalter are the work of an Italo-Byzantine artist. The rich bishopric of Winchester was held at this time by Henry of Blois (1129–71), who is known to have imported antiquities from Rome, and it is tempting to see in him a personal channel of influence for the Italo-Byzantine style. He was, besides, a Cluniac, and the mother-house of the Cluniac order, the abbey of Cluny, had early been influenced by the Byzantine style.

In the longer term, however, the importance of the Byzantine impact on England must be that it acted as a catalyst for the softening of the monumental Romanesque style and for the revival of the Anglo-Saxon *mouvementé* linear style. The Guthlac Roll in the British Library (Harley Roll Y.6, probably drawn at Crowland Abbey, Lincolnshire, in the early thirteenth century) is one instance of the English skill at combining outline drawing with a sense of freshly-observed activity; it is both a classic example of the English Romanesque style, and at the same time may also be said to anticipate the drawings of Matthew Paris at St Alban's Abbey in the 1240s and 1250s (see the illustration below).

Almost all artistic styles will affect all media – painting and sculpture as well as architecture. The speed at which a style will make its impact is variable, however; the more portable works of art, such as books, may well be the first to reflect a new influence. Yet this was not really the case with the Gothic style, despite its highly linear nature, which might be expected to have given it an immediate appeal to English artists; instead, the Gothic style was brought to England by William of Sens, a French master mason who was appointed by the monks of Canterbury Cathedral to rebuild the eastern part of their church after it had been severely damaged by fire in 1174. They were, of course, in a position to pay for such a costly undertaking, thanks to the offerings of pil-

Building St Alban's church. Tinted drawing in the style of Matthew Paris, illustrating the Life of St Alban that he translated from Latin into Anglo-Norman in about the 1240s. The scene is set in the time of King Offa, but the workmen are shown as if they were Matthew's contemporaries.

grims coming in rapidly-escalating numbers to the tomb of Thomas Becket, murdered barely four years previously. William of Sens was appointed after a kind of competition between different masters, and so it can safely be assumed that the monks knew precisely what they were letting themselves in for. One of the monks, Gervase, wrote a detailed account of the fire and rebuilding, enabling the progress of events at Canterbury to be traced in exceptional detail, year by year, from 1174 to 1184.[4]

The Gothic style of architecture is in a sense a masonry idiom: it depended on the working of the masonry, upon the cutting of the stones that formed load-bearing arches and window tracery according to outlines that a master prepared and then gave to his masons to follow. Williams of Sens will have done as all subsequent Gothic and Perpendicular architects did: he will have made 'moulds' or outlines, presumably of wood, and then handed these to the masons who cut the stones. Medieval architects would create their stock of drawings for moulds during their working career, taking them from one commission to another – thus permitting modern architectural historians to track their progress: Only if the architects worked for, say, the Crown's office of works at Westminster, would they have made use of an existing archive of drawings (and, presumably, have had to contribute some of their own drawings to it).

William of Sens remodelled the Canterbury choir in just three years, but in 1177 he fell from a lofty piece of scaffolding and appears to have been crippled; he returned to France and died there in 1180. His successor at the Cathedral, William the Englishman, was described by Gervase as 'small in body, but in workmanship of many kinds acute and honest'. He was actually more of an innovator than William of Sens, for the Trinity Chapel and Corona which he designed are stylistically far more advanced than the choir (see the illustration opposite). The English Gothic style which developed over the next half-century and more is distinguished by a richness of decoration of its arch mouldings that was far greater than that prevailing elsewhere in Europe; it depended both on thick walls (as in Romanesque buildings) and – metaphorically – on deep purses. French Gothic buildings might be taller, but their profiles were far simpler. Architecturally, the English Gothic style remained isolated from the Continent until the 1240s, when the rebuilding of the church of Westminster Abbey was undertaken at Henry III's behest. And virtually without exception, after William of Sens the architects of English buildings were all English.[5]

In manuscript illumination and the decorative arts, the Gothic style was established only from around 1220 onwards, developing from the English Romanesque style. But the enormous prestige of the Parisian court style that led Henry III into undertaking his great schemes for Westminster Abbey and the royal palaces also led to a change of style and design by the English book artists. Bibles, Psalters (traditionally, the books from which the children of the rich learnt to read, and which the rich themselves read for devotional purposes) and Apocalypse texts (of less explicable popularity, except that they lent themselves to illustrations) from about the 1260s show how quick English artists were to evolve an insular variant of the French styles: the English workshops, whether in Oxford or elsewhere, were alert to changes of fashion.

Yet workshops respond to fashions; they do not usually innovate. The finest illuminated books were probably painted in London, by members of a relatively small number of artists drawn there by the presence for much of the

The Trinity Chapel, Canterbury Cathedral, was rebuilt under the direction of the architect William the Englishman, *c.* 1181–84; the work proceeded from west to east. In the foreground is the archbishop's marble throne, also 12th-century.

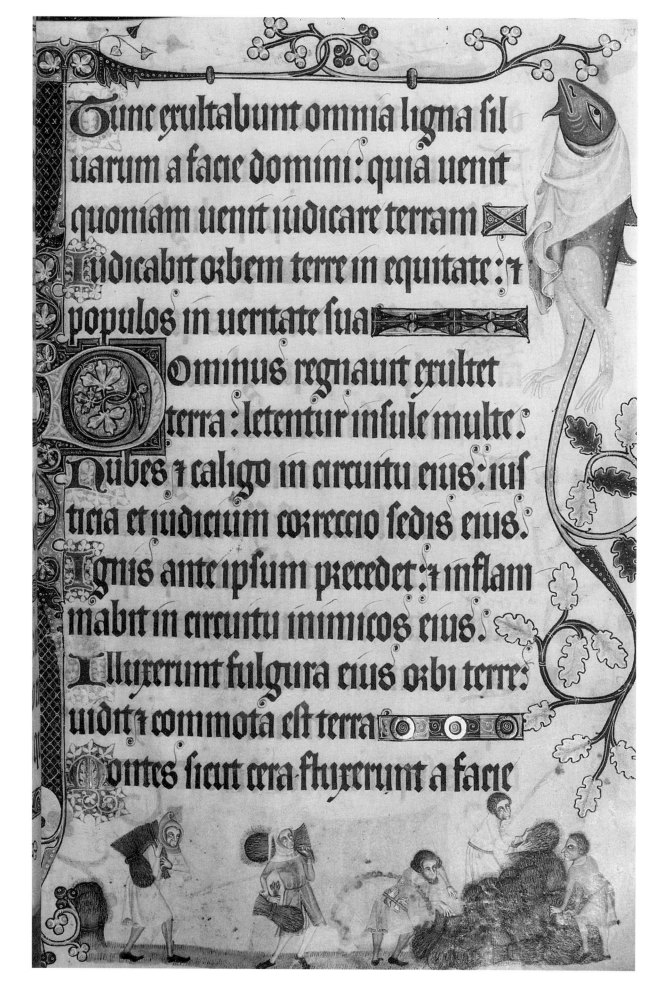

Tunc exultabunt omnia ligna sil
uarum a facie domini: quia uenit
quoniam uenit iudicare terram
Iudicabit orbem terre in equitate: ⁊
populos in ueritate sua

Ominus regnauit exultet
terra: letentur insule multe.
Nubes ⁊ caligo in circuitu eius: ius
ticia et iudicium correccio sedis eius.
Ignis ante ipsum precedet: ⁊ inflam
mabit in circuitu inimicos eius.
Illuxerunt fulgura eius orbi terre:
uidit ⁊ commota est terra
Montes sicut cera fluxerunt a facie

time of Henry III's court. The so-called Westminster Psalter (British Library, Royal MS 2 A. XXII) belonged to Westminster Abbey from the time that it was first made, *c.* 1200, and so the very fine tinted drawings that were added to it *c.* 1250 can safely be assumed to have been executed by an artist based in Westminster, or at least in London. Of no less high quality are the paintings of the Westminster Retable, the famed painting that has already been mentioned as long hidden from view by serving as a table-top; it is an attractive hypothesis that this was made for the Abbey's high altar and was in place for the dedication of the sanctuary in 1269.[6] On the other hand, although its paintings are of an outstanding quality, it is hard to credit that a retable made merely of wood and set round the edge with cameos that were only of glass would have been regarded as appropriate for such a setting; a silver-gilt retable, set with precious or semi-precious stones, would have been more likely, by any European country's standards. The medieval aesthetic was not the same as the present century's, and placed a far higher value upon quality of materials (which were esteemed for more than just their monetary value). The Coronation Chair, of *c.* 1300, also chances to survive at Westminster Abbey, having been made to enclose the Stone of Scone which Edward I had removed from Scotland in 1296 (see the illustration on p. 238); here, documentary evidence suggests that the wooden chair was only intended as a temporary creation, made to serve until a bronze version had been cast.[7]

In the fourteenth century the Court style of painting and drawing continued for another generation, into the 1320s; the name of the principal artist has not yet been identified, and he is referred to by art historians as the Queen Mary Master, after his masterpiece, the Queen Mary Psalter (British Library, Royal MS 2 B.VII; it owes its name to its having been seized by a customs official and presented to Queen Mary in 1553), in which he made all 223 tinted drawings. A number of artists worked in the same style as this prolific master, gentle and restrained, graceful and delicately linear; it was not uncommon for a major book commission to be shared among several artists, and the Queen Mary Master himself collaborated with other artists on at least two books. A style might be shared by different members of one workshop or even by rivals who had once worked together, perhaps as fellow apprentices.

The Queen Mary Master is assumed to have worked in London, but, artists being peripatetic, there can be no certainty that it was even the principal base either for him or for the practitioners of his style. The leading alternative style of the period, now termed the East Anglian, was far from being limited to books produced in or for Norfolk, Suffolk and the adjacent Fenland; it was, however, a coherent although developing style, marked above all by its exuberant marginal decoration. In its richness of decoration, it – and not the Court or Queen Mary style – matches the Decorated style that was now the fashionable architectural and sculptural idiom throughout England.[8]

The disappearance of the Queen Mary style after the 1320s – seemingly to be replaced at Court by commissions being given to a diverse variety of practitioners – left the East Anglian as the prevailing national style. And the end of both the East Anglian and Decorated styles in the 1340s has led art historians to blame the Black Death of (especially) 1348–49 for creating this void. It is very difficult to know how to measure the plague's impact on art, since it raises questions not only of human mortality but also of the unquantifiable – artistic style. Far too few works of art are reliably dated, and so there has at times been a tendency for art historians to date their execution

Facing page Detail from the Luttrell Psalter, made for Sir Geoffrey Luttrell of Irnham (Lincolnshire) between *c.* 1325 and 1340. The illustration in the lower margin shows men bringing in and stacking the sheaves of corn at harvest-time.

to shortly before the Black Death, on the ground that they could not postdate it and yet came late in terms of development of the style that they are in. The most celebrated East Anglian production of all, the Luttrell Psalter (British Library, MS. Add. 42,130; see the illustration on p. 152), can – exceptionally – be dated with confidence to not later than 1340, since it shows its patron, Sir Geoffrey Luttrell's wife, as alive, and she is known to have died in 1340; yet its date of execution has been variously put between *c.* 1325 and 1340.[9] The richness of the Luttrell Psalter and certain other East Anglian works, as well as of some Decorated sculptural works, has at times been labelled 'decadent', and so it has even been implied in a judgemental sense that the Black Death was somehow appropriate as a punishment.

Such moralising is as absurd as suggesting that the image of Charles I in Van Dyck's portraits somehow reveals a foresight of his execution. The Black Death had a dramatic effect on English art, but it was by wiping out large numbers of artists and patrons, and not by leading in any direct sense to a change of stylistic direction. In the 1350s and 1360s there were quite simply very few patrons, individual or institutional, with money to spare for works of art; and there were probably very few artists available to execute such commissions as there were. It may have been, for instance, because of a lack of native monumental brass makers that some English patrons in the third quarter of the fourteenth century turned to Flemish workshops for their memorials.[10] The Flemish brasses, as it happens, were larger and richer in detail than their contemporary English counterparts, and were no doubt costlier, too.

The Perpendicular style of architecture can be traced back to the early fourteenth century; if there is any one individual with whom its early genesis should be connected, it is a Kentish master mason, Michael of Canterbury (d. 1321?). He is first recorded in the 1270s as an architect in the employ of Canterbury Cathedral Priory, but in the early 1290s he made one of the Eleanor Crosses for Edward I (as part of Edward's commemoration of his wife, Eleanor of Castile) and at almost the same date he began to design the royal chapel of St Stephen in Westminster Palace; it was the tracery grid on the outside of St Stephen's chapel that in the 1330s became the basis for Perpendicular architecture, being followed in the design for the chapter house and cloister of St Paul's Cathedral, London (destroyed in the Fire of London but recorded in seventeenth-century engravings by Wenceslas Hollar). The Perpendicular style's aesthetic and its highly linear emphasis may well have been a reaction to the lively exuberance of the Decorated style; it was certainly not a response to the mortality caused by the Black Death.

It would be hazardous, too, to associate with the bubonic plague's after-effects some of the societal changes that can be discerned in the later fourteenth century. How, for example, is one to explain the greater emphasis on realistic portraiture which becomes more evident from this period? Can it be related to a greater value that (supposedly) was placed on the individual? And what were the factors that led Richard II into promoting his regal office? The trends towards realism in portraiture can equally be explained in terms of contemporary continental artistic fashion; the vogue had already taken root in France, and Richard, like all his aristocratic contemporaries in England, looked to Paris as the centre of all that was fashionable. Furthermore, realistic portraiture was an obvious counterpart to the no-less-fashionable International Gothic style in painting in which the leading English artists participated fully in the closing years of the fourteenth century and the opening years of the fifteenth. The supreme exemplar of this style in England is the Wilton Diptych (see the colour plate on p. 227), which is a brilliant anonymous masterpiece that has defied all efforts to pin its artist to any single country's tradition, and which is also both a palpable, recognisable portrait of Richard II and a symbolic and idealised representation that may be intended to show the monarch either as he was at the time or as he had been, or perhaps even as he might be, if conceived as a soul about to enter Heaven.[11] All that has been established with reasonable certainty is that it cannot have been painted earlier than 1396 (or possibly 1395), since it shows Richard wearing a collar of broom-pods, and these were a French livery or device that he was presented with by Charles VI in 1396 (and possibly also in the previous year). The outer sides of the two panels are painted with Richard's device of a white hart lying amid branches of rosemary, and, on the other panel, his coat of arms, the English royal arms impaled with the arms attributed to Edward the Confessor. When closed, the diptych would thus have seemed a purely secular work of art.

The insides of the panels, however, have a self-evidently devotional purpose: they show, on the left side, Richard, kneeling, with, gesturing towards him, three saints for whom he is known to have had a particular devotion – Edmund, martyred king of the East Angles, Edward the Confessor and Richard's patron saint, John the Baptist. On the facing panel are St Mary the Virgin holding the infant Christ, and, standing or kneeling around her, a group of angels. One of the angels carries a banner that is of white with a red cross, such as was commonly shown in medieval paintings as being carried by Christ at His Resurrection. All the angels are wearing broom-pod collars and white hart badges, although these are not bejewelled like those worn by Richard. Overall, the impression is given that Richard is being presented by the three saints to the Virgin, that Christ and the Virgin are looking at him (though Christ's eyes are possibly looking a little above Richard's and conceivably are intended to be focused on the banner's staff or one of the saints), and that Christ either is beckoning Richard towards Himself or perhaps is blessing him.

The diptych's meaning or significance is highly uncertain: too little is still known about medieval gestures for it to be possible to say with any confidence what is intended by the hand movements either of Richard or of Christ. Is Richard shown as having just given or received something, or are his hands open in wonderment and adoration? Only from the answers to such questions of detail can it be said how the diptych's overall subject-matter and purpose were intended to be understood. Nor need there have been just one meaning or level of meaning; the work may well have been meant to be 'read' in both a secular and a spiritual way, for to any medieval person the two worlds were inextricably fused. And Richard, of all English rulers, was perhaps the most fully conscious of the sacred character of his regal office.

The name of the artist responsible for painting the Wilton Diptych may yet be discovered by research in Richard's accounts in the Public Record Office. It would not be surprising if it proved to be that of a Frenchman or Italian, perhaps an Italian resident for some years in England. If so, the diptych could also be said to foreshadow the trend for the next century and a half in English painting, for most of the identifiable leading artists in England seem then to have come from the Continent. Ironically enough, it was only after the iconoclastic sixteenth century that there emerged a vigorous English tradition in painting that was capable of reaching the highest level of painterly skills. The succession of continental artists, many of them from the Low Countries or Germany, from Herman Scheere at the start of the fifteenth century to Hans Holbein the Younger in the 1520s and 1530s, had no English pupils or followers of comparable talent. Ironically, too, the practitioners of the highly insular Perpendicular style of architecture continued to be capable of evoking new variants that attained new heights of structural ingenuity and technical virtuosity, and, in the early sixteenth century, they successfully adopted the style to a new material, brick.

Many of the finer exponents of the English linear tradition were not artists of the book, still less of panel-painting, but were practitioners of sculpture and especially of the decorative arts. Linear designs are of course perfectly suited to textiles, and the English were always renowned for their skill at producing embroideries – 'English work', as it was known abroad (*opus anglicanum*; the French, by contrast, were characterised by their architecture, *opus francigenum*).[12] In the thirteenth and fourteenth centuries especially, it was sought after throughout Europe; a very detailed papal inventory of 1295 includes far more pieces of *opus anglicanum* than of any other kind of embroidery. The English embroiderers' workshops undoubtedly produced a wide range of heraldic and other secular pieces, for these figure in many inventories and accounts, but virtually none survive; some fragments in the Musée de Cluny, Paris, showing leopards, are perhaps the remains of a horse-trapper made for royal use (and if so, and if lilies were not on a missing portion, they can be dated to before 1340, when Edward III had the French arms of fleurs-de-lis quartered with the leopards of England as the new English royal arms).[13] Far better preserved are a considerable number of copes (see the illustration opposite), chasubles and other ecclesiastical vestments; these characteristically display a lavish use of silk and gold or silver-gilt thread, decorated with pearls and precious stones, and would accordingly have been extremely expensive. They remain in fine condition because, like regalia and the finest books, they were displayed or used only on special occasions.

Much cheaper, and far more widespread on the Continent, were another characteristic English product: panels and figures of alabaster, carved as religious imagery (see the illustration on p. 166). In Derbyshire and Staffordshire there were some of the best deposits in Europe of alabaster (a form of limestone, most prized when pure white and free from discoloration), and from the later fourteenth century onwards the panels and figures were marketed abroad with increasing success.[14] Their sales became a very considerable commercial enterprise, and in the fifteenth century a decline in general sculptural quality is undeniable, although the alabaster carvers were still capable of producing very fine work for special commissions, be it as devotional imagery or for tomb effigies. What happened was simply that the alabaster salesmen found that they were competing abroad with other mass-producers – for instance, the limewood carvers of north Germany and the scribes and illuminators of Books of Hours in the Low Countries – and they adapted their product accordingly. The English embroiderers were also faced with increasing competition in the fifteenth century, from the silks and velvets with woven patterns that were being produced in Italy and Spain; their response was to abandon their traditional technique of fixing gold threads by underside couching and to use instead the simpler method of surface couching. Simpler designs were also followed, with identical motifs, such as angels and conven-

tional flowers, being spread out over the plain materials (quite commonly, dark red velvet).

Goldsmiths – that is, makers of silver and gold plate and jewellery – must have prospered increasingly in the fourteenth and fifteenth centuries, as ownership of their wares became more widespread. It is true that the Crown and the aristocracy tended to buy their costliest plate either directly from Parisian goldsmiths or, much more commonly, from English goldsmiths or other merchants who imported it from abroad; but that was only at the top of the market, dominated by considerations of fashion. So little medieval plate survives that it is hard to assess it in stylistic terms, and, besides, for some of the goldsmith's products a style was followed that was *sui generis* (and so not easily dated). For a few products, such as censers and croziers, the detailed intricacies of Gothic architecture were an obvious challenge to a goldsmith's craftsmanly skills: the silver-gilt Ramsey Abbey censer of *c.* 1325 (Victoria and Albert Museum; see the colour plate on p. 174) is in the form of a miniature polygonal chapter-house and is presumably an example of the style occasionally referred to in documents as 'of masonry'.[15] Of architec-

The Pienza Cope: detail, showing the Nativity (left) and the Angel appearing to the Shepherds (right). This fine example of *opus anglicanum*, embroidered between *c.* 1315 and 1335, was doubtless exported shortly afterwards. It was given to Pienza Cathedral in 1462 by Pope Pius II; he is said to have received it from the Byzantine ruler Thomas Palaeologus, Despot of the Morea.

Christ has almost completely disappeared into the Heavens in this early fifteenth-century alabaster panel of the Ascension. Around the square platform from which He has ascended are the Apostles: Peter (centre left), with his key, kneels opposite Andrew, with the cross that was his attribute in medieval iconography.

There are several hundred medieval alabaster panels and figures in British museums, galleries and churches; all have either been rediscovered (after being concealed at the Reformation) or have been brought back from the Continent in the last three centuries.

tural inspiration, too, is the banding round some late medieval cups, such as the Lacock cup (on loan from Lacock church, Wiltshire, to the British Museum), a silver-gilt covered cup made for secular use in the first half of the fifteenth century, and preserved thanks to its having been put to use as a communion chalice.

Consideration of the decorative arts leads naturally into a discussion of questions of technique and artistic organisation. Yet similar questions equally deserve to be raised by an examination of painting and architecture. It is not merely a matter of styles and techniques cutting across the borders that in more recent times have come to separate the fine arts from the decorative arts and to isolate both from architecture; it is also that the constraints and opportunities inherent in all artists' working methods can best be understood if looked at from the widest perspective.

Common to all medieval commissions of art and architecture, for instance, was a separation of the cost of the materials and the artist's time. Unless an article was bought ready-made, its bill would always be broken down into these two distinct categories of cost. Hence, in the accounts of a late fifteenth-century dean of St Paul's Cathedral, William Worsley, a payment of £5 11s 8d to a London goldsmith for work on two dishes is broken down into 75s for the silver (22½ oz at 3s 4d per oz), 30s for his labour, and 6s 8d for burnishing the silver and for some mercury.[16] This payment, run-of-the-mill as it is, is suggestive too of another general trait of the artistic world, the tendency to specialise. A goldsmith was not a burnisher, but a rather more expensive kind of craftsman, and unless a goldsmith had a burnisher working in his own workshop or under contract to him, a patron or customer would have expected to have to pay separately for the burnisher to polish up brightly what the goldsmith had made. Only towards the end of the Middle Ages, and especially in London, did workshops tend to become so large that they contained several specialists as well as journeymen (ex-apprentices who had not set up on their own) who could undertake a range of related activities, although still all within the same medium. Thirteenth- and fourteenth-century records abound with references to craftworkers whose occupation may seem unnaturally specialised – forcermakers (makers of caskets and coffers), sheathers (makers of leather sheaths) and quernpeckers (indenters of the surface of millstones), as well as the more familiar horners, wimplers and bell-makers. Occasionally there were artists whose skills extended to several kinds of work – like Henry Yevele, the late fourteenth-century architect and sculptor (or at least, designer of sculpture), or the thirteenth-century draughtsman, engraver and *littérateur* Matthew Paris, monk of St Albans Abbey – but such geniuses were rare, and they tended to be amateurs, like Matthew Paris or master Hugo, monk of Bury St Edmunds Abbey in the twelfth century, who was lauded as a carver of wood and stone and as a bell-founder. Though the issue was hotly disputed earlier in this century, it is now accepted that from about the first half of the twelfth century onwards almost all craftsmen were lay professionals.

Most artists and craftsmen belonged to a guild. There were benefits in this both for them and for the public who acquired their products. The guilds set up monopolies, or at least tried to do so, but that was a necessary precondition to their being able to control and regulate their particular area of activity; those who belonged to a guild were protected from interlopers, while the guild itself served to protect the consumer by enforcing the maintenance of certain standards of production. Guilds were, of course, unable to regulate what happened in towns other than the ones where they were located, and so those artists and craftsmen who habitually travelled around the country – masons and, to a lesser extent, scribes and book-illuminators, were only marginally affected by the guild-system. Who is to say whether this benefited either their art or the consumer? It is arguable that the tighter guild structure in Paris resulted in books being produced there in the late twelfth and thirteenth centuries to a more highly standardised level of fineness; and yet it is not really possible to make a valid comparison, since English book production at that time was probably centred largely outside London, and Europe's

The interrelationship of designs, in this case by their having an ultimate common source, is shown by a tile from Tring (Hertfordshire) with miraculous scenes from the Infancy of Christ, and illustrations of the same two scenes in an Anglo-Norman text. In the first scene Jesus sows corn and an abundant harvest is gathered; in the second he is told of some pigs that have been locked in an oven. Both tile and illuminations are of the same date, *c.* 1315–25.

guilds were always at their most effective in the larger cities.

It is arguable, too, that the master masons did not need to be protected or coerced by a guild, both because their work was plain for all to see and judge, and because their greatest patrons were the Crown, the aristocracy and the wealthier ecclesiastics and ecclesiastical institutions, all of which also existed outside the world of the guilds. Those who wished to work for the Court, whether as painters, carpenters, glaziers or architects, had to impress their own peers; the Court, and above all the Crown, being the greatest fount of artistic patronage, there must always have been a stream of those who were eager to gain commissions from it. And just as the guilds of London drew constantly on a flow of people coming in from the countryside, so too the Court drew on different parts of England for its favoured few. Different regions were to the fore at different times: in the footsteps of Michael of Canterbury came a succession of other Kentish architects (unsurprisingly, perhaps, since Kent was a county full of stone quarries and masons), while East Anglia and Lincolnshire provided a sizeable proportion of the Crown's painters over the course of the fourteenth century. The London guilds' members generally stayed in London for the rest of their working lives, but the artists who worked on commissions for the Crown would doubtless often return to the region that they came from. It has been pointed out that several of those who worked as painters on the Painted Chamber at Westminster in 1307 had surnames indicating that they came from towns or villages in Lincolnshire, Norfolk and Suffolk, and that from this it may – very tentatively – be possible to infer a court origin for the 'East Anglian' style of book illumination.[17] More certainly, the master John Bernetby who in 1341 was paid the large sum of £15 for painting the retable and tabernacle of the high altar of Thornton Abbey, Lincolnshire, can be identified with John Barneby, who worked at St Stephen's Chapel, Westminster.[18] By such means, the fashionable style of the Court could trickle back to the provinces.

Judged by today's standards, the medieval aesthetic was contrary in the extreme. Works of art were valued because of the intrinsic value of their component parts – their break-up value, as well as the special value or virtue that was attached for example to each of the precious and semi-precious stones and even to the precious metals, gold and silver – and because of the skill with which they were made. Since there was also a preference for the symbolic and ideal, as opposed to the naturalistic and what counterfeited reality, it is not surprising that representations of individual mortals were slow in making their appearance. Innovation was almost the last quality to be prized by a patron. Of the many dozens of medieval contracts that survive, none specifies novelty, but many require the architect or craftsman to copy an existing work.[19] Patrons wished to know exactly what they were going to get, and they were not concerned that it was going to replicate with minor variants something that was several years old. Hence, no doubt, the various 'near-pairs' of some surviving books and other works of art (see also the illustrations opposite and on p. 162).[20]

John de Grandisson, bishop of Exeter from 1327 to 1369, has been posited as a leading and influential patron of the arts. So in many ways he was. He built up a collection of books, totalling several dozen (a very large collection at the time); these were mostly just texts, but they included a few that were richly decorated. He was evidently particularly proud of an illuminated psalter

Neck of a gittern. Wood, carved in the early fourteenth century, probably in England. The scenes of hunters with dogs are paralleled in contemporary English manuscript illustrations. The gittern (or cithern) is a guitar-like musical instrument; its bow is on the left.

that he owned (British Library, MS Add. 21,926, now known as the Grandisson Psalter; see the illustration opposite), for he had a tinted drawing added at the front, of a standing angel holding a shield with his arms, and he ultimately bequeathed the book to Edward III's daughter Isabella. Yet the psalter was far from new when he acquired it, having been written and illuminated, perhaps within the diocese of Chichester, in about the 1270s, a full fifty years earlier.[21] He was a notably diligent bishop of his diocese, travelling much within it and rarely outside it, save when he went to sessions of Parliament or the Convocation of the Canterbury province; to his cathedral church he apparently contributed the cost of completing the nave and adding the whole west front, with its profusion of statuary. He also refounded and built the church of Ottery St Mary, Devon. The Grandissons were a Savoyard family, and John de Grandisson studied both civil law, probably in Oxford, and theology, in Paris, and then, like many civil lawyers, he acted as a diplomat; he was thus a widely travelled man by the time he was consecrated bishop of Exeter at the age of about 35. His will mentions an impressive number of textiles, and several of these survive, identifiable as having been made for him by the presence of his coat of arms. Art historians have found particularly interesting his commissions of three ivories (see the illustration on p. 172), each of which, though carved by an Englishman, shows a clear indebtedness to near-contemporary Italian works of art:[22] the representation on one, of the Virgin and Child embracing, is almost certainly based on a painting by Ambrogio Lorenzetti. It would, however, be misleading to infer from these that Grandisson held advanced artistic views, or had an interest in the exotic, or was in any sense 'forward-looking'; he was cosmopolitan in that he was well-travelled, and hence had been able to acquire works of art in Paris or made 'in the Roman manner', but in his taste he was utterly conventional, with an inor-

Grandisson Psalter. Historiated initial 'B', for the opening word, 'Beatus', of Psalm 1; illuminated in England, possibly at Chichester, in about the 1270s. Within the initial are shown scenes from the life of David (above) and the Judgement of Solomon (below). The psalter subsequently belonged to John de Grandisson, bishop of Exeter (d. 1369), who added his initials and two drawings of his coat of arms.

Ivory triptych, carved in England in about the 1330s. Its general format and such iconographic motifs as the swooning Virgin Mary and onlookers at the Crucifixion (below) and the Virgin's resigned acceptance of her divine role, in the Annunciation (above), are reminiscent of contemporary Italian panel-paintings. It was commissioned by John de Grandisson, bishop of Exeter (d. 1369), as is shown by the heraldry and the identity of the saints: at upper left and right, Peter and Paul (to whom Exeter Cathedral is dedicated); at lower left, Stephen (dedicatee of an altar in Exeter Cathedral); and at lower right, Thomas Becket (of whom Grandisson wrote a Life). Grandisson's arms are above Stephen and Becket.

dinate fondness for seeing his own coat of arms. His importance as a patron, then, is that he was typical of his age, and that, by chance, a considerable number of his commissions have come down to us, more or less intact.

Some artistic practices positively militated against innovation. For one thing, there was an increasing tendency in the later Middle Ages to separate the execution of works from their design. The master-masons' practice of preparing moulding-profiles came to have its counterpart in the artists' and craftsmen's resort to sheets of patterns. These had the benefit of allowing what might be called the cross-over of designs or motifs from one medium to another. The sole surviving medieval English pattern-book, the Pepysian Sketchbook at Magdalene College, Cambridge, has designs for architecture, for paintings and perhaps tapestries, all brought together at some point in the fifteenth century. Goldsmiths doubtless used drawings to show to patrons; in 1331 Queen Philippa paid the London goldsmith Simon de Berking 2s for the drawing of a ship on parchment, to have a model by which a ship for alms (or

Initial by William de Brailes. The initial letter in this Book of Hours shows a tonsured man; the inscription reads: 'w de brail qui me depeint' ('W. de Brailes who drew me'), and is a vital clue for the elucidation of the activity of this Oxford artist of the mid-thirteenth century. His tonsure shows that he was at least in minor orders, and his inscription indicates that he was bilingual, since he must also have been fluent in English.

Ramsey Abbey censer and boat.
The design of the upper half of the
censer is like that of a monastic
chapter-house. Both censer and
boat may well have belonged to
Ramsey Abbey (Huntingdonshire),
since the boat has finials in the
form of rams' heads, and both were
discovered *c.* 1850 in the nearby
Whittlesey Mere. They are of silver-
gilt, the censer of *c.* 1325 and the
boat of *c.* 1350.

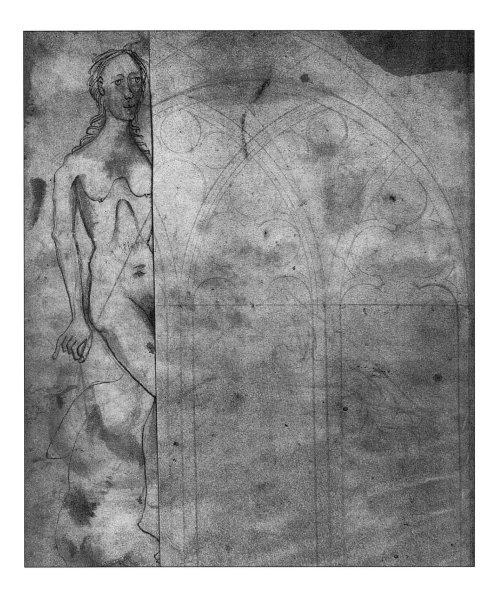

Drawings of varying dates and purposes were bound up as the Pepysian Sketch-book (so called from its having belonged to the diarist Samuel Pepys). On this sheet of parchment, experimental designs for window tracery are combined with a naturalistic drawing of a nude woman, of the late fifteenth century.

nef) could be made. One implication here is that the goldsmith in question was not necessarily going to make the *nef* personally.

Furthermore, while the transfer of designs from one medium to another may in the short run have been invigorating to the recipient medium (and the invention of the woodcut was to make this an extremely common practice in the Renaissance, rendering the designs of, say, Dürer almost universally familiar), in the longer term its effect was probably stultifying. The occasional use of pattern sheets would tend to descend into reliance on a limited range of designs which would be used time and again over what might be a period of many years – just as goldsmiths might use the same moulds for a generation or more. The drawings in the Pepsyian sketchbook (see the illustration above) range over a period of several decades, from the late fourteenth century onwards, while some may actually be copies of late thirteenth-century works of art. J. A. Knowles thought that one reason for the decline in the quality of later medieval stained glass in England was the abandonment of specialist stained-glass designers in favour of the repetition of figures, poses and gestures from the stock of cartoons in the glazier's workshop. If such a wholesale abandonment did take place in any workshops, it was certainly an end to what had been the master glazier's principal role, for he would not have painted any glass himself.

It is hard to assess how the growing commercialism or, at least, attempts at mass production in the late Middle Ages affected the position of the artists themselves.[23] Aesthetic standards were not lowered, nor were the richer patrons any less demanding, just because run-of-the-mill works of art were more cheaply and readily available. Talented artists were always scarce and were presumably valued accordingly, although architects remained the most highly esteemed, considerably ahead of sculptors. Painters were only highly regarded from the time in the sixteenth century when they became appreciated for their skill at capturing people's likenesses; before then, they could hardly expect to be ranked ahead of other image-makers, since their principal output was for the ecclesiastical world. Patrons who wanted to impress their visitors commissioned tapestries or goldsmiths' work, not paintings, throughout the Middle Ages; both cost far more than paintings.

It would be misleading to seek to categorise rigidly each artistic medium's practitioners, however, for the nature of their various activities was liable to change enormously. Glaziers in the fifteenth century ceased to be producers of a translucent architectural adjunct, and became instead exponents of a branch of the painter's art. Goldsmiths and other metalworkers, and probably also the majority of book-artists, came to be organised in workshops located in London, and their status reflected the commercial reality of whether they owned and ran the workshop or merely worked for it. If they ran the business, then they very likely operated as merchants, rather than craftsmen, and they may have imported from abroad quite as much as they either subcontracted or had made under their own eyes. Of architects alone can it simply be said that their societal standing remained high, and perhaps – thanks to the perception of their knowledge of applied geometry and sophisticated draughtsmanship – edged higher. In the 1330s John de Grandisson referred to Thomas of Witney, the architect in charge of the building works at Exeter Cathedral as a 'dearly loved member of our household' (*dilectus familiaris noster*).[24] William de Ramsey, the first exponent of the Perpendicular style in his work at St Paul's Cathedral, had by the time of his death in 1349 a finely cut seal with his own coat of arms: a pair of compasses between two rams' heads erased in chief and a gateway in base. A good many goldsmiths had their own seal (which they doubtless made themselves), and a few also laid claim to a coat of arms, but no other craftsman is known to have matched the architects William Wynford (architect of the nave of Winchester Cathedral) and Henry Yevele (architect of the reconstruction of Westminster Hall, and of much else for the Crown and other patrons) in dining frequently at high table in New College, Oxford, at the invitation of Bishop William of Wykeham.

In the Middle Ages, works of art were valued most for the richness of their materials; the artist therefore was judged according to his skill in working as a craftsman with the materials in which he specialised. By the early sixteenth century, however, there was a new criterion: the artist's ability to use his materials to represent the natural world and those who inhabited it. Where once an artist had been judged on the sense of richness and virtue evident in his creation, he was now esteemed according to his ability to transcend his materials. He might not be representing another world; but whatever he drew, he needed to represent with apparent fidelity.[25]

POLITICS AND
THE NATION

THE POLITICAL INSTITUTIONS OF THE REALM

Ralph Griffiths

The political institutions of later medieval England were largely the king's institutions, directed either by him or in his name. This goes for those institutions which were lodged in or near the Great Hall of the royal palace at Westminster, or in or near the Tower on the edge of the city of London; it goes, too, for those provincial institutions which were a focus of political life in the shires, the county court especially. Only those institutions – the households and councils of nobles, archbishops and bishops – that had political significance because of the influence which particular nobles and great ecclesiastics enjoyed locally and in the realm at large were not the king's. England, then, was a highly personal and relatively compact monarchy, and there was little – if anything – that a king did or said, publicly or in private, which did not have a political dimension. It was a commonplace in the later Middle Ages to compare the king's realm to the human body, and the following excerpt from a speech prepared by Bishop John Russell for the opening of Parliament in 1483 would have been readily and widely understood (though the Parliament itself never met): 'In this politic body of England there be .iii. estates as principal members under one head – the estate of the lords spiritual, the estate of the lords temporal, and the estate of the commonalty. The head is our sovereign lord the king here present.'[1] In the later Middle Ages, this king was a person of flesh and blood who at the same time embodied an institution – the Crown, the monarchy. Ever since the Norman Conquest, kings had owned vast lands, the royal demesne, the Crown estate; and by the thirteenth century lawyers and politicians were able to separate in their minds an individual king from the institutional Crown, especially when exasperated by the actions of Henry III (who faced civil war in the 1250s and 1260s) and Edward II (who was deposed and murdered in 1327). Such ideas were less popular in later years, for the fourteenth and fifteenth centuries saw the public

The coronation of Edward III, from an Order of Service of *c.* 1330–39. The crowned king, holding the sceptre and orb, is seated on an elaborate throne in Westminster Abbey. He is surrounded by bishops, lay lords, lawyers and clerks, some of whom offer gifts. In the background, the general public is shown as if peering through a grille.

elevation of kings and monarchy to heights of majesty not previously attained, by means of ceremony, symbolism and theory, and by the hardening custom of hereditary succession and the special reverence accorded to those of royal blood, 'the royal stock', the dynasty. Later medieval kings used the royal 'we' and Richard II spoke of 'our crown' as if they and he were special trustees of a unique institution which they embodied. They did so whether they were infantile or senile or prostrate with illness: the English Crown was a perpetual institution. No longer were justiciars or regents appointed to rule in place of young kings or kings who were absent from their realm for long periods; rather were 'keepers', 'guardians' or 'protectors' nominated merely to safeguard the interests of monarchs who retained their regal powers, no matter where they were or how old or sane they were. This was, it is true, an age of unprecedented turbulence around kings, even of civil wars, depositions and the murders of kings and the children of kings; yet the Crown as an institution seemed scarcely damaged in any permanent way by this turbulence, and usurpers and pretenders claimed to be no lesser kings than those whom they sought to displace. Kingship, Crown and the monarchy were deeply complex phenomena, full of paradoxes, and central to English political life.[2]

Certain qualities were expected of all these kings. They included traditional qualities that harked back centuries; others emerged from more recent developments. In the later Middle Ages, warfare was still a frequent resort of politics, and since kings swore at their coronation (see the illustration opposite) to defend the liberties of their subjects and the Church, they were expected to lead their subjects into battle when necessary and to win victories. Only the boy-king Edward V, who reigned for just ten weeks in 1483, and the pacific Henry VI, whose reign of thirty-nine years (1422–61) is one of the longest in English history, never commanded an army against an enemy or in defence of their dominions; Henry's omission helped to produce the tide of dissatisfaction with his rule that led to his deposition in 1461. Edward II's crushing defeat by the Scots at Bannockburn in 1314 tarnished his reputation, and the turning of the tide of the Hundred Years War against England in the 1370s and 1380s helped to sour relations between the new young king, Richard II, and his greater subjects. By the same token, the resounding successes of both Edward III and Henry V against the French so elevated their reputations at home and abroad that they were regarded by contemporaries – and historians have frequently agreed with them – as paragons among medieval kings. Effective defenders and victorious warriors were still exemplars of good kingship.[3]

English kings were expected to be staunch defenders of the Church, as their coronation oath again made clear. Indeed, success in war was a most persuasive sign of God's favour; contrariwise, a king's defeat in battle might encourage rivals to challenge or deny his kingship and, as with Henry Tudor in 1485, to do so with the apparent approval of the Almighty. In cold reality, this spiritual quality of kingship may have been less compelling than it had once been in an age of deeper faith, for in the later Middle Ages kings were increasingly successful in bending the English Church as an institution – its resources and personnel – to their own practical, political purposes. This meant that after the clashes between Edward I and Pope Boniface VIII over the rights of the Church and papacy in England, and between the youthful Edward III and Archbishop John Stratford over how to govern England when the king was warring abroad, the Church gave steadfast support to English kings and supplemented spiritual endorsement with practical aid. Statutes of Edward III and Richard II curbed the pope's temporal authority in England, but this did not stop archbishops and bishops from mobilising the clergy and people, by means of sermons, processions, prayers and taxation, in support of the king and his policies. It was about this time, from Richard II's reign onwards, that kings placed great store by anointment at their coronation with the 'holy oil' said to have been given 200 years earlier to Thomas Becket by an angel despatched from the Virgin Mary – the 'balm [of] an anointed king', as Shakespeare memorably put it. A haughty Richard, when pressed to abdicate by his cousin, Henry Bolingbroke, duke of Lancaster, at the most dangerous moment of his life, in 1399, declared that he could not surrender what God had laid upon him, and both kings and pretenders to the English Crown affected to embrace this belief during the dynastic crises of the following century. It enhanced and sustained the pretensions of kingship in England, and underlined the special quality of the royal blood.[4]

English kings' insistence that they were emperors in their kingdom was quite recent too. It had greater force following the loss of English lands in France in King John's day, and it was reflected in the more robust attitude to the pope's temporal claims in England, as well as in English kings' determination to match the claims of French monarchs since about 1200 that they enjoyed independent, self-contained sovereignty in their kingdom (or empire). By the mid-fifteenth century, English publicists like Sir John Fortescue, Henry VI's chief justice, were insisting that 'from of old [English kings] have reigned independently, and acknowledged no superior on earth in things temporal'. This was a popular refrain in poem and song, and the new style of closed (or arched) crown designed for Henry V, and worn by his successors, epitomised this quality of English kingship.[5] The commons in Parliament understandably became apprehensive about the place which England might occupy in any dual Anglo-French monarchy that a victorious Edward III or Henry V might create, and in 1363 Edward also proposed the creation of a dual Anglo-Scottish monarchy. They need not have worried that the English monarchy would lose its identity as a consequence. None of these schemes came to pass, and in any case their planning took place at Westminster and Windsor, not even in Rouen or Paris following Henry V's great victories in 1417–19. English kings clung, with increasing unreality, to their claim to be kings of France until 1802; towards Scotland, they periodically insisted (until 1603) only on superior lordship over the northern monarchs.

At the same time, English kings came to rule more than the realm of England. After the death of Llywelyn, the last independent prince of Wales (1282), the king gained a principality that covered half of Wales and was 'annexed and united' to the realm, thereafter to be administered by the king or his eldest son. The rest of Wales belonged to English nobles, the lords of the Welsh marches, and the politics of the principality and marches were often central to English political life, for the marcher lords were among the greater nobles, present in Parliament and prominent in the king's counsels and at his court. Ireland, where the king was lord (before Henry VIII declared himself king in 1541), had its royal territories too, while English nobles like the Mortimers had large lordships there. These and other interests – including Calais and Gascony – were part of English politics and were managed by English political institutions, as Edward I recognised as early as 1275, when he declared it to be his obligation to offer justice to all his subjects.[6] The machinery of government and politics was adapted to the needs of 'Greater England' following the collapse of the Angevin empire at the beginning of the thirteenth century.

Acceptance of hereditary succession in the male line gave continuity and stability to England's kingship. It facilitated a peaceful transition from one reign to the next, even when the reigning king's eldest son – or grandson, in the case of Richard II – was a minor. The accession in 1216 of Henry III, the 9-year-old son of King John, proved to be an important precedent. Not only was his accession notable for taking place in the midst of civil war – though it was politically astute to acclaim a blameless lad at a time when Prince Louis of

France was invading the country – but this was the first time since the Norman Conquest that a minor had been accepted as king. The example of Henry's accession helped to ensure that the 10-year-old Richard II, Edward III's grandson, should succeed in 1377 with scarcely a murmur of dissent, rather than one of Edward's younger sons. And yet in 1399 and several times thereafter, the custom appears to have been breached. This was the result of the political and personal failures of individual kings, particularly Richard II himself and Henry VI, or else of the ambitions of royal relatives (as with Richard, duke of Gloucester, who took advantage of the minority of his nephew, Edward V, to seize the Crown for himself in 1483), and the readiness of certain nobles to exploit the political circumstances of 1399, 1461 and 1483 in their own interests. When Edward II was deposed in 1327, the custom of hereditary succession in the senior male line was not breached, because his eldest son replaced him as Edward III. But in 1399 Richard II had no children or younger brothers, and there was room for argument as to whether the usurper, Henry IV, who was descended from Edward III in the male line, or whether Richard's other cousin, the earl of March, who was descended from Edward in a senior though female line, was the rightful heir. The earl of March's descendant, Richard, duke of York, challenged Henry IV's grandson for the Crown in 1460. After the lords in Parliament declined to offer an opinion on a matter that was 'so high and of such weight that it was not right for any of the king's subjects to enter into communication thereof' alone, and the king's justices regarded it as 'above the law and passed their learning', there seemed no alternative but a resort to arms.[7] The constitutional custom of hereditary succession was not sufficiently developed to cope with this uncertainty, which muddied the political waters during the fifteenth century and threatened to place a check on royal powers.

In 1485, when Henry Tudor won a decisive victory at Bosworth Field, not all were convinced that the descendant of a female, illegitimate line from Edward III could be truly king of England. Matters were still unsettled in the sixteenth century, yet every one of those who claimed the Crown after 1399 maintained that his hereditary right was sound and sought to justify his actions by appealing to custom – though Henry VII wisely preferred to say as little as possible about heredity. In 1399 Henry IV went to elaborate and inventive lengths to demonstrate his claim, though Edward IV declared that the Lancastrian kings were no more than usurpers and merely kings *de facto*. Richard III resorted to even more outrageous fictions to justify his removal of 'the princes in the Tower', denouncing them and their father, Richard's own brother, Edward IV, as bastards. Richard's actions in 1483 could have undermined custom even further, for whereas minor kings – even a 9-month-old Henry VI in 1422 – had succeeded in the past, now a combination of fear, ambition and political ruthlessness led Richard to set aside the 12-year-old Edward V. In brief, it seems that so long as kings ruled as well as reigned, the succession of kings in England might be the occasion for political manoeuvre or dispute at critical moments. And yet no one seems to have championed an alternative to hereditary kingship: election produced neither stability nor strength in the Holy Roman Empire, while urban republicanism had no roots in England and, to judge by developments in northern Italy, was likely to result in tyranny.

None of this – not even God's sanction – meant that an English king had absolute or unchallengeable power. The way in which kings discharged their regal functions provided much of the stuff of politics; for the character and abilities of an individual king, along with the powers and obligations of his kingly office, were at the heart of political life in later medieval England. These powers and obligations were matters of frequent discussion among intellectuals, royal officials and the nobility and bishops, and the oath sworn by a king at his coronation summed them up: to provide justice as well as protection for all his subjects and for God's Church. Proposals that Edward II and Richard II, who tested their subjects' patience by their behaviour on more than one occasion, should swear the oath more than once suggest that it was an adequate touchstone of good government. There were available, too, from the thirteenth century onwards, manuals of theoretical and practical instruction on the regal qualities – 'Mirrors for Princes', as some of them were known.[8] Yet there was no acknowledged means on earth by which a king could be corrected or removed if he failed to discharge his obligations adequately. Moral and practical pressures were exerted on kings on many occasions in the three centuries following Magna Carta (1215), and on seven occasions between 1327 and 1485 kings were deposed and, save on one occasion (Henry VI's first dethronement in 1461), even killed.

By such means, limitations were placed on the king's powers at the same time as the scope of the king's authority in law-making and government was being broadened and the machinery of royal administration elaborated. And these limitations and the institutions that were intended to impose them were the outcome of political discussion and sometimes political conflict. According to Henry de Bracton, the notable legal writer and king's councillor in the mid-thirteenth century, 'The king ought not to be under any man but under God and the law, because the law makes the king . . . For there is no king where will rules and not law . . . For the king has a superior, namely God. Also, the law by which he is made king.' Two centuries later, Sir John Fortescue was in no doubt as to the value of such limitations, which in his view made England superior to other Western monarchies:

> There be two kinds of kingdoms, of the which that one is a lordship called in Latin *dominium regale* [regal dominion], and that other is called *dominium politicum et regale* [political and regal dominion]. And they are different in that the first king may rule his people by such laws as he makes himself. And therefore he may set upon them taxes and other impositions, such as he will himself, without their assent. The second king may not rule his people by other laws than such as they assent unto. And therefore he may set upon them no impositions without their own assent . . .
>
> But blessed be God, this land is ruled under a better law [than under regal law]; nor thereby hurt in their persons, but they be wealthy, and have all things necessary to the sustenance of nature. Wherefore they be mighty, and able to resist the adversaries of this realm, and to beat other realms that do, or would do, them wrong. Lo, this is the fruit of *Jus politicum et regale* [political and regal law] under which we live.[9]

The kings of England in the later Middle Ages – there were no queens regnant before Mary Tudor (1553) – are a motley group. Their individual personalities and abilities powerfully determined the politics of their reigns, including relations with their subjects. Yet, even in a hereditary monarchy, the hazards of life made it difficult to ensure that kings were educated and trained for kingship. Whereas Edward I was schooled in the politics and civil strife of his father's later years (which may have helped to make him a determined and overbearing king after 1272), he so distrusted his son, later Edward II, that he denied him much experience of government and politics before 1307. Some kings mounted the throne as boys, and others, like Henry V, were carefully educated not as prospective kings but as the sons or grandsons of nobles. This had its advantages, for it gave kings like Henry IV, Henry V and Edward IV an appreciation of aristocratic attitudes and expectations. Along with the distinctive status of the royal family from Edward I's reign onwards, and the role of the king's Court as a social and political environment (see the illustration on p. 188), it also had the effect of binding Crown and nobility together in what was, after all, a predominantly aristocratic society centred on the king. Over-mighty subjects existed: witness the rebellious Thomas, earl of Lancaster, in Edward II's reign and Warwick the Kingmaker in Edward IV's. But what is just as striking is the way in which during Henry VI's long minority (1422–36), the nobility did not dissolve into warring factions but co-operated sufficiently to preserve peace at home and continue Henry V's war in France. During Edward III's later years, it was not noble over-mightiness but scandalous royal officialdom that brought the king's government into disrepute. Over-mightiness arose, rather, from unusual ambition – like that of the disgruntled Percys in 1403 and the treacherous duke of Buckingham in 1483 – or disastrous rulership, like that of Henry VI, which led his cousin, York, to challenge him for the Crown. As Richard II observed, the nobles shed lustre on the king himself.[10] The least experienced of adult kings at his accession, Henry Tudor (1485), proved to be one of the most successful. His was no conventional aristocratic upbringing, and he had no training for kingship; yet aside from qualities nurtured in exile, he made skilful use of his family, and his obedient Court was the hub of English politics.

The Court was where the queens consort had influence. They had no particular public role in politics or government, they were rarely nominated as keeper or guardian of the realm when their husbands were abroad, and when Margaret of Anjou demanded to be regent for her sick husband, Henry VI, in 1454, many nobles were hostile. Queens were expected to provide kings with children, especially a male heir, and to cement the diplomatic alliances of which their marriage was a part. Any other influence or activities depended on their individual characters and abilities, and on the inclinations of their husbands. Eleanor of Provence was a powerful influence on Henry III, Isabella of France led rebellion against her husband, Edward II, and Margaret of Anjou assumed leadership of the Lancastrian family when Henry VI was incapacitated; on the other hand, Eleanor of Castile is best remembered for the crosses which Edward I erected to mark the journey of her corpse from Lincolnshire to Westminster, Joan of Navarre was too unpopular to have much influence with Henry IV, and Katherine of Valois barely had time to give birth to a son before her husband, Henry V, died. Queens had a prominent and honoured place at the king's Court; they helped to set its tone and brought up the royal children, they had patronage to dispense, and who knows what wifely pressure might have been exerted in the bedchamber. They were frequently distrusted as the foreigners they invariably were before 1464, and then Edward IV's bride, Elizabeth Woodville, attracted odium for advancing the interests of her numerous English relatives.

Still less did queens have an acknowledged role after their husbands died. Most royal widows lived in comfortable retirement. They had no position in the ruling councils during the minorities of Henry III and Henry VI. The corrupt régime of Isabella of France, following the deposition of her

The king and his Court. John Talbot, earl of Shrewsbury, his robe decorated with the
Garter emblem, is shown presenting the queen, Margaret of Anjou, with a book of
romances in the presence of King Henry VI, on the occasion of their marriage in 1445.
The scene is a chamber in the royal palace, and the courtiers include two of the queen's
ladies, and perhaps (left) the steward of the king's Household holding his staff of office
(William de la Pole, marquess of Suffolk, who brought Margaret to England) and, wearing
a circlet, the elderly Humphrey, duke of Gloucester, together with other lords.

husband, Edward II, was bitterly resented, not least by her son, Edward III; and Elizabeth Woodville's meddling after Edward IV's death in 1483 contributed to the dethronement of her son, Edward V, and the usurpation of Richard III. The first priority was to treat dowager queens honourably and control their activities. Several were young enough to attract (or pursue) new husbands, and such liaisons might prove politically factious. Eleanor of Provence made no trouble for her 'sweetest son', Edward I, whose own widow, Margaret of France, took no steps to remarry though still in her twenties in 1307; but in 1428 a statute was passed to determine the marriage of queens dowager because Henry VI was an only child and his mother, Katherine of Valois, was not 'able to fully curb her carnal passions' and had set her cap at one of the powerful Beaufort family before lighting on the less provocative (but still controversial) Welsh squire, Owen Tudor. The second major concern was the dower estate of queens, which was worth £4,500 a year and was generally enjoyed till death. It was increased to £6,500 in 1402 for Joan of Navarre, but in 1419 her stepson, Henry V, who was fighting a great war and contemplating his own marriage, accused Joan of witchcraft and seized her possessions. Not even ageing queens were safe when politics supervened, as Margaret of Anjou discovered, most tragically of all, after Henry VI's death in 1471; she died in France in 1482 in utter poverty.[11] Over-mightiness in queens, like over-mightiness in nobles, was a discordant factor in English politics, and the wise queen was content to exercise her influence in private, away from the gaze of critical and male contemporaries and inquisitive historians. Both queens and nobles were central elements of the king's Court and the royal Household, to which the queen's own establishment was closely linked.

The Court encompassed the king's Household, which organised his domestic life (including his personal finances, religious devotions and daily round) and his military needs; it also played an important part in the politics and government of the realm. It was the Household which spawned most of the organs or departments of administration – the Chancery, the Exchequer and the central courts of law. In this propensity for creating bureaucratic, professional, routine offices lay the genius of English government. In this way, the Household, chameleon-like, adapted to changing circumstances, yet at the same time remained the place where the king's family, friends, advisers, visitors and petitioners consorted, though its precise role depended on the king himself. The Household could be large and expensive, cliqueish and corrupt; as a result, it was frequently distrusted, envied or resented. Those who were senior members of the Household were often the most influential people in the land; those whom it shunned often its bitterest critics. Most influential of all were the officials of the Household, headed by the steward, the chamberlain and the treasurer, who rubbed shoulders with those who visited the Court and might be wined, dined and accommodated in the Household; they were served from 'below stairs' by a large staff of clerks and servants. These senior officials were close to the king, regulated access to him, and influenced his attitudes and decisions. The steward maintained the general discipline of the Household; the chamberlain supervised its most important department, the Chamber; and the treasurer of the Wardrobe managed its income and expenditure. The Court and the Household together provided the king's personal environment, where he ate, played, prayed and slept, consulted his counsellors and friends, gave rewards and favours, and received visitors and envoys, usually in a confidential manner. Its outer trappings and formalities concealed serious personal and political business.

The Household had a military air about it for much of the Middle Ages, and the knights, esquires and serjeants with whom the king consorted in his Court were a reliable core of his armies; on such people the king relied for advice, and some of them were his friends. Many developed interests as country land-owners, shire officials and castle constables, and in due time the military nature of the Household lessened, partly as a result of newer methods of raising large armies more frequently for longer periods of service from the fourteenth century onwards, and partly because of the expansion of royal government by ordinance and statute, which required a reliable provincial establishment linked with the departments at Westminster and the king's Household. The personal military needs of the king grew less after 1360 as Edward III abandoned the life of a warrior, and subsequent monarchs (with the signal exception of Henry V) campaigned abroad only on rare, brief occasions, and were in need of good counsel rather than military muscle at Court. True, knights and esquires continued to be attached to the Household and were present at Court in substantial numbers, but for less militaristic purposes, and by Edward IV's reign according to a rota system which linked Westminster and the provinces in ways that created a royal affinity for effective government and political control rather than for war. Some of them were the king's confidants or councillors or officials of his Household. With Parliament meeting almost exclusively at Westminster from the mid-fourteenth century, such men, who figured largely among the commons' representatives, felt increasingly at home in the vicinity of the Court and were adept at serving their own and the king's purposes there. At the same time, the Court became more ceremonious, secular and civil, though no less the hub of English politics and society.[12]

At the heart of the king's government was his Chancery or writing-office or secretariat. In 1200, it had been in existence as part of the king's Court for more than two centuries. Only relatively recently had the Chancery clerks taken to keeping systematic records – in the shape of hefty rolls and thick files, many of which still exist today – of the orders, appointments and grants that were the stuff of royal business; these instruments were authorised by the king's great seal, and they concerned both domestic and foreign affairs. The Chancery was evidently increasingly busy after 1200, and it became a distinct, permanent, bureaucratic office 'out of Court'. It grew in size and professionalism, so that well before the end of the fourteenth century some 100 clerks were employed in the Chancery, in several grades that provided a career structure for them. The Chancery's headquarters was in the palace of Westminster (see the illustration opposite), and rarely did these clerks accompany the king on his travels after 1200 as they had done before; indeed, a certain amount of routine business was undertaken without reference to the king himself or his closest advisers. It was this tendency towards routine executive action that gave the Chancery great political importance, for the chancellor had considerable initiative and a prominent place among the king's councillors and at meetings of Parliament. In one major respect, these powers of initiative continued to grow in the fifteenth century and impinged directly on political affairs: in a 'court' of Chancery, the chancellor developed a jurisdiction as a judge (his 'equity' jurisdiction) in cases of serious violence

Facing page The Court of King's Bench in session. This fifteenth-century illumination gives a vivid impression of a cramped and busy court that shared Westminster Hall with Common Pleas. Below the royal arms there sit the Chief Justice and four puisne judges on the king's bench, gorgeously attired in scarlet and with coifs on their heads. In front of them two-tone clerks write up the records on awkward rolls and a crowd of spectators press around the table, on which coifed counsel dispute, while the fettered prisoner stands between warders and serjeants at the bar. The further six shaggy defendants also scheduled for trial that day remind us how swift, summary and fatal justice could be for defendants who appeared in court.

The painted chamber of the Palace of Westminster, looking east, from a drawing made (in 1799) by William Capon, before the palace was largely destroyed by fire in 1834. The chamber, eighty feet long and twenty-six feet wide, was built by Henry III in 1236 as his personal apartment or Great Chamber; it was decorated with scenes from the Old Testament. In the later Middle Ages, the chamber became the more public focus for those attending the king's Court.

and unrest that threatened the king's peace but for which there seemed no effective remedy available in the courts of common law. The chancellor, then, was crucial to the functioning of English government and central to political life: he often presided at Council meetings in the king's absence; he frequently opened Parliament and set its agenda with a well-chosen biblical text; and he was often at the Court, dined in the Household and negotiated with foreign envoys.[13]

A chancellor's appointment was of the first importance to the king and was made by him personally. For most of this period, the chancellor was either a bishop or an archbishop, which ensured that he was literate, experienced, well-connected at home and abroad, could be conveniently and economically rewarded with Church benefices, and was unlikely to turn the office into a family fiefdom. On rare occasions – for example, when Henry III was keen to promote his Household servants in the Chancery, or when Edward III faced political crises in the 1340s and 1370s, or when Henry VI was desperately ill in the 1450s – a prominent knight or an earl might be appointed; but, in general, the clerical pattern persisted to Henry VIII's reign. A study of the chancellors as a group is revealing.[14] Robert Burnell, Edward I's closest confidant, was chancellor for eighteen years (1274–92), a record of service brought to an end

Facing page The Court of Chancery in session. Chancery was a civil court, handling cases between parties, and sought to offer fair remedies not available at common law. It was the court of the Chancellor, normally a bishop. Beneath the royal arms sit two judges, one a cleric, flanked by four masters in chancery. Clerks preparing rolls and writs surround a table, on which a clerk reads from documents, while five counsel including three serjeants plead their case.

only with Burnell's death, and for all but the first four months of his term he was bishop of Bath and Wells. The assassination of Richard II's chancellor, Simon Sudbury, archbishop of Canterbury, by the peasant insurgents in London in June 1381 was a stark reflection of the power of his office and his vast responsibilities. Another long-serving chancellor, John Stafford (1432–50), also bishop of Bath and Wells and then archbishop of Canterbury, led Henry VI out of his minority but, despite his abilities, fell in the torrent of protest against Henry's government in 1450. The record of Archbishop Rotheram as chancellor (1474–83 and 1485) demonstrates that experience in managing the principal office of state was more important to Henry Tudor after Bosworth Field than Rotheram's earlier Yorkist allegiance.

The stability and strength of the English monarchy depended on its ability to collect the king's rents and dues, impose taxes and manage his expenditure. These had been functions of the king's Court in the past. As the business and commitments of royal government expanded from the twelfth century onwards, so its financial organisation – known as the Exchequer after the chequered cloth on which financial calculations were made – became more complex as a department 'of state', headed by the king's treasurer, who was assisted by senior figures known as barons of the Exchequer and served by a permanent staff in an office at Westminster (see the illustration below). We are fortunate in having a description of the Exchequer's procedures, written about 1178 by Richard FitzNigel, then the king's treasurer. This 'Dialogue of the Exchequer' describes its functions at a time of rapid expansion.[15] These functions remained fundamentally unaltered in the centuries that followed; the Exchequer received revenue from estates, rights of jurisdiction and taxation which was deposited in the treasury, and it audited the activities of the king's financial agents throughout the realm, especially the sheriffs in the early days and, later, other officials too. The Exchequer produced the most famous series of English royal records, the Pipe Rolls, for sound financial manage-

The interior of the Exchequer in the Palace of Westminster, looking south, from a drawing made by William Capon before the great fire of 1834. The original Exchequer had overlooked the Thames, and *c.* 1244 this large building, about eighty feet long, was constructed against the north-west end of the Great Hall of the palace. As the Exchequer's business grew, the buildings for the clerks were extended from this main building.

ment depended on detailed information, efficient machinery and a systematic will to pursue the king's rights. These characteristics placed the Exchequer at the heart of royal politics.

It proved a resilient and resourceful department 'of state', for all the careful and methodical nature of its proceedings, which could be mistaken for slowness or inefficiency. By the 1230s, when Henry III began his personal rule, reforms were introduced to bring the Exchequer's operations up-to-date; a century later, in the 1320s, an innovative treasurer, Walter Stapledon, rationalised and simplified some of its procedures to cope with the greater volume and complexity of work that arose from frequent taxation and intensive government; war finance was especially demanding, not to speak of more difficult economic circumstances in the fourteenth century. On both these occasions, Exchequer reforms had political implications, for there was nothing like finance and the pursuit of efficiency to arouse the suspicions of those who owed the king money or whom the king pressed for extra money.[16] Further reforms were felt necessary in Henry VI's reign, by which time the financial pressures on English government had led to a shift away from the receipt and expenditure of cash to credit operations, loans and the management of royal debt. At the same time, political crises and military disasters counselled against major structural reforms, and Henry in his later years, and his successors more consistently, turned to the more accessible and responsive departments of the king's Household to ease their financial problems. To develop the Chamber in the Household as a financial office was in a long tradition of bureaucratic development.[17]

The treasurers of England were key figures in English politics and government, for they were close to the king, present at his Court, welcome in the Household and, like the chancellors, they were among the most senior of the king's advisers. Usually clerics in the thirteenth and fourteenth centuries, when the clergy's education, experience and literacy were highly prized in government, it was not unknown, especially during political crises, for kings to prefer someone even more reliable and intimate. By the fifteenth century the educated layman had made greater inroads in the Exchequer than in the Chancery, for laymen, especially noblemen, were often no less experienced in the arts of estate and financial management. This development also advanced the politicisation of the Exchequer's officialdom.

By Edward I's reign, the treasurers were frequently of great consequence, men like Walter Langton, treasurer from 1295 to 1307, and bishop of Coventry and Lichfield for almost as long; and Walter, Lord Hungerford, treasurer from 1426 to 1432, one of Henry V's companions in arms and a stalwart figure in his young son's régime after 1422; and Ralph, Lord Cromwell, who, while he was treasurer from 1433 to 1443, championed sound financial management at a time of military defeat in France, and yet also made his fortune. The treasurer's staff rose to about 100, organised in grades which suggest a career structure, though it was one generally separate from that of the Chancery. The political role of the treasurer lay less in his own powers of initiative than in his control of purse-strings and in the consequences of good (and bad) financial discipline.[18]

Unlike the Chancery and Exchequer, the king's Chamber and Wardrobe in his Household did not go entirely 'out of Court' during the later Middle Ages, partly because the Chancery and Exchequer continued to be under the king's control and responsive to his wishes, and partly because kings from Henry III onwards had less need to spend time across the Channel. The king did require a means of immediate communication from his Court and Household to the bureaucratised offices 'of state', and by 1200 a small, secret or private seal was being used in addition to the great seal of England (see the illustration opposite) which the chancellor kept. The official who had custody of this 'privy seal' in time acquired a pivotal influence through his access to the king and his role in authenticating the king's wishes. With Edward I frequently on campaign, especially in the 1290s, the privy seal was used more often, and its modest secretariat gradually acquired a routine function that led it, too, 'out of Court' as another bureaucratic department by the mid-fourteenth century; its keeper was almost always a clerk. It continued to be the seal used by the king's Council to communicate its decisions, summon councillors together, and often to instruct the chancellor to issue charters and letters under the great seal; indeed, one of the clerks in the privy seal office served as clerk of the Council. This being so, it is not surprising that there should have arisen need of a more intimate method by which the king could make his wishes immediately known: Richard II used his signet or 'secret seal', which was kept by his secretary who was close at hand in the Household and who generally accompanied the king on his travels; Richard's successors followed his example. Although lower in status than the chancellor and the treasurer, the keeper of the privy seal and the secretary were involved in some of the most important and private political matters; for that reason they were sometimes mistrusted, and critics of royal rule and its expense occasionally claimed that they abused their position.[19]

By 1200 the Chamber and Wardrobe in the Household were larger than the king's purely domestic needs justified; they had staffs of officials and wide responsibilities. In Edward I's reign, for example, the Wardrobe seemed well suited to organising and financing the king's wars in Wales, France and Scotland, not least because its staff could join the king on campaign. It served him well and was used to similar purpose by Edward III and Henry V. The Chamber also shouldered additional responsibilities, most notably as a finance office, and when the signet seal was introduced in Richard II's reign it was kept there at the king's beck and call. In the later fifteenth century it was used (as we have seen) as a speedier, more accessible financial office to supplement the work of the more stately Exchequer. The Household thus made available offices – which grew into institutions – to meet the practical political and governmental needs of English kings, and this gave its senior officials political importance. It meant, too, that the Household was at the heart of political life, open to criticism, especially when Parliament provided a representative forum and the king's wars made him heavily dependent on his subjects' co-operation.[20]

Political issues in the later Middle Ages mostly arose out of interpretations of the king's duties and the way in which he discharged them. Decisions on such issues were taken at the highest level by the king himself in the light of whatever advice he chose to seek – from family and friends at Court or living in the Household, from the chief officers of Chancery, Exchequer and the law courts, from others nominated to be his councillors and drawn from the nobility, the higher clergy and distinguished military commanders, and other men who had proved their worth in Parliament or elsewhere. Political decisions were implemented by the administrative departments, most notably the

Chancery, Exchequer and the newer offices of privy seal and, from the later fourteenth century, the signet.

The emergence of a Council as an identifiable group of royal advisers appears to be connected with interlocking developments of the early thirteenth century: greater specialisation in government since Angevin days, greater concentration on the affairs of England, the ending of rule by a justiciar, and Henry III's coming of age. From the 1230s onwards, certain advisers 'swore upon oath that they would give faithful counsel to the king'; they met frequently in the king's Household, with the chief officers of Chancery and Exchequer, the law courts and the Household taking a leading role.[21] The Council thereafter was at the centre of royal government. As a result, it was criticised when things went wrong, for it was easier and safer to condemn the councillors rather than the king himself. Some councillors were ill-chosen, notably Henry III's foreign relatives and the kinsfolk of Edward IV's Englishborn queen, Elizabeth Woodville, which suggests that it was less their social origins that jarred than the use or abuse of their position as councillors. If restraints on the king's actions were thought desirable, influence over his choice of councillors was one way of imposing them, and critics tended to champion a balanced Council of earls, barons, bishops and chief officers, 'who would not hesitate to speak the truth and act profitably' (as the commons put it in 1376).[22] Such considerations had been in the barons' minds in 1258 when, by the Provisions of Oxford, a Council of fifteen was selected and expected to account formally for their activities three times a year. Political crises in later decades – under Edward II, Edward III, Richard II and Henry IV – led to similar attempts to influence the choice and behaviour of the king's councillors. But in normal circumstances, it was the monarch who

Impressions of Edward I's Great Seal of England. Kept by the chancellor of England, this most important of the royal seals was used to authenticate the most formal of the king's charters, writs and letters. The reverse (left) shows the warrior king; the obverse (right) the enthroned king holding the sceptre and orb to symbolise the king as ruler, judge and protector of his subjects and the Church.

Facing page A modern plan of the Palace of Westminster. This shows the evolution of Westminster as the king's chief residence and administrative capital during the Middle Ages; the proximity of the great abbey (where the parliamentary commons frequently met); and the water gate to the Thames (close to the present Westminster Bridge) and the great gateway to the road leading to London. The government offices gradually took over much of the palace, especially around the Great Hall which still stands.

chose his councillors; it was he who decided when to consult them and what to refer to them – whether issues of diplomacy and defence, war and peace, trade and finance, administration and justice, or grievances, crime and proposed legislation. Under a masterful king like Edward I, the Council was imprecise in membership and function, with hardly an independent, executive role; other kings had different inclinations. Gradually, the Council's role expanded, and as a result of the protests at Edward II's régime and of Edward III's lengthy absences in France, it became more of an institution, settled at Westminster, its members taking a salary and meeting almost daily, from the 1340s in a specially constructed 'Star Chamber'. By then, too, it had become an executive body, and sometimes the king was not even present at its deliberations.

We know little of what went on at Council meetings, partly because the discussions were confidential and partly because few records survive. From one chronicler, however, we have a glimpse of a discussion about war with France in 1294: Anthony Bek, bishop of Durham, exclaimed, 'Mount the war-horses, take your lance in your hands', and his enthusiasm swept along with him all the barons who were present.[23] During the minorities of Richard II and Henry VI, 'continual' Councils, sworn, salaried and formally nominated, seemed best to conduct the king's affairs in his name. A number of lords and royal relatives were prominent, for they were widely regarded as the king's 'natural councillors', taking responsibility though leaving detailed administrative work to the experienced officers who were also there. Adult kings followed their own inclinations, Edward III favouring some knightly soldiers, Edward IV several gentry from his Household, and Henry VII a number of able young companions of his exile. The Council was served by a clerk or two; by 1392 a designated clerk of the Council was in office, and the king's privy seal was used to convey its authority.

What contemporaries valued in the king's Council was its 'sad and substantial' nature, its wisdom and the sense of responsibility of its members. When such qualities seemed lacking, the protests were loud, as in the 1370s and 1380s and in the 1440s.[24] Some kings, like Edward IV, were inclined to seek advice from their councillors but to limit their executive role; in Edward's case, this may have been a reaction to the experience of Henry VI's reign, when Council meetings had sometimes degenerated into rivalries and faction. Yet, despite all, there is no gainsaying the importance of the Council in the government of the realm or its value to the king. The growth in the amount of Council business, especially in relation to order and justice, seems to have led to the appearance of *ad hoc* committees of relevant, expert councillors to deal with particular matters. This was a natural, practical and effective development that, under Edward IV and especially Henry VII, produced a rash of what may be called 'delegated councils' to tackle specific problems, both in the provinces and Wales, and at Westminster (see the illustration opposite).

Parliament was one of the most significant and characteristic developments of later medieval England. Historians dispute its early nature and importance, partly because it emerged in response to needs and pressures rather than institutional or political theories, partly because contemporaries held an imprecise view of its role in the first century and a half of its existence, and partly because it has left few or patchy records. These uncertainties cannot conceal Parliament's growing importance in English society, government and

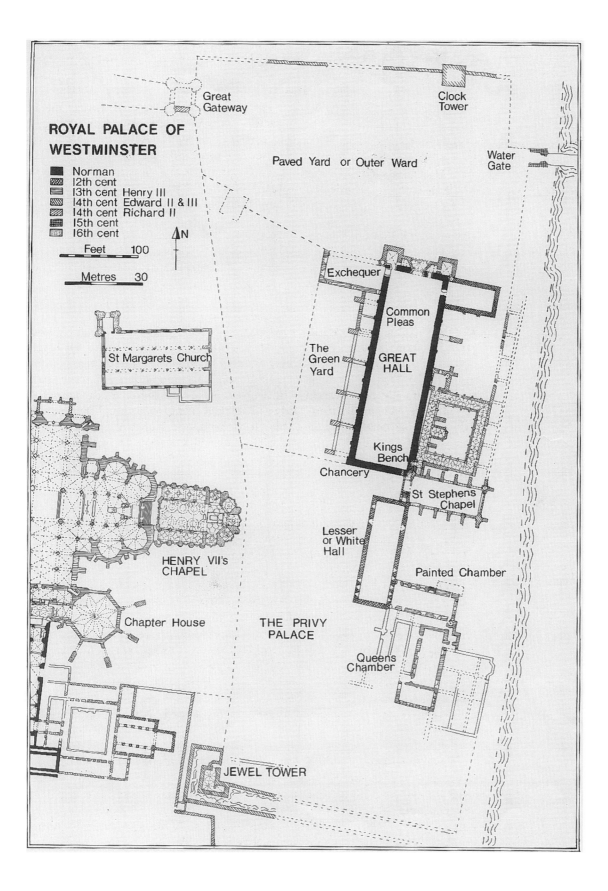

ROYAL PALACE OF WESTMINSTER

Norman
12th cent
13th cent Henry III
14th cent Edward II & III
14th cent Richard II
15th cent
16th cent

Feet 100

Metres 30

N

Great Gateway

Clock Tower

Paved Yard or Outer Ward

Water Gate

Exchequer

Common Pleas

GREAT HALL

The Green Yard

St Margarets Church

Kings Bench

Chancery

St Stephens Chapel

Lesser or White Hall

Painted Chamber

HENRY VII's CHAPEL

Chapter House

THE PRIVY PALACE

Queens Chamber

JEWEL TOWER

politics from the thirteenth century onwards (the earliest officially-recorded reference to Parliament is dated 1236), even though the pace of its development was not uniform.[25] Throughout the later Middle Ages, Parliament was a royal institution: the king decided when it should meet, how long it should last, who should attend (at least until membership became formalised from the mid-fourteenth century) and what it should discuss; and individual kings differed markedly in the way in which they made these decisions.

The years between the 1290s and the 1340s are a profoundly important watershed in the history of this distinctively English (and British) institution. These decades saw vigorous English campaigns in France after half a century of comparative peace, ambitious political and military schemes in Wales and Scotland that strained England's resources, political crises at home connected with these enterprises as well as with the quality of rulership, the deposition of Edward II (1327) after a spell of civil war, and all at a time of economic and social distress. These experiences were closely connected with Parliament's development, which was evolutionary and improvisory, seeking to forge a co-operative and collaborative relationship between the king and his influential subjects, both lay and clerical, throughout the realm.

The single most significant – and detectable – factor at the heart of this process was the king's frequent need for extra direct taxation, his 'great necessity'; this and the political strains to which it gave rise were responsible for several parliamentary developments in these years. Before the 1290s, such taxes had been imposed periodically, and from John's reign consent had been sought usually from the barons, though occasionally also from meetings with knights and yeomen from the shires and burgesses from certain towns, for these rural and urban communities were the backbone of a society that was increasing in size and wealth. Early Parliaments had a further role in providing justice to petitioners, whether individuals or groups, in cases that were difficult, delicate or important, for as the anonymous but well-informed writer of the lawbook called *Fleta* put it in the 1290s,

> the king has his court in his council in his parliaments in the presence of prelates, earls, barons, magnates and others learned in the law, where doubts of the judges are concluded and new remedies are provided for new injuries that have arisen, and where justice is done to each according to his merits.

Yet already by 1280, Edward I had realised that this role threatened discussion of 'the great demands of his realm and his foreign lands'.[26] Early Parliaments, too, had a link with the counties and towns. Since King John's time, magnates and lesser folk at assemblies and, later, Parliaments provided the king and his officials with knowledge about the realm and a channel through which to convey the king's will to the provinces. Edward I especially valued this particular function, and the scope and success of his law-giving in the first two decades of his reign owed much to his promulgation of statutes in Parliament (see the illustration opposite) and to the dissemination and publication of their contents far and wide.

The significance of Parliament was underlined during the baronial rebellion of 1258–65, when the barons insisted that Parliament should meet regularly and frequently (three times a year, according to the Provisions of Oxford, 1258) in order to deal with the business of king and kingdom; they also recognised the value of including in some of their discussions representatives from the shires and towns. These early Parliaments were not simply

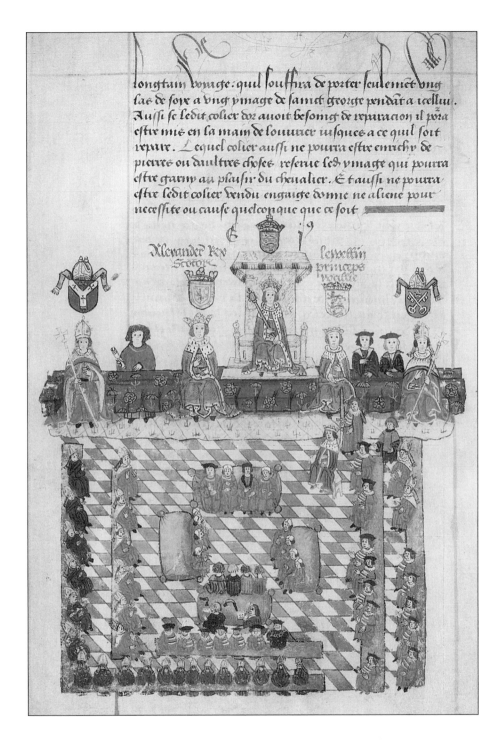

longtam voyage: quil souffira de porter seulemet ong
las de soye a bng ymage de samct george pendat a icellui.
Auisi se sedit colier dor auoit besoms de reparacion il pora
estre mie en la main de souurer iusques a ce quil soit
repare. Lequel colier aussi ne pourra estre enrichy de
pierres on aultres choses, reserue sed ymage qui pourra
estre garny au plaisir du cheualier. Et aussi ne pourra
estre sedit colier vendu engaige domne ne aliene pour
necessite ou cause quelconque que ce soit

Alexander Rex Scotoie

Lewellin princeps wallie

Edward I in Paliament, *c.* 1278, according to the Garter Book of *c.* 1534. It shows the ecclesiastical and lay lords seated before the crowned king, who is flanked on either side by the archbishops of Canterbury and York, and by Alexander III (died 1286), king of the Scots, and Llywelyn ap Gruffydd (d. 1282), prince of Wales, who, though they never attended a Parliament together, symbolise in this picture King Edward's claims to dominion. The sword of state is held by a lay lord. On four woolsacks, symbolising the most valuable commodity of England's trade, are seated the justices and several clerks, two of whom record the proceedings. At this stage, there were no commoners present.

taxing and judicial assemblies, but rather enlarged meetings of royal councillors, extending the feudal obligation of tenants-in-chief to advise their
suzerain. As such, they dealt with all sorts of issues of government, politics
and diplomacy at the king's invitation. To quote A. L. Brown, they were

> largely regular, working meetings where administrative and judicial cases were
> decided, where petitions were handled and where wider issues of policy and
> government were discussed, often in the presence of small numbers of magnates,
> councillors and officials, occasionally with considerably larger numbers specially
> summoned.[27]

The half-century between the 1290s and the 1340s converted these fluid (and,
to us, shadowy) arrangements into a complex, formalised institution. In the
1290s, Edward I's need for large sums of money was urgent, and Parliament
was the forum for frequent negotiation with representatives of his wealthier
subjects, lay and clerical, and the political nation. This made it well designed
for the discussion of political issues and crises, and the presentation of
common grievances. Parliaments were thenceforward summoned regularly
and on average once a year between 1327 and 1437; counties and towns were
invariably represented from 1325, and a complementary membership of lords
and commons gave the institution a permanent importance. It became a
forum in which royal policy was discussed: foreign and domestic issues, and
questions of war and peace, relations between Church and State and with the
papacy; grievances were advanced and legislation promulgated, and economic
and social measures were devised, as well as major questions affecting individuals treated. At the same time, the specifically judicial business was curtailed
in Edward II's reign, many cases being referred to appropriate courts or to the
king's Council. The greater formality of membership and the invariable presence of representatives created by 1340 two distinct chambers (or houses) of
lords and commons. They communicated with each other as a matter of
course, and in 1376 the nomination of a commons' speaker, Sir Peter de la
Mare, facilitated the expression of collective views by the numerous
commons' representatives – and created a new official of unique standing and
influence. The clergy mostly withdrew to meetings of Convocation (of
Canterbury and York) which usually met about the same time as Parliament to
deal with some common business. The archbishops, bishops and a select
group of abbots and priors continued to be summoned as lords. Thus,
Parliament had become an assembly of the king and his ministers with his
officials and councillors, magnates and prominent landowners and townsmen
drawn from throughout the realm; it acquired enormous political and governmental authority in contributing through consultation to peaceable and effective royal rule. It also provided a convenient forum for complaints and
protests, including some directed at the king's ministers and occasionally at
the king himself.

By the end of Edward III's reign (1377), Parliament was a fully-fledged
institution, with developing procedures and an appreciation of its own role in
public affairs. Its consent to extraordinary taxation was essential, and its role
in law-giving by statute was significant. It monitored the conduct of the king's
government and the behaviour of his officials; and lords and commons
enjoyed privileges and protection. On rare occasions – as in 1330 with Roger
Mortimer – it sought to condemn a prominent politician, and resort to parliamentary impeachment in 1376, involving accusation by the commons and trial

before the lords, made it possible to secure the condemnation (even execution) of particularly corrupt or hated royal ministers in a public 'state trial'. Both lords and commons took part in discussions of policy, criticising and exploiting the king's need for taxes by demanding concessions or imposing conditions, but almost never did Parliament seek to take the initiative in politics and government away from the king; rather it put its faith in 'good and abundant governance' (1406) and 'politique rule and governance', preferring to see the king discharge his obligations well and in concert with Parliament (see the illustration on p. 214). It had status and authority as an assembly of 30–50 lords and 200–300 commons, broadly representative of the political community of the realm. Theirs was 'participation in government at the sovereign's command', to quote J. S. Roskell.[28]

When the king's need was less urgent, Parliament was summoned less often (once every three years on average between the end of the Hundred Years War in 1453 and Henry VII's death in 1509), and that had consequences for the pace of its development as a political forum.[29] It is worth noting, too, that some functions of Parliament were fulfilled by large meetings of king's councillors (or Great Councils), which were distinct assemblies by the 1340s and continued to meet in the fourteenth and fifteenth centuries. These might not have the standing of a Parliament, but they discussed particular major issues – such as war with France in 1415, and the ending of Henry VI's minority in 1436 – and representatives as well as magnates were sometimes present. But taxation and legislation had to wait for a Parliament to assemble.

Of all the political institutions of the realm, Parliament was pre-eminently the one that forged strong links between the capital and the provinces (and the dominions beyond), between the departments of government and the king's Court and Household, and his subjects in the localities. As such, its role was unique in ensuring order, stability and effective government in later medieval England. We know tantalisingly little of how these links operated in detail, whether through the county court or through baronial and town councils. By the fourteenth century, the election of commons' shire representatives was arranged by sheriffs in the county courts, and incidental references suggest that local landowners were consulted and sometimes polled, and that there were some contested elections. Connection and influence, rather than political attitudes, doubtless marked one candidate off from another, and baronial and town councils may have discussed the political implications of parliamentary elections; the famous Paston letters indicate that this happened in the 1450s, and town records of Hull, York and elsewhere suggest this too.[30] How such MPs reacted when they attended Parliament, and what were their relations with the king's councillors and officials and with the lords nearby are largely shrouded from us. Such bodies of powerful and privileged men commonly attract criticism, and the satirist who described a parliamentary meeting *c*. 1399–1400 was probably a jaundiced eyewitness:

> Some members sat there like a nought in arithmetic . . . Some had taken bribes . . . Some were tattlers, who went to the king and warned him against men who were really good friends of his . . . Some members slumbered and slept and said little. Some stammered and mumbled and did not know what they meant to say. Some were paid dependents, and were afraid to take any step without their masters' orders. Some were so pompous and dull-witted that they got hopelessly involved before they reached the end of their speeches.[31]

King, Lords and Commons. Henry VI is represented crowned and kneeling before the Virgin Mary at the beginning of the foundation charter of King's College, Cambridge, which was issued on 16 March 1446 during a meeting of Parliament. The ecclesiastical lords (archbishops, bishops and abbots) and the lay lords (in order of precedence) are shown kneeling behind the king, who is surmounted by his coat of arms and the closed, imperial crown of England; members of the commons, headed by their speaker, are shown kneeling below.

Yet by the fifteenth century landowners and lawyers, merchants and officials were eager to gain election – and for a borough if a county seat were not available – and that must reflect the importance they set on Parliament and the place it had come to occupy in the political firmament of later medieval England.

In 1500, England's political institutions were sophisticated ones. They provided the realm with effective government, not least because their development had been pragmatic and adaptive, with few radical or revolutionary changes but with significant adjustments every generation or two. The king's powers were immense and in some respects were growing – for example, in relation to the Church and law enforcement. The monarchy was striving to become hereditary in the male line, making the royal blood, as a result, more exclusive and distinctive. The king remained the mainspring of government and politics throughout the later Middle Ages, advised by those whom he chose or was accustomed to consult. His will was executed by those departments 'of state' which had developed out of his predecessors' Court and by those Household departments that were close at hand, and by the monthly meetings of shire courts which published and implemented annually hundreds of writs and proclamations conveyed to them by royal messengers from Westminster. For, as Sir John Fortescue appreciated, 'the might of the land, after the might of the great lords thereof, standeth most in the king's officers'.[32] Yet this very sophistication made the English monarchy a co-operative structure, with acknowledged obligations on the part of both king and subject. It developed, too, channels of communication, advice and service, of which Parliament was the most prominent, whereby a wide community could play its part in political discussion and administration. This Edward IV fully appreciated when he addressed the commons in his first Parliament (1461) after winning the crown by force of arms:

> And if I had any better good to reward you with all than my body, you should have it, the which shall always be ready for your defence, never sparing nor letting for no jeopardy; praying you all of your hearty assistance and good continuance, as I shall be unto you your very rightwise and loving liege lord.[33]

The significant changes in these institutions occurred in response to problems and pressures. Among these was the reorientation of the monarchy's focus after the Angevin age. The attempt to extend its dominion in the British Isles and to maintain a hegemony in certain French provinces produced stresses with political and institutional consequences; so too did lengthy wars and the resources needed to wage successful campaigns. Nor must we forget that this was an age of plague, demographic change, and economic and social turbulence, and an age, also, of scholarly debate about sovereignty, good government and the common weal, and about consultation and consent. The most obvious changes took place following the collapse of the Angevin 'empire', in the decades following Edward I's robust rule and in the early years of the Hundred Years War, and perhaps, too, as a consequence of defeat in France and disastrous rule by Henry VI.

What is remarkable is the vitality of these institutions, their genius for adaptation and development, and the propensity of the king's Court to create offices of government and administration without much violence. Like all institutions, the more complex they became, the slower and more stately in operation they seem, but adaptation provided its own solvent in the interests of effectiveness, efficiency and social peace. It is testimony to the worth of these institutions that none was swept away by protest and all were able to meet the changing needs of new generations.

LAWMAKERS AND LAWBREAKERS

Michael Hicks

It is lawbreaking rather than lawmaking that is usually associated with late medieval England. Here was an era of violence, of Livery and Maintenance, of private and civil war; a time when judges were convicted of corruption, bound themselves in service to contending litigants, and when even a Chief Justice could take pride in the unruly lawlessness of Englishmen! King and Parliament received constant complaints about lawlessness and ever more crimes were reported to the courts. Parliament legislated, apparently ineffectively, the law failed to reform itself, and unscrupulous lawyers heaped up the fortunes that established landed families in opulent castles and country houses.

There, however, is the central paradox in this traditional stereotype. Complainants resorted ever more to the courts. Judges could be corrupt and lawyers successful precisely because such a flood of litigants provided them with ever more business. It was not just that people were more litigious, that a more complex society required greater regulation, or that quarrels henceforth were conducted in the courts rather than by force of arms. Activities hitherto acceptable or merely anti-social had become unacceptable, were proscribed and hence prosecuted. There were many new offences and new crimes to be committed. The burgeoning plea rolls confirm the complaints of lawlessness from those seeking ever more regulation of everyday life and ever higher standards of enforcement. Late medieval England was actually a much regulated country and was subject to the international codes of arms and the Church as well as the purely English law that is discussed here.

Crime is created by laws that forbid particular activities as anti-social. Laws themselves embody the standards of those who made them. Already unacceptable in the Garden of Eden, murder sometimes resulted in blood-feuds and payments of blood-money, such as the Anglo-Saxon wergild. Kings were responsible for doing justice; pre-Conquest kings such as Ine and Cnut framed law-codes to regulate the righting of such wrongs. By the twelfth century, murder, felonies and misdemeanours were regarded as breaches of the king's peace, crimes against the king, and hence were for him alone to prosecute. This was a crucial development in the elimination of self-help, although the blood-feud and blood-money persisted in outlying areas such as Wales, and even a seventeenth-century Lord Chancellor recognised revenge as legitimate where the law offered no remedy.[1] As ever more litigants came to the king, Parliament and the courts for the redress of newly-identified wrongs, so new remedies were provided under both criminal and civil law and royal justice became a universal system. First, however, it had to supplant or adapt the systems that already existed.

There was already a system of local government and local justice before the Norman Conquest. Each Anglo-Saxon shire or county possessed its county court, presided over by the shire reeve or sheriff, and each was subdivided into districts with their own courts, variously called hundreds, wapentakes, lathes and rapes in different regions of England. It was these subdivisions that administered the frankpledge system, whereby all males aged 12 or more whose good conduct was not guaranteed by their lords were arranged in tithings of ten men, who pledged themselves not to tolerate theft or thieves or other crime and to produce in court suspected offenders from their tithings.

Unfortunately this universal system was broken down by a myriad exceptions by the thirteenth century. The Normans had established feudal courts – courts of the honour, the barony, and the manor – that exercised jurisdiction over their tenants and which cut across the existing system. Public rights of jurisdiction were granted to private individuals; thus frankpledge for particular manors was often viewed in private courts leet. Lords were granted other franchises, the right to a gallows or the forfeited property of felons, within their manor, hundred or whole county. In County Durham or the Welsh marcher lordships the privileges (regalian rights) were so extensive that the lords stood in place of the king, whose writ did not run, and exercised jurisdiction over all inhabitants, whether their tenants or not. Such franchises existed everywhere, even in London or Suffolk, but were most extensive in northern England, where Durham stood out as the greatest among many liberties such as Allertonshire, Beverley, Elandshire, Norhamshire, and Tynedale. The fragmentation of local government offered refuge for fugitives, who could take sanctuary for many years, dodge across franchise boundaries, and even use their new homes as bases for criminal careers outside. In 1470 the sanctuarymen of St Martin-le-Grand near St Paul's Cathedral emerged to exploit the political dislocation of yet another dynastic revolution.

Every church, of course, was a sanctuary for malefactors. If even a resident of County Durham could reach the splendid knocker on the door of Durham Cathedral, he was assured of the protection of St Cuthbert (see the illustration on p. 218). Elizabeth Woodville, queen to Edward IV, twice took sanctuary in Westminster Abbey. A particularly privileged fugitive, she took her daughters and her furniture and was allowed to stay indefinitely. More normal fugitives, mere criminals, could be starved out and obliged to go abroad (abjure the realm). Churchmen and the literate claimed benefit of clergy and thus escaped the worst penalties on consignment to the much tenderer mercies of the Church. Canon law, the international law of the Church, administered in its own courts with ultimate appeal to the pope, covered cases

The lion door-knocker of Durham Cathedral, 1180. County Durham was the greatest of the northern liberties. Within it the cathedral, like all churches, offered sanctuary even against the local lord, the Bishop of Durham. Malefactors fleeing to sanctuary who grasped the splendid knocker were immune from arrest except, under Henry VII, for treason. Such fugitives could live indefinitely in churches, like Edward IV's queen, unless starved out, when they were expelled from the country (abjured the realm).

arising from sin such as adultery, matrimonial affairs, defamation, and proof of wills (probate) from which the common law was excluded.

Existing systems of justice were increasingly superseded by the legal reforms of the Angevin kings (1154–1216) and by the justices of the peace two centuries later. To the Angevins can be attributed the emphasis on civil law, cases between party and party, that were greatly encouraged by the so-called possessory assizes (novel disseisin, mort dancestor, and darrein presentment) that initiated disputes over property. Private lordship lost ground to public justice. Even in the twelfth century feudal courts needed royal permission to try cases involving free land and increasingly required royal writs before embarking on cases. By about 1250 most feudal courts had lost out to the king's; even frankpledge was in decay by 1300. The Quo Warranto proceedings of Edward I forced lords to justify their liberties and caused many to be terminated or abandoned as obsolete. What remained was almost everywhere subject to royal supervision and intervention until Edward IV and Henry VII could even rip traitors from sanctuary and execute them! County and hundred courts lost much of their criminal jurisdiction during the thirteenth century and were largely restricted to petty cases worth 40s or less from 1278. But the institutions themselves and their officials had many centuries service ahead as the bottom administrative level of a now centralised national legal and judicial system. It was still the sheriff and the hundred bailiffs who served writs, distrained chattels, empanelled jurors, arrested, imprisoned and hanged convicted offenders.

It was the new central courts, the common law that they administered, and their procedures that were the framework for criminal justice and civil litigation for the rest of the Middle Ages. This was the era when the law emerged as a learned profession, when there evolved a cheaper system of local justice and flexible remedies for new wrongs. Late medieval developments, however, were much less formal, more flexible, and respected the realities of contemporary society. Law and justice do not operate in a vacuum. They cannot merely respond to grievances with remedies, but must operate within contemporary power structures. Power in late medieval England was shared between the king and his greater subjects, the aristocracy: magnates, nobility and gentry. The strongest of kings hesitated before offending them. Such men sat on the royal council and in Parliament, shared in the formulation of the law and exercised a veto on its implementation in the localities. Increasingly, as we shall see, it was they who judged cases and implemented decisions in their own 'countries'.

'Lo! To fight and to judge is the office of a king' declared Chief Justice Fortescue. A medieval king was the source of justice. At his coronation an English monarch took an oath to see justice was performed; an oath that Richard III for one took very seriously.[2] It was a king's task to remedy grievances, to right wrongs and to punish offenders. Normally he was portrayed seated on his throne (in a posture recalling God at the Last Judgement) receiving and determining petitions which were often judicial pleas. It is no accident that even so unimpressive a ruler as Henry VI was depicted on a plea roll presiding with two judges (see the illustration on p. 210). The principal criminal court was appropriately called King's Bench – King Edward IV still occasionally presided – and the authority that it exercised was that which the king had delegated to it. As Chief Justice Gascoigne explained in Shakespeare's *Henry V* to the king he had arrested when mere Prince Hal:

> I then did use the person of your father.
> The image of his power lay then in me.
> And in the administration of his law,
> Whiles I was busy with the commonwealth,
> Your highness pleased to forget my place,
> The majesty and power of law and justice,
> The image of the king whom I presented,
> And struck me in the very seat of judgement,
> Whereon, as an offender to your father,
> I gave bold way to my authority,
> And did commit you.

Contempt of court was contempt to the king himself. And no offence was more heinous than treason against the king, which entailed not only the most frightful death but the disinheritance of one's heirs.

Sessions of King's Bench were thus solemn occasions that aped both king and God in judgment. A Chief Justice in the same pose as Henry VI features on one of Henry VII's plea rolls (see the illustration on p. 211). Meeting in Westminster Hall, its judges were gorgeous in their scarlet robes and close-fitting coifs (caps) beneath the royal arms. Before them clerks composed writs

Henry VI and two justices from the coram rege roll of the court of King's Bench, 1460. However inadequate as a person, the king was the fount of justice and was entitled to preside over his courts, thus making overt the royal and indeed divine authority under which justice was administered. Hence the king's splendid throne was set higher than the judicial bench. The scene may be symbolic, since Henry VI – unlike Edward IV – is not known to have presided over King's Bench, though he often attended the fearsome execution and dismemberment of traitors.

and plea rolls on a table. Beyond them was the defendant and at the bar bounding the court were a group of prisoners in chains flanked by armed guards (see the colour plate on p. 191). Their presence reminds us how summary medieval justice could be once the accused were in the clutches of the law; perhaps only a few minutes for the trial before proceeding to the execution. In one sense, however, their presence is unrealistic. By far the most difficult task was to arrest the suspects: perhaps as many accused appeared voluntarily at King's Bench to plead their pardons and to be excused *sine die* (without a day to appear).

The criminal side of King's Bench, however, was not the busiest of the royal courts. When the Angevin kings reformed the royal judicial system along the lines that prevailed for the rest of the Middle Ages, it was civil cases that took pride of place. Already by 1230 there were three distinct central courts,

Sir William Husy, Henry VII's Chief Justice of King's Bench, is depicted seated, within an initial letter at the beginning of the King's Bench roll for Hilary term 1487. The chief judicial officer of the Crown, with more than a say in the Crown's legal policy and its enforcement, Husy is depicted in his gown and coif that distinguished him, all professional judges, and serjeants at law from lesser men.

which later became King's Bench, Common Pleas and the Exchequer, sitting in law terms at Westminster. By 1290 all were staffed by professional judges: Chief Justices and puisne justices in the first two and a Chief Baron with lesser barons in the Exchequer. King's Bench, as we have seen, handled the criminal prosecutions: both felonies and the less serious trespasses or misdemeanours. In practice most trespasses were prosecuted in the king's name by individuals seeking damages. Common Pleas, the most popular court, concentrated on disputes about land, debt and covenants. The third court, a mere by-product of the king's principal finance office, was the Exchequer of Pleas. It handled financial cases affecting the king or his agents, such as smuggling or default on tallies. In the fourteenth and fifteenth centuries each produced four substantial rolls of proceedings each year; those of Common Pleas are

The brass of Chief Baron Sir John Cassy and his wife, *c.* 1400, at Deerhurst reminds us that late medieval judges were laymen and family men with local estates and domiciles. Judge Cassy wears his gown and coif of office. The Chief Baron presided over the third of the common law courts, the Exchequer, which concerned itself mainly with financial cases involving the Crown, such as smuggling.

vast. As befitted the senior court, King's Bench could correct the errors of Common Pleas.

Civil suits were begun by purchase of a writ from Chancery; the details of the suit were commonly elaborated only when the defendant appeared in court. Ideally the writ was served, the defendant came to court, pleaded, and a jury gave its verdict. However, what was called the mesne process, which separated the original writ from the actual trial, became extremely complex and protracted, involving much to-ing and fro-ing between central and county court for essoins (excuses), distraint, arrest and outlawry. Technicalities abounded and could easily determine a case; lawsuits generally took years and were correspondingly expensive.

If the common law courts relieved the king of much legal business, much nevertheless remained. As further cases came to him that were not covered by existing courts, they were heard as convenient in Parliament, in the royal council, by particular councillors, or by the chancellor. Demarcation lines were blurred and flexible. Gradually the activities of the chancellor evolved into a new court, Chancery, the first of what much later became known as the prerogative courts. The case-load multiplied several times in the fifteenth century. Instead of starting with writs, Chancery suits commenced with bills or petitions in which the plaintiff stated his case; defendants responded in kind. Potentially there were five bills per case, or more where there were several defendants or affidavits. Normally it is only the bills themselves that survive, seldom all for any case, infrequently filed together. They are difficult to date and rarely endorsed with verdicts, which survive systematically only with the decree rolls and books of post-medieval centuries. Almost nothing survives of the newer prerogative courts such as Star Chamber or Requests before 1500.

Plaintiffs in Chancery habitually claimed to have suffered some wrong that could not be settled at common law, often because of the might of their opponent. Only in the fifteenth century did Chancery become a genuine court of equity, to which plaintiffs appealed when they had no claim at common law but only at conscience. The notion of conscience was borrowed from academic civil law, presumably by a chancellor who was not only a churchman, as most were, but a graduate in academic law. Our only picture of Chancery in session reveals a tonsured judge (see the colour plate on p. 192). Conscience opened up new avenues in areas for which there was hitherto no remedy, such as mercantile debt. The classic example is enfeoffments to uses (trusts), where the common law recognised only seisin, and thus regarded the occupant as the rightful holder even if only the feoffee (trustee) of someone else.[3] Defaulting trustees were commonplace defendants in Chancery.

Although very different in scope and procedures, all these courts emanated ultimately from the king's own judicial role. This, however, was not always apparent, particularly to common lawyers, and later the common lawyers and prerogative courts saw themselves as rivals. Since no serious attempt was made in the later Middle Ages to create a judicial *system*, in which courts complemented one another rather than conflicting, and since English law developed piecemeal from precedent to precedent, there came to be considerable overlaps that led to acrimony in later centuries.

All such developments presumed the emergence of an abstract law and of a legal profession, neither of which really existed in 1200, still less in 1100. In mid-twelfth-century England the only professional legal experts practised

canon law; only canon and civil law were subjects of academic study in the late medieval universities. Surprisingly, perhaps, English common law developed largely independently of these rival systems. The king's justices were numerous under Henry II partly because they were part-time amateurs, who doubled as administrators and presided over courts rather than judged the not very complex cases. From 1176–77 royal justices were called on to judge, soon after formal records commenced, and the practice of the law become ever more complex. The fourteen standard writs of Henry II became the hundred of about 1300. There was a much wider choice of actions, pleadings and tactics at every stage, which called for expert advice, and it became possible for cases to be pleaded on one's behalf. Coupled with continual sessions and an enormous expansion of business, professional judges and then professional pleaders became essential.

Both existed by about 1290, when the serjeants at law, so it appears, were already a closed circle with a monopoly of pleading in the most lucrative court, Common Pleas.[4] Like the justices, who were generally and then exclusively recruited from them, their badge of office was the coif. Some judges were portrayed in their coifs, as in the brass of Justice Cassy (see the illustration above). An illumination of about 1300 depicts two serjeants disputing before a judge, probably in the court of Common Pleas (see the illustration above). Apart from judges and serjeants, there were apprentices, at this stage learning the law. If there was indeed a legal profession by 1300, as Dr Brand has argued, it was limited to the relatively small numbers practising in the

A judge presiding in debate between two serjeants at law *c.* 1300. This illumination presumably depicts a case in the court of Common Pleas, the busiest court handling suits between parties, where serjeants at law had the lucrative monopoly in pleading. As the common law became increasingly complex, the more interesting arguments and decisions being recorded in the Year Books, so suitors had to rely more heavily on professional lawyers to act for them. Pride of place went to the serjeants, experts selected by the Crown, who wore special caps (coifs) to distinguish them from other lawyers, acted as assize judges, and were assured, if they lived long enough, of becoming royal justices or exchequer barons themselves.

Westminster courts. If there was one by 1500, it was larger and more varied, including many provincials as well, though not yet clearly differentiated into barristers and solicitors.[5] From 1340 the inns of court and inns of chancery emerged – Lincoln's, Gray's, Furnival's inns and the rest – which offered corporate premises, self-government, and more organised training. Like Oxbridge colleges, the principals disciplined their members and upheld standards of behaviour. Apart from eating together – hence the splendid new hall of 1490–92 for Lincoln's Inn (see the illustration opposite) – members came together to manage their affairs, for elections, readings and disguisings. Among members there was certainly the corporate spirit nowadays expected of professions. Such institutions, however, still served mainly those who manned the central courts, who remained relatively few. There were far more *legis periti*, men learned in the law, who appear as councillors, trustees and conveyancers, who may never have attended an inn, and who called themselves 'esquire' or 'gentleman' from choice.

To be a lawyer, it seems, did not necessarily confer status in the eyes of others. The poet Langland and the rebels of 1381 were highly critical. Clearly, as Langland deplored, the law offered pecuniary opportunities. The successful lawyers of the thirteenth century, like Chief Justice Hengham, were successful pluralists; two generations later his counterparts, the two Chief Justices Scrope, were laymen who founded landed families that made it to the peerage.[6] Similar good fortune awaited the Stonors, the Gascoignes, the Pastons, the Townshends, and Serjeant Thomas Keble. The salaries, retaining fees and expenses of successful practice rivalled the incomes of important landowners and gave the recipients the liquid capital to operate extensively on the land market. It is no wonder that lawyers put their sons to the law, like the Townshends, Mores or Catesbys; William Catesby the younger, Richard III's notorious agent (see the illustration on p. 216), the legally trained son and nephew of judges, was heir to a substantial Northamptonshire estate and need not have worked for his living. Acquaintance with the law was obviously advisable for any landowner who had to fight for what he had, or was destined to be a JP, but it was not until late in the sixteenth century that a period at the inns of court rivalled the universities as the higher education expected of any gentleman. Nor was success confined merely to lawyers at the central courts. There were certainly many less well-recorded than the minor Wiltshire lawyer Thomas Troponell, who documented his purchases of land in his cartulary and constructed about 1480 a comfortable stone mansion at Great Chalfield.

Inevitably the central courts handled a mere fraction of the total number of criminal and civil cases: those brought to them by litigants, referred or transferred to them by subordinate jurisdictions, or those from the immediate vicinity, such as the Middlesex cases that bulk so large in the criminal cases before King's Bench. How, then, can we speak of a national system? How could the king's justice prevail everywhere? This considerable problem exercised the Crown regularly throughout the Middle Ages. Several alternatives were explored: to send the central courts to the localities; to intervene locally whenever particularly required; or to establish a system of local justice under direct supervision of the centre.

The first option, probably the most effective, involved visits by the central courts to the localities. This took three forms. Already in the thirteenth century royal justices descended on the localities on what was called the

Facing page The Old Hall of Lincoln's Inn, 1490–92. As the common law became more professional, so lawyers in the central courts associated themselves together in inns of court which acquired land and buildings, provided facilities such as dinners and training, and emerged as self-governing and self-regulating bodies. Their development was important for the emergence of the common law as a discipline and the common lawyers as a profession. The splendid Old Hall at Lincoln's Inn demonstrates both the resources that the inns commanded and the prestige to which they aspired.

general eyre and on assizes. Eyres were extremely thorough; they covered all outstanding criminal cases – all other courts were suspended – and they took up to a year and involved literally thousands of people. Although much feared, not least for the large sums in amercements that they raised for the Crown, they were too expensive in skilled manpower to occur even at intervals of seven years or more. They were seldom held after 1294 and finally ceased in the 1330s. Alternatively, King's Bench itself might descend on a particular locality, such as Shropshire and Staffordshire in 1414.[7] It, too, could ill be spared, so such visitations were unusual and ceased in 1421. More enduring – indeed, still with us today – were the assizes, when royal justices, later supplemented by serjeants at law and local lawyers, visited the localities. Initially concerned with civil cases, especially land disputes initiated by Henry II's assizes and from 1285 including many cases delegated from Common Pleas, the assizes added criminal jurisdiction over prisoners (gaol delivery) in 1299, abuses of local officials, and many trespasses too. As the sole regular oversight exercised by royal justices in the localities, the assizes were much more important than their paltry surviving records reveal.

The second option consisted of special commissions such as trailbaston and oyer and terminer. Commissioners were appointed by the Crown for specific purposes: a particular crime, in response to a particular plaintiff, to deal with the lawlessness of a particular place. Emerging late in the thirteenth century, oyer and terminer commissions became the normal response of the Crown to any notable crime or outbreak of disorder and were used, for example, to investigate the private wars of the 1450s, treasonable plots in the 1460s and the composition of the army vanquished at Barnet in 1471. Commonly consisting of local magnates, judges, gentry and lawyers, they were a prestigious, economic and focused way of dealing with disorders. Any indictments left over after their brief sessions were acted on by King's Bench. Such commissions, especially trailbaston, were feared and therefore presumably effective. Since such commissions could be solicited by individuals, who could nominate commissions favourable to themselves, such sessions could be perverted to private ends, to pursue particular quarrels or to obtain political advantages, and proved no adequate substitute for political consensus and co-operation. Jurors would not always indict or convict.

The end of the eyres left a large gap in local peacekeeping, and a whole series of expedients were tried, ending, successfully, with the establishment of the justices of the peace. Building on the keepers of the peace, able to try offenders and from 1389 always authorised to determine their suits, JPs consisted of a core or quorum of professional lawyers supplemented by a majority of local aristocrats. They gradually acquired wide powers over felonies, trespasses and administrative matters, which later made them into the real government of the counties, and were even able to impose the death penalty. While Crown and Parliament clearly had qualms about delegating such powers to laymen, in practice sessions seem to have been dominated by the professions; presumably, however, the amateurs were active out of court in binding over, market regulation and exercising other statutory powers little recorded in the scanty surviving plea rolls.

What emerged by the end of the Middle Ages, therefore, was a system of regular quarter sessions and assizes that brought royal justice to the localities, which was largely administered by the local elites and which enjoyed local consent. Oversight was exercised through the justices of assize, through the transmission of unfinished cases to King's Bench and by its review of doubtful or suspicious cases, and through the special commissions that were targeted on particular areas. Abuses of power, even by the king's brother, could not easily escape detection.

Yet there were constant complaints about crime and lawlessness, the absence of legal remedies, the corruption and oppression of lawyers, the costs and partiality of the law. In 1381 and 1470 rebellious peasants saw lawyers as their enemies and oppressors. Royal justice could be an unwelcome intruder to be resisted, as in 1414 when local jurors refused to convict local men of piracy in Devon or illegal livery in Shropshire.[8] Attempts to extend the scope and remedies of the judicial system through the emergence of Chancery failed to compensate for the deficiencies of the courts of common law: by the 1480s, observed Dr Blatcher, the court of King's Bench was more ineffective than it could afford, if it was to survive.[9] Self-help through violence and private arbitration offered more hope than a legal system that was unable to reform itself.

Moreover, from 1261 at least,[10] there were constant complaints that great men (magnates) were able to defy the law, to overawe the courts and legal officials with their liveried (uniformed) retainers, and to pervert justice for their own ends. There were complaints about maintenance (the support of suits in the courts) and embracery (the bribery of jurors). Jurors, sheriffs and even judges were retained in their service. Private disputes escalated into private and even civil wars, such as the Wars of the Roses themselves. Victorian historians and some more recent ones have attributed the problems of law and order directly to this combination of livery and maintenance,[11] but that, as we shall see, is to oversimplify.

The magnates, nobility and gentry, whom historians collectively call the aristocracy, were the holders of large estates which conferred on them wealth, influence and territorial power. They lived in extravagant splendour, a key feature of which was the large entourage of servants that surrounded them. They kept large households, tens, scores or even hundreds strong, almost entirely able-bodied males. They had large numbers of tenants who owed them service, and these were supplemented by non-resident retainers – lawyers, estate officials and lesser aristocrats of standing. Such men were rewarded with keep and/or pay – often in the form of annual retaining fees or annuities – and the promise of the lord's good lordship in their just cause, for example, maintenance. Characteristically but not universally, formal written contracts called indentures of retainer set out the terms of service and employment of more valued retainers for life, most commonly lesser aristocrats, but on occasion experts in the law, cookery, minstrelsy or gunnery. This system of retaining is known as Bastard Feudalism.[12]

Late medieval lords travelled less than their Anglo-Norman predecessors and resided in a few comfortable residences on their estates: sometimes real castles that had been modernised, with light and airy rooms and panelled chambers; more often in mock castles or palaces. Even at Warkworth Castle in Northumberland, an important fortress for defence against the Scots, the Percy Earls of Northumberland constructed a large tower well away from enemy gunfire, that had thin walls, large windows, and the private airy rooms that conformed to modern standards of domestic comfort. Tattershall Castle foreshadows many Tudor houses, such as Thornbury Castle, Layer

Facing page William Catesby is best known as one of the notorious henchmen of Richard III, but he was also a successful provincial lawyer. So profitable was the law that in Catesby's case it brought him a substantial Northamptonshire estate, with a distinguished pedigree and coat of arms. Education at the inns of court prepared him for extensive legal practice in his home area, where he counselled such local notables as Lord Hastings and the Duke of Gloucester – who as king continued his employment and rewarded him on a lavish scale. Catesby, however, committed himself too closely and shared Richard's III's violent death.

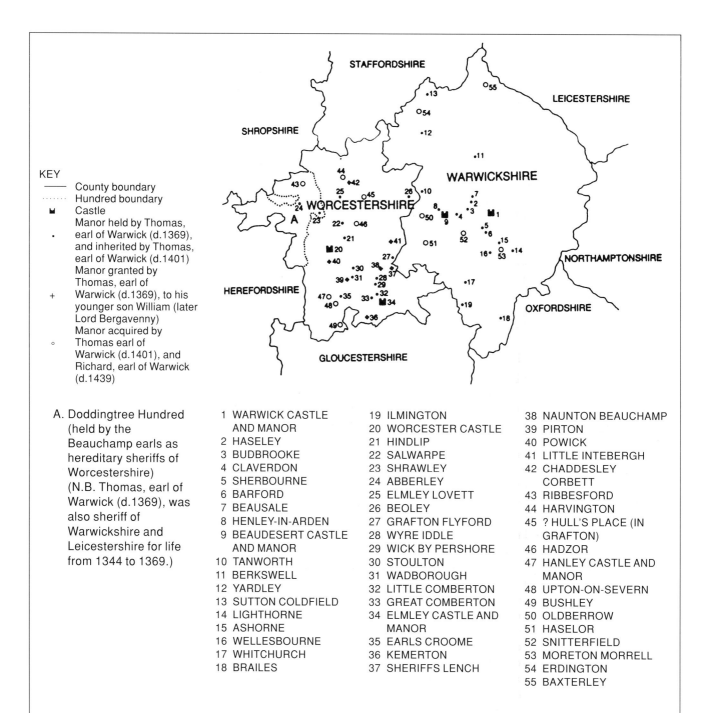

A. Doddingtree Hundred
   (held by the
   Beauchamp earls as
   hereditary sheriffs of
   Worcestershire)
   (N.B. Thomas, earl of
   Warwick (d.1369), was
   also sheriff of
   Warwickshire and
   Leicestershire for life
   from 1344 to 1369.)

1 WARWICK CASTLE AND MANOR	19 ILMINGTON
2 HASELEY	20 WORCESTER CASTLE
3 BUDBROOKE	21 HINDLIP
4 CLAVERDON	22 SALWARPE
5 SHERBOURNE	23 SHRAWLEY
6 BARFORD	24 ABBERLEY
7 BEAUSALE	25 ELMLEY LOVETT
8 HENLEY-IN-ARDEN	26 BEOLEY
9 BEAUDESERT CASTLE AND MANOR	27 GRAFTON FLYFORD
10 TANWORTH	28 WYRE IDDLE
11 BERKSWELL	29 WICK BY PERSHORE
12 YARDLEY	30 STOULTON
13 SUTTON COLDFIELD	31 WADBOROUGH
14 LIGHTHORNE	32 LITTLE COMBERTON
15 ASHORNE	33 GREAT COMBERTON
16 WELLESBOURNE	34 ELMLEY CASTLE AND MANOR
17 WHITCHURCH	35 EARLS CROOME
18 BRAILES	36 KEMERTON
	37 SHERIFFS LENCH

38 NAUNTON BEAUCHAMP	
39 PIRTON	
40 POWICK	
41 LITTLE INTEBERGH	
42 CHADDESLEY CORBETT	
43 RIBBESFORD	
44 HARVINGTON	
45 ? HULL'S PLACE (IN GRAFTON)	
46 HADZOR	
47 HANLEY CASTLE AND MANOR	
48 UPTON-ON-SEVERN	
49 BUSHLEY	
50 OLDBERROW	
51 HASELOR	
52 SNITTERFIELD	
53 MORETON MORRELL	
54 ERDINGTON	
55 BAXTERLEY	

Map of the lands of the Beauchamp Earls of Warwick in the West
Midlands. The Beauchamps were the dominant family in Warwickshire
and Worcestershire about 1400, but the map shows that their properties
were unevenly distributed and that they held only a minority of the land.
They actually held more land in Worcestershire than Warwickshire, where
Warwick was on the edge of their estates. A monopoly or majority of
land and income was not needed to dominate their 'country'.

Marney Towers and Titchfield Abbey, that use crenellation merely as decoration. Household, estates and tenants, and non-resident retainers from the locality gave most retinues a distinctly regional flavour. About 1400 the Beauchamp Earls of Warwick held fifty-five properties in Warwickshire and (mainly) Worcestershire (see the map opposite), altogether only a fraction of the total land, but comprising an estate that in size, wealth and manpower was without parallel and which made them the dominant family in the whole region. All lords, large or small, had their own 'countries' which they dominated – sometimes mere villages or districts, like the Berkeleys' Vale of Berkeley, but often much more extensive. Within these areas, their influence and authority were difficult to gainsay; it is surprising how often plaintiffs record the irresistible dominance of provincial lords of merely parochial importance!

If lands and money were the source of noble power, manpower was the instrument, and it was important to be seen to have men at one's command, particularly men of standing. Twice a year each lord issued his retainers with his livery – uniform gowns in his chosen colours – and sometimes also with his badges. In times of crisis, when hundreds of these badges were issued – 2,000 Stafford knots in 1454 and silver bears-and-ragged staffs at 5d each in the 1430s – they were presumably of little value and have been lost. Heralds were able to catalogue the badges of each family (see the illustration on p. 220). Some surviving examples, however, were valuable jewels, which were cherished by recipients and recorded on their monuments: examples are the SS collar of the house of Lancaster or the collar of Yorkist sunbursts boasted by Sir Robert Harcourt (see the illustration on p. 221). A handful of original badges survive; silver boars of Richard III (see the illustration on p. 222) and the white swan of Queen Margaret of Anjou. Either the badges given by kings were most valuable, or such marks of service were most memorable when the lord was a king. Always to be attended by a liveried entourage at home, on journeys or on important occasions, was an essential attribute of lordship; a source of prestige and hence of influence and authority. It was also potentially useful both at law and in war.

It was always possible for the elite – those with property and in authority, the hereditary aristocracy – to override or otherwise infringe the rights of others. In the twelfth century men complained of abuses of power by royal sheriffs. Abuses multiplied as the rights of others were defined, as more rights were recognised and thus became eligible for infringement, as more crimes were created, and more jurisdiction passed into the hands of the Crown, even if it was administered in practice by the elite as royal officials. Aristocrats were indicted and convicted of crimes against social inferiors and were sued by them in the common law courts for infringing their rights. It was a common law principle that all were equal before the law; judicial officials of Richard III were required to swear to treat everyone the same way.

This notion of law as an important arbiter reached its apogee after the Middle Ages; an eighteenth-century Earl Rivers was executed for killing his butler. It is hard to think of any precise medieval parallel; it was remarkable and unprecedented when the king's cousin, Thomas of Lancaster, was executed for treason in 1322. The nobility were great men and were not treated quite as others were. They were less likely to be tried; quite unlikely to be whipped, put in stocks, or hanged; more likely to be pardoned, to be consigned to prison for a 'cooling-off period'; and were beheaded as a final

Badges of the Dukes of Norfolk and Suffolk. All important lords inherited coats of arms, crests and badges from their ancestors, which they used to distinguish their houses, books and other possessions, and their retainers. Such emblems were so well known that poets often used them to identify their owners, so that the bear denoted the Earl of Warwick, and observers instantly recognised who monumental effigies represented and who had patronised churches that were so adorned.

my lord of norfolk

John Mowbray
Duke of Norfolk
1461.

my lord of Suffolk

John de la Pole
Duke of Suffolk
1450 — 1491.

privilege. Parliament was an assembly of rural and urban property-owning elites. Many medieval laws sought to preserve or reinforce the hierarchy and conferred rights on social superiors that were denied to their inferiors. This was true of the Ordinance and Statute of Labourers (1349, 1351), which reinforced landholders' rights to employ their own tenants, fixed maximum wages and restricted freedom of movement; the sumptuary laws, which in 1363 sought to distinguish dress by rank, restricting smarter kit to top people, and in 1483 even distinguished the attire of the royal family from the high nobility; the game laws; and the 1390 ordinance of livery that limited the retaining of non-residents to the peerage. The authority that heads of household exercised over their domestic servants was especially extensive when the head was a lord and the household scores or even hundreds strong. Obedience to one's master could constitute a valid excuse even for treason. Landowners were still securing rights of jurisdiction, to hunt (free warren) and to fortify (crenellate) their houses, that were denied to others. There were minimum qualifying incomes to enter the peerage, to become JPs, MPs, jurors or voters in parliamentary elections. The Church allowed those of rank to have private chapels, portable altars and private confessors, and the heralds recognised their coats of arms. Those who killed – betrayed – their master were guilty not of mere murder but of petty treason, and were liable to the same penalties as traitors against the Crown.[13]

It is hardly surprising, therefore, that judges, law officers and noblemen alike considered that the great should be treated differently. After all, if people could be punished for *scandalum magnatum* – bringing the nobility into disrepute – was it not presumptuous of them to sue, disobey, or otherwise offend their superiors and governors? Simple and straightforward though the legal system itself may have been, it was susceptible to unfair influence at all levels. It was easy to buy writs, hard to serve them, and more difficult yet to pursue one's suit through all the legitimate delays and technical minefields of the common law. Moreover, many a defendant failed to play by the rules – or, perhaps, by rules that we would recognise. Despite all the legislation of the later Middle Ages, there was still a place for legal maintenance, and jurors were still expected to bring their own information to a case. A determined and powerful litigant could bribe or overawe judges, jurors, witnesses, sheriffs, broaden the dispute by violence or vexatious suits in other courts or thwart the implementation of unfavourable verdicts. The law itself was so uncertain, lawsuits so time-consuming and litigation so expensive that those with deep purses could expect to outlast their opponents. The emergence of the Court of Requests about 1480 sought to offer remedies to the poor hitherto almost confined to the rich.

For lords were as capable of committing crime as lesser men. Not for them, perhaps, the petty larcenies or the casual killings of lesser men, but instead the poaching, violent assaults, riots, maintenance and even private warfare that are commonly considered much more serious. These were social crimes specific to their class – 'fur-collar crime' as Professor Hanawalt calls them[14] – the equivalent of the white-collar crime of today. Bred to self-importance, believing manual labour to be demeaning, trained in arms, and, if younger sons, often lacking their own livelihoods, such men had great potential as lawbreakers. At certain periods of particular disorder, like those following periods of foreign war, groups of aristocrats set up criminal gangs who engaged in highway robbery, terrorised particular localities, and even captured, ransomed

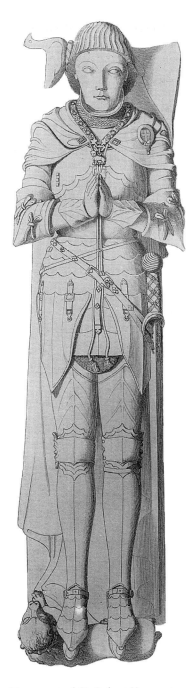

Monument of Sir Robert Harcourt, showing his collar of Yorkist sunbursts. Service to a lord, especially the king, did not lower a gentleman but was a distinction that he often recorded in his will or on his monument. Although Harcourt was an important landowner and a distinguished man in his own right, his monument boasts his service to Edward IV. The Lancastrian SS collar and the Yorkist sunburst collar, like the order of the Garter itself, were valuable jewels that were reserved for the most important retainers.

or killed cardinals and judges. The Coterels and Folvilles were particularly active in the 1320s and 1330s.[15] Sometimes such men were brought to book, like Hampshire's William Wawe in 1427.[16] More commonly they were indicted, pardoned, and found congenial employment in English armies abroad. Their immunity owed much to their own numbers and qualities, but something also to the protection derived from noble connections, sympathies and perhaps even maintenance.

Such men had their uses for lords anxious to threaten force or even to deploy it. Violence could be an alternative or even a complement to litigation. The retinues of lords increased in size with rank and wealth, giving, for example, a squire the capacity to coerce mere husbandmen and to the Duke of Norfolk the private army capable of besieging Sir John Paston's Caistor Castle. As Sir Thomas More observed, the mere existence of such men was conducive to disorder.[17] The ancient indictments of King's Bench reveal the constant infringement of property rights, the forcible seizure of land and cutting down of hedges, mass poaching of game, violence and riot. Among the worst *causes célèbres* the most notorious, perhaps, were the capture and ransom of the bishop of Durham and robbing of two cardinals by Sir Gilbert Middleton in 1317, the murder of Henry Radford in 1455 by the future earl of Devon, and the seizure and judicial murder of the widow Ankarette Twynho by the king's own brother in 1477. If this was what lords wanted retainers for, then known criminals were especially suitable instruments and may therefore have been attractive recruits for some lords. Moreover, once clad in their lord's livery and virtually immune from prosecution, retainers could embark on crime on their own behalf, though surviving records make it difficult to distinguish such cases from those initiated by lords. Professor Bellamy's book on *Crime and Public Order in the Later Middle Ages* gives pride of place to crimes and corruption associated with Bastard Feudalism.

Contemporaries often made the connection between lawlessness, perversions of justice and illegal retaining; hence a whole series of statutes that outlawed maintenance and its associated abuses. Hence, too, the bans on retaining of royal judges in the fourteenth century and of JPs by Elizabeth I, a whole series of ordinances and statutes of livery between 1390 and 1504 and, finally, the measures taken to simplify and speed up procedures for dealing with riot, livery and related issues that enabled JPs to take summary action without need for consent by juries that could be suborned.[18] Some historians argue that the Commons, consisting mainly of the gentry, saw their interests as conflicting with those of the Lords and were anxious to restrict their power and influence. Such legislation indicates a growing understanding of the problems and more effective countermeasures designed to block up loopholes. The need for further legislation, repeating or amplifying what went before, the rarity of prosecutions using the new procedures, and the continuance of abuse has been taken as evidence that such legislation was ineffective – that there were problems of enforcement – and that tinkering with the problem was not enough. Outright abolition of retaining was

Boar badge of Richard III as Duke of Gloucester and as king. The white boar of Richard III is one of the best-known emblems of a magnate affinity and was notoriously equated with Richard himself in rhyme: 'The Cat, the Rat and Lovell the Dog / Rule all England under a Hog.' This badge was found by the moat at Middleham Castle, one of Richard's principal seats before his accession. Badges of this design distinguished his war retinue for the invasion of France in 1475. That 13,000 were cheaply mass-produced in latten for his son's investiture as Prince of Wales in 1483 indicates that the level of commitment to be expected of recipients was much less than for those aristocrats, who were given such valuable jewels as the Dunstable swan or the Lancastrian SS collar.

the only cure. Where earlier historians gave a key role in this suppression to Henry VII, it is now generally recognised that Bastard Feudalism and its abuses persisted into the sixteenth century and beyond.

Such an interpretation is both too complex and too pessimistic. Society was to be hierarchical for centuries after 1500. Given the importance of the bonds between lords or masters and their servants or retainers, it was not practical to abolish retaining altogether, or to prevent people from keeping domestic servants. Nor was it necessary. Households were authoritarian institutions directed by their heads, who accepted responsibility over their servants. The earliest statutes of livery restricted retaining to noble lords, their households, and aristocratic retainers, who knew how to behave and could be held to account. They outlawed casual ties with non-residents contracted by mere gentry or their inferiors with those below them. The Commons, in short, did not restrict the nobility's capacity to retain. The gentry did not see their interests as incompatible with those of the nobility – how could they, when they were all members of a single class, separated by little more than titles of honour? Indentured retaining for life was banned in 1468. Neither in 1390 nor in 1468 did such measures have much effect on the great, who relied increasingly on more binding obligations created by service in their ever-burgeoning households. Cases of illegal retaining did occur in the fifteenth century, but those involved were few in number and humble in rank. They did not represent a significant proportion of all retainers.[19]

Moreover, aristocrats had important roles in maintaining the law. Perhaps royal justice never took over from private justice as completely as historians have usually supposed. Apart from retaining their franchises, private officials sometimes acted as coroners, and most significant lords were JPs or sheriffs. They insisted on decorum in their households. Lords and their councils often feature as mediators and arbiters in disputes among retainers and neighbours. 'Good lordship' in a retainer's 'just cause' evidently need not mean maintenance in his unjust one! Far from relying primarily or solely on physical force and bastard feudal corruption of justice, great lords were important users of the king's civil courts, both in their countries of dominance and elsewhere. Resort to the courts was not a sign of weakness; it was a sign of confidence in their efficacy.

That the ineffectiveness of the royal courts drove potential litigants to violence or arbitration is no longer believed. The legal system was not incapable of reforming itself, though development does not take the most obvious forms. Professor Bellamy has identified the introduction and refinement of new summary procedures. That few cases in the central courts resulted in verdicts need not mean, as Blatcher supposed, that the courts were ineffective. They stopped prematurely because settled out of court, by mediation or arbitration, which were commonplace. Moreover, such cases were probably initiated not to secure judgements, but, by threatening costs and inconvenience, to bring defendants to terms.[20] Arbitration was an alternative to litigation, but it was not a rival. Often arranged by the so-called prerogative courts as well as by noblemen, private individuals and towns, arbitration offered speedier and more flexible procedures to the same end; the law that was administered was the same. The arbiters were often common lawyers and even judges, who certainly did not see arbitration and the courts as rivals. Both were integral parts of a single system collaborating to restore domestic peace. Arbiters characteristically relied on the common law to enforce their decisions. Of course arbitration had its failures – usually thorny cases that resisted all efforts at remedy – but failure was not the norm.

Despite all the deficiencies in the law, there were more cases and more litigants before the central courts by the late fifteenth century than ever before. These lawsuits were not merely frivolous and vexatious, as has sometimes been suggested, but resulted principally from disputes over titles to property and inheritance, issues of paramount importance for any aristocratic family. Peaceful litigation about property contrasts sharply with the more usual impression of disorder and lawlessness in the localities, which has been much exaggerated. The violence and litigation experienced by the Pastons was as exceptional, no doubt, as the utterly tranquil existence of their neighbour John Hopton. Just as misleading, however, are the records of the central courts. The adversarial nature of the English legal system was already stressing friction and conflict. To qualify cases for particular actions litigants had to couch their cases in terms of numbers, violence and weapons that related little with reality. Actually violence was unusual in civil suits. That Bellamy's summary procedures were seldom employed was because there was rarely any need for them: only thrice in the 1430s in Bedfordshire and East Anglia![21] Bastard feudal abuses had become uncommon and were virtually to disappear in the next century,[22] and the really notorious cases, always unusual, were ever more uncommon. The gratuitous violence of the Coterels, Folvilles and *Gest of Robin Hood* was already archaic.

By 1500, therefore, England was a society with great respect for the law, in which aristocratic violence and bastard feudal abuse had become sufficiently unusual for even relatively minor incidents to occasion remark. Why, then, was there so much recorded crime and why were there so many complaints about lawlessness? As more records survive, so more crime is recorded. Crime itself proliferated as more activities became illegal. Practices that had been legal in 1200, if perhaps anti-social, had been outlawed, and new laws had been required to regulate new activities. Maintenance was not illegal until it was made a crime. Such changes resulted from higher standards of order and lower thresholds of tolerance within society. While there was a solid basis to the complaints of lawlessness in almost every decade of the fifteenth century, they most probably arose from higher expectations among the plaintiffs rather than because conditions had actually deteriorated. Almost certainly they had improved. Petty crime among the lower orders, the poor preying on the poor, undoubtedly persisted and perhaps even increased, as the hungry and unemployed sought the means to live. 'Fur-collar' crime and bastard feudal abuse persisted, though on an ever-diminishing scale. Such offences, however, occurred within an atmosphere of disapproval and condemnation, of growing respect for and increasing resort to the law. Propertied England especially was an orderly and law-abiding society; perhaps already as much so, by the standards of the time, as when peace, order and the rule of law were eighteenth-century commonplaces.

Harlech castle from the south. Harlech was one of the 'ring of stone' castles which Edward I built in the 1280s to encircle Snowdonia. Its location by the sea and its commanding position over the surrounding countryside made it virtually invulnerable, though it was captured by the Welsh rebel leader Owen Glendower in 1404 and used by him as the base for his operations in north Wales (and as the meeting-place for one of his 'parliaments') until 1409, when it was recaptured by the English.

Edward I creating his son Prince of Wales in 1301. Edward I conquered the native principalities in the north and west of Wales between 1276 and 1284 and in 1284 annexed them to the English Crown. In 1301, however, he decided to combine them into one principality for his eldest son, the future Edward II, thus inaugurating the custom, which lasts to this day, of the heir to the English throne being styled Prince of Wales.

The Wilton Diptych, which is the most famous and technically the finest painting to survive from the medieval period in England, is a portable altarpiece painted for King Richard II about 1395–6. The left panel shows the king kneeling, being presented by SS Edmund, Edward the Confessor and John the Baptist to (in the right panel) the Virgin and Child surrounded by eleven angels wearing Richard's livery of the white hart. The name of the artist is unknown, but it is likely that he was either French or Italian.

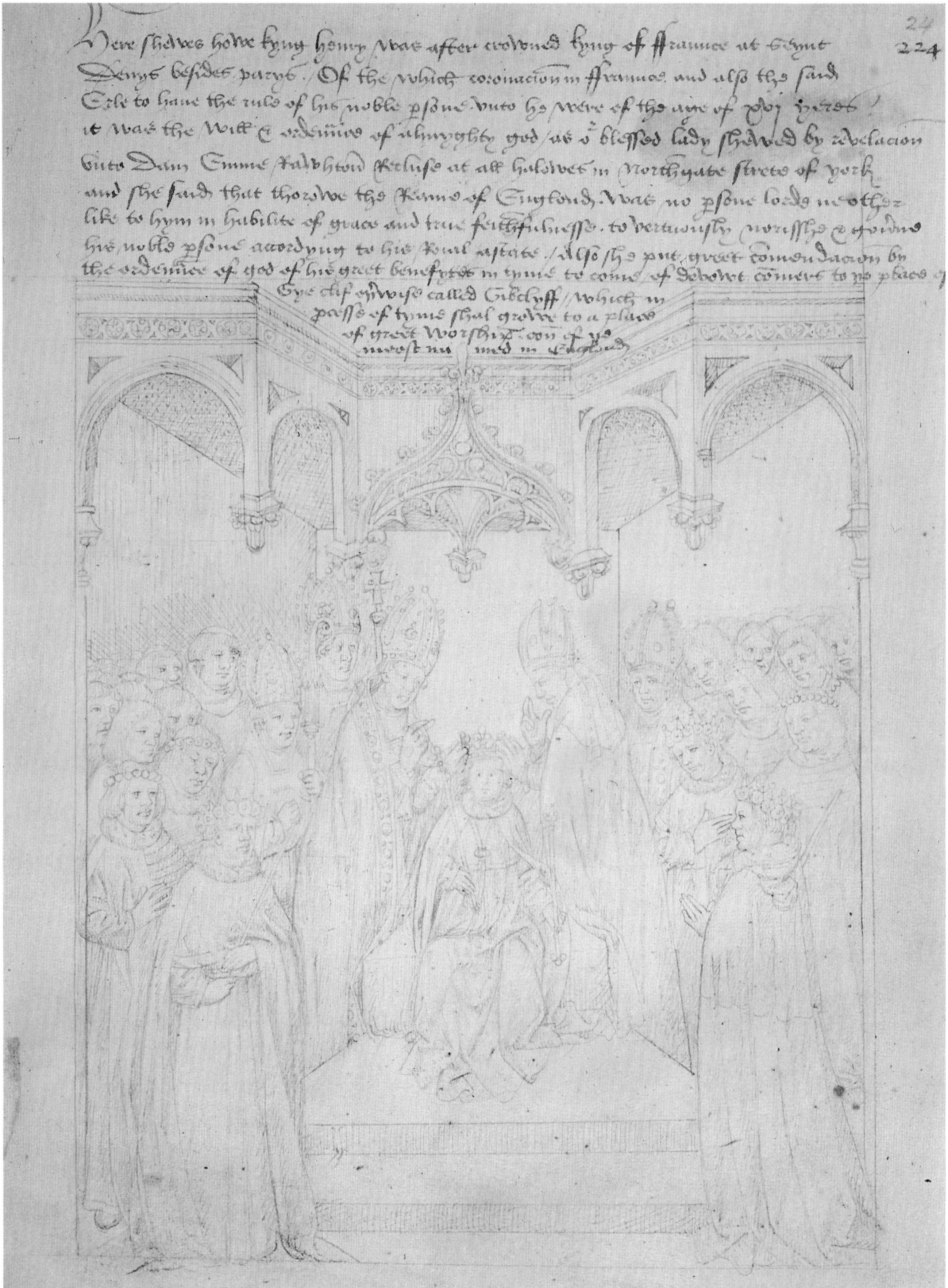

CIVIL WAR AND REBELLION

Simon Walker

Writing a little before 1470, Sir Thomas Malory drew a clear lesson for his own time from the tale of the civil war between King Arthur and Sir Mordred that destroyed the fellowship of the Round Table:

> Lo! you, all Englishmen. See you not what a mischief here was? For he that was the most King and noblest Knight of the world and most loved the fellowship of noble knights and by him they were all upholden, and yet might not these Englishmen hold them content with him. Lo! thus was the old custom and usages of this land, and men say that we of this land have not yet lost that custom. Alas! this is a great default of us Englishmen, for there may us nothing please no term.[1]

Malory was not alone in condemning the restless and violent search for novelty he saw as characteristic of his countrymen. The Cornish clerk John Trevisa compared the English to the Romans, who could only be overcome in their own land, while the harassed Milanese ambassador in Paris, seeking to explain the latest twist of English dynastic fortunes to his paymasters in 1471, wished that 'the people and their country were plunged deep into the sea, because of their lack of stability'.[2] When Philippe de Commynes attributed the troubles of Henry VI's reign to an excess of natural aggression on the part of his subjects, he was only the most articulate in a long line of French commentators on the violence and uncertainty of English political life. What most impressed them was the unfortunate fate of so many English kings. The Chancellor of France informed the Estates-General in 1484 that the English had suffered twenty-six changes of dynasty since the foundation of their monarchy,[3] and there were sufficient recent examples – Edward II, Richard II, Henry VI and Edward V, all done to death by their captors – to lend plausibility to his estimate.

Contemporary commentators, at home and abroad, had no doubts that civil

Facing page Henry VI crowned king of France in 1431. Although all the medieval kings from Edward III onwards claimed the French kingdom, Henry VI was the only one actually to be crowned king of France, at Paris in December 1431, when he was aged 10. Within a few years of his coronation, however, the English position in France had begun to crumble, and by 1453 Henry had lost almost all his French possessions.

war and rebellion were among the defining features of English political life in the later Middle Ages. This is an analysis that historians have generally accepted, seeking to draw from the study of these periodic breakdowns in political co-operation more general conclusions about the nature of the English monarchy in this period. Richard Kaeuper has argued, for example, that a distinction should be drawn between the political troubles of the thirteenth century, which were the result of a temporary disequilibrium in the balance between the costs and benefits of royal government, and the rebellions of the fourteenth and fifteenth centuries, which were brought about by a more corrosive disillusion with the ability of the monarchy to perform the tasks expected of it. E. B. Fryde has made a similar point more bluntly in explaining the popular rebellions of the period as a result of 'the worst deterioration in the quality of internal government that England had experienced since the civil wars of the thirteenth century'.[4] As these quotations make clear, the frequent incidence of civil war and rebellion in the later Middle Ages stands at the centre of a debate about the nature of English society: was the disruption they embodied pathological, the result of structural weaknesses in the English state that rendered political violence inevitable, or was it accidental, a sign of short-lived disturbance within a generally peaceful and effective political system? In order to reach a conclusion, a series of related questions needs first to be answered. Were there any recurrent situations or grievances that provoked political violence in England? Was there an increasing disposition over time to resolve political differences by a resort to arms? Were the civil wars of late medieval England more frequent, or more destructive, than in the other monarchies of Western Europe during the same period?

As a starting-point, some distinctions should be drawn between the motivations and objectives of the various rebellions and insurrections. Four principal types of disturbance can be identified. First, 'reformist' rebellions, intended to correct what were perceived to be abuses in the king's government and to remove from his presence those advisers considered responsible for the abuses. Such movements characteristically generated a set of formal demands, to which the king was requested, or compelled, to acquiesce, such as those embodied in Magna Carta (1215), the Provisions of Oxford (1258) and the Ordinances (1311). Each of these documents proved to be the occasion for an outbreak of civil war, though violence was not the inevitable result of such reformist proposals. There were similar sets of demands, such as the so-called Paper Constitution (1244) or the Remonstrances, a list of grievances circulated following a meeting of many of the higher nobility at Montgomery in June 1297, presented to the king in an atmosphere of great political tension, whose explosive potential was nevertheless successfully defused. What distinguished these more peaceful protests was less the content of the demands made on the king than the degree of flexibility that both sides were prepared to show in negotiating around them. Henry III refused to accept the reform proposals in 1244, but dropped the demand for an aid from the baronage that had initially provoked them, while the crisis of 1297 ended with the issue of the *Confirmatio Cartarum*, a concession by the king's council that embodied a number of the demands of the Remonstrances.

Such accommodations were as frequent as the breakdowns of consensus that issued in violence, and they were facilitated, in the later part of this period, by a shift in the focus of reformist ambition away from the attempt to manipulate the institutional details of royal government that characterised the thirteenth-century reform movements, towards a concentration on the task of removing from the king's presence those of his advisers who were held responsible for the misgovernment. 'Evil counsellors' had always been one of the targets for reform – Magna Carta called for the exile of Gerard d'Athée and his numerous kindred, while Henry III's most unpopular advisers, Guy and Geoffrey de Lusignan, together with William and Aymer de Valence, were forced to leave the kingdom in 1258 – but concentration on purging the personnel of royal government became the central characteristic of reformist rebellions in the later fourteenth and fifteenth centuries. The actions of the Appellants against Richard II had their origins in a widespread anger at the king's failure to implement a programme of administrative reform proposed in Parliament in October 1385, yet the bulk of their lengthy indictment of Richard's rule concentrated on itemising the misdeeds of the five named counsellors whom they held responsible for the king's derelictions. Richard duke of York's protests against Henry VI's conduct of government in the 1450s were expressed in similarly personal terms, ascribing its shortcomings to the dominance that his great rival, the duke of Somerset, enjoyed in the king's counsels. It was this growing concentration on the personalities rather than the principles of royal government that led William Stubbs to characterise the political struggles of the later Middle Ages as 'contests of personal and family factions, not of great causes'.[5] In reality, the change was more one of tactics than of substance. It sprang from a realistic recognition, born of experience, that however ingenious the administrative constraints laid upon the monarchy, an adult king in his right mind could only be effectively prevented from doing what he wanted by force. Removing a ruler's favourite advisers was, in the final analysis, less drastic than imposing a permanent restraint upon his prerogative powers, and correspondingly less likely to lead to the violence all parties wished to avoid.

Reformist movements could nevertheless be transformed, in the appropriate circumstances, into the second major category of rebellions to be considered: dynastic risings, whose declared intent stretched beyond the criticism of royal policies to an attempt to remove the king held responsible for them from power. Richard duke of York's relations with the Lancastrian government provide the clearest instance of this transformation, for they progressed from protestations of injured loyalty in 1450, through an armed demonstration of dissatisfaction in 1452, to the defeat in open battle of the king's party in 1455 and finally to his claim to the throne of England in 1460. Between the 'Epiphany rising' of 1400, an attempt by a group of his former intimates to restore the deposed Richard II, and the final defeat of Perkin Warbeck, the self-styled duke of York, in 1499, such dynastic rebellions were largely a fifteenth-century phenomenon, given sanction and plausibility by the successful Lancastrian deposition of Richard II in 1399. The loyalty of the English to the Plantagenet dynasty was not absolute; nearly three-quarters of the baronage were prepared to support the claim of Louis, son of Philip-Augustus of France, in preference to that of the young prince Henry in 1216, on the grounds that they had previously renounced their allegiance to Henry's father, John (see the illustration on p. 232). With that one exception, however, dynastic rebellions were animated by the belief that the ruler of the kingdom was king 'in fact, but not by right' and sought to replace the usurper with a claimant more directly descended from the true blood of the Plantagenets.

Richard duke of York made his claim on the grounds that, as the great-grand-son of Lionel of Antwerp, duke of Clarence, he was descended from Edward III by a line of blood senior to that of the reigning Lancastrian dynasty. The justification for doing so, clearly articulated in the declaration of the Yorkist title in Edward IV's first Parliament, was that this would itself effect a reform of the kingdom's government, putting an end to the 'unrest, inward war and trouble, unrighteousness, shedding and effusion of innocent blood' and other evils that were the inevitable result of a disturbance in the divinely-ordained succession.[6] Only in 1212, when Eustace de Vesci and others allegedly plotted to assassinate John and replace him with the elder Simon de Montfort, and again in 1327, when Roger Mortimer threatened Edward II with a successor who was not of the royal line if he did not abdicate in favour of his son, was there ever a suggestion that the accepted rules of inheritance, to which every landowner looked to guarantee the secure transfer of his own property to his children, should be set aside in the case of the Crown.

The third major group of rebellions consists of the popular risings: pre-eminently the 'English rising' of 1381 and Cade's rebellion in 1450, both insurrections by the peasantry of south-eastern England which succeeded in gaining temporary control of the capital, though there were also significant disturbances among the commons of Yorkshire between 1469 and 1471 and again in 1489, while the south-western rebellion in 1497 was serious enough to put Henry VII's control of the kingdom in question, at least for a moment. Though these popular risings were concentrated in the later part of the period, this does not mean that the common people had previously been politically passive. Many peasants were involved in the civil wars of 1264–65, and their actions were, at least on occasion, informed by an understanding and support for the cause of baronial reform such as that displayed by the villag-ers of Peatling Magna (Leicestershire), who accused one royalist captain of acting 'against the welfare of the community of the realm and against the barons'.[7] It was principally the changed economic conditions after 1350, notably the relative abundance of land and the high daily wages created by the fall in population, that gave the later medieval peasantry the confidence and resources to co-ordinate the independent expression of their grievances at a regional, even national, level. None of the risings in this group was, in fact, exclusively a revolt of the peasantry; the participation of the Londoners was a

The Battle of Sandwich, 1217. Though Matthew Paris's illustration of his own *Chronica Majora* depicts the naval encounter off Sandwich as a national struggle between English and French, it was also an episode in an English civil war, between those barons who wished to extend their renunciation of allegiance to King John to his son and heir as well, and those who did not. The victory of prince Henry's fleet, commanded by Hubert de Burgh, was instrumental in bringing both sides to the negotiating table; a final peace was concluded three weeks after the battle.

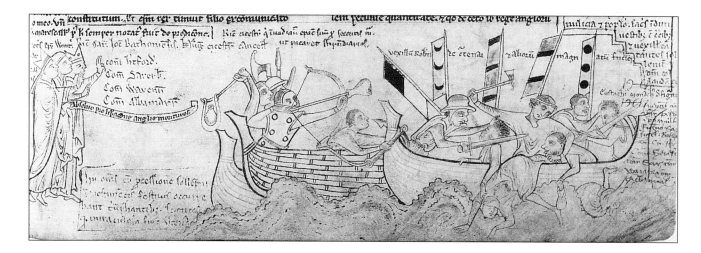

significant element in 1381 (see the illustration above), while Cade's rebellion enjoyed a significant measure of support from the lesser Kentish gentry, and the 'Robin of Redesdale' rising in 1469 included many gentry partisans of the earl of Warwick among the participants. They were, nevertheless, 'popular' risings in the sense that, in contrast to the two previous types of rebellion, which were invariably led by members of the aristocracy, the most prominent rebels were drawn from social levels below the nobility and gentry – Wat Tyler and John Ball in 1381, the pseudonymous Jack Cade in 1450, Ralph Flammanck in 1497. As a consequence, there was in all these revolts a substantial element of social and economic grievance against the operation of a lordship, whether seigneurial or royal, that was perceived as unjust and oppressive. In 1381 the rebels sought to abate this lordship by demanding the abolition of villeinage and a fixed rent of 4*d* an acre for tenanted land, while the high rents and entry fines exacted by landlords, together with their continued enforcement of labour services, remained a grievance for many of the Cade rebels in 1450. In general, however, the peasant rebellions sought to moderate the oppressions of lordship by claiming for their participants a place within the existing political process, not by seeking to create a new one, and their demands followed the same agenda as those of their social superiors, concentrating on the reform of particular abuses in the king's government and the removal of those royal advisers held responsible for them –

Rebels in London in 1381. The rebel leader, Wat Tyler, is shown riding into the king's presence at Smithfield – 'mounted on a little horse so that the commons might see him' – to present the second list of rebel demands. These were considerably more radical than the first set, presented at Mile End the previous day, and included demands that all lordship should be abolished, that much of the wealth of the Church be divided among the people, and that all men should be free of the bonds of villeinage. The rebels' profession of continuing loyalty to the Crown is represented in this illustration by the arms of England and the flag of St George under which they are mustered.

John of Gaunt, duke of Lancaster, together with the great officers of state in 1381, the 'false progeny and affinity' of the duke of Suffolk in 1450.

It was left to the last group of rebellions, the religious risings, to articulate a more radical set of social and political demands. Both the rebellion of Sir John Oldcastle in 1414 and the rising at Abingdon in 1431, led by the weaver William Perkins, sought a complete overthrow of the existing secular and ecclesiastical hierarchies and an inauguration of the rule of the godly – in this case, the adherents of the body of heretical doctrine associated with the teachings of John Wyclif, who sought to cleanse the Church of its corruption by a forcible disendowment of its temporalities. Oldcastle's alleged intention was to kill the king and his magnates, force the clergy into secular occupations and distribute the wealth of the churches among his followers. Though the project appears a far-fetched one, the contemporary success of the Hussite rebels in Bohemia in implementing a programme of clerical disendowment directly inspired by Wyclif's teachings meant that the threat of religious rebellion was always taken seriously by the ecclesiastical authorities – the archbishop of Canterbury's vigilance was thought to have prevented a further rising in 1428 – and exercised an influence on their actions far greater than the rebels' real prospect of success ever warranted.

Similar considerations affected the conduct of secular affairs, for the prospect of a further rising by the common people was, in the aftermath of 1381, an ever-present element in the calculations of the king's advisers. It was only the rumour of such a rising among the commons of Kent that finally allowed the Appellants to overcome Richard II's stubborn resistance to the execution of his favourite, Sir Simon Burley, in 1388. Frequent though rebellions were in later medieval England, therefore, the record of their actual incidence is only a partial guide to their political importance and influence. Fear of rebellion was, itself, a significant factor in the formulation of state policy. Behind the legislative and administrative reforms of Edward I's early years lay the anticipation of a renewal of Montfortian resistance in the Midlands, while the principal brake on Edward III's financial demands between 1336 and 1340 was his ministers' fears that any further taxation would provoke a general rising of the people. There was a further concern that a rebellion, once begun, would release the generalised social tensions that underlay medieval society, creating a downward spiral of widespread violence. The chronicler Adam Usk viewed the death of the rebellious lord Despenser at the hands of the townsmen of Bristol in 1400 with foreboding, fearing 'that they will make this an excuse to wield the sword against their lords more often in future' (see the illustration opposite).[8] Such fears were at their height during Edward II's reign, when the king's general failure to maintain an acceptable standard of public order meant that the frequent armed demonstrations against his actions made by Thomas earl of Lancaster and his allies could not be contained within the bounds of the political process. Indiscriminate violence accompanied the harrying of the Despensers' estates in the March of Wales during 1321–22, while a series of local risings broke out in Bristol, Bury St Edmunds and St Albans, Hampshire, south Lancashire and Glamorgan, adding a further element of local grievances and jealousies to the general disorder of the reign and its aftermath.

It was to guard against such dangers that, however frequently practice failed to live up to theory, the political ideal subscribed to by all sides in later medieval England – including the peasant rebels of 1381 – was one of monar-

Facing page Peasants as descendants of Cain. The continuing distrust with which the ruling authorities regarded their lesser subjects is well caught in this scene, from the Holkham Bible, in which Cain – distinguished by his 'mark', the horns protruding from under his hood – and his children are represented as peasant cultivators, busily engaged in the work of the fields. John Gower expressed an attitude widespread among landowners when he described the violence of the 'lesser people' as a sharp nettle, as uncontrollable as fire or flood.

chical authority, limited only by certain customary expectations. These expectations are well exemplified in the opening clauses of the Dictum of Kenilworth, drawn up in October 1266 as an instrument of pacification following the Monfortian civil war: the king was to rule freely and without the impediment or contradiction of anyone, provided always that he observed the liberties of the Church and the provisions of Magna Carta (see the illustration on p. 236) and the charter of the Forest (in the reissues of 1225); he also undertook to appoint worthy men to 'strengthen the throne and royal majesty with justice' by administering the realm according to its praiseworthy laws and customs.[9] Justice was, indeed, the quality most valued in a king, and contem-

Magna Carta. Concluded in June 1215, this agreement between King John and his baronial opponents sought to codify for the first time the acceptable limits of royal authority. It remained at the centre of political debate over the following century. Though it was rapidly modified into a document more acceptable to the Crown, it remained a potent symbol for those who sought to restrain royal actions; Archbishop Pecham sought to defend ecclesiastical liberties by posting the Charter in parish churches, while its confirmation was one of the concessions Edward I had to offer his opponents in 1297. The copy illustrated here is an exemplification of the enrolled version confirmed in 1297.

porary understanding of the term encompassed both the unhindered operation of the due process of law and a broader sense of an expectation of equitable, and hence predictable, treatment. Robert Grosseteste, bishop of Lincoln, succinctly expressed this ideal – in a tract known to Simon de Montfort – when he wrote that 'all things connected with rule should be directed by reason, the guardian of justice and equity'.[10] Denial of justice, whether it was the kind of favouritism alleged against Henry III in cases affecting the Lusignans, when 'he who should have been a propitious judge . . . became a terrible enemy',[11] or the more generalised abuse of legal procedure for the private advantage of Henry VI's household men complained of by the Cade rebels, or the setting aside of the fundamental customs of inheritance that drove the Marcher barons to arms in 1321–22, was the course of action most calculated to provoke a violent response from the king's subjects. Closely related to the denial of justice, and scarcely less fatal, was the misdirection of royal resources in the king's gift, since this inevitably implied a failure to act equitably by rewarding the deserving as well as punishing the unworthy. The emergence of a favourite, towards whom a disproportionate amount of royal patronage was directed, was a certain source of political tension. This was the case with William de Valence at Henry III's court, Piers Gaveston and Hugh Despenser in Edward II's reign, Robert de Vere in Richard II's, and William de la Pole under Henry VI. Each aroused the apprehension and hostility of the aristocracy and each was forcibly removed from his favoured prominence. With the possible exception of Piers Gaveston, it was not the position and actions of the favourite alone that created the conditions for rebellion. Rather, it was the existence of a single, and apparently easily remediable, grievance shared by a wide body of opinion that provided a focus for otherwise disparate discontents and alienated the king from his natural body of supporters. In 1258, for example, dissatisfaction with Henry III's government ranged over a variety of issues: the financial burdens of the general eyre then in progress; the actions of the royal sheriffs and, more generally, the oppressive policy of the Exchequer that lay behind their misdeeds; the king's inability to resist the encroachments of Llywelyn in the March of Wales; and the anticipated fiscal and military burden created by Henry's undertaking to enforce papal overlordship in Sicily. Yet it was the widespread dislike of the Lusignans, and the fear that the young prince Edward was about to fall under their control, that led to the sworn confederation of April 1258 and the confrontation with the king that followed.

What was at stake in these cases was not simply the resources favourites were able to gather to themselves, though this was always a significant consideration. Neither the Despensers' ability to triple the value of their estates in the decade after 1317 nor the Woodvilles' startling success in the marriage-market after 1464 went unnoticed by their enemies. Equally important was the more general denial of access to the king that a favourite's position supposed; a particular charge against the Despensers was that they would not allow anyone to approach Edward II unless one or other of them were present. Complaints about the distribution of patronage were, in this respect, more a symptom of discontent than a cause of rebellions, for what was distinctive about the king's distribution of his favour was that it was the principal attribute of his kingship still to depend – in a way that, after John's reign, the doing of justice could not – on the exercise of his unfettered will. In order to harness and domesticate this disturbing liberty the monarch was expected to be accessible and receptive to the advice of his greater subjects; in contemporary terms, to take good counsel. Failure to take counsel was the third great dereliction of which English kings could be guilty and it features frequently in the complaints preferred against them. Usually the failure was blamed upon 'evil counsellors', such as those Richard earl of Cornwall rose against in 1238 and the lords Ordainer sought to expel from the realm in 1311, estranging the king from his natural, noble, companions, though this convenient fiction did not free every ruler from a share of the blame; the Lancastrian deposition articles complained in 1399 that Richard II would not accept advice in Council, sharply censuring those who attempted to give it (see the illustration on p. 238). Questions of counsel and patronage were, of course, intimately related, for kings tended to reward most generously those whose advice they

The capture of Richard II. On campaign in Ireland in the summer of 1399, Richard II was caught off his guard by the sudden return of his exiled cousin, Henry of Lancaster, to England and his swift seizure of the kingdom. Richard's surrender, deposition and subsequent death in captivity inaugurated a century of dynastic instability. Richard's right to the throne of England had been undisputed but his style of rule was bitterly contested; impulsive and autocratic, he lost the respect and trust of his nobility as a teenager and, despite his best efforts, never succeeded in regaining them.

valued most highly, but the issue of counsel was especially important to the king's opponents for the public dimension it possessed, introducing questions of national interest – decisions over taxation and foreign policy – into the essentially private dialogue between the king and his greatest tenants. The imposition of a named and approved body of councillors, sworn to maintain the common good and charged with the control of appointments and overall supervision of the administration, was the favourite remedy for rebels faced with the practical problem of reforming royal government. It was an expedient attempted in 1258, 1311, 1385–88 and advocated, in a vaguer fashion, by the Cade rebels in 1450 when they called upon Henry VI to gather round himself 'the true Lords of his royal blood of this his realm'.[12]

The ability to do justice, a disposition to act equitably and a ready accessibility to his greater subjects were, then, the three qualities most valued in a king. If he could provide them, it was likely that the common advantages to be derived from maintaining the political concord and social harmony that guar-

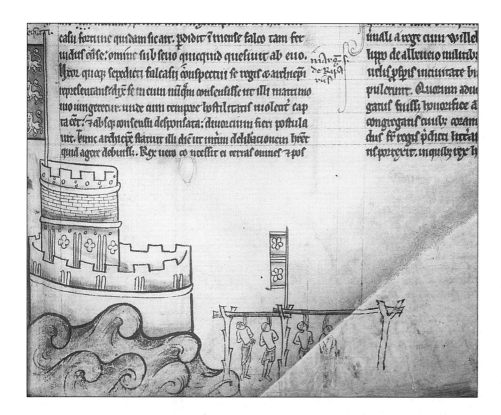

The siege of Bedford castle, 1225. Bedford was the stronghold of Fawkes de Breauté, one of King John's Norman captains, who achieved fame and notoriety in the confused early years of Henry III's reign. Largely responsible for the royalist victory at Lincoln in 1217, Fawkes turned his military success to material advantage, creating for himself a Midlands power-base that called into question the effectiveness of royal authority. Faced with the gradual dissolution of his influence, Fawkes reacted in 1225 by capturing a royal justice and having him imprisoned at Bedford. The subsequent siege of the castle was substantial enough to require a grant of taxation and, while it was in progress, the young Henry III swore by the soul of his father that he would hang the defending garrison. He kept his word, but such reprisals were rare in English civil conflicts; the fate of Bedford's defenders was sealed by the desire of the justiciar, Hubert de Burgh, to make an example of those who questioned his authority.

anteed the privileged position of both Crown and nobility would outweigh whatever grievances might be entertained against him. For every baronial rebellion in later medieval England, there was another armed demonstration that failed to attract sufficient support to present a serious threat to the kingdom's rulers, such as Henry earl of Lancaster's protest against the rule of Isabella and Mortimer in 1328–29 or Richard duke of York's march on the court in 1452. Yet when rebellion and civil war did break out, this was not solely the fault of incompetent kings. Aristocratic restraint was as important as royal sensitivity in maintaining the peace and it, too, was sometimes lacking. Political circumstance and private interest could combine to create as great an intransigence on the part of the king's opponents as Edward II or Richard II ever displayed. The shifting demands of the northerners, growing in scope and ambition as John's position weakened between 1212 and 1215, did as much to create the conditions for a civil war as the king's fiscal and administrative excesses. Purely factional disturbances, designed to further the concerns of their protagonists alone and conducted without reference to a wider political vocabulary, were rare, largely because their chances of success were slim. The rising of William de Forz in 1221 and Fawkes de Breauté's attempt to preserve his position as 'more than a king in England'[13] four years later (see the illustration above) were two such incidents, but on both occasions the collective discipline of the English nobility proved durable enough to withstand their challenges.

Some magnates were, nevertheless, violent and self-seeking by nature and their single-minded pursuit of their own ambitions in a highly-charged political context could act as a catalyst for violence, as the careers of Robert Ferrers, earl of Derby, during the period of baronial reform, and of Henry

Thomas of Lancaster as a saint.
Vindictive and rapacious in his
lifetime, Thomas earl of Lancaster
seems one of the least likely
candidates for sanctity. Yet his
inflexible defence of the provisions
of the Ordinances (1311),
combined with his execution by the
forces of the unpopular Edward II
in 1322, made his tomb at
Pontefract an object of veneration
and pilgrimage until the
Reformation. Shown here facing St
George in the first of a series of
miniatures depicting pairs of
popular saints, the equality of
treatment accorded Thomas is
usually taken to represent an
assumed equality of status.
Lancaster's cult, like that of Simon
de Montfort before him, never
received official ecclesiastical
recognition, but its early popularity
is evidence of the esteem in which
some opponents of the Crown
could be held.

Holland, duke of Exeter, in Henry VI's reign, demonstrate. If they were the exceptions to a general rule of responsible acceptance of royal lordship, even the most inflexible opponents of royal tyranny sometimes aroused the suspicion that adherence to constitutional principle could come close to the protection of private interest. Simon de Montfort incurred criticism for the generosity with which he rewarded his family and servants, while Thomas of Lancaster (see the illustration opposite) used his years of dominance in government to pursue a family quarrel with the earl Warenne. Even within the wider political struggle, the pursuit of personal advantage and the settling of old scores remained a priority; William de Ferrers and Brian de Lisle sought to use each turn of events in the civil war of 1216–17 to assert their control over the disputed castle of the Peak, while Roger Mortimer's summary execution of the Despensers in 1326 was a further violent episode in a feud between the two families stretching back at least two generations. Such struggles were the common currency of landed society and, given a degree of responsibility on the part of the protagonists, could usually be resolved through the traditional channels of royal and magnate lordship. Yet there can be little doubt that unchecked local disputes, such as the struggle for dominance in the south-west between William lord Bonville and Thomas Courtenay, earl of Devon, during Henry VI's reign, or the feud between the Stanley and Harrington families in Lancashire under Edward IV, served to undermine traditional loyalties and contributed to the polarisation of the political community. Similar considerations of self-interest lay at the root of a further source of conflict – the reluctance of loyal magnates, elevated to a position of unusual eminence by the support they had lent their king in a crisis, to surrender any of the political and financial advantages they gained in consequence as normal circumstances returned. This was the common characteristic shared by the revolts of the Percys in 1403, of the earl of Warwick in 1469 and of the duke of Buckingham in 1483.

Relations between kings and their nobles therefore continued to be vulnerable to occasional failures of political management by both sides, though the frequent rebellions against the rule of the Anglo-Norman kings and the prolonged instability of Stephen's reign make it seem unlikely that there was any general deterioration in the ability of the political nation to withstand and absorb these frictions over time. Yet there were two additional circumstances of political life, specific to the later Middle Ages, which contributed to its volatility. One was the dynastic uncertainty created by the deposition of Richard II in 1399. Under the canon law, deposition was a legitimate recourse for a king's subjects, provided that he could be shown to be insufficient to the task of ruling, incorrigible in his faults, and guilty of great crimes. The ceremonies removing Edward II and Richard II were careful to advertise the ways in which both kings satisfied these criteria. Edward II's abdication was, however, less of a threat to political stability than Henry of Lancaster's deposition of Richard II, which involved a break in the accepted line of succession to the throne. The difficulties this could entail had already been foreshadowed in December 1387 when the victorious Appellants, having apparently resolved to renounce their allegiance to the king, were forced to restore Richard to the throne because they could not agree among themselves on his rightful successor. The disruptive effect of the Lancastrian usurpation on fifteenth-century political life was felt in several ways. At times when the king had no son – which was, in practice, for just over half the century – it created an uncertainty and debate over the succession which was, in itself, unsettling. Richard duke of York's belief that he should be publicly recognised as Henry VI's heir-apparent served to sharpen the political differences between himself and his rivals for that recognition, the Holland and Beaufort families. As an almost inevitable corollary, the existence of alternative candidates with a claim to the Crown undermined the basis of mutual trust that should ideally have existed between a ruler and his greatest subjects, creating suspicion on the part of the king and unease among the suspected nobles. Even Archbishop Arundel, Henry IV's closest ally, was accused of supporting the Mortimer claim to the throne during Henry IV's early years, while the fate of Edward earl of Warwick, the great-nephew of Edward IV, held in captivity for fourteen years by Henry VII and finally executed on fabricated charges in 1499, was a striking illustration of the dangerous distinction royal blood conferred. Less directly, the dynastic instability of the century increasingly created among the nobility and gentry a wary reluctance to commit themselves irrevocably to any single claimant to the throne which, in turn, made the task of satisfying the political nation's appetite for firm rule all the harder. Richard duke of Gloucester sought to justify the pre-emptive deposition of his nephew, the young Edward V, on the grounds that he alone could maintain the precarious stability the Yorkist dynasty had achieved, and lost his throne when he failed to deliver the peace he had promised.

The second, and more important, development specific to the later Middle Ages was the increasing demand made by the English monarchy upon the resources of its subjects. Before 1215, baronial rebellions in medieval England had either arisen as adjuncts to a dispute over the succession to the throne, such as those that occurred immediately after the accession of both Henry I and Stephen, or as the result of the exclusion of too powerful an individual or too numerous a group from the king's favour – a state of affairs that prompted the risings of Odo of Bayeux (1088), Robert of Mowbray (1095) and Henry the Young King (in both 1173 and 1182). Though these two motives were, at times, scarcely distinguishable, the rebellions they fuelled were essentially disputes over the extent and destination of what the king had to give, rather than protests against the burden of what he was taking. It was not until the reign of John that, in response to the king's determined efforts to raise sufficient capital to recover his lost duchy of Normandy, the fiscal and administrative exactions of royal government were first placed at the centre of the demands of the king's opponents. Thereafter, the cost of defending the continental possessions of the English Crown by military and diplomatic means escalated rapidly, and the financial burden that the Crown's subjects were required to bear increased commensurately. Henry III spent some £80,000 on his campaign to regain Poitou in 1242, whereas Edward I had to set aside approximately £750,000 for his military commitments between 1294 and 1298 and Edward III spent a similar sum on his campaigns against the French between 1337 and 1341. Henry III had initially sought to meet these costly commitments by a more rigorous exploitation of the traditional fiscal prerogatives of the Crown; the failure of this policy underlay many of the grievances – such as the abuses of Forest law, the exactions of the justices in eyre and the excessive farms imposed on the shires – expressed in the Petition of the Barons. It soon became clear that such high levels of expenditure could only be met by the creation of a national system of regular direct and indirect taxation, which England possessed in all its essentials by 1300. The effect of this was to endow the Crown, even in peacetime, with unprecedented resources. Edward I had approximately £40,000 p.a. at his disposal before the onset of the military crisis of 1294–97, but his response to that crisis nearly doubled the sums available to him annually for the remainder of his reign and created a set of financial precedents that his son and grandson successfully exploited. Direct and indirect taxation, which had produced no more than 15 per cent of the Crown's income in the early twelfth century, was accounting for 80 to 90 per cent of all Exchequer receipts by the reign of Henry IV.

The search for such sums was itself bound to cause hardship and create resentment – the barons were complaining to Henry III, as early as 1244, that all in the kingdom were so oppressed by amercements and aids that they had little left to give. Resistance to the Crown's financial demands was, in consequence, an element common to many rebellions in the late Middle Ages. This element of fiscal protest is clearest in the risings of the commons; resentment at the heavy and inequitable incidence of the three 'poll taxes' imposed since 1377 was the catalyst for the great rebellion of 1381, while the regional risings of 1489 and 1497 were both protests against attempts to collect Parliamentary subsidies. Nor were high levels of taxation the only burden that the Crown's military ambitions laid upon its subjects. The feudal obligation of service in the king's army remained a contentious one, whose scope the king's opponents consistently sought to limit. The considerable resistance John encountered over the issue in 1213–14 was repeated when Edward I demanded service from his tenants-in-chief in Flanders, while the lords Ordainer went one step further in 1311 by seeking to deny altogether the king's ability to make war or to leave the country without the consent of the baronage in Parliament. Equally, the king's acknowledged right to purvey goods for the sustenance of his household was extended, under the pressure of war financing, into a quasi-national levy for victualling the royal armies. As a consequence, purveyance became another familiar target for the king's opponents. The Petition of the Barons complained that purveyors were taking two or three times as much as the needs of his household required, and similar complaints were echoed in the Remonstrances, the Ordinances, the manifesto issued by Archbishop Scrope in 1405 and the petitions of the Cade rebels.

It was not, however, simply the burden of royal demands that created the conditions for rebellion and civil war, though the heavy incidence of such demands was the justification most commonly cited by the rebels themselves. The social group most prominent in seeking to restrain the claims of the English state upon its subjects, the higher nobility, was itself only marginally affected by the fiscal aspect of the Crown's commitment to overseas warfare; Roger Bigod, earl of Norfolk, who led the resistance to Edward I's demands in 1297, paid less than 5 per cent of his estate revenue in taxation during the crisis years of 1294–97. More important was the gradually altered relationship between the king and the political community created by the era of intensive warfare that followed the loss of Normandy. The threat of attack and invasion by a common enemy – whether Scots, Welsh or French – conferred on the Crown's defensive measures a representative authority to speak and act on behalf of the English nation as a whole that it had not previously possessed. This had several significant consequences. It served to accentuate the traditional expectation that individual kings would discharge their duty of defence successfully and to intensify the penalties of failure. 'The road from Bouvines to Runnymede was direct, short and unavoidable';[14] the loss of Gascony and

Scotland through 'bad counsel and bad custody' was one of the justifications cited for the deposition of Edward II;[15] the fear of a French invasion of the south coast and the widespread perception that the natural defenders of the national interest were failing in their duty were important elements in the risings of 1381 and 1450. At the same time, the growth of direct taxation sanctioned by a representative assembly enlarged the circle of those who could claim a legitimate voice in how that duty of defence should be fulfilled. Against the enormous new resources conferred on the Crown by the growth of national taxation was balanced a novel justification for resistance to its demands, appeal to the interests of the 'community of the realm'. Concern for the provision of an effective national defence inevitably expanded from an initial preoccupation with the raising and funding of suitable forces to debate over the strategic priorities that underlay the Crown's demands. Disagreement over the direction of foreign policy, first openly manifested in the unanimous baronial opposition to Henry III's commitment to the conquest of the Sicilian kingdom, became an increasingly dangerous fault-line in English politics; readily comprehensible, highly emotive and capable of uniting disparate groups of the disaffected into an effective political alliance, as Richard II in 1387 and Henry VI in the 1450s both discovered to their cost.

Finally, the prominence of warfare in the Crown's calculations gave the king's opponents a new ability to make their misgivings effective. This arose from changes in the Crown's methods of military recruitment during the fourteenth century. Once the English kings ceased to depend upon the obligations of feudal tenure for a substantial part of their forces and chose, instead, to rely upon a contract army, in which the principal captains were paid at fixed rates for the troops they brought with them, the Crown was rendered technically indebted, often for quite substantial sums, to its principal subjects. Indebtedness had previously been one of the means by which successive kings, especially John and Edward I, had sought to discipline their recalcitrant magnates. Now it became a source of political leverage for the magnates, even, on occasion, a reason for rebellion; the Percys cited the £120,000 allegedly owed them by Henry IV as a justification for their rising in 1403. More significant, though, was the personal stake in the issue of Crown solvency this system of war financing gave the nobility and the additional incentive it provided to concern themselves with the details of royal income and expenditure – details that inevitably raised the issues of patronage, counsel and prerogative that formed the staple of debate between the king and his subjects. The debts Edmund Mortimer, earl of March, contracted in financing his campaigns abroad fuelled his support for the impeachment of Edward III's courtiers in the Good Parliament (1376), while the £26,000 owed Richard duke of York by 1446 for the costs of his lieutenancy in France only increased his determination to secure a more influential place in Henry VI's counsels.

In certain circumstances, therefore, the development of a 'war state' in later medieval England, highly taxed and intensively governed, does seem to have generated additional political tensions, and these sometimes spilled over into armed resistance to the demands of the Crown. Yet there were opportunities as well as dangers in this turn of events. Defeat abroad was perennially damaging, but victory was now doubly beneficial, not only enhancing the prestige of the individual ruler, but also confirming the representative legitimacy of the monarchy. It is no accident that the longest periods of domestic peace later medieval England experienced – from 1327 to 1381 and 1415 to 1450 –

were ushered in by the spectacular victories of Edward III and Henry V in France. How the balance of advantage between opportunity and danger is to be struck largely depends upon an estimate of the seriousness of the civil wars and rebellions considered in this chapter. It can be argued that, for all the strictures of contemporary commentators, the civil disturbances England experienced in this period were a relatively small price to pay for the development of the financial and administrative capacities of the state that the enterprise of war necessitated and for the sense of common political purpose it fostered.

When the record of English rebellions is set against the experience of other Western monarchies, there is little to suggest that English politics were uniquely violent or unusually prone to civil strife. The dynastic disruption so remarked upon by French observers was equally evident elsewhere: most notably in the German kingdom, which suffered a long interregnum between 1254 and 1273, followed by depositions in 1298 and 1400 and the murder of a third king in 1308; but also in Castile, where revolts of the nobility saw the actual deposition of one king in 1366 and the attempted deposition of another in 1465, and in Scotland, where James I was assassinated in 1437 and James III killed in battle agaisnt his nobles in 1488. Although France was unusual in escaping a change of dynasty, its political life suffered at least as much from court factions, noble feuds and royal incapacity as England's. Princely resistance to the regency of Blanche of Castile between 1226 and 1234; the provincial leagues of 1314–15; the Navarrese crisis (1356–58); the highly damaging struggle between Armagnac and Burgundian factions for control of Charles VI's court; the 'war of the public weal' (1465) and the *Guerre Folle* (1488): these were only the most spectacular instances of the French monarchy's failure to reach a lasting accommodation with an exceptionally powerful and independent noble caste, while the popular insurrections that disturbed the kingdom, such as the *Pastoureaux* movements in 1251 and 1320, or the *Jacquerie* (1356), were notably more destructive than their English equivalents.

Measured against these standards, the level of destruction that inevitably accompanies civil war seems to have been contained within generally acceptable bounds in England. Though the forces involved were sometimes considerable, as were the casualties at battles like Evesham and Towton, campaigns were usually short, and deliberate destruction of the countryside, a standard tactic of the English armies in France, was rare – Henry of Lancaster's punitive ravaging of Cheshire in 1399 and the depredations of Margaret of Anjou's army in 1460–61 are, in this respect, exceptional. Towns were occasionally sacked and looted, as happened at Winchester in 1265 and Stamford in 1461, but prolonged siege warfare, a staple of continental civil strife, was infrequent, as a result of the unprepared condition of most urban defences. In the treatment of defeated enemies, the rigours of the laws of war were often mitigated; John's decision to spare the defenders of Rochester in 1216 was more typical than Edward II's execution of the garrison of Leeds castle in 1321. When reprisals were unavoidable, prudent commanders, aware that popular support for their cause was a considerable political asset, sought to spare the commoners caught up in the quarrels of their masters.

In the light of these European comparisons, three features of English rebellions in the later Middle Ages stand out as distinctive: that there were no exclusively urban risings; that every rebellion became, however it began, a matter of national concern, defining its aims and demands by reference to the debates of national politics rather than simply seeking a remedy for regional grievances; and that this was as true of popular insurrections as of noble revolts. The internal politics of English town life was often contested and occasionally explosive, resulting in such spectacular demonstrations of defiance as occurred at Bristol (1312–16) and Norwich (1443), yet the matters under dispute were usually so specific that it was only at times of national political disturbance, notably in 1263–65 and 1381, that urban unrest took on a general significance. Equally, certain regions proved, by reason of their tenurial geography or the reserves of military manpower they possessed, particularly fertile breeding-grounds for rebellion. One such area was the March of Wales, where Richard Marshall was able to oppose Henry III with impunity in 1233, the baronial opponents of Edward I met to discuss their grievances in 1297 and a coalition of local barons first defeated Hugh Despenser in 1321. Yet though the March provided the setting for a show of defiance, the object of each of these protests was to effect a significant change in the course of national politics, not to resolve a local difficulty. Even a rising as localised and eccentric as the disturbances in Oxfordshire at Easter 1398 possessed a wider political dimension, for its leader, Thomas Gildesowe of Witney, claimed to be 'the young earl of Arundel'[16] – the son of a popular magnate unjustly executed by Richard II six months earlier.

This was partly a matter of geography, partly a matter of history. England was a small country, its extreme nothern border less than a week's hard ride away from London. Even a remote regional rising posed a potential threat to the execution of government, which the authorities had to treat correspondingly seriously; it took the south-western rebels less than a month to march from Taunton to Blackheath in 1497. Conversely, it was what happened at the political and administrative centre that was decisive in determining the outcome of many revolts. The keys to the kingdom lay in control of London, the capital city and the only commercial metropolis the country possessed, and it was the point towards which every rebel force sought to gravitate. It was the alliance between London and his opponents that finally forced John to concede Magna Carta and the Londoners' consistent support for reform that saved Simon de Montfort in 1263 and forced a compromise with the Disinherited on Henry III in 1267. The rising of the Londoners in October 1326 paralysed the attempts of the Despenser regime to organise any resistance to Queen Isabella's invasion, while the refusal of the London oligarchs to support him condemned Richard II to defeat in December 1387. Wise kings sought to purchase the capital's approval and support; Richard III's promise to bring Southwark within the jurisdiction of the City was only the most generous of many royal favours. Popular rebellions were no different in this respect from noble risings, seeking to gain control of the capital as a means of enforcing their demands; the willingness of the Londoners to admit the rebel forces in 1381 and 1450 ensured their short-term success, just as their refusal to open the gates to Thomas Fauconberg led to the dissolution of his forces in 1471.

Yet although England was a small, highly centralised state, in which control of the country was largely dependent upon control of a single city, there was no core of professional administrators – similar to the *baillis* and *intendants* of the Valois kings, or the *pesquisdores* and *corregidores* of the Castilian monarchy – to manage the machinery of government. In their absence, the Crown had to

rely upon a broad group of greater and lesser landowners to staff the local administration of the shires and to develop, through the county courts and quarter sessions, regular channels of communication between centre and locality. This inevitably bred a responsive political culture, in which a relatively extensive ruling class possessed a vested interest in the political health and fiscal credit of the Crown, and the political leverage to make their views effective. Political awareness was widely disseminated and the issues at stake between the king and his opponents well understood; petitions and complaints to the king and council made frequent and generally accurate reference to the great reforming measures of 1215, 1258 and 1311. The inevitable result of this was that any substantial failure of political management – whether at the king's court, in Parliament, or in dealing with the individual communities of city and county – generated widespread friction, of a kind that successive kings, dependent for much of their effective authority on the co-operation of the political classes and vulnerable to any withdrawal of goodwill, were ill-prepared to resist. This balance of power created conditions conducive to frequent civil strife, but it was only on rare occasions, and for brief periods (1264–65, 1321–22, 1459–61), that the protagonists in such conflicts abandoned the disposition to negotiate and compromise bred into them by the experience of self-government at the king's command (see the illustration above). Rebellion and civil war in later medieval England should not, therefore, be regarded as evidence of a serious deterioration in the quality of government, but as the price to be paid for the development of a cohesive and generally successful political culture. They were a vindication of the belief in the identity of interest between successive kings and their subjects, expressed with vigour by a group of Kentish sailors in 1450, that 'the crown of England . . . was the community of the said realm, and that the community of the realm was the crown of the realm'.[17]

Death and mutilation of Simon de Montfort. The mutilation of Simon de Montfort's body – and still more the subsequent presentation of his head and testicles to the widow of one of his enemies – after his death in battle at Evesham (August 1265) was an unaccustomed barbarity that shocked even his critics. It is also a measure of the unusual degree of polarisation in English politics that the earl of Leicester's policies had created over the previous two years. His insistence that Henry III observe the letter of the undertakings given in 1258 made him seem to some to be 'fighting bravely like a giant for the liberties of the kingdom' and to others to be no more than 'a lover and inciter of war'. Even in defeat, his ideals still had their adherents; it was nearly ten years before the heartland of de Montfort's support in the Midlands was fully pacified.

ENGLAND AND ITS NEIGHBOURS

Chris Given-Wilson

Rebellions, depositions, even civil wars were not infrequent in late medieval England, but its integrity as a nation-state was never really in question. The only occasions during this period when it was seriously threatened were in 1216–17, when the French Prince Louis invaded, and during the second decade of the fourteenth century, when the near-continuous Scottish raids under Robert Bruce made a mockery of the English king's claim to govern the northern counties. On each occasion it survived, and with something to spare. Yet England's experience in this respect was markedly different from that of its neighbours: France, Ireland, Scotland and Wales all faced political disintegration on at least one occasion between the thirteenth and fifteenth centuries, and the catalyst in each case was the same – English military and territorial ambition. It was, arguably, the uncommonly centralised and unitary nature of the English state which allowed it to behave in this way towards its neighbours, but it was also a consequence of events which in some cases had occurred long before 1200.

This is most obviously true in the case of France. The Norman Conquest established territorial links between England and France which were to endure for almost five hundred years (see the map opposite). Throughout this time, every king who ruled England also ruled a part of France, and although the extent of that part varied enormously – from the 'Angevin Empire' of 1154–1204, which encompassed about a third of the French kingdom, to the single town of Calais, to which the English hold in France was reduced after 1453 – it meant that for much of this period the overriding consideration behind the framing of English policy was likely to be the reaction of the French monarchy. This raises the fundamental question of what medieval English rulers regarded as foreign. Between 1066 and 1204, most English kings spent more time in France than they did in England. For William the

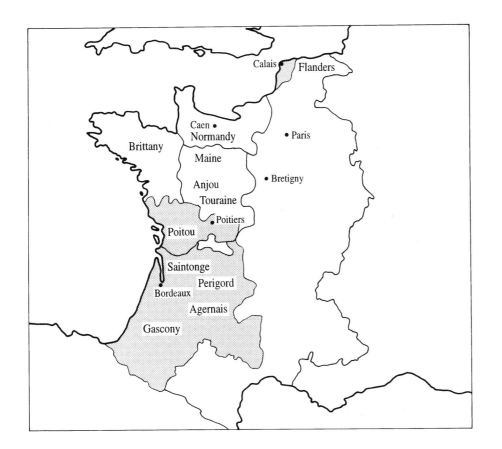

France after the Treaty of Bretigny, 1360. Between 1154 and 1204, the 'Angevin Empire' held by the English kings encompassed about a third of the French kingdom, including Normandy, Maine, Anjou, Touraine, Poitou, Gascony, and for a time Brittany. The northern lands of the Angevin Empire were lost to the French kings during the early thirteenth century, but, following his military successes against the Valois kings, Edward III was granted an expanded duchy of Gascony (the shaded area) and Calais and other territories in the north, in full sovereignty, by the Treaty of Bretigny in 1360.

Conqueror or Henry II, the idea that France was a 'foreign' country would have seemed absurd: Normandy and Anjou respectively were the heartlands of their empires (William is buried at Caen, Henry at Fontevrault), and French was the language they spoke. On the other hand, there was still a sense in which, as kings of England, they regarded the king of France as the head of a foreign power. In fact, most medieval English kings had a dual relationship with the kings of France, for while, as kings of England, they were his equals and frequently his adversaries, as holders of lands in France (that is, as dukes of Normandy or Gascony, or counts of Anjou or Ponthieu) they were simultaneously his vassals, and were thus numbered among the peers of the French kingdom. What they held in England, they held autonomously, but what they held in France, they held by feudal tenure from the king of France.

The ambiguity of this relationship was one of the primary causes of the Anglo-French warfare which dominated the politics of north-western Europe in the later Middle Ages. However, from the beginning of the thirteenth century a gradual change occurred in Anglo-French relations, brought about by the English kings' loss during the first quarter of that century of most of their French lands. Between 1204 and 1224, under Philip II 'Augustus' (1180–1223) and his son Louis VIII (1223–26), the French monarchy first confiscated and then overran Normandy, Anjou, Maine, Touraine and Poitou, which meant that the only part of Henry II's French empire now left to the English king was the south-western duchy of Gascony; and although the reality of these losses was not to be acknowledged by Henry III until 1259, its effect was in one sense immediate, for it meant that from now on English kings lived in, and operated primarily from, England. A prized possession Gascony might be, but it was never the heartland of an Anglo-French empire in the way that Normandy or Anjou had been. England's kings were becoming more truly English.

England was also the major power in the British Isles, and was not slow to assert itself as such. Military penetration of Wales had begun soon after the Norman Conquest, and in the 1170s it was carried to Ireland: by 1200, substantial parts of both countries were under the control of lords of Anglo-Norman stock who owed their allegiance to the king of England, and who existed in an uneasy and generally hostile relationship with the local inhabitants. This is not to say that the local ruling dynasties had been eliminated: Irish kings and Welsh princes – there were many of both – continued to hold land and exercise authority over their native subjects, but they were obliged to recognise English overlordship, and the area which they controlled was relentlessly diminished by waves of English migration. In Scotland, English pressure was more insidious, the chief difference being that Scotland was a unitary kingdom. Moreover, there were times in the twelfth century – most notably during the troubles of Stephen's reign – when Scottish kings effectively asserted their claim that Northumberland, Westmorland and Cumberland were really a part of Scotland. Nevertheless, English cultural and economic influence in Scotland increased markedly in the twelfth century, accompanied when necessary by sharp reminders of English claims on the obedience of its northern neighbour: in 1174, for example, having rashly joined a rebellion against Henry II, King William the Lion of Scotland (1165–1214) was forced by the Treaty of Falaise to make a humiliating public submission at York, to acknowledge that he was 'the liegeman of [King Henry II] against all men, for Scotland, and for all his other lands', and to surrender five Scottish castles to Henry's officers.[1] Henry did not try to exploit this submission, and in fact relations between England and Scotland were generally quite amicable for much of the thirteenth century, but there was no doubting the English view of the terms upon which they might remain so: namely, continuing Scottish acceptance that England was the senior partner.

By about 1230, then, England's relations with its neighbours were governed by two principal considerations. In France, the aim was to maintain control of Gascony as freely as possible from French interference, and if possible to recover the other Angevin lands recently lost. Within the British Isles, it was to preserve English authority in those areas which had been seized by English lords, and to continue to insist on the recognition of English overlordship elsewhere.

The second half of the thirteenth century saw a number of changes to this picture, the most significant of which was the Treaty of Paris in 1259 between Henry III and Louis IX (1226–70) of France. The principal terms of this treaty were that while Henry III abandoned his claims to the northern lands of the Angevin Empire – Normandy, Anjou, Touraine, Maine and Poitou – Louis IX would reverse the confiscation of Gascony decreed by Philip Augustus in 1202 (which had never been put into effect). This was in many ways simply a recognition of the status quo; in one crucial respect, however, it altered the status quo, for it was a condition of the treaty that if Henry was to be recognised as duke of Gascony, he must hold it from the French king by liege homage, which was, at least in theory, a more binding form of vassalage than had been agreed hitherto. Precisely what liege homage entailed was not spelt out, and was later to be a source of much disagreement between English and French kings. Nor did it prove easy to define the limits of the duchy of Gascony, and there remained a peripheral borderland in areas such as Saintonge, Perigord and Agenais where the competing claims of French and English overlordship provided an almost constant source of friction. Nevertheless, the Treaty of Paris did provide the basis for peace for much of the next eighty years: its great virtue was that it narrowed the area of potential Anglo-French disagreement to the question of Gascony.

The second half of the thirteenth century also saw the intensification of English claims to overlordship within the British Isles. This has at times, understandably, been interpreted as a conscious change of direction following the improvement in Anglo-French relations in the 1250s, but it is probably more correct to see it, in Ireland and Wales at least, as a gradual evolution from what might be described as a primary phase of lordship – recognition of English sovereignty, colonial plantation, the taking of tribute and hostages, and so forth – to a secondary phase entailing the annexation and integration of the conquered lands into the permanent judicial and governmental structure of the occupying power. The 1240s and 1250s were especially significant in this respect: Henry III led a number of campaigns to Wales during these years – insisting on his own feudal overlordship of both English-held and Welsh-held lands there, demanding that disputes be settled at Westminster – and in 1254 he granted Ireland to his eldest son, the future Edward I, with the proviso that 'the land of Ireland shall never be separated from the Crown of England'.[2] In both countries, the Crown rather than the aristocracy was now the driving force behind English colonial enterprise.

Under Edward I these developments reached a climax, most notably with his conquest of Wales. Llywelyn ap Gruffudd, prince of all Gwynedd from 1256, took advantage of the disturbed state of English politics between 1258 and 1265 to lead a native Welsh revival and establish his power through much of Wales, even securing recognition as 'Prince of Wales' from Henry III in 1267, but when he began to flout Edward I's authority in the 1270s, he was quickly brought to heel, and when he and his brother David rebelled again in 1282 they were shown no mercy. Llywelyn was killed in a skirmish, David executed as a traitor. That brought the direct line of the princes of Gwynedd to an end, and Edward now determined on full integration: by the Statute of Rhuddlan (1284), north and west Wales – the area not already held by English lords – was annexed to the English Crown (see the map on p. 252). An English administration directly accountable to Westminster was established at Caernarvon, Welsh criminal law was abolished, and a ring of massive castles was constructed around Snowdonia to enforce English rule in this most impenetrable of Welsh strongholds (see the colour plate on p. 225). Welsh independence was at an end. In 1301, to emphasise the fact, the title of 'Prince of Wales' was conferred by Edward upon his eldest son, the future Edward II, a title which is still borne by the heir to the English throne (see the colour plate on p. 226). The effect of Edward I's conquest was permanent: since then, Wales has remained more fully integrated into the English governmental structure than Scotland or any part of Ireland. It also brought a degree of stability to late medieval Wales which had been lacking during the previous two centuries. It can hardly be imagined that the Welsh

Wales following Edward I's conquest: between *c.* 1100 and 1270 eastern Wales, and much of the south, was brought under the rule of English lords (the 'Marchers'). Thus Edward I's 'Conquest of Wales' in the 1270s and 1280s was really the culmination of a process which had been going on for some 200 years. The map shows the Principality of Wales annexed to the Crown in 1284 and the ring of castles constructed by Edward I around Snowdonia (the heartland of Welsh resistance) to enforce his conquest.

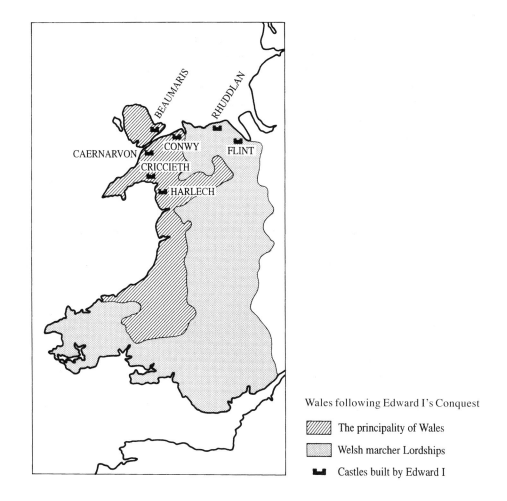

Wales following Edward I's Conquest

▨ The principality of Wales

▦ Welsh marcher Lordships

▄ Castles built by Edward I

welcomed their subjection to the English, but they were made brutally aware of the futility of kicking against it, for the strength of English lordship there, and Wales's proximity to the south-eastern centres of English power, usually made it relatively simple to crush what opposition arose. More than anything, it was this simple fact of geography that gave the story of English colonialism in Wales an outcome so different from those in Ireland and Scotland.

For if the conquest of Wales was – from the English point of view – Edward I's greatest triumph, his attempts to conquer Scotland ended in frustration. This is not to suggest that Edward set out to conquer Scotland, any more than he had set out to conquer Wales – although conquest certainly became his goal in both countries. In fact, there was little to suggest during the first fifteen years or so of his reign that Anglo-Scottish relations would not continue to be characterised by that harmony which had prevailed through much of the thirteenth century; Scottish claims to the northern English counties had been abandoned by the re-establishment of the Tweed–Solway border in the Treaty of York (1237), and the Scottish kings Alexander II (1214–49) and Alexander III (1249–86) busied themselves with the building of an effective and relatively unified kingdom on England's northern border. But, as so often, it was dynastic tragedy that opened the door to intervention. Alexander III's two sons and one daughter all predeceased him, so that when, on the night of 19 March 1286, his horse plunged over a cliff near Kinghorn in Fife, carrying the king to his death, his heiress was his grand-daughter Margaret, the 'Maid of Norway'; and when, in 1290, the 7-year-old Margaret, to whom Edward had hoped to marry his own son, also died, Scotland was thrown into a succession crisis.

The 'Great Cause' to determine the succession to the Scottish throne was thus set in motion, and Edward now began to throw his weight around. Claiming his rights of feudal suzerainty, he made it clear that he intended to use this opportunity to impose English overlordship on Scotland once and for all. Strictly speaking, Edward acted within the law, and there can be little doubt that John Balliol, upon whom the choice fell, had the best claim to the Scottish throne, but nor is there much doubt that Edward's bullying attitude stirred up considerable resentment among the Scots, especially those who supported Balliol's chief rival for the throne, Robert Bruce lord of Annandale. Nor did he stop there: once Balliol had become king (in November 1292), Edward insisted upon the exercise of his rights of over-lordship; appeals from Scottish courts were transferred to Westminster, and demands were sent ordering the Scottish king to attend English parliaments and to perform military service in the English army. Balliol was in effect treated like any other English magnate, and his position soon became intol-erable. Caught between the intransigence of Edward I on the one hand, and growing Scottish impatience at English presumption on the other, he was forced in 1295 to hand over effective power in Scotland to a council of twelve, and in February 1296 an alliance was concluded between Scotland and France. By this time, Edward was at war with France, and such an alliance could mean but one thing: war between England and Scotland was now unavoidable.

It was not only unavoidable, it was also, so it was to prove, almost unstop-pable. Nine English armies were sent to Scotland during the last twelve years of Edward I's reign; Balliol was deposed, Berwick-upon-Tweed (Scotland's chief port) captured, the Stone of Destiny – the ancient coronation seat of the Scottish kings – removed from Scone to Westminster abbey (see the illustration on p. 254), and Scotland itself demoted in Edward's eyes from a kingdom to a 'land' (*terra*), governed by lieutenants appointed by the English king. Yet, despite this massive military effort, the resistance of Scottish parti-sans led by popular leaders such as William Wallace and the Morays meant that Edward was unable to subdue Scotland. By 1305, the year in which Wallace was horrifically executed at Smithfield, it seemed as if he might have done so, but in the following year Robert Bruce (the grandson of the man who had claimed the throne in 1290) led a fresh rebellion and had himself crowned at Scone; and when, in the summer of 1307, the ageing Edward tried to take an army north to crush the revolt, he got only as far as Carlisle before dying. Bruce's reign (1306–29) marks the high point of Scottish kingship in the Middle Ages. He raided northern England at will, inflicted a crushing defeat on the feeble Edward II at Bannockburn on Midsummer Day 1314, recap-tured Berwick in 1318, and even succeeded, shortly after Edward II's deposi-tion, in forcing the English government to recognise him as king of an independent Scottish realm (the 'shameful peace' of Edinburgh, 1328). His success was unparalleled, and whatever doubts one might have about how much he could have achieved against a more formidable English opponent, to him must nevertheless go much of the credit for instilling among Scotsmen that sense of nationhood and self-belief so eloquently expressed in 1320 at the Declaration of Arbroath:

> For as long as a hundred men are left, we will never submit in the slightest to the dominion of the English. It is not for glory, riches or honours that we fight, but only for liberty, which no good man loses but with his life.[3]

Yet scarcely had Bruce been laid to rest in Dunfermline abbey when such sentiments were put to the test, for Edward III was of far sterner stuff than his father, and immediately began scheming to overturn the Treaty of Edinburgh. Circumstances were propitious for Edward, for Bruce's heir David was just 5 years old. In 1333 the English king invaded Scotland, won a bloody victory at Halidon Hill, retook Berwick, and installed Edward Balliol – the son of the deposed John Balliol, who had died in 1313 – on the Scottish throne. In return, Balliol handed over the eight southern counties of Scotland

The Coronation Chair, Westminster Abbey: the wooden Coronation Chair used by the kings and queens of England was constructed for Edward I between 1297 and 1300, and was designed to enclose the 'Stone of Destiny' (visible in this photograph), the ancient stone upon which kings of Scotland had been proclaimed as monarchs at Scone (near Perth). Edward I seized it and brought it south during his invasion of Scotland in 1296. It has remained at Westminster ever since, apart from a few months in 1951 when it was 'kidnapped' by Scottish nationalists, being found a few months later in Arbroath abbey. The Coronation Chair was decorated by Walter of Durham.

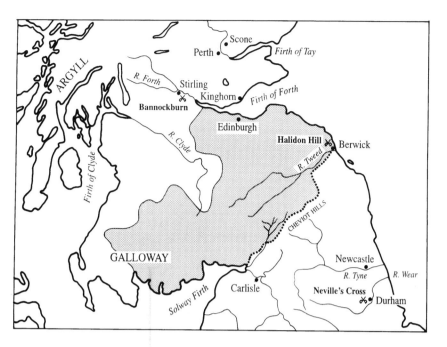

to Edward, 'to be annexed to the crown of England for all time to come' (see the map above).[4] And although a nationalist faction soon gathered around Bruce's heir, the boy was nevertheless obliged to flee for protection to France, where he landed in May 1334. As a result, the Anglo-Scottish dispute became entangled in Anglo-French affairs, which since the 1290s had also taken a distinct turn for the worse.

The war that had broken out between England and France in 1293–94 was concerned almost exclusively with the issue of Gascony. For the previous half-century or so, there had been a striking degree of amity and cultural interchange between the English and French courts, but the issues left unresolved by the Treaty of Paris were no closer to resolution by the 1290s, and once goodwill evaporated, the potential for conflict was ever-present. The principal issue was that of the French king's sovereignty, especially his judicial sovereignty: to what extent might appeals from Gascon subjects of the king of England be referred to the Paris *Parlement*, the high court of the king of France? It was a question upon which both Edward I and the French king Philip IV (1285–1314) had decided views (see the illustration on p. 256). Edward was determined to maintain sovereignty in his dominions: if appeals from Gascon courts were to be heard anywhere, it was in his own parliament. Between 1273 and 1275 he held a great 'Gascon inquest', the object of which was to tighten up English administration in Gascony and make it more directly accountable to Westminster, and in 1286–89 he visited the duchy again to reinforce his lordship. Perhaps this was because he understood the temper of the new French king, but Philip IV's attitude to Gascony must also be seen in the context of the development of the French state in the thirteenth century. Since the destruction of the Angevin Empire, the French monarchy had moved relentlessly towards the creation of a more unified and centralised state, the result of which had been to transform the fragmented and strife-torn kingdom of the twelfth century into the foremost power in

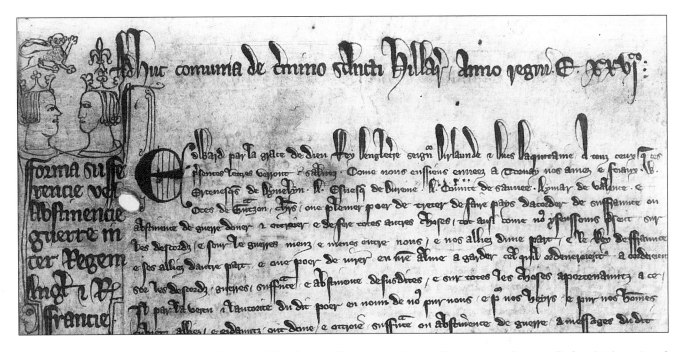

Edward I (on the left) confronting Philip IV of France (1285–1314), an illustration drawn by a clerk in the margin of an exchequer memoranda roll in 1297. Both kings were forceful characters and acutely aware of their competing claims in Gascony, over which they were at war with each other for ten years, between 1294 and 1303.

Europe. Yet there still remained a small number of great fiefs which resisted control from Paris – most notably Gascony, Flanders, Brittany and Burgundy. Philip IV was determined to be the master of his kingdom, and it was in such a spirit that he contemplated the independence of the great fiefs, Gascony included.

Flanders was a second area in which Anglo-French tensions were coming to a head in the 1290s. Flanders, with its rich cloth-manufacturing towns of Ghent and Ypres, and its busy international port of Bruges, was the wealthiest and most urbanised region of northern Europe. It was also of vital importance to both France and England: politically, the county of Flanders was a fief of the king of France, and its position on the nothern border of the French kingdom gave it considerable strategic significance. Economically, however, Flanders was dependent upon England for the supplies of raw wool – England's chief export – which fed its cloth-manufacturing industry. When England and France went to war, therefore, Flanders was peculiarly vulnerable. Urbanisation and industrialisation had also created deep social tensions within Flanders, where the powerful townsmen, natural allies for England on account of their economic needs, frequently saw their interests as different from those of the more Francophile count and nobility.

The war which broke out between Edward I and Philip IV in 1293–94 brought these issues to a head, and created a series of alliances in north-western Europe which were to set the pattern in times of conflict for the next century or so. Scotland turned to France, and the 'Auld Alliance' was born; the Flemish, seeking an ally to help them resist French centralisation, allied with England in 1297. The message to Philip was clear: if he proposed to interfere in England's 'backyard', Edward would reply in kind. Yet the war failed to solve any of the underlying problems: Gascony was occupied by French forces for a number of years, but following the French defeat by the Flemish at Courtrai in 1302, both sides agreed to abandon their allies, and in 1303 an Anglo-French peace which more or less restored the status quo ante was sealed by the marriage of the future Edward II and Isabella, the daughter of Philip IV.

Nevertheless, a pattern had been set, and it was to prove difficult to break. Over the next forty years, with continuing war between England and Scotland, continuing French attempts to bring the Flemish to heel (a further five French armies were sent to Flanders between 1313 and 1328), and continuing tension in Gascony – where another brief Anglo-French conflict flared up in 1324–25 – England and France were never far from open warfare. Edward III's well-known claim to the French throne – which came to him through his mother Isabella, following the death of Charles IV of France in 1328 – had little to do with the outbreak of war in 1337. He had shown himself willing in 1331 to acknowledge Philip VI (1328–50) as the rightful king of France by agreeing to perform liege homage for Gascony. At the same time, the two kings decided to set up a commission (the 'Process of Agen') to try to sort out the problem of Gascony. This suited Edward well: he was more interested in the early 1330s in trying to reassert English control of Scotland. It was Philip VI's decision in 1334 to help David Bruce which precipitated the breakdown in Anglo-French relations, for Edward wanted to deal with Scotland and Gascony separately. Philip, afraid that Edward would, if allowed his own way, all too rapidly succeed in Scotland before returning, strengthened, to the Gascon question, told Edward in 1334 that he would not reach any agreement over Gascony unless Scotland were included too. The 'Process of Agen' broke up in acrimony, and Edward began to rebuild the anti-French coalition in the Low Countries. Although unable to win the count of Flanders to his side, he employed the economic weapon of a wool embargo on Flanders to such good effect that the Flemish townsmen turned against their count and sought their own alliance with England. The ostensible reason for the outbreak of war in 1337 was Philip VI's fury at the fact that Edward had harboured the French rebel Robert of Artois, but what really lay behind it was the inability to contain the regional conflicts in Gascony, Scotland and Flanders any longer.

The Hundred Years War, as it came to be known (though not until the nineteenth century) was to dominate England's relations with its neighbours for the rest of the Middle Ages. Its traditional dates are 1337 to 1453. It was, of course, a very spasmodic affair, including long stretches of military inactivity, truce and even one period of Anglo-French peace (1360–69). It is perhaps best seen as a series of episodic conflicts with certain unifying characteristics, the most obvious of which was the continuing hostility of the two principal protagonists, England and France. Yet it was also both more and less than an Anglo-French war: more, because not just England and France but much of western Europe was dragged into it at various times; Scotland and the Low Countries especially, but also Germany, the papacy, and the Iberian kingdoms: less, because it is also possible to view the Hundred Years War as a French civil conflict, although this is an approach which on the whole has been favoured more by French historians than English. It was also the approach favoured by the French monarchs of the time, and not surprisingly, since it was self-evidently in their interests to present the conflict as a feudal one between a sovereign and his vassal (the duke of Gascony), whereas it was in the English king's interests to present it as a national and dynastic struggle. This is why, from an early stage in the war, Edward III's claim to the French throne came to assume the importance which it did. His claim was, in fact,

The French Succession in 1328: Edward III's claim to the French Crown in 1328 was a good one, since he was at the time the only surviving grandson of Philip IV. However, it was decided by the French nobles that a woman could neither accede to the throne nor transmit her claim to it to her children (regardless of their sex), so the Crown passed instead to the nearest claimant through a male line, Edward's cousin Philip de Valois (Philip VI).

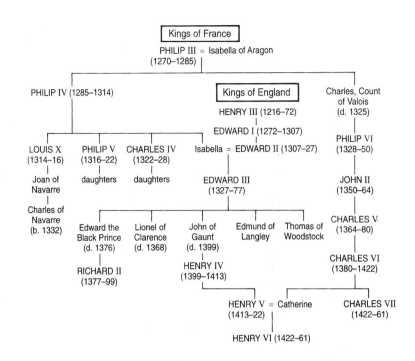

quite a good one, for following the extinction of the Capetian dynasty in the direct male line with the death of Charles IV in 1328, he was the only living grandson of Philip IV (see the illustration above). Yet it should hardly come as a surprise that it was rejected, not only because of the fact that he was king of England, but also because his claim came through a female line, and if one matrilineal claim were to be allowed, how many more might follow? What, for example, if Joan of Navarre, the daughter of Louis X (1314–16) were to marry and have a son? (which, as it turned out, she soon did).

Nevertheless, Edward's title as 'king of France' – formally assumed at Ghent in January 1340 – was more than a weighty bargaining counter (which it certainly was) in the negotiations with the French. It also provided many of those who lived within the borders of the French kingdom with a legitimate excuse for opposition to the Valois regime, particularly the many disaffected in the great fiefs such as Brittany and Flanders, who now took advantage of the war to try to regain the autonomy which they had lost during the thirteenth century. And as the war went from bad to worse for the French, disillusionment with the early Valois kings and doubts about the legitimacy of their rule grew apace, and ever more Frenchmen looked to Edward III for relief, so that there were times when the war really did have more of the aspect of a civil war than a national one.

This French disunity goes some of the way towards explaining the astonishing success which Edward enjoyed in the 1340s and 1350s, though naturally his own qualities of leadership and military organisation also played a major part. The standard English tactic for much of the fourteenth century has come to be known as the *chevauchée*, a raid through France under the king or one of his captains with an army usually numbering about 5,000 to 10,000 men, the chief objects of which were to plunder and destroy, amass booty, lower the morale and taxable capacity of the regions through which it passed, demonstrate the inability of the French king to protect his people and entice him to battle. There was also much siege warfare, mainly of towns in Brittany (where a war of succession broke out in 1342, with the French supporting one claimant and the English the other) and on the fringes of Gascony, though the most famous siege of all was the eleven-month blockade which resulted in the surrender of Calais in August 1347 and its occupation by the English for the next two hundred years. Battles were infrequent; the three most famous during this first phase of the war were the naval battle off Sluys (Flanders) in 1340, and the engagements at Crecy in 1346 and Poitiers in 1356. All three were English victories. At Crecy Edward III himself was in command, but at Poitiers the English army was led by the king's eldest son, Edward the Black Prince, and not only did he inflict a terrible slaughter on the French nobility, he also captured the French king John II (1350–64). Devastated by twenty years of warfare, France was brought to its knees by the defeat at Poitiers, and negotiations for peace now began in earnest, though they took nearly four years to conclude. The resulting Treaty of Bretigny (near Chartres) of May 1360 reflected the extent of English success: King John, who had spent the past four years in English captivity, was ransomed for the outrageous sum of £500,000 – four or five times the average annual income of the English Crown – and Gascony and its debatable borderlands, even including Poitou, were given to Edward III in full sovereignty, as were Calais and a number of neighbouring towns and lordships in the north of France. King John had been forced to dismember his kingdom. The only concession made by Edward in return was to forgo his claim to the throne of France. It was a diplomatic triumph to match the military triumphs of the past fifteen years, and it established England as the foremost military power in western Europe. It also brought to an end the opening phase of the Hundred Years War, and ushered in nine years of Anglo-French peace.

The magnitude of their defeat at Poitiers was what forced the French to begin serious negotiations for peace; it also convinced the Scots that, for the moment at least, there could be no expectation of help from France. Since Edward III had first begun to champion the cause of Edward Balliol in the early 1330s, the fortunes of the Anglophile (Balliol) and nationalist (Bruce) parties in Scotland had swung back and forth. By 1341, when they recaptured Edinburgh, David Bruce's supporters had recovered enough ground to enable the young king, now 17, to return from his French exile, and during the next five years a number of expeditions were launched into England. There was no doubt about the seriousness with which the English regarded the Franco-Scottish alliance; at the Westminster parliament of 1344, for example, it was announced that

> the Scots, who are allies of the said Adversary [of France], say openly that whenever the said Adversary lets them know that he does not wish to keep the truces, they will not keep them either, but will ride into England and inflict what evil they can.[5]

It was in pursuit of just such an objective, however – a request from the French king to invade England while Edward was besieging Calais – that disaster struck: on 17 October 1346, a Scottish army led by King David was defeated at Neville's Cross outside Durham, and the Scottish king taken captive. He remained a prisoner in England for the next eleven years. Yet although David's capture reduced the threat from the Auld Alliance, in some ways it raised as many problems as it solved. Should he be ransomed, or should Edward III now press for Scottish acceptance of Edward Balliol – on behalf of whose rights he had, at least ostensibly, been warring with the Scots – as their king? As it turned out, Scottish resistance under the guardianship of Robert the Steward remained undiminished, and Balliol failed to press home the advantage, so that the English king soon began to conceive of a new plan. As early as 1350 it seems that Edward was prepared to negotiate David's release on various conditions, including the stipulation that should he die childless, the king of England or one of his sons would be recognised as his heir. Edward Balliol had outlived his usefulness, and was now, like his father before him, to be discarded: on 20 January 1356, in a theatrical gesture at Roxburgh, he lifted the Scottish crown from his head and handed it to Edward III, together with a handful of earth and stones, thereby signifying the resignation of his Scottish claims to the English king in return for a life pension of £2,000. Yet an English succession was unacceptable to most Scotsmen, and although the diminished prospects of effective French support after Poitiers convinced them of the necessity to treat with Edward III, all that was agreed at the 'Treaty' of Berwick in October 1357 was that King David would be allowed back to Scotland in return for a ransom of £66,666, payable over ten years, during which a truce would prevail. In this sense at least, the Auld Alliance had served its purpose: it was Edward's pre-occupation with French affairs that convinced him of the necessity to settle for a ransom alone, and to abandon his hopes of a Scottish crown for himself or one of his children.

Yet, as the events of the 'peaceful' 1360s were to show, the aggrandisement of his dynasty continued to occupy Edward III's mind. In 1362, Gascony and its borderland were erected into the principality of Aquitaine and granted to the Black Prince, the heir to the English throne. Negotiations were also set in motion to try to secure the hand of Margaret, heiress to the county of Flanders, for the king's fourth son, Edmund of Langley, though these were ultimately to prove fruitless; and in 1371, following military intervention in the Castilian civil war, Edward's third son, John of Gaunt, was married to the daughter of the murdered King Peter, whereby Gaunt acquired a claim to the throne of Castile. Although this claim was never to be realised either, it was a sign of the prestige and self-confidence of the English king that he could entertain such grandiose schemes for the advancement of his family in Europe. But there were also problems closer to home to be dealt with, and the ending of the war with France provided the opportunity to do so. The most pressing of these was Ireland, and it was to his second son, Lionel of Clarence, that Edward turned.

The 'English of Ireland', as they called themselves, spent much of the fourteenth century on the retreat. Since the time of Edward I, when English lordship in Ireland had reached its greatest extent, and a more rigorous system of financial and judicial control from Westminster had been established over the Dublin administration (see the illustration opposite), English migration to Ireland had dried up, and the native revival had steadily pushed back the Anglo-Irish settlers, all but expelling them from Ulster in the north and Connacht in the west. The reaction of some was to return to England (complaints from the Anglo-Irish about absentee landlords and falling land prices became ever more insistent as the fourteenth century progressed), while those

The Irish Exchequer in action, from the Red Book of the Exchequer, *c.* 1400. The Exchequer was based at Dublin, the administrative centre of English rule in Ireland, which by this time was shrinking steadily. Those who owed money to the Crown, or were owed money by it, came here to settle their accounts with the royal officials, the chequered cloth being used as an abacus to assist calculations. The heading at the top of the page, in Anglo-Norman, reads 'Welfare for the people' (*Bone estate pour le people*).

Late medieval Ireland: between *c.* 1170 and 1300, more than half the surface area of Ireland was brought under English rule, centred at Dublin. During the fourteenth and fifteenth centuries, however, the area of English administrative control gradually dwindled, until in 1484 it was defined by statute as consisting of the 'Pale' (shaded in the map). Elsewhere, the native Irish kings competed with Anglo-Irish lords such as the earls of Desmond, Ormond and Kildare for control of land and people.

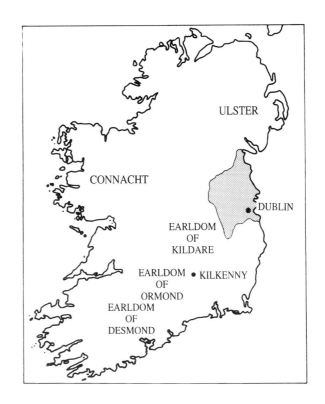

who chose to stay such as the Geraldine earls of Desmond and Kildare, and the Butler earls of Ormond, came to form a more distinctly Irish nobility with few interests in England and a frequently hostile and carping attitude towards a Westminster government which they believed was allowing English rule in Ireland to slip away (see the map above). It was increasingly to this compact group of great families that the English government was obliged to entrust the responsibility of maintaining English rule in Ireland, and they exercised it on their own terms: the native Irish chieftains might be permitted to rule in the north and west, but the English political and legal system remained closed to them, and they had practically no contact with the administration in Dublin. As a result, by the mid-fourteenth century Ireland contained in effect two communities, and English rule there was in danger of becoming the preserve of the great Anglo-Irish families. Equally disturbing was the fact that revenues from Ireland to the English Exchequer had fallen sharply since the early fourteenth century.

Edward III's decision to send Clarence to Ireland in 1361 marked the beginning of a forty-year period during which much English money and effort was spent on trying to recover, or at least to stabilise, English rule there – but to little avail. Between 1361 and 1376, the English Exchequer spent £71,000 on Ireland; Clarence himself remained there for five years, to be succeeded by the notorious William of Windsor, the husband of Edward III's mistress Alice Perrers. Richard II also showed much interest in Irish affairs, promoting his favourite Robert de Vere to be duke of Ireland in 1386 (it was even rumoured that he planned to make de Vere king of Ireland),[6] and leading expeditions there himself in 1394–95 and 1399, the first royal expeditions to Ireland since that of King John in 1210. Richard's policy in Ireland, although unsuccessful in the long term, was at least different: he met the Irish chieftains face to face, took submissions from them, and tried to draw them into a more direct relationship with the English Crown. He was, in effect, trying to create 'a polity that took in all the powerful elements in the island',[7] but history was against him. To attempt to reintegrate the native Irish and Anglo-Irish communities was not only to resurrect the host of irreconcilable claims which divided the two communities, but also to threaten the privileges upon which the security of the Anglo-Irish was based. Neither side could compromise, and when Richard hurriedly departed in July 1399 – shortly to lose his throne – he left Ireland much as he had found it. The legacy of English rule in fourteenth-century Ireland was not Richard II's attempted settlement in the 1390s but the Statute of Kilkenny, passed in 1366 during the last months of Clarence's lieutenancy, 'a programme designed to protect the Englishness of the English of Ireland',[8] which excluded the 'wild Irish' from ecclesiastical office, forbade intermarriage between them and the English settlers, and prohibited the latter from using the Irish language, dress or pastimes. Confirmed on numerous occasions between 1366 and 1495, it was not to be repealed until 1613.

Within three years of the passing of the Statute of Kilkenny, however, England was back at war with France, and Irish affairs took second place again. This phase of the Hundred Years War, which lasted from 1369 until 1389, was to prove a dispiriting affair for England. By the time he died in 1377, Edward III had already lost most of what he had won at Bretigny, and although the English sustained few further setbacks over the next twelve years, they were not able to recover what they had lost. There were various reasons for this. Most obviously, political leadership in England was lacking, with the senility of Edward III and the premature death of the Black Prince in 1376 being followed first by the minority of Richard II and then by the domestic turbulence of his majority. English foreign policy became fragmented. John of Gaunt, who by 1377 was the new king's senior surviving uncle (Clarence had died in 1368), hoped to use English resources to press his claim to the throne of Castile. Richard himself increasingly favoured a moderate attitude towards France, but his policy found little sympathy with his uncle, the duke of Gloucester, who discounted any settlement which did not reaffirm the terms agreed at Bretigny. Lack of resources also hampered the English war effort at this time, especially once the Peasants' Revolt of 1381 had demonstrated how explosive the reaction to excessive taxation might be. And when English expeditions were sent abroad, they were frustrated by the tactics adopted by the resourceful new French king Charles V (1364–80), who, instead of trying to defeat them in battle, concentrated on a policy of harassment, scorched earth and grinding siege warfare. Denied thereby the psychological boosts which they had gained from victories such as Crecy and Poitiers, the English also found themselves fighting the war on a wider front. This was partly because of the failure of Edward III's diplomacy in the 1360s: English intervention in Iberia had resulted in a Franco-Castilian alliance which created a dangerous new threat to English shipping from the Castilian navy; failure to secure the hand of Margaret of Flanders for Edmund of Langley was followed by her marriage to the French prince Philip the Bold, the first Valois duke of Burgundy, as a result of which Flanders moved gradually but perceptibly into the French orbit; and after the death of David Bruce and the succession of the first Stewart king, the

Anglophobe Robert II, in 1371, the Scots too re-entered the war, and by 1400 had recovered almost everything that Edward III had taken from them in the middle years of the century. Thus diplomatically isolated, militarily humiliated and riven by internal dissension, the gap between England's claims and the reality of its position became ever wider as the fourteenth century drew to a close.

Yet although Richard II continued to style himself king of France, the war of 1369–89 was no longer really about the French throne, but about the Treaty of Bretigny. Sovereignty over Gascony remained the crucial issue, but in a different form: Bretigny had separated Gascony from France and created an English-held duchy there. That was precisely why, in the long term, it could never be acceptable to the French monarchy. Nor was it popular with the native Gascon lords, who valued the opportunities which their relationship with both the French and English kings offered to play off one against the other; indeed, it was the appeals of the Gascon nobles to Charles V against the impositions of the Black Prince which had provided the French king with his *casus belli* in 1369, and it was this question of sovereignty in Gascony which continued to provide the main stumbling-block to peace during Richard II's reign. Richard, an admirer of French culture and manners, was anxious to make peace with France: once a truce had been agreed in 1389, a series of negotiations was held during the early 1390s to discover whether a peace formula might be found. Unfortunately it could not. It may be – the evidence is not conclusive – that Richard himself would have been prepared to relinquish English sovereignty over Gascony in return for its hereditary grant to John of Gaunt (who in 1388 had bartered his Castilian claim for a life pension), but a volte-face of this magnitude from the terms of Bretigny was unacceptable to many of the Gascon lords, who rebelled when they heard that it was under consideration. The French king Charles VI's first attack of insanity in 1392 also thwarted the negotiations, and in the end the two sides had to settle for a twenty-eight-year truce, sealed by Richard's marriage in 1396 to Isabella, the 7-year-old daughter of Charles VI. This at least promised a period of harmony during which a final peace might be worked out. Yet despite the undoubted desire for peace on both sides, the intractability of the Gascon question had demonstrated once again how difficult it was to find a formula for ending the conflict; and when, three years later, Richard himself was deposed, Anglo-French relations were once more thrown into the melting-pot.

It was from closer to home, though, that the first real challenge to English rule came following Henry IV's usurpation. Wales, which for over a century appeared to have been undergoing a fairly painless assimilation to English rule, suddenly in September 1400 exploded into a rebellion which was to stretch English lordship in the principality to its limits and drastically reduce its profitability to the English landlords who until then had so successfully exploited it. The leader of the revolt was Owen Glendower, an esquire descended from the ancient princes of Powys who typified the fortunes of many Welshmen in the fourteenth century; for although a relatively prosperous native landholding and administrative class had established itself under English lordship in the wake of Edward I's conquest, a strong sense of alienation remained both because of the economic and legal privileges enjoyed by English settlers and the fact that, at the highest levels, landlordship was kept firmly in English hands. Glendower enjoyed widespread support: between 1402 and 1406 he controlled much of Wales, made an alliance with France which led to the landing of a French force at Milford Haven in 1405, summoned 'parliaments' to meet at Machynlleth and Harlech, and drew up plans for an independent Welsh Church. He also wrote to the Scottish king and the Irish lords asking them to join him in liberating their peoples from 'the tyranny and bondage of mine and your mortal foes the Saxons'.[9] After 1406, however, with Henry IV more secure on his throne, English military power once again proved too strong, and by 1410 the revolt was all but over. Owen himself was never captured; he probably died in 1417, but the date and place of his burial have never been discovered. And although it might appear that his revolt was nothing short of a disaster for Wales – for economically it was devastated, families had been divided against themselves, and fearsome anti-Welsh laws were passed at Westminster, which remained in force long after it was quelled – yet there is no denying that Glendower had, in his own way, done for Wales what Robert Bruce had done for Scotland – restored a nation's self-respect. To later Welshmen he was a national hero, and to many he still is.

The decade following Richard II's deposition was a testing time for the English monarchy. Not only in Wales, but in Ireland and Gascony too, local groups of disaffected attempted to take advantage of the political turmoil in England, and both Anglo-French and Anglo-Scottish relations entered a new period of crisis. Charles VI's horror at the deposition of his son-in-law led to the dispatch of a number of French forces to Gascony between 1403 and 1407, while the Scottish situation was aggravated by the continuing rumours that Richard II had not, as Henry IV claimed, died at Pontefract in February 1400, but was alive and well in Scotland and awaiting his chance to return. Glendower's dreams of an anti-English coalition appeared far less unrealistic at the time than they do now. In 1406–07, however, the tide turned: on 14 March 1406 the 11-year-old James, the heir to the Scottish throne, was fortuitously captured off Flamborough Head; three weeks later he became king of Scotland, but he was to spend the first eighteen years of his reign a prisoner in England. Of far greater significance, though, was the assassination in Paris on 23 November 1407 of Louis, duke of Orleans, the brother of the French king, by agents of John the Fearless, duke of Burgundy, which marked the effective start of what has come to be known as the Armagnac-Burgundian civil war, the vicious struggle which was to tear France apart during the first third of the fifteenth century and open the way for the last significant expansion of English power during the Middle Ages.

The turn-round in England's fortunes during the second decade of the fifteenth century was astonishing. Much of the credit for this is usually given to Henry V, and rightly so, for although it was the Armagnac-Burgundian war which really underlay his success, he exploited it mercilessly and to great effect (see the illustration on p. 266). Hardly was he crowned when he reopened negotiations for the restoration of the terms of Bretigny, playing the French factions off against each other in an attempt to maximise their bids for his support; when these failed to match his expectations, he took an army to France and won a stunning victory at Agincourt in October 1415. Agincourt was as momentous a psychological blow to the French as Poitiers had been, and with Charles VI now almost continuously insane, France was falling headlong towards political disintegration. Following further negotiations in 1416, during which a deal of sorts was struck with John of Burgundy,

Portrait of Henry V (Royal Library, Windsor Castle), by an unknown artist. Henry was known for his orthodox piety. His successes in France – most notably his victory at Agincourt in 1415, and the Treaty of Troyes in 1420 – have made him the archetypal English hero-king, but he did not live to enjoy his triumphs, dying in 1422 at the age of 35 and bequeathing his kingdom to his 9-month-old son, Henry VI.

Henry took another army to France in 1417 and began the conquest of Normandy. It is his Norman campaign of 1417–19 which reveals Henry's qualities as a leader. This was no old-style *chevauchée*, but a systematic drive for land. For over a year and a half the English army remained in the field, reducing town after town and castle after castle; garrisons were installed, English nobles were granted lands to be held from the English king, and an English administration set up throughout the duchy. With the fall of Rouen in January 1419, Normandy became an English colony, and Henry turned his sights on Paris.

By this time, however, fear of what Henry might achieve was beginning to outweigh even the bitter legacy of a decade of French civil war. With Charles VI incapacitated, it was left to his son the Dauphin, the future Charles VII, to rally those Frenchmen still loyal to the Valois monarchy. Tentatively the two French factions edged towards an accord. On 10 September 1419, a meeting was arranged between the Dauphin and John of Burgundy on the bridge at Montereau, fifty miles south-east of Paris. Once again, however, events conspired in Henry's favour. The two sides met in the middle of the bridge, but as Duke John knelt to greet the Dauphin, one of the latter's attendants stepped forward and stabbed him to death. It was a terrible deed, and whether or not the Dauphin had any foreknowledge of it, the consequences for him were to be far-reaching. Hopes of French reconciliation evaporated. Within a few months, the tacit Anglo-Burgundian agreement of 1416 was ratified by Duke John's son, Philip the Good, as a formal pact; by the Treaty of Troyes (May 1420), Charles VI – who was in Burgundian custody, but who hardly knew what he was doing – agreed to disinherit his own son, the Dauphin, to marry his daughter Catherine to Henry, and to acknowledge Henry as regent during his lifetime and as heir to the kingdom of France after his death. Henry had achieved all he had sought – perhaps more.

The Treaty of Troyes broke new ground in the war. For the first time since Edward III initially put forward his claim in 1328, a French government had recognised the right of an English king also to be king of France. Yet it created as many problems as it solved, for it also raised the stakes in the French civil war, as well as shackling the English government with an open-ended commitment to military action in pursuance of its terms. It was, as has been pointed out, 'an unusual peace treaty because it required the continuance of war'.[10] Northern France was effectively divided between an English zone in the west and a Burgundian zone in the east, but further south (with the exception of Gascony), the country was still largely loyal to the Dauphin, and Henry's ability to enforce his claim as the next king of France would depend upon his capacity to defeat the Dauphin by military force. Whether he might have accomplished it we shall never know, for in August 1422 he died, predeceasing Charles VI by just two months, and leaving a 9-month-old infant, Henry VI, as his heir.

For some years after Henry V's death, under the capable French regency of his brother John duke of Bedford, the English maintained their hold on Normandy, pushing downwards into Maine in 1424 and further southwards thereafter, while Philip of Burgundy consolidated his hold on the Low Countries and the north-east of France. By 1429 the Loire had been reached, and the earl of Salisbury was besieging Orleans. However, 1429 was to mark the limit of English expansion in France. Encouraged by Joan of Arc, the Dauphinists took heart and raised the siege of Orleans. Charles himself recaptured much of Champagne, had himself crowned at Rheims, and marched towards Paris. Worse still, the Anglo-Burgundian alliance – the rock upon which English success in France had been built – began to show signs of fragility, and eventually, at the Treaty of Arras in 1435, it crumbled: Duke Philip and King Charles made their peace, and uneasy though it may have been, it was to last until the English were hounded out of France. Bedford died in the same year, and in May 1436 Paris was lost. It was into this increasingly precarious inheritance that Henry VI entered when, in November 1437, he declared himself of age.

Given the events of the early 1430s, it would be unfair to lay too much blame on Henry VI for the loss of his French possessions (see the colour plate on p. 228). Yet it cannot be said that he served his country well. In fact, the situation which developed during the 1440s was strikingly similar to that of the 1380s. The king himself became increasingly convinced that an agreement with France, even if it fell short of the terms of Troyes, was preferable to indefinite war, and by the time the Truce of Tours brought a cessation of hostilities in 1444, there were signs of a shift in the English view: Gascony and Normandy in full sovereignty, rather than the throne of France, now seemed to constitute Henry's negotiating position. Yet as in the 1380s, the king's capacity to deliver on a commitment of this nature depended as much on his ability to convince his own subjects of its worth as it did on his ability to convince the French, for a powerful faction among the nobility – led by a new duke of Gloucester, his uncle Humphrey – advocated a much harder line against the 'adversary of France'. Foolishly, Henry deceived them: some time in 1445, he secretly promised to surrender Maine to Charles VII. When the news leaked out, it provoked fury in England and refusals by the captains of English-held castles in Maine to hand them over. Maine, they claimed, was Normandy's buffer-zone; if it were lost, the French would be at the gates of the duchy – and so it proved. Under Henry's orders, Maine was eventually given over to the French in 1448. Charles VII had used the years of truce to reorganise his army, and in August 1449 he launched his assault on Normandy. It fell within a year, to be followed in 1451 by most of Gascony; and when Bordeaux finally fell in 1453, the 'tresvictorieux roy' Charles VII had expelled the English from France, with the sole exception of Calais. In the end, it had all been extraordinarily sudden.

The Hundred Years War was over. Not that this was obvious at the time, but by the end of the fifteenth century it had become so. Within two years of the fall of Bordeaux, the first skirmishes of the Wars of the Roses had rendered any prospect of effective English intervention in France unlikely. Events within France also strengthened the French kings' hand. Following the English collapse the chief threat to the French monarchy came from the duchy of Burgundy, but with the defeat and death of Duke Philip's son, Charles the Rash, in 1477, Burgundy and various lands in the Low Countries reverted to the Crown; and when Brittany was annexed by marriage in 1492, it meant that three of the great fiefs whose separatist pretensions had so enervated French royal power during the fourteenth and fifteenth centuries had, within the space of forty years, fallen under the sway of the monarchy. It was a fact which Henry VII of England tacitly recognised. In November 1492, at Etaples, he concluded a treaty with Charles VIII of France which, although it did not entail his explicit renunciation of either the French throne or the former English lands in France, nevertheless established peace between the two realms. Already, some ten years before this, English royal documents had begun to refer to the French ruler not as 'our adversary of France' – as they had done for most of the previous two centuries – but as 'the king of France'. The 400-year-old Anglo-French empire was at an end. Western Europe in the sixteenth century was to be dominated by the rivalry of Habsburg and Valois, in which England, although often enough a valued ally, was never a leading player.

If nations are 'imagined communities', the community which lived in the imaginations of most Englishmen by the year 1500 was rather different from that of three or even two hundred years earlier. When King John succeeded Richard I in 1199, it was not merely as king of England, but as the overlord of a vast Franco-British empire stretching from the Cheviots to the Pyrenees, with its heartland in Normandy and Anjou and its claws reaching deep into the Celtic lands to the west. A hundred years later, in the last years of Edward I's reign, the focus had shifted significantly. Gone were Normandy and Anjou, but Scotland, Wales and Ireland were being drawn ever more tightly into the English net. The Scottish lowlands, the Welsh highlands, and large parts of Ireland were gripped by English-held castles; at Berwick, Caernarvon and Dublin, English exchequers collected the profits of conquest and the dues rendered by economically-privileged English townsmen. Had subsequent kings of England concentrated their ambitions here, the future of the British Isles might have been very different. But English dreams of a French empire refused to die: a century and a half after the Treaty of Paris, Henry V could still demand from the French not only all the lands granted to Edward III at Bretigny, but Normandy, Maine, Anjou and Touraine too: in other words, the old Angevin Empire. It is arguable – although such an argument would have cut little ice at the time – that it was the late medieval English kings' pre-occupation with France which saved Scotland and Ireland from English domination. This is, perhaps, most obviously true of Anglo-Scottish relations in the 1330s and 1340s, when Edward III's continental pretensions diverted him from what until then had seemed to be his principal task. By 1400, the Scots had more or less managed to restore the 'true and ancient' Tweed–Solway border,[11] and although it was not until 1560 that the English eventually dropped their demand for homage from the Scottish kings, Scotland's independence was not in serious doubt during the fifteenth century. In Ireland too, English attempts to recover ground were half-hearted and spasmodic during the fourteenth and fifteenth centuries, although in this case falling population and the consequent decline in the number of English wishing to settle in Ireland were also to blame. As it was, the area of English administration continued to shrink during the fifteenth century, until in 1488 it was defined by statute as consisting only of parts of the four eastern counties of Louth, Meath, Dublin and Kildare, protected by 'the Pale' (a fortified earthen rampart). Not until the later sixteenth century were the English to show how deep were the inroads they could make into Ireland when they put their minds to it.

England's relations with its neighbours during the later Middle Ages were determined by a variety of factors. Old claims were rarely allowed to drop, at least not explicitly, but there was usually more to it than this: Gascony was not merely the last remnant of the Angevin Empire, it also had important trading links with England, and control of the Gascon ports ensured a measure of security to English shipping in the Bay of Biscay. In Ireland and Wales, English colonies founded initially by land-hungry nobles, enterprising traders or zealous churchmen increasingly looked to English kings for protection and definition of their privileges, so that settlement and overlordship hardened into conquest and landlordship. Grandiose as were the ambitions of kings such as Edward I, Edward III or Henry V, they were only part of the story; many English nobles also took a distinctly imperialist attitude towards their neighbours, and, as kings like Richard II and Henry VI found to their cost, any backsliding on the part of the monarchy in its perceived role outwith England was liable to have dire repercussions. Lesser subjects of the king – merchants, knights, even the humbler town and country-dwellers who were encouraged to settle in Ireland or Wales in the thirteenth century, Calais in the fourteenth or Normandy in the fifteenth – also stood to gain from a policy which saw the influence of the English Crown pushed onwards and outwards. Nor can it be denied that the urbanisation, trading links and cultural interchange which accompanied English expansion sometimes brought benefits to the inhabitants of those regions, or that native rulers did not at times welcome, even invite, English intervention. Whether they spoke for their peoples or understood the tiger that they were thereby unleashing is a different matter: it is difficult to avoid the conclusion that Robert Bruce and Owen Glendower were more representative of the true feelings of most of their countrymen. The passions which they articulated were of a universal and enduring quality, and it was in part due to their efforts that, by 1500, the tiger had been leashed – for the moment. Wales may have been subdued, but Scotland remained independent, Ireland was slipping away, and the Treaties of Bretigny and Troyes were dead letters. England's political community was more Anglocentric than it had been for many centuries past, or was to be again for some time to come.

PICTURE CREDITS

CREDITS FOR COLOUR PLATES

Entry for *anulus* in the encyclopaedia of James le Palmer (British Library MSS. Royal 6. E. vi and vii). By courtesy of the British Library (MS. Royal 6. E. vi, fo. 104)

Seating at meals. By courtesy of the British Library (MS. Add. 42,130, fo. 208)

Entry for *adulterium* in the encyclopaedia of James le Palmer. By courtesy of the British Library (MS. Royal 6. E. vi, fo. 61)

Propitious times for operations and medication. The volvelle in the Book of the Barber-Surgeons of York. By courtesy of the British Library (MS. Egerton 2,572 (fifteenth century), fo. 51)

Bloodletting. By courtesy of the British Library (MS. Harley 3,719 (fifteenth century), fos 158v–159)

The toothpuller, from the encyclopaedia of James le Palmer. By courtesy of the British Library (MS. Royal 6. E. vi, fo. 503v)

The crucifixion and other scenes from the life of Christ. By permission of the Warden and Fellows of Keble College, Oxford (MS. 39, fo. 105v)

Dreamer and Pearl-Maiden. By courtesy of the British Library (MS. Cotton Nero A. x., fo. 42v)

Initial by William de Brailes. By courtesy of the British Library (MS. Add. 49,999, fo. 43)

Ramsey Abbey censer and boat. By courtesy of the Victoria and Albert Museum, London

The Court of King's Bench. By courtesy of the Masters of the Bench of the Inner Temple and ET Archive

The Court of Chancery in session. By Courtesy of the Masters of the Bench of the Inner Temple and ET Archive

Harlech castle from the south. CADW Welsh Historic Monuments. Crown copyright

Edward I creating his son Prince of Wales. By courtesy of the British Library (MS. Cotton Nero D. ii, fo. 191v)

The Wilton Diptych. By courtesy of the National Gallery

Henry VI crowned king of France, from the *Life and Acts of Richard Beauchamp, earl of Warwick*, by John Rous, *c.* 1485. By courtesy of the British Library (MS. Cotton Julius E. iv, art. vi, fo. 24)

CREDITS FOR BLACK AND WHITE ILLUSTRATIONS

East Witton (Yorkshire). Cambridge University Collection of Air Photographs: copyright reserved

Laxton (Nottinghamshire). Cambridge University Collection of Air Photographs: copyright reserved

Brassington (Derbyshire). Cambridge University Collection of Air Photographs: copyright reserved

How Moor (Cambridgeshire). Cambridge University Collection of Air Photographs: copyright reserved

Orford (Suffolk). Cambridge University Collection of Air Photographs: copyright reserved

Ermine Street. Cambridge University Collection of Air Photographs: copyright reserved

Herstmonceux castle (Sussex). Cambridge University Collection of Air Photographs: copyright reserved

Fountains abbey (Yorkshire). Cambridge University Collection of Air Photographs: copyright reserved. © British Crown copyright/Ministry of Defence. Reproduced with the permission of the Controller of Her Britannic Majesty's Stationery Office

Hockwold (Norfolk). Cambridge University Collection of Air Photographs: copyright reserved. © British Crown copyright/Ministry of Defence. Reproduced with the permission of the Controller of Her Britannic Majesty's Stationery Office

A medieval coalmine (Hartington, Derbyshire). Cambridge University Collection of Air Photographs: copyright reserved

Hammer-lake at Mannings Heath (Sussex). Cambridge University Collection of Air Photographs: copyright reserved. © British Crown copyright/Ministry of Defence. Reproduced with the permission of Her Britannic Majesty's Stationery Office

Medieval quarrying at Collyweston (Northamptonshire). Cambridge University Collection of Air Photographs: copyright reserved

Claimants to the throne of Scotland. By courtesy of the Conway Library, Courtauld Institute of Art (former Phillipps MS. 25,422 (sold at Sotheby's, 29 November 1966), fo. 134)

The descendants of the kings of England. By courtesy of the Conway Library, Courtauld Institute of Art (MS. 'Chronicle of the kings of England' (sold at Sotheby's, 24 June 1980))

The south porch of Aylesham church (Norfolk). By courtesy of the Conway Library, Courtauld Institute of Art

Marriage ceremony. By courtesy of the Bodleian Library, University of Oxford (MS. e. Mus. 60, fo. 78)

Husband bashing. By courtesy of the British Library (MS. Add. 42,130, fo. 60)

Securing annulment. By courtesy of the British Library (MS. Royal 11. D. ix, fo. 284)

Child maintenance. By courtesy of the Conway Library, Courtauld Institute of Art (British Library, MS. Add. 15,452)

Arbor consanguinitatis. By courtesy of the British Library (MS. Harley 3,644, fo. 164)

The ape physician, from the Metz Pontifical, French, early fourteenth century. By courtesy of the Fitzwilliam Museum, Cambridge (MS. 298, fo. 25)

Laxatives and astrology. A copy of the *Secretum Secretorum* made by Walter de Milemete for presentation to Edward III in 1327. By courtesy of the British Library (MS. Add. 47,680, fo. 54v)

John of Arderne's clyster pipe. By courtesy of the British Library (MS. Sloane 56, fo. 24v)

Armour-bearer after spasm. By courtesy of the British Library (MS. Add. 29,301, fo. 5)

John of Arderne probes a fistulous hole. By courtesy of the British Library (MS. Sloane 2,002, fo. 24v)

Procedures and instruments for fistula in ano. By courtesy of the British Library (MS. Add. 29,301, fo. 25)

The aggressive owl or *bubo*, from John Bradmore, *Philomena* (early fifteenth century). By courtesy of the British Library (MS. Sloane 2,272, fo. 59)

Wooden funeral effigy of Anne of Bohemia. By courtesy of the Dean and Chapter of Westminster

Botiller's tomb, Warrington (Cheshire). By courtesy of Warrington Library, Cheshire County Council

Archdeacon Sponne's skeleton-tomb, Towcester (Northamptonshire). By courtesy of Northamptonshire County Library

Thame church (Oxfordshire). By courtesy of the Bodleian Library, University of Oxford (MS. Top. Oxon. d. 852, fo. 9v)

Rycote chapel (Oxfordshire). By courtesy of English Heritage

Roger Cheyne's brass. By courtesy of the Bodleian Library, University of Oxford (MS. Top. Oxon. d. 852, fo. 9v)

Wall-painting of St Christopher. By courtesy of Buckinghamshire County Library

Relic hand. By courtesy of Canon Anthony Griffiths, St Peter's Church, Marlow

John Schorne. By courtesy of Dr R. P. Hagerty

Ely misericord. By courtesy of Mr Ken Hitch

Dialect map of Middle English. Reproduced by courtesy of Prentice Hall

Vomiting glutton. By permission of the Master and Fellows of St John's College, Cambridge (MS. B. 9 (31))

Abraham worshipping the Trinity. By permission of the Master and Fellows of St John's College, Cambridge (MS. K. 26, fo. 9)

The Hoccleve portrait of Chaucer. By courtesy of the British Library (MS. Harley 4866, fo. 88)

Frontispiece to *Troilus and Criseyde*. By courtesy of the Master and Fellows of Corpus Christi College, Cambridge (MS. 61, fo. 1v)

Canterbury pilgrims, from John Lydgate's *Siege of Thebes*. By courtesy of the British Library (MS. Royal 18 D. ii, fo. 148)

Fornicating lovers and cuckolded husband. By courtesy of New College Library, Oxford (MS. 208, fo. 241)

Illuminated initial with Archbishop Arundel and monks of Christ Church, Canterbury. By courtesy of the Bodleian Library, University of Oxford (MS. Laud Misc. 165, fo. 5)

Opening of Nicholas Love's *Mirror*. By courtesy of the Librarian of Glasgow University Library (MS. Hunter, fo. 3v)

Scenes from the Life of Christ. By courtesy of the Bodleian Library, University of Oxford (MS. Barlow 22, fo. 13)

St Katherine and her wheels. By courtesy of the British Library (MS. Royal 2. B. vii, fo. 283v)

St Agatha and her tormentors. By courtesy of the British Library (MS. Royal 2 B. vii, fo. 242)

John Gower firing satirical arrows at the world. By courtesy of the Librarian of Glasgow University Library (MS. Hunter 59, fo. 6v)

Terracotta aquamanile. By courtesy of Sotheby's

The Middleham Jewel (Yorkshire Museum). Photograph by courtesy of the Trustees of the British Museum

The death of Harold, from the Bayeux Tapestry (Musée de la Tapisserie, Bayeux). By courtesy of the Bridgeman Art Library

Building St Alban's church. By courtesy of Trinity College, Dublin (MS. 177, fo. 60)

Trinity Chapel, Canterbury Cathedral. By courtesy of Dr C. Wilson

Detail from the Luttrell Psalter. By courtesy of the British Library (MS. Add. 42,130, fo. 173)

The Pienza Cope. By courtesy of Pienza Cathedral

The Ascension. By courtesy of the Burrell Collection, Glasgow

The interrelationship of designs. By courtesy of the British Museum (Medieval and Later Antiquities, 1922, 4–12, 1) and the Bodleian Library, University of Oxford (MS. Selden supra 38, fos 21v, 22v)

Neck of a gittern. By courtesy of the British Museum (Medieval and Later Antiquities, 10–2, 1)

Illuminated initial from the Grandisson Psalter. By courtesy of the British Library (MS Add. 21,926, fo. 26)

Ivory triptych. By courtesy of the British Museum (Medieval and Later Antiquities, 61, 4–16, 1)

Drawings from the Pepysian sketch-book. By courtesy of Magdalene College, Cambridge (Pepys Library 1916, fo. 17v)

The Coronation of Edward III. By courtesy of the Master and Fellows of Corpus Christi College, Cambridge

The king and his court. By courtesy of the British Library

The painted chamber of the Palace of Westminster. By courtesy of the Society of Antiquaries of London

The Exchequer in the Palace of Westminster. By courtesy of Westminster City Archives

The Great Seal of Edward I. By courtesy of the Dean and Chapter of Durham

Plan of the Palace of Westminster. By courtesy of J. M. Steane (after Brown, Colvin and Taylor)

Edward I in Parliament. The Royal Collection © Her Majesty The Queen

Henry VI in Parliament. Reproduced by permission of the Provost and Scholars of King's College, Cambridge

The lion door-knocker of Durham Cathedral. By courtesy of the Dean and Chapter of Durham

Henry VI and two justices. By courtesy of the Public Record Office (KB27/796)

Sir William Husy, Chief Justice of King's Bench. By courtesy of the Public Record Office (KB27/902)

Brass of Chief Baron Sir John Cassy and his wife. By courtesy of the Victoria and Albert Museum

A judge presiding over a debate between two serjeants at law. By courtesy of the Board of Trinity College, Dublin

The Old Hall of Lincoln's Inn. By courtesy of A. F. Kersting, Architectural Photographer

William Catesby. By courtesy of Geoffrey Wheeler

Map of lands of the Beauchamp family. By courtesy of Chris Given-Wilson

Badges of the Dukes of Norfolk and Suffolk. By courtesy of the British Library

Monument of Sir Robert Harcourt. By courtesy of the National Portrait Gallery

Boar badge of Richard III. By courtesy of the Yorkshire Museum

The Battle of Sandwich, 1217. By courtesy of the Master and Fellows of Corpus Christi College, Cambridge (MS. 16, fo. 52)

Rebels in London in 1381. By courtesy of the British Library (MS. Royal 18 E. 1, fo. 165v)

Peasants as descendants of Cain. By courtesy of the British Library (MS. Add. 47,682, fo. 6)

Magna Carta (1297 exemplification). By courtesy of the Public Record Office (DL10/197)

The capture of Richard II. By courtesy of the British Library (MS. Harley 4380, fo. 181)

The siege of Bedford castle, 1225. By courtesy of the Master and Fellows of Corpus Christi College, Cambridge

Thomas of Lancaster as a saint. By courtesy of the Bodleian Library, University of Oxford (MS. Douce 231, fo. 1)

The death and mutilation of Simon de Montfort. By courtesy of the British Library (BL, Cotton Nero D II f. 177)

The Coronation Chair, Westminster Abbey. By courtesy of the Dean and Chapter of Westminster

Edward I confronting Philip IV of France. By courtesy of the Public Record Office (E368/69, m. 54)

The Irish Exchequer in action. By permission of the Syndics of Cambridge University Library (reproduced from Tab. b. 253, part 3, Facsimiles of National Manuscripts of Ireland)

Portrait of Henry V. The Royal Collection © Her Majesty the Queen

FURTHER READING

The broad topics covered by the chapters, and many of the examples used to illustrate them, are considered in greater detail in the texts which are recommended for further reading.

Notes refer to specific examples which have been taken from sources outside these core texts.

THE ENGLISH LANDSCAPE

G. Astill and A. Grant, eds, *The Countryside of Medieval England* (Oxford, 1988).

M. Aston, D. Austin and C. Dyer, eds, *The Rural Settlements of Medieval England* (Oxford, 1989).

L. Butler and C. Given-Wilson, *Medieval Monasteries of Great Britain* (London, 1979).

L. M. Cantor, ed., *The English Medieval Landscape* (London, 1982).

R. E. Glasscock, ed., *Historic Landscapes of Britain from the Air* (Cambridge, 1992).

W. G. Hoskins, *The Making of the English Landscape* (revised edition, London, 1988).

H. H. Lamb, *Climate: Present, Past and Future* (London, 1977).

C. Platt, *The English Medieval Town* (London, 1986).

C. Platt, *The Parish Churches of Medieval England* (London, 1986).

O. Rackham, *The History of the Countryside* (London, 1986).

T. Rowley, *The High Middle Ages 1200–1550* (London, 1986).

M. W. Thompson, *The Decline of the Castle* (Cambridge, 1987).

POPULATION AND ECONOMIC RESOURCES

J. L. Bolton, *The Medieval English Economy 1150–1500* (London, 1980).

R. H. Britnell, *The Commercialisation of English Society 1000–1500* (Cambridge, 1993).

B. M. S. Campbell, 'Land and people in the Middle Ages, 1066–1500', in R. A. Dodgshon and R. A. Butlin, eds, *An Historical Geography of England and Wales* (second edition, London, 1990).

H. C. Darby, ed., *A New Historical Geography of England before 1600* (Cambridge, 1976).

C. Dyer, *Standards of Living in the Later Middle Ages: Social Change in England c. 1200–1520* (Cambridge, 1989).

J. Hatcher, *Plague, Population and the English Economy 1348–1530* (London, 1977).

M. M. Postan, *The Medieval Economy and Society* (Harmondsworth, 1975).

T. Rowley, *The High Middle Ages 1200–1550* (London, 1986).

P. T. H. Unwin, 'Towns and trade 1066–1500', in Dodgshon and Butlin, eds, *Historical Geography of England and Wales*.

FAMILY AND INHERITANCE, WOMEN AND CHILDREN

J. M. W. Bean, *The Decline of English Feudalism, 1215–1540* (Manchester, 1968).

Joseph Biancalana, 'Widows at Common Law: The development of Common Law Dower', *The Irish Jurist*, vol. xxiii (new series) (1988), pp. 255–329.

James A. Brundage, *Law, Sex and Christian Society in Medieval Europe* (Chicago, 1987).

Barbara A. Hanawalt, *Growing up in Medieval London: the Experience of Childhood in History* (Oxford, 1993).

Barbara A. Hanawalt, *The Ties that Bound: Peasant Families in Medieval England* (Oxford, 1986).

R. H. Helmholz, *Canon Law and the Law of England* (London, 1987).

R. H. Helmholz, *Marriage Litigation in Medieval England* (Cambridge, 1974).

George C. Homans, *English Villagers of the Thirteenth Century* (Cambridge, Mass., 1941, reprinted 1968).

R. C. Palmer, 'Contexts of marriage in medieval England: evidence from the King's Court c. 1300', *Speculum* 59, no. 1 (January 1984), 42–67.

Sue Sheridan Walker (ed.) *Wife and Widow in Medieval England* (Ann Arbor, 1993).

HEALTH, DIET, MEDICINE AND THE PLAGUE

C. Dyer, *Standards of Living in the Later Middle Ages: Social Change in England c. 1200–1520* (Cambridge, 1989).

F. M. Getz, 'The Faculty of Medicine before 1500', in *The History of the University of Oxford*, vol. 2, edited by J. Catto and R. Evans (Oxford, 1992), pp. 373–405.

R. S. Gottfried, *Doctors and Medicine in Medieval England, 1340–1530* (Princeton, 1986), and the critical review by F. M. Getz in the *Bulletin of the History of Medicine*, 61 (1987), 455–61.

R. S. Gottfried, *Epidemic Disease in Fifteenth-Century England* (Leicester, 1978).

B. Harvey, *Living and Dying in England 1100–1540* (Oxford, 1993).

R. Horrox, *The Black Death* (Manchester, 1994).

T. Hunt, *Popular Medicine in Thirteenth-Century England* (Cambridge, 1990).

P. M. Jones, 'John of Arderne and the Mediterranean tradition of scholastic medicine', in *Practical Medicine from Salerno to the Black Death*, edited by L. Garcia-Ballester, R. French *et al.* (Cambridge, 1994), pp. 289–321.

P. M. Jones, *Medieval Medical Miniatures* (London, 1984).

C. Rawcliffe, 'The profits of practice: the wealth and status of medical men in later medieval England', *Social History of Medicine*, 1 (1988), 61–78.

S. Rubin, *Medieval English Medicine* (Newton Abbot, 1974).

C. H. Talbot, *Medicine in Medieval England* (London, 1967).

C. H. Talbot and E. A. Hammond, *The Medical Practitioners in Medieval England: a biographical register* (London, 1965).

P. Ziegler, *The Black Death* (London, 1969).

RELIGIOUS SENSIBILITY

A. Brown, *Popular Piety in Later Medieval England* (Oxford, 1995).

E. Duffy, *The Stripping of the Altars* (New Haven and London, 1992).

C. Haigh, *English Reformations* (Oxford, 1993).

C. Harper-Bill, *The Pre-Reformation Church in England, 1400–1530* (London, 1989) (introductory).

P. Heath, *Church and Realm, 1272–1461* (London, 1988).

P. Heath, *The Church and the Shaping of English Society, 1215–1535* (London, 1995).

R. N. Swanson, *Church and Society in Later Medieval England* (Oxford, 1989).

R. N. Swanson, *Catholic England* (Manchester, 1993) (an anthology of source-material).

J. A. F. Thomson, *Early Tudor Church and Society* (London, 1993).

LANGUAGE AND LITERARY EXPRESSION

Alexandra Barratt, ed., *Women's Writing in Middle English* (London, 1992).

Piero Boitano and Jill Mann, eds, *The Cambridge Chaucer Companion* (Cambridge, 1986).

J. A. Burrow, *Medieval Writers and their Work: Middle English Literature and its Background 1100–1500* (Oxford, 1982).

J. A. Burrow, *A Reading of Sir Gawain and the Green Knight* (London, 1965).

A. C. De la Mare and B. C. Barker-Benfield, eds, *Manuscripts at Oxford: an Exhibition in memory of Richard William Hunt* (Oxford, 1980).

A. S. G. Edwards, ed., *Middle English Prose: A Guide to Major Authors and Genres* (New Brunswick, NJ, 1984).

Anne Hudson, ed., *Selections from English Wycliffite Writings* (Cambridge, 1978).

Carol Meale, ed., *Women and Literature in Britain 1100–1500* (Cambridge, 1993).

A. J. Minnis and A. B. Scott with the assistance of David Wallace, *Medieval Literary Theory and Criticism c. 1100–c. 1375: The Commentary-Tradition* (Oxford, 1988).

O. Pächt and J. J. G. Alexander, eds, *Illuminated Manuscripts in the Bodleian Library*, vol. III (Oxford, 1973).

Lee Patterson, *Negotiating the Past: The Historical Understanding of Medieval Literature* (Madison and London, 1987).

Derek Pearsall, *Old and Middle English Poetry* (London, 1977).

Wolfgang Riehle, translated by Bernard Standring, *The Medieval English Mystics* (London, 1981).

Elizabeth Salter, *Fourteenth-Century English Poetry: Contexts and Readings* (Oxford, 1983).

FORMS OF ARTISTIC EXPRESSION

J. J. G. Alexander and P. Binski, eds, *The Age of Chivalry: Art in Plantagenet England, 1200–1400* (exhibition catalogue) (London, 1987).

John Blair and Nigel Ramsay, eds, *English Medieval Industries: Craftsmen, Techniques, Products* (London, 1991).

R. Allen Brown, H. M. Colvin and A. J. Taylor, *The History of the King's Works*, vols I–II, *The Middle Ages* (London, 1963).

Nicola Coldstream, *The Decorated Style: Architecture and Ornament, 1240–1360* (London, 1994).

Joan Evans, *English Art, 1307–1461* (Oxford History of English Art) (Oxford, 1949).

Dillian Gordon, *Making and Meaning: The Wilton Diptych* (London, 1993).

John H. Harvey, *English Mediaeval Architects: A Biographical Dictionary down to 1550*, 2nd edn (Gloucester, 1984).

Donald King, *Opus Anglicanum: English Mediaeval Embroidery* (exhibition catalogue, Victoria and Albert Museum) (London, 1963).

Richard Marks, *Stained Glass in England during the Middle Ages* (London, 1993).

Andrew Martindale, *The Rise of the Artist in the Middle Ages and Early Renaissance* (London, 1972).

Nigel Morgan, *Early Gothic Manuscripts*, 2 vols (A Survey of Manuscripts Illuminated in the British Isles, vol. IV) (London, 1982–88).

Margaret Rickert, *Painting in Britain: The Middle Ages* (Pelican History of Art), 2nd edn (Harmondsworth, 1963).

Lucy F. Sadler, *Gothic Manuscripts, 1285–1385*, 2 vols (A Survey of Manuscripts Illuminated in the British Isles, vol. V) (London, 1986).

Lawrence Stone, *Sculpture in Britain: The Middle Ages* (Pelican History of Art), 2nd edn (Harmondsworth, 1972).

Francis Wormald, *Collected Writings*, edited by J. J. G. Alexander *et al.*, 2 vols (London 1984–88).

George Zarnecki *et al.*, eds, *English Romanesque Art, 1066–1200* (exhibition catalogue) (London, 1984).

THE POLITICAL INSTITUTIONS OF THE REALM

A. L. Brown, *The Governance of Late Medieval England, 1272–1461* (London, 1989).

J. Cannon and R. Griffiths, *The Oxford Illustrated History of the British Monarchy* (Oxford, 1988).

S. B. Chrimes, *English Constitutional Ideas in the Fifteenth Century* (Cambridge, 1936).

S. B. Chrimes, *An Introduction to the Administrative History of Medieval England* (Oxford, 1952).

A. Crawford, ed., *Letters of the Queens of England, 1100–1547* (Stroud, 1994).

R. G. Davies and J. H. Denton, eds, *The English Parliament in the Middle Ages* (Manchester, 1981).

C. Given-Wilson, *The Royal Household and the King's Affinity: Service, Politics and Finance in England, 1360–1413* (New Haven and London, 1986).

G. L. Harriss, *King, Parliament and Public Finance in Medieval England to 1369* (Oxford, 1975).

A. R. Myers, *The Household of Edward IV* (Manchester, 1959).

A. R. Myers, ed., *English Historical Documents, 1327–1485* (London, 1969).

H. Rothwell, ed., *English Historical Documents, 1189–1327* (London, 1975).

T. F. Tout, *Chapters in the Administrative History of Medieval England*, 6 vols (Manchester, 1920–33).

W. L. Warren, *The Governance of Norman and Angevin England, 1086–1272* (London, 1987).

B. Wilkinson, *The Chancery under Edward III* (Manchester, 1929).

B. Wilkinson, *Constitutional History of England in the Fifteenth Century (1399–1485)* (London, 1964).

B. Wilkinson, *Constitutional History of Medieval England, 1216–1399*, 3 vols (London, 1948–58).

J. F. Willard, W. A. Morris and W. H. Dunham, eds, *The English Government at Work, 1327–1336*, 3 vols (Cambridge, Mass., 1940–50).

LAWMAKERS AND LAWBREAKERS

J. G. Bellamy, *Bastard Feudalism and the Law* (London, 1989).

J. G. Bellamy, *Crime and Public Order in Late Medieval England* (London, 1972).

J. G. Bellamy, *Criminal Law and Society in Late Medieval and Tudor England* (Gloucester, 1984).

P. Brand, *The Origins of the English Legal Profession* (Oxford, 1992).

A. L. Brown, *The Governance of Late Medieval England* (London, 1989).

M. A. Hicks, *Bastard Feudalism* (London, 1995).

M. A. Hicks, ed., *Profit, Piety and the Professions in Later Medieval England* (Gloucester, 1990).

E. W. Ives, *The Common Lawyers of Pre-Reformation England* (Cambridge, 1983).

H. M. Jewell, *English Local Administration in the Middle Ages* (Newton Abbot, 1972).

J. R. Lander, *English Justices of the Peace, 1461–1509* (Gloucester, 1989).

P. C. Maddern, *Violence and the Social Order* (Oxford, 1992).

J. R. Maddicott, *Law and Lordship: Royal Justices as Retainers in Thirteenth- and Fourteenth-Century England* (*Past & Present* supplement) (1978).

C. E. Moreton, *The Townshends and their World* (Oxford, 1992).

R. C. Palmer, *The County Courts of Medieval England, 1150–1350* (Princeton, NJ, 1992).

R. C. Palmer, *English Law in the Age of the Black Death, 1348–81* (Chapel Hill, NC, 1993).

E. Powell, 'Arbitration and the law in England in the later Middle Ages', *Transactions of the Royal Historical Society*, 5th series, xxxiii (1983).

CIVIL WAR AND REBELLION

T. H. Aston and R. H. Hilton, eds, *The English Rising of 1381* (Cambridge, 1984).

D. A. Carpenter, *The Minority of Henry III* (London, 1990).

N. Fryde, *The Tyranny and Fall of Edward II, 1321–1326* (Cambridge, 1979).

J. Gillingham, *The Wars of the Roses: Peace and Conflict in Fifteenth-Century England* (London, 1981).

R. A. Griffiths, *The Reign of Henry VI* (London, 1981).

I. M. W. Harvey, *Jack Cade's Rebellion of 1450* (Oxford, 1991).

J. C. Holt, *The Northerners: a Study in the Reign of King John* (Oxford, 1961).

R. Horrox, *Richard III: a Study of Service* (Cambridge, 1989).

J. R. Maddicott, *Simon de Montfort* (Cambridge, 1994).

A. Tuck, *Richard II and the English Nobility* (London, 1973).

ENGLAND AND ITS NEIGHBOURS

C. T. Allmand, *The Hundred Years War* (Cambridge, 1988).

A. Cosgrove, *Medieval Ireland 1169–1534* (Oxford, 1987).

A. Curry, *The Hundred Years War* (London, 1993).

R. R. Davies, *Conquest, Coexistence and Change: Wales 1063–1415* (Oxford, 1987).

R. R. Davies, *Domination and Conquest: the Experience of Ireland, Scotland and Wales 1100–1300* (Cambridge, 1990).

R. Frame, *Colonial Ireland 1169–1369* (Dublin, 1981).

R. Frame, *The Political Development of the British Isles 1100–1400* (Oxford, 1990).

K. Fowler, *The Age of Plantagenet and Valois* (London, 1967).

R. Nicholson, *Scotland: the Later Middle Ages* (Edinburgh, 1974).

M. Vale, *The Angevin Legacy and the Hundred Years War 1250–1340* (Oxford, 1990).

M. Vale, *English Gascony 1399–1453* (Oxford, 1970).

NOTES

THE LATE MIDDLE AGES IN ENGLAND

1 Quoted in Denys Hay, *The Italian Renaissance in its Historical Background* (2nd edn, Cambridge, 1977), p. 12.

2 *Ibid.*, p. 13.

3 *The Black Death*, ed. Rosemary Horrox (Manchester, 1994), p. 84.

4 N. J. G. Pounds, *The Medieval Castle in England and Wales* (Cambridge, 1990), pp. 32–3.

5 K. B. McFarlane, *The Nobility of Later Medieval England* (Oxford, 1973); C. Given-Wilson, *The English Nobility in the Late Middle Ages* (London, 1987).

6 *Calendar of Patent Rolls 1345–48*, p. 480.

7 *Calendar of Patent Rolls 1381–85*, p. 542.

8 Michael Prestwich, *Edward I* (Berkeley, 1988), p. 422.

9 Pierre Chaplais, *Piers Gaveston: Edward II's Adoptive Brother* (Oxford, 1994).

10 R. Allen Brown, *English Castles* (2nd edn, London, 1976), p. 208.

11 *Chronicon Adae de Usk*, edited by E. M. Thompson (London, 1876), p. 100.

12 Dillian Gordon, *Making and Meaning: The Wilton Diptych* (London, 1993).

13 *Polychronicon Ranulphi Higden Monachi Cestrensis*, ed. C. Babington and J. R. Lumby (9 vols, London, 1865–86), ii, 161.

THE ENGLISH LANDSCAPE

1 T. Tusser, *Five Hundred Points of Good Husbandry* (various editions), chapter 52. I am grateful to Dr Duncan Bythell for his general comments on early drafts of my two chapters.

2 C. Dyer, *Standards of Living in the later Middle Ages* (Cambridge, 1989), chapter 10; M. Bailey, '*Per impetum maris*: natural disaster and economic decline in eastern England 1275–1350', in B. M. S. Campbell, ed., *Before the Black Death: Essays in the Crisis of the Early Fourteenth Century* (Manchester, 1991), pp. 184–208.

3 D. P. Dymond, *The Norfolk Landscape* (London, 1985), p. 101.

4 C. Dyer, *Everyday Life in Medieval England* (London, 1994), pp. 73–4; D. P. Dymond and E. Martin, eds, *An Historical Atlas of Suffolk* (Ipswich, 1989), p. 48.

5 Suffolk Record Office, Bury St Edmunds Branch, HA 504/1/3 m.12.

6 Suffolk Record Office, Ipswich Branch, V11/2/1.1.

7 A. J. L. Winchester, *Landscape and Society in Medieval Cumbria* (Edinburgh, 1987), pp. 68–77.

8 M. Bailey, 'Sand into gold: the evolution of the foldcourse system in west Suffolk 1300–1600' *Agricultural History Review* 38 (1990), pp. 40–57.

9 O. Rackham, *The History of the Countryside* (London, 1986), p. 78.

10 For medieval forests, see C. R. Young, *The Royal Forests of Medieval England* (Leicester, 1979).

11 Bradgate Park is discussed in W. G. Hoskins, *Leicestershire: the History of the Landscape* (London, 1957), pp. 36–8, 49.

12 Public Record Office, DL43/14/3, m.25.

13 K. P. Witney, 'The woodland economy of Kent, 1066–1348', *Agricultural History Review* 38 (1990), pp. 20–39; Winchester, *Medieval Cumbria*, pp. 105–7.

14 Winchester, *Medieval Cumbria*, pp. 92–6.

15 R. A. L. Smith, *Canterbury Cathedral Priory: a Study in Monastic Administration* (Cambridge, 1969), chapter 11. For the general exploitation of the East Anglian Fenland, see H. C. Darby, *The Medieval Fenland* (Cambridge, 1940).

16 R. Leech, 'Small medieval towns in Avon', Committee for Rescue Archaeology in Avon, Gloucestershire and Somerset, *Survey* 1 (1975), pp. 15–19.

17 *Rotuli Hundredorum* (Record Commission, London, 1812), p. 194.

18 C. Platt, *The English Medieval Town* (London, 1976), p. 40.

19 J. Langdon, *Horses, Oxen and Technological Innovation* (Cambridge, 1986).

20 W. G. V. Balchin, *The Cornish Landscape* (London, 1983), p. 178.

21 J. F. Edwards and B. P. Hindle, 'The transportation system of medieval England and Wales', *Journal of Historical Geography* 17 (1991), pp. 123–34; J. Langdon, 'Inland water transport in medieval England', *Journal of Historical Geography* 19 (1993), pp. 1–11.

22 S. Oosthuisen, 'Isleham: a medieval inland port', *Landscape History* 16 (1994), p. 34.

23 Dymond, *Norfolk Landscape*, p. 131.

24 R. Morris, *Churches in the Landscape* (London, 1989), p. 351.

25 H. S. A. Fox, contribution to M. Aston, D. Austin, and C. Dyer, eds., *The Rural Settlements of Medieval England* (Oxford, 1989), p. 101.

POPULATION AND ECONOMIC RESOURCES

1 The early fourteenth century is an enigmatic and controversial period; for a useful background, see B. M. S. Campbell, ed., *Before the Black Death: Essays in the Crisis of the Early Fourteenth Century* (Manchester, 1991).

2 See the example of Wormleighton, in M. W. Beresford, *The Lost Villages of England* (Lutterworth, 1954), pp. 128–9.

3 Britnell, *Commercialisation*, p. 97.

4 D. P. Dymond, ed., *The Register of Thetford Priory*, Norfolk Records Society (forthcoming).

5 For recent urban estimates, see B. M. S. Campbell, J. A. Galloway, D. Keene and M. Murphy, *A Medieval Capital and its Grain Supply: Agrarian Production and Distribution in the London Region, c. 1300*, Historical Geography Research Series 30 (1993), pp. 9–11.

6 Britnell, *Commercialisation*, p. 123.
7 M. Bailey, 'A tale of two towns: Buntingford and Standon in the later Middle Ages', *Journal of Medieval History* 19 (1993), p. 361.
8 R. H. Britnell, *Growth and Decline in Colchester 1300–1525* (Cambridge, 1986), pp. 152–62 and 262–4.
9 A complaint accepted by the Royal Commissioners; *Calendar of Inquisitions Miscellaneous 1399–1422* (London, 1968), p. 165.
10 M. W. Beresford, *New Towns in the Middle Ages: Town Plantation in England, Wales and Gascony* (London, 1967), p. 480.
11 M. Bonney, *Lordship and the Urban Community: Durham and its Overlords 1250–1540* (Cambridge, 1990), p. 148.
12 For woollen cloth manufacture, see E. M. Carus-Wilson, 'Evidences of industrial growth on some fifteenth-century manors', *Economic History Review*, second series, 12 (1959); A. R. Bridbury, *Medieval English Clothmaking: an Economic Survey* (London, 1982).
13 For the fishing industry, see P. Heath, 'North Sea fishing in the fifteenth century: the Scarborough fleet', *Northern History* 3 (1968); A. Saul, 'The herring industry at Great Yarmouth 1280–1400', *Norfolk Archaeology* 38 (1981); M. Bailey, 'Coastal fishing off south-east Suffolk in the century after the Black Death', *Proceedings of the Suffolk Institute of Archaeology and History* 37 (1990).
14 W. G. V. Balchin, *The Making of the Cornish Landscape* (London, 1983), pp. 130–1.
15 J. Hatcher, *The History of the British Coal Industry*, vol. 1: *Before 1700* (Oxford, 1993), p. 22.
16 W. Childs, 'England's iron trade in the fifteenth century', *Economic History Review* 34 (1981).
17 For the tin industry, see J. Hatcher, *English Tin Production and Trade before 1550* (Oxford, 1973).
18 See I. Blanchard, 'Labour productivity and work psychology in the English mining industry 1400–1600', *Economic History Review* 31 (1978).

FAMILY AND INHERITANCE, WOMEN AND CHILDREN

1 Public Record Office, CP 40/129, m. 75. For earlier evidence of a similar group of kinsmen making arrangements for the custody of the lands and property of a much younger man incapable of managing his affairs, see Public Record Office, JUST 1/365, m. 25d.
2 Public Record Office, JUST 1/622, m. 9d.
3 Public Record Office, JUST 1/492, m. 39d.
4 British Library, MS. Add. 5,925, fos 9v–10r.
5 British Library, MS. Egerton 2,811, fo. 100r–v.
6 Public Record Office, KB 27/191, m. 7.
7 Public Record Office, CP 40/81, m. 48d.
8 Public Record Office, CP 40/160, m. 203.
9 Public Record Office, JUST 1/14, m. 2.
10 Public Record Office, JUST 1/726, m. 3d.
11 Public Record Office, CP 25(1)/215/34, no. 25.
12 Public Record Office, CP 25(1)/282/7, no. 135.
13 Public Record Office, JUST 1/408, m. 24d.
14 Public Record Office, C 145/49, no. 3, m. 30; CP 40/72, m. 14d; CP 25(1)/215/40, no. 7.

HEALTH, DIET, MEDICINE AND THE PLAGUE

1 B.L. Additional Ms. 47680, esp. fos. 53–76v.
2 For Galenic medicine and its importance in medical learning in the universities, see N. Siraisi, *Medieval and Early Renaissance Medicine* (Chicago, 1990).
3 Langland, *Piers the Ploughman*, ed. and trans. J. F. Goodridge (London, 1966), p. 44.
4 Froissart, *Chronicles*, ed. and trans. G. Brereton (London, 1968), p. 331.
5 Chaucer, *Canterbury Tales*, ed. N. Coghill (London, 1977), p. 233.
6 Langland, *Piers the Ploughman*, p. 89.
7 *Ibid.*, p. 88.
8 John of Arderne, *Treatise of Fistula in Ano, Haemorrhoids and Clysters*, ed. D'Arcy Power, Early English Text Society, vol. 139 (London, 1910), pp. 74–6.
9 John of Arderne, *De Arte Phisicale et de Cirurgia*, ed. and trans. D'Arcy Power (London, 1922), p. 2.
10 Froissart, *Chronicles*, p. 331.
11 Arderne, *Fistula in Ano*, p. 103.
12 C. H. Talbot, *Medicine in Medieval England* (London, 1967), p. 131. See also C. H. Talbot, 'A medieval physician's *Vade Mecum*', *Journal of the History of Medicine and Allied Sciences*, 16 (1961), pp. 213–33.
13 P. H. S. Hartley and H. R. Aldridge, *Johannes de Mirfield of St Bartholomew's, Smithfield* (Cambridge, 1936), pp. 139–43.
14 British Library, MS. Sloane 2,435.
15 H. P. Cholmeley, *John of Gaddesden and the 'Rosa Medicinae'* (Oxford, 1912).
16 *Ibid.*, p. 41.
17 S. J. Lang, 'John Bradmore and his book, *Philomena*', *Social History of Medicine*, 5 (1992), pp. 121–30. I am grateful to 'Tig' Lang for her generosity in supplying all subsequent references relating to the Bradmore manuscript (British Library, MS. Sloane 2,272).
18 *Johannes de Mirfield*, p. 131.
19 Henri de Mondeville, *Chirurgie*, ed. and trans. E. Nicaise (Paris, 1893), p. 201.
20 Arderne, *Fistula in Ano*, pp. 1, 21–8, 6.
21 *Ibid.*, p. 41; British Library, MS. Sloane 56, fo. 34; Arderne, *De Arte Phisicali*, p. 8.
22 Arderne, *Fistula in Ano*, p. 74; *De Arte Phisicali*, pp. 35–6.
23 Arderne, *Fistula in Ano*, pp. 44, 49.
24 *Ibid.*, pp. 71, 100.
25 *Ibid.*, pp. 69, 100.
26 British Library, MS. Royal 6 e. vi (fourteenth-century).
27 British Library, MS. Harley 1,735, fos 29v–50v. See J. K. Mustain, 'A rural medical practitioner in fifteenth-century England', *Bulletin of the History of Medicine*, 46 (1972), pp. 469–76.
28 *The Brut Chronicle*, ed. F. W. D. Brie, Early English Text Society (London, 1906, 1908), vol. 2, p. 303.
29 British Library, MS. Sloane 3,489, fo. 44. See F. M. Getz, 'Charity, translation and the language of medical learning in medieval England', *Bulletin of the History of Medicine*, 64 (1990), pp. 1–17.

RELIGIOUS SENSIBILITY

1 See R. O'Day, *The Debate on the English Reformation* (London, 1986), and for a bibliographical review of recent work on the later medieval Church, P. Heath, 'Between Reform and Reformation', *Journal of Ecclesiastical History* 41 (1990), pp. 647–78. A. G. Dickens, *The English Reformation* (2nd edn, London, 1989) remains the best, and formidably best, cross-examination of a Church badly in need of reform. Throughout this chapter, the key works listed as 'Further Reading' should be assumed as references.

2 See, for example, E. Duffy, *The Stripping of the Altars* (New Haven and London, 1992); C. Carpenter, 'The Religion of the gentry of fifteenth-century England', in *England in the Fifteenth Century*, ed. D. Williams (Woodbridge, 1987), pp. 53–74.

3 See R. Horrox, *The Black Death* (Manchester, 1994) for specific source material and bibliography. M. E. Aston, 'Popular religious movements in the Middle Ages', in her *Faith and Fire* (London, 1993), pp. 1–26, and R. N. Swanson, 'In search of Pre-Reformation English spirituality', in his *Catholic England* (Manchester, 1993), pp. 1–43, are sensitive insights. See also R. G. Davies, 'Lollardy and locality', *Transactions of the Royal Historical Society*, 6th series, 1 (1991), pp. 191–212; R. Whiting, *The Blind Devotion of the People* (Cambridge, 1989); L. R. Poos, *A Rural Society after the Black Death* (Cambridge, 1991).

4 See Duffy, *The Stripping of the Altars*, R. Hutton, *The Rise and Fall of Merry England* (Oxford, 1994), M. Rubin, *Corpus Christi* (Cambridge, 1991) and note 3 above.

5 Among much else, see Davies, 'Lollardy and locality' above; J. Bossy, 'The Mass as a social institution', *Past and Present* 100 (1983), pp. 29–61; *idem*, 'Blood and baptism: kinship, community and Christianity in Western Europe from the fourteenth to the seventeenth centuries', in *Sanctity and Secularity*, ed. D. Baker (Oxford, 1973), pp. 129–43; G. Rosser, 'Parochial conformity and voluntary religion in late-medieval England', *Transactions of the Royal Historical Society* 6th series, 1 (1991), pp. 173–89; N. Orme, 'Children and the Church', *Journal of Ecclesiastical History* 45 (1994), 563–87; C. Barron, 'The parish fraternities of medieval London', in *The Church in Pre-Reformation Society*, ed. C. M. Barron and C. Harper-Bill (Woodbridge, 1985), pp. 13–37; B. McRee, 'Religious guilds and regulation of behaviour in late medieval towns', in *People, Politics and Community*, ed. J. T. Rosenthal and C. Richmond (Gloucester, 1987), pp. 108–22.

6 Overviews by K. Thomas, *Religion and the Decline of Magic* (London, 1971), Duffy, *The Stripping of the Altars* and R. Hutton, *The Rise and Fall of Merry England*. For comparative European studies, see B. Ankerloo and G. Henningsen (eds), *Early Modern Witchcraft* (Oxford, 1990), especially the essays by J. C. Baroja, S. Clark and R. Muchembled.

7 R. Hutton, *The Rise and Fall of Merry England* has brought much of this work together. Subsequent paragraphs are a gloss around this fine work.

8 J. Bossy, 'The Social history of confession in the age of the Reformation', *Transactions of the Royal Historical Society* 5th series, 25 (1975), pp. 21–38.

9 M. Rubin, *Corpus Christi*.

10 The most extreme compilation from such material of complaint remains H. Maynard-Smith, *Pre-Reformation England* (London, 1938). A. Hudson, in *The Premature Reformation* (Oxford, 1988) demonstrated, however, that Lollard critiques are not so lightly to be dismissed.

11 Unpublished papers and work in progress by Mrs J. Carnwath (University of Manchester) and Mr R. Lutton (University of Kent) point to optimism. Meanwhile, see C. Marsh, 'In the Name of God? Will-making and faith in early modern England', in *The Records of the Nation*, edited by G. H. Martin and P. Spufford (Woodbridge, 1990), pp. 215–49 (mainly post-Reformation); C. Burgess, '"By quick and by dead": wills and pious provision in late medieval Bristol', *English Historical Review* 102 (1987), 837–58; *idem*. 'Late medieval wills and pious conventions: testamentary evidence reconsidered', in *Profit, Piety and the Professions*, ed. M. Hicks (Gloucester, 1990), pp. 14–37.

12 This is on the assumption that most testaments were drawn up entirely on the death-bed, rather than at least drafted well beforehand; an assumption that may be challenged one day. Henry Brudenell (d. 1431), of the well-known Northants family, is one at least who trimmed and snipped over the course of life.

13 J. Le Goff, *The Birth of Purgatory* (English translation, Aldershot, 1991), especially chapter 9; C. Burgess, '"A fond thing vainly invented"', in *Parish, Church and People*, ed. S. Wright (London, 1988), pp. 59–70.

14 See, among a considerable literature, C. Gittings, *Death, Burial and the Individual in Early Modern England* (London, 1984); Burgess, '"By quick and by dead"' and '"A fond thing vainly invented"'; J. T. Rosenthal, *The Purchase of Paradise* (London, 1972); R. Houlbrooke (ed.), *Death, Ritual and Bereavement* (New York, 1989), chapters 1 and 2. There is much yet to do in this field.

15 Information supplied by J. Carnwath, whose study of the Dormer papers at Rowsham (Oxfordshire), by invitation of Mr and Mrs T. Cotterill-Dormer, promises rare holistic sight of the social interaction of a later medieval town and church (Thame).

16 See W. K. Jordan, *Philanthropy in England, 1480–1660* (London, 1959); much criticised for its use of evidence, badly neglected as to its perceptions.

17 The theme ran through their writings from before 1395, via their Twelve Conclusions and 'parliamentary petition' of 1410, to the forlorn and eccentric revolt of 1430; see M. E. Aston, '"Caim's Castles": poverty, politics and disendowment', in *Church, Politics and Patronage*, ed. R. B. Dobson (Gloucester, 1984), pp. 45–67.

18 C. L. Scofield, *Life and Reign of Edward the Fourth* (London, 1923) vol. I, pp. 268–9, vol. II, pp. 167–8; A. Payne, 'The Salisbury Roll of Arms of *c.* 1463' in D. Williams (ed.) *England in the Fifteenth Century*, p. 187, note 3; J. B. Post, 'The obsequies of John of Gaunt', *Guildhall Studies in London History* 5 (1981), 1–12; P. Coulstock, *The Cathedral Church of Wimborne Minster* (Woodbridge, 1993), chapter 10.

19 E. A. R. Brown, *The Monarchy of Capetian France and Royal Ceremonial* (Aldershot, 1991), part 2, 'Death, royal dying and succession to the crown of France', collects her several classic essays.

20 G. L. Harriss, *Cardinal Beaufort* (Oxford, 1988), p. 398; P. Aries, *Images of Man and Death* (trans., Cambridge, Mass., and London, 1985), especially chapter 5; K. Cohen, *Metamorphosis of a Death Symbol* (for the *transi* tomb); H. Colvin, *Architecture and the After-life* (New Haven and London, 1991), especially chapter 5.

21 C. Richmond, 'Religion and the fifteenth-century gentleman', in R. B. Dobson (ed.) *Church, Politics and Patronage*, pp. 194–5.

22 See, e.g., J. T. Rosenthal, *The Purchase of Paradise*; C. Richmond, 'Religion and the fifteenth-century gentleman'; M. Hicks, 'Chantries, obits and almshouses: the Hungerford foundations' and 'Piety and lineage in the Wars of the Roses: the Hungerford experience', in his *Richard III and his Rivals* (London, 1991), pp. 79–98, 163–84; M. G. A. Vale, *Piety, Charity and Literacy among the Yorkshire Gentry, 1370–1480*, Borthwick Papers 50 (York, 1976).

23 P. W. Fleming, 'Charity, faith and the gentry of Kent, 1422–1529', in *Property and Politics*, ed. T. Pollard (Gloucester, 1984), pp. 36–57.

24 See W. F. Carter, *The Quartermains of Oxfordshire* (Oxford, 1936), plate facing p. 52 (identified incorrectly).

25 C. Richmond, 'Religion and the fifteenth-century gentleman'; K. Mertes, 'The household as a religious community', in Rosenthal and Richmond, *People, Politics and Community*, pp. 123–39.

26 M. Rubin, *Corpus Christi*, especially chapters 2 and 5.

27 M. E. Aston, '*Corpus Christi* and *Corpus Regis*: heresy and the Peasants' Revolt', *Past and Present* 143 (1994), 3–47.

28 See above, note 2.

29 K. B. McFarlane, *Lancastrian Kings and Lollard Knights* (Oxford, 1972), pp. 207–20.

30 *Kent Sede Vacante Wills*, ed. C. E. Woodruff (Kent Archaeological Society, 1914), pp. 81–5 (Arundel); *Testamenta Eboracensia*, ed. J. Raine I (Surtees Society, 1836), pp. 306–17 (Skirlaw), 398–402 (Bowet); *Historiae Dunelmensis Scriptores Tres*, ed. J. Raine (Surtees Society, 1839), ccxli–ccxlvii (Langley).

31 Buckinghamshire Record Office, Aylesbury; Enrolled Wills, D/A/We 3/53, William Grover of Blackwell Hall (probate 15 July 1533); 3/166, Thomas Grover of Whelpley Hill (probate 30 March 1536).

32 J. Bossy, 'Blood and baptism; kinship, community and Christianity', in *Studies in Church History* 10 (1973), 129–43. P. Heath, *The English Parish Clergy on the Eve of the Reformation* (London, 1969) reached the conclusions other historians have been rediscovering since.

33 For well-edited examples of parochial visitations, see *The Courts of the Archdeaconry of Buckingham*, ed. E. M. Elvey (Buckinghamshire Record Society, 19, 1975), especially pp. 2–10, 264–6, 285–99; *Kentish Visitations of Archbishop William Warham and his Deputies, 1511–12*, ed. K. L. Wood-Legh (Maidstone, 1984), pp. 50–292.

34 The only good modern evaluation is by J. Carnwath, 'The Churchwardens' accounts of Thame, Oxfordshire', in *Trade, Devotion and Governance*, ed. D. Clayton *et al.* (Manchester, 1994), pp. 177–97, but cf. R. Hutton, *The Rise and Fall of Merry England*.

35 See K. Mertes, 'The household as a religious community'.

36 For impressive lists of those buried, see J. Stow, *Survey of London*, ed. C. L. Kingsford (Oxford, 1908) I, 319–22; C. L. Kingsford, *Grey Friars of London* (Aberdeen, 1915), pp. 124–44; *idem.*, 'Additional material for the history of the Grey Friars, London', *Collectanea Franciscana II* (Manchester, 1922), 61–149.

37 R. C. Finucane, *Miracles and Pilgrims: Popular Beliefs in Medieval England* (London, 1977), is not focused on the later medieval period, but lacks a sequel. E. Duffy, *The Stripping of the Altars*,

38 *The Book of Margery Kempe*, ed. B. A. Windeatt (Harmondsworth, 1985), especially chapters 27–42; *Two Wycliffite Texts*, ed. A. Hudson (EETS, o.s., 1993), pp. 61–6.

39 For aspects of the place of women, see M. E. Aston, 'Segregation in churches'; E. Duffy, 'Holy Maydens, Holy Wyfes: the cult of women saints in fifteenth–sixteenth-century England'; D. M. Wells, 'Women and home: the domestic setting of late medieval spirituality'; all in *Women in the Church*, edited by W. J. Sheils and D. Wood (Oxford, 1990), pp. 237–94, 175–96, 159–73. E. Duffy, *The Stripping of the Altars*, B. McRee, 'Religious guilds and regulation of behaviour in late medieval towns', C. Barron, 'The parish fraternities of medieval London' and A. Hudson, *The Premature Reformation* give firm leads on the other themes.

40 See R.N. Swanson, *Church and Society*, chapter 3; R. L. Storey, 'Episcopal king-makers in the fifteenth century', in Dobson, *Church, Politics and Patronage*, pp. 82–98; R. G. Davies, 'The Church and the Wars of the Roses', in *The Wars of the Roses*, ed. A. J. Pollard (London, 1995), pp. 134–61.

41 See note 37 above.

LANGUAGE AND LITERARY EXPRESSION

1 For the history of the language during the Old English period, see Albert C. Baugh and Thomas Cable, *A History of the English Language*, 4th edn. (London, 1993), pp. 41–104. For an introduction to the literary culture of this period, see *The Cambridge Guide to Old English Literature*, edited by Malcolm Godden and Michael Lapidge (Cambridge, 1991).

2 This section on the history of English, French and Latin in England draws on Baugh and Cable, pp. 105–94. For another helpful account of the language, see J. A. Burrow and Thorlac Turville-Petre, *A Book of Middle English* (Oxford, 1992), pp. 1–55.

3 See Derek Pearsall, *The Life of Geoffrey Chaucer: A Critical Biography* (Oxford, 1992), pp. 64–5.

4 For the complete text, see *Laȝamon: Brut*, edited by G. L. Brook and R. F. Leslie, EETS o.s., I, 250 (1963); II, 277 (1978). For an edition of the Arthurian section with a facing-page modern English translation, see *Laȝamon's Arthur: The Arthurian Section of Laȝamon's Brut (Lines 9229–14297)*, edited and translated by W. R. J. Barron and S. C. Weinberg (London, 1989); from which this chapter quotes. For this quotation from the opening lines of the poem, see the editors' introduction, pp. viii–ix.

5 For surveys of romance, see W. R. J. Barron, *English Medieval Romance* (London, 1987) and John Stevens, *Medieval Romance: Themes and Approaches* (London, 1973).

6 *Boethius, De Consolatione Philosophiae, translated by John Walton, Canon of Oseney*, edited by Mark Science, EETS o.s. 170 (1927), III. Met. 12, stanzas 8–9.

7 For analysis of this metre, see I. R. Johnson, 'Walton's Sapient Orpheus', in *The Medieval Boethius: Studies in the Vernacular Translations of De Consolatione Philosophiae*, edited by A. J. Minnis (Cambridge, 1987), pp. 139–68.

8 An accessible modern edition of the poem is in Burrow and Turville-Petre, *A Book of Middle English*, pp. 110–29, from which I quote.

9 See *Six Middle English Romances*, edited by Maldwyn Mills (London, 1973), pp. 148–68, from which I quote.

10 Both Middle English text and contemporary English translation are taken from *Middle English Prose for Women: Selections from the Katherine Group and Ancrene Wisse*, edited by Bella Millett and Jocelyn Wogan-Browne (Oxford, 1992), pp. 112–15.

11 *The Cloud of Unknowing and The Book of Privy Counselling*, edited by Phyllis Hodgson, EETS o.s. 218 (1944). For a modern English translation of this work, see *The Cloud of Unknowing and Other Works*, translated by Clifton Wolters (Harmondsworth, 1978).

12 For the Short Text, see *Julian of Norwich's Revelations of Divine Love*, edited by Frances Beer, *Middle English Texts* 8 (Heidelberg, 1978). For the Long Text, see *Julian of Norwich: A Revelation of Love*, rev. edn, edited by Marion Glasscoe (Exeter, 1993). Quotations are taken from this edition. Both versions of Julian's text are edited with considerable notes and commentary in *A Book of Showings to the Anchoress Julian of Norwich*, 2 vols, edited by Edmund Colledge and James Walsh (Toronto, 1978).

13 Quotations are from *William Langland, The Vision of Piers Plowman; A Critical Edition of the B-text*, edited by A. V. C. Schmidt (London, 1987). An extremely helpful guide to this challenging poem is James Simpson, *Piers Plowman: An Introduction to the B-text* (London, 1990).

14 For discussion of the Trinity in this passage, see Simpson, *Piers Plowman*, pp. 200–2.

15 See *Sir Gawain and the Green Knight, Pearl, Cleanness, Patience*, edited by A. C. Cawley and J. J. Anderson (London, 1983), pp. 1–47, from which quotations are taken. *Pearl* is also available in *The Poems of the Pearl Manuscript: Pearl, Cleanness, Patience, Sir Gawain and the Green Knight*, edited by Malcolm Andrew and Ronald Waldron (Exeter, 1987), pp. 53–110.

16 Cawley and Anderson, *Sir Gawain and the Green Knight*, pp. 157–254, from which quotations are taken. The poem is also available in Andrew and Waldron, *The Poems of the Pearl Manuscript*, pp. 206–300.

17 All Chaucer quotations are from *The Riverside Chaucer*, 3rd edn, general editor Larry D. Benson (Oxford, 1988).

18 The circumstances attending the 'disambiguation' of English poetry in the fifteenth century have recently been given a new focus by Nicholas Watson, who is currently engaged on a substantial study of vernacular theology in England at this time. For discussion of the relationship of the court to the establishment of an orthodox national tradition of vernacular literature, see Derek Pearsall, 'Hoccleve's *Regement of Princes*: The Poetics of Royal Self-Representation', *Speculum* 69 (1994), 386–410; and John Fisher, 'A Language Policy for Lancastrian England', *PMLA* 107 (1992), 1,168–80.

19 *Nicholas Love's Mirror of the Blessed Life of Jesus Christ*, edited by Michael G. Sargent (New York and London, 1992), from which quotations are taken, with slight alteration to the punctuation.

20 For discussion of the competing strategies of Love and the Wycliffites, see Ian Johnson, 'Vernacular Valorizing: Functions and Fashionings of Literary Theory in Middle English Translation of Authority', in the proceedings of the Symposium on Medieval Translation, held at the 28th International Congress on Medieval Studies, Western Michigan University, Kalamazoo, May 1993, edited by Jeanette Beer (Kalamazoo, forthcoming).

21 For a survey of Middle English Lives of Christ, see Elizabeth Salter, *Nicholas Love's 'Myrrour of the Blessed Lyf of Jesu Christ'*, *Analecta Cartusiana* 10 (Salzburg, 1974), pp. 73–118. For a study of hagiography, see Thomas J. Heffernan, *Sacred Biography: Saints and Their Biographies in the Middle Ages* (New York, 1988).

22 *The Life of St Katherine of Alexandria by John Capgrave, D.D.*, edited by Carl Horstmann, EETS o.s. 100 (1893).

23 *Legendys of Hooly Wummen by Osbern Bokenham*, edited by Mary S. Serjeantson, EETS o.s. 206 (1938), lines 7,130–7. For a modern English version of this work, see *A Legend of Holy Women: Osbern Bokenham, Legends of Holy Women*, translated by Sheila Delany (Notre Dame and London, 1992).

FORMS OF ARTISTIC EXPRESSION

1 If a person's possessions were forfeit to the Crown, they would be taken into the keeping of the royal Exchequer or of local escheators or other officials, and they would be listed by or for the Exchequer or Chancery clerks.

2 For a recent survey of Westminster Abbey's history, see Christopher Wilson *et al.*, *Westminster Abbey*, The New Bell's Cathedral Guides (London, 1986). The bishop of London from 1044 to 1051 was a Norman, Robert of Jumièges, who perhaps advised or encouraged Edward.

3 The case for the Bayeux Tapestry as a *chanson de geste*, a work of secular narrative art, is made by C. R. Dodwell, 'The Bayeux Tapestry and the French Secular Epic', *Burlington Magazine*, cviii (1966), pp. 549–60.

4 Gervase's account of the burning and rebuilding of Christ Church, Canterbury is printed in *The Historical Works of Gervase of Canterbury*, edited by W. Stubbs, 2 vols (Rolls Series, 73, 1879–80), I, pp. 3–29; there are translations by Robert Willis, *The Architectural History of Canterbury Cathedral* (London, 1845), pp. 32–62, and Charles Cotton, *Of the Burning and Repair of the Church of Canterbury in the Year 1174, From the Latin of Gervase . . .*, Canterbury Papers, no. 3, 4th edn (Canterbury, 1956).

5 One exception is Berengar, the master mason who was in charge of the building works at Hailes Abbey (Gloucestershire) in 1272–73; his name strongly suggests that he came from France, and the building works at the abbey included the continental feature of a chevet (a set of chapels radiating out from the apse), as at Westminster Abbey.

6 Thus Pamela Tudor-Craig in *The Age of Chivalry: Art in Plantagenet England, 1200–1400*, edited by J. Alexander and P. Binski (London: Royal Academy of Arts, 1987), p. 133.

7 P. Binski, *The Painted Chamber at Westminster*, Society of Antiquaries, Occasional Papers, n.s. ix (1986), p. 74, who claims, however, that it was 'counterfeited in painted wood after the example (*ad exemplar*) of a bronze prototype'.

8 See Jean Bony, *The English Decorated Style: Gothic Architecture Transformed* (Oxford, 1979); Nicola Coldstream, *The Decorated Style: Architecture and Ornament, 1240–1360* (London, 1994).

9 L. F. Sandler, *Gothic Manuscripts, 1285–1385*, 2 vols, A Survey of Manuscripts Illuminated in the British Isles, vol. V (London, 1986), II, pp. 118–21, no. 107; *The Age of Chivalry*, edited by Alexander and Binski, pp. 455–6, no. 575. Good illustrations are in Janet Backhouse, *The Luttrell Psalter* (London, 1989).

10 P. Binski, 'Monumental brasses', in *The Age of Chivalry*, edited by Alexander and Binski, pp. 171–3 (p. 173).

11 The most recent discussion, with a marshalling of the evidence and summaries of the theories, is by Dillian Gordon, in *Making and Meaning: the Wilton Diptych* (London (The National Gallery), 1993).

12 The most recent general treatment of *opus anglicanum* is by Donald King, *Opus Anglicanum: English Medieval Embroidery*, catalogue of exhibition at the Victoria and Albert Museum (London (Arts Council), 1963).

13 *The Age of Chivalry*, edited by Alexander and Binski, no. 12.

14 See further N. L. Ramsay, 'Alabaster', in *English Medieval Industries: Craftsmen, Techniques, Products*, edited by W. J. Blair and N. L. Ramsay (London, 1991), pp. 29–40.

15 Cf. Marian Campbell, 'Gold, silver and precious stones', in *English Medieval Industries*, edited by Blair and Ramsay, pp. 107–66 (p. 161).

16 London, Guildhall Library, MS 25166/1, an account perhaps datable to 1479–80.

17 Francis Wormald, *Collected Writings*, edited by J. J. G. Alexander, T. J. Brown and Joan Gibbs, II, *Studies in English and Continental Art of the Later Middle Ages* (London, 1988), pp. 86–7.

18 N. L. Ramsay, 'Artists, craftsmen and design in England, 1200–1400', in *The Age of Chivalry*, edited by Alexander and Binski, pp. 49–54 (p. 50).

19 See, for instance, T. D. Atkinson, *Local Style in English Architecture* (London, etc., 1947), pp. 159–61, which lists buildings, tombs and other works specified in contracts to be in imitation of others.

20 'Near-pairs' resulted from works of art being made a few years apart. See N. J. Barker, *Two East Anglian Picture Books* (London, 1988)

21 N. J. Morgan, *Early Gothic Manuscripts*, pt 2, *1250–1285*, A Survey of Manuscripts Illuminated in the British Isles, vol. IV (London, 1988), pp. 162–4, no. 165.

22 See, e.g. *The Age of Chivalry*, edited by Alexander and Binski, pp. 463–7.

23 Printing might be called the supreme example of mass production of works of art, and it resulted in the creation of a new category of artist, the printer.

24 J. H. Harvey, *English Mediaeval Architects: a Biographical Dictionary down to 1550*, 2nd edn (Gloucester, 1984), p. 339.

25 A good example of the application of the new criteria can be seen in a letter from Sir William Fitzwilliam to Henry VIII: writing from Paris in 1521, he complained that 'the painter did not do my portrait well, but I hope he will do better in England, as he made mine in haste' (*Letters and Papers, Foreign and Domestic, of the Reign of Henry VIII*, III, pt 1, no. 1227). Even the best foreign artists – and this one was, perhaps, Clouet of Navarre, as Mme Cécile Scaillérez advises me – could fail to live up to the new expectations.

THE POLITICAL INSTITUTIONS OF THE REALM

1 British Library, MS. Cotton Vitellius e. x, printed in S. B. Chrimes, *English Constitutional Ideas in the Fifteenth Century* (Cambridge, 1936), p. 180.

2 See J. Cannon and R. Griffiths, *The Oxford Illustrated History of the British Monarchy* (Oxford and New York, 1988), chapter 3 ('Monarch and Nation, 1216–1509').

3 On the duties of kings, see Chrimes, *English Constitutional Ideas*, chapter 1, section 1 ('The conception of the kingship').

The coronation oath sworn by Edward II in 1308 is translated in *English Historical Documents, 1189–1327*, edited by H. Rothwell (London, 1975) p. 525.

4 R. N. Swanson, *Church and Society in Late Medieval England* (Oxford, 1989), chapter 3 ('The Church and the political order'); T. A. Sandquist, 'The holy oil of St Thomas of Canterbury', in *Essays in Medieval History presented to Bertie Wilkinson*, edited by T. A. Sandquist and M. R. Powicke (Toronto, 1969), pp. 330–44.

5 *The Works of Sir John Fortescue, Knight*, edited by Thomas, Lord Clermont (2 vols in 3, London, 1869), I, 513 ('Defensio Juris Domus Lancastriae'); P. Grierson, 'The origins of the English sovereign and the symbolism of the closed crown', *British Numismatic Journal*, 33 (1969), 118–34.

6 *Statutes of the Realm* (Record Commission, 1810–28), I, 31; R. A. Griffiths, 'The English Realm and Dominions and the King's Subjects in the later Middle Ages', in *Aspects of Late Medieval Government and Society*, edited by J. G. Rowe (Toronto, 1986), pp. 83–105.

7 *Rotuli Parliamentorum* (7 vols, Record Commission, 1783–1832), V, 375–6, quoted in *English Historical Documents, 1327–1485*, edited by A. R. Myers (London, 1969), p. 416.

8 See *Four English Political Tracts of the Later Middle Ages*, edited by J.-P. Genet (Camden Society, 4th series, 18, 1977), especially pp. ix–xix.

9 Quoted from Henry de Bracton's 'On the laws and customs of England', in B. Wilkinson, *Constitutional History of Medieval England, 1216–1399*, Vol. III (London, 1958), pp. 102, 104; *The Governance of England by Sir John Fortescue*, edited by C. Plummer (Oxford, 1885) pp. 109, 115.

10 'the more we bestow honours on wise and honourable men, the more our crown is adorned with gems and precious stones' (1385) (*Reports from the Lords' Committees touching the Dignity of a Peer of the Realm* (5 vols, Record Commission, 1829), V, 64–5, quoted in A. Tuck, *Richard II and the English Nobility* (London, 1973), p. 84).

11 See *Letters of the Queens of England, 1100–1547*, edited by A. Crawford (Stroud, 1994), especially pp. 67, 118; R. A. Griffiths, 'Queen Katherine of Valois and a missing statute of the Realm', *Law Quarterly Review*, 93 (1977), 248–58.

12 C. Given-Wilson, *The Royal Household and the King's Affinity* (New Haven and London, 1986); A. R. Myers, *The Household of Edward IV* (Manchester, 1959); R. A. Griffiths, 'The king's Court during the Wars of the Roses: continuities in an age of discontinuities', in *Princes, Patronage and the Nobility*, edited by R. G. Asch and A. M. Birke (London, 1991), chapter 2.

13 B. Wilkinson, *The Chancery under Edward III* (Manchester, 1929); N. Pronay, 'The Chancellor, the Chancery and the Council at the end of the fifteenth century', in *British Government and Administration*, ed. H. Hearder and H. R. Loyn (Cardiff, 1974), pp. 87–103.

14 For a list of chancellors, see the *Handbook of British Chronology*, edited by E. B. Fryde *et al.* (Royal Historical Society Guides and Handbooks, 3rd edn, 1986), pp. 82–92.

15 *De Necessariis Observantiis Scaccarii Dialogus qui vulgo dicitur Dialogus de Scaccario*, edited and translated by C. Johnson (rev. edn, Oxford, 1983).

16 F. M. Powicke, *King Henry III and the Lord Edward* (Oxford, 1966 repr.), chapter III; M. Buck, *Politics, Finance and the Church in the Reign of Edward II* (Cambridge, 1983), especially chapters 7, 8.

17 R. A. Griffiths, *The Reign of King Henry VI* (London and Los Angeles, 1981), pp. 785–90; B. P. Wolffe, *The Royal Demesne in English History* (London, 1971), chapters VI, VII.

18 *Handbook of British Chronology*, pp. 101–9.

19 T. F. Tout, *Chapters in the Administrative History of Medieval England* (6 vols, Manchester, 1920–33); A. J. Otway-Ruthven, *The King's Secretary and the Signet Office in the Fifteenth Century* (Cambridge, 1939); *Handbook of British Chronology*, pp. 92–101.

20 G. L. Harriss, *King, Parliament and Public Finance in Medieval England to 1369* (Oxford, 1975), especially chapters VIII, IX.

21 Annals of Dunstable, in *Annales Monastici*, Vol. III, edited by H. R. Luard (Rolls Series, 1866), pp. 145–6, as quoted in Wilkinson, *Constitutional History of Medieval England*, III, 141.

22 *Rotuli Parliamentorum*, II, 323, as quoted in A. L. Brown, *The Governance of Late Medieval England, 1272–1461* (London, 1989), p. 236.

23 *The Chronicle of Pierre de Langtoft*, edited by T. Wright (2 vols, Rolls Series, 1886), II, 200–4, as quoted in M. Prestwich, *Edward I* (London, 1988), pp. 386–7.

24 For Henry VI's promise in 1450 to 'stablish with sad and so substancial consaile', see R. A. Griffiths, 'Duke Richard of York's intentions in 1450 and the origins of the Wars of the Roses', *Journal of Medieval History*, I (1975), 205.

25 J. C. Holt, 'The prehistory of Parliament', in *The English Parliament in the Middle Ages*, edited by R. G. Davies and J. H. Denton (Manchester, 1981), p. 6.

26 *Fleta*, edited and translated by H. G. Richardson and G. O. Sayles (Selden Society 72, 1953), II, 109, as quoted in Brown, *The Governance of Late Medieval England*, p. 165; W. Stubbs, *The Constitutional History of England* (4th edn, 3 vols, Oxford, 1906), II, 276, note 2 (from a Chancery warrant, 1280).

27 Brown, *The Governance of Late Medieval England*, p. 165.

28 J. S. Roskell, 'Perspectives in English Parliamentary history', *Bulletin of the John Rylands Library*, 46 (1964), 474.

29 See *Handbook of British Chronology*, pp. 525–81, for lists of Parliaments.

30 *Paston Letters and Papers of the Fifteenth Century*, Part II, edited by N. Davis (Oxford, 1976), pp. 54–5; S. J. Payling, *Political Society in Lancastrian England* (Oxford, 1991), pp. 158–67.

31 Quoted in H. M. Cam, *Liberties and Communities in Medieval England* (London, 1963), p. 230.

32 Fortescue, *The Governance of England*, pp. 150–1.

33 *Select Documents of English Constitutional History, 1307–1485*, edited by S. B. Chrimes and A. L. Brown (London, 1961), p. 326, from *Rotuli Parliamentorum*, V, 487.

LAWMAKERS AND LAWBREAKERS

1 F. Bacon, 'Of revenge', in *The Works of Francis Bacon*, edited by J. Spedding *et al.*, vi (London, 1858), 385.

2 A. Sutton, 'The Administration of Justice whereunto we be professed' in *Richard III: Crown and People*, edited by J. Petre (Richard III Society, 1985).

3 M. Beilby, 'The profits of expertise: the rise of the civil lawyers and Chancery equity', in *Profit, Piety and the Professions in Later Medieval England*, edited by M. A. Hicks (Gloucester, 1990).

4 P. Brand, *The Origins of the Legal Profession* (Oxford, 1992), especially pp. 106–9.

5 N. Ramsay, 'What was the legal profession?', *Profit, Piety and the Professions*, chapter 5.

6 B. Vale, 'The profits of the Law and the "rise" of the Scropes', *ibid.*, chapter 7.

7 E. Powell, 'The King's Bench in Shropshire and Staffordshire in 1414', in *Law, Litigants and the Legal Profession*, edited by E. W. Ives and A. H. Manchester (London, 1983).

8 *The English Rising of 1381*, edited by T. Aston and R. H. Hilton (Cambridge, 1984), chapter by A. Harding; 'The Chronicle of the Rebellion in Lincolnshire 1470', in *Three Chronicles of the Reign of Edward IV*, edited by K. Dockray (Gloucester, 1988), p. 6; E. Powell, *Kingship, Law and Society* (Oxford, 1989), pp. 201–2.

9 M. Blatcher, *The Court of King's Bench 1450–1550* (London, 1978), p. vii.

10 D. Carpenter, 'Bastard Feudalism revised: debate', *Past and Present* 131 (1991), 182.

11 For earlier historians, see M. A. Hicks, *Richard III and his Rivals* (London, 1991), pp. 3–6, 11.

12 The latest analysis is to be found in M. A. Hicks, *Bastard Feudalism* (London, 1995).

13 J. G. Bellamy, *The Law of Treason in England in the Later Middle Ages* (Cambridge, 1970), appendix II.

14 B. A. Hanawalt, 'Fur-collar crime: the pattern of crime among the fourteenth-century English nobility', *Journal of Social History* viii (1974).

15 J. G. Bellamy, *Crime and Public Order in England in the Later Middle Ages* (London, 1973), p. 70ff.

16 R. A. Griffiths, *King and Country* (London, 1991), chapter 14.

17 T. More, *Utopia*, edited by P. Turner (Harmondsworth, 1965), p. 45.

18 J. G. Bellamy, *Criminal Law and Society in Late Medieval and Tudor England* (Gloucester, 1984).

19 Hicks, *Bastard Feudalism*, chapter 4.

20 C. E. Moreton, *The Townshends and their World* (Oxford, 1992), pp. 102–3.

21 P. C. Maddern, *Violence and the Social Order* (Oxford, 1992), p. 174.

22 Hicks, *Bastard Feudalism*, chapter 8.

CIVIL WAR AND REBELLION

1 *The Works of Sir Thomas Malory*, edited by E. Vinaver (Oxford, 1947), iii, 1,229.

2 *Polychronicon Ranulphi Higden*, edited by C. Babington and J. R. Lumby (Rolls Series, 1865–66), ii, 169; *Calendar of State Papers and Manuscripts existing in the archives and collections of Milan* (London, 1912), p. 154.

3 P. S. Lewis, 'Two pieces of fifteenth-century political iconography', *Journal of the Warburg and Courtauld Institute*, xvii (1964), 319.

4 R. W. Kaeuper, *War, Justice and Public Order: England and France in the Later Middle Ages* (Oxford, 1988); E. B. Fryde and N. Fryde, 'Peasant rebellion and peasant discontents', in *The Agrarian History of England and Wales, 1348–1500*, edited by E. Miller (Cambridge, 1991), p. 744.

5 W. Stubbs, *The Constitutional History of England* 4th edn (Oxford, 1906), ii, 319.

6 *Rotuli Parliamentorum* (London, 1783), v, 464.

7 *Select Cases of Procedure without Writ under Henry III*, edited by H. G. Richardson and G. O. Sayles, Selden Society, lx (1941), 43; D. A. Carpenter, 'English peasants in Politics 1258–1267', *Past and Present*, cxxxvi (1992), 3–42.

8 *Chronicon Adae de Usk*, edited by E. M. Thompson (London, 1904), p. 203.

9 W Stubbs, *Select Charters and other illustrations of English Constitutional History* 9th edn (Oxford, 1913), pp. 407–8.

10 D. A. Carpenter, 'Simon de Montfort: the first leader of a political movement in English history', *History*, lxxvi (1991), 20.

11 *Annales Monastici*, edited by H. R. Luard (Rolls Series, 1864–69), i, 459.

12 *The Peasants' Revolt of 1381*, edited by R. B. Dobson (London, 1983), p. 342.

13 *Annales Monastici*, i, 64.

14 J. C. Holt, *The Northerners: a Study in the Reign of King John* (Oxford, 1961), p. 100.

15 M. V. Clarke, *Medieval Representation and Consent* (London, 1936), p. 183.

16 *Oxfordshire Sessions of the Peace in the Reign of Richard II*, edited by E. G. Kimball, Oxfordshire Record Society, liii (1983) 85.

17 R. Virgoe, 'The death of William de la Pole, duke of Suffolk', *Bulletin of the John Rylands Library*, xlvii (1964–65), 501.

ENGLAND AND ITS NEIGHBOURS

1 *Anglo-Scottish Relations 1174–1328*, edited by E. L. G. Stones (Oxford, 1965), p. 3.

2 R. R. Davies, *Domination and Conquest: the Experience of Ireland, Scotland and Wales 1100–1300* (Cambridge, 1990), p. 84.

3 *English Historical Documents*, iii (1189–1327), edited by H. Rothwell (London, 1975), p. 542.

4 R. Nicholson, *Scotland: The Later Middle Ages* (Edinburgh, 1974), p. 130.

5 *Rotuli Parliamentorum*, ii, p. 147.

6 Thomas Walsingham, *Historia Anglicana*, edited by H. T. Riley, 2 vols (London, 1863–64), ii, p. 147.

7 R. Frame, *The Political Development of the British Isles 1100–1400* (Oxford, 1990), p. 216.

8 *Ibid.*, p. 214.

9 *Chronicon Adae de Usk 1377–1421*, edited by E. M. Thompson (London, 1904), p. 240.

10 A. Curry, *The Hundred Years War* (London, 1993), p. 107.

11 As it was described in 1245; see Stones, *Anglo-Scottish Relations*, p. 55.

INDEX

administration, royal, 190–4
aesthetic, medieval, 168, 176–7
ages of the world, 1
Agincourt, battle of (1415), 14, 92, 265
agricultural production, 39–40, 44–8
Alexander II, king of Scotland (1214–49), 252
Alexander III, king of Scotland (1249–86), 252–3
Alexander the Great, 82
Alnwick (Northumberland), 33
Anagni, 3
Ancrene Wisse, 132
Angevin Empire, 9, 248–9, 269
apothecaries, 91, 96–7
Aquitaine (Gascony), 9, 11, 15, 184, 249–52, 255–60, 264–70
    Eleanor of, 9
Arbroath, Declaration of (1320), 254
architecture, 157–64, 176
Arden, forest of (Warwickshire), 24
Arderne, John of, surgeon, 88–9, 92–7
Aristotle, 82
Armagnac-Burgundian civil war, 265–78
armies, 8, 190, 222, 243–5
Arras, treaty of (1435), 268
art and artists, 152–77
Arthur, King, 130, 137–8, 147, 229
Artois, Robert of, 257
Arundel, earls of, 7, 13, 113, 242
    Thomas, archbishop of Canterbury, 118, 122, 144–5, 242
astrology, 82, 85
Athée, Gerard d', 231
Augustine, St, 1, 111, 145
Avignon papacy, 2, 3
Aylesham (Norfolk), 62

Baker, Geoffrey le, chronicler, 93
Ball, John, 233
Balliol, Edward, 254–5, 259–60
Balliol, John, king of Scotland (1292–96), 253
Bannockburn, battle of (1314), 8, 10, 183, 253
Barnack (Northamptonshire), 56
Barnet, battle of (1471), 16, 216

barons, 6
'Bastard Feudalism', *see* feudalism
Bayeux, Odo bishop of, 155–6
    Tapestry, 155–6
Bayle, George, 96
Beaufort, Lady Margaret, 112
Becket, St Thomas, 152, 158, 183
Bedford, John duke of, 267–8
Bek, Anthony, bishop of Durham, 198
Bekynton, Thomas, 114–15
Berking, Simon de, goldsmith, 172
Bernetby, John, painter, 168
Berwick-upon-Tweed, 253–4
Bigod, Roger, earl of Norfolk, 243
Blackburn, Adam of, and his wife Alesia, 78
    Henry, 90
Black Death, 2, 4–5, 12, 16, 27, 31, 39, 43, 45, 49, 52, 86, 97–9, 104, 161–2
Blois, Henry of, bishop of Winchester, 157
bloodletting, 89
Bodiam castle (Sussex), 36
Bokenham, Osbern, 147
Boniface VIII, pope, 3, 183
Book of the Duchess, 140
Bordeaux, 268
Bosco, John de, 93
Bosworth, battle of (1485), 7, 16
Botiller, Sir John and Lady, 113–14
Bowet, Henry, archbishop of York, 118
Bracton, Henry de, 186
Bradgate park (Leicestershire), 28
Bradmore, John, surgeon, 92, 97
Braham, Andrew of, and Alice his wife, 58
Brandon (Suffolk), 26
Braose, Richard and Alice de, and their daughter Mary, 78
brasses, memorial, 117–18, 162
Brassington (Derbyshire), 27
Bray, John, physician, 92
Bréaute, Fawkes de, 239
Brétigny, treaty of (1360), 11, 259–60, 264, 270
bridges, 35
Bridlington, John of, 122
Brok, Richard de, and his daughter Agnes, 68

Bruce, Robert, king of Scotland (1306–29), 10, 60, 248, 253–5, 265, 270
Brut, of Layamon, 129–30
Brutus, 130
Buckingham, duke of, 187, 233
Buntingford (Hertfordshire), 49
Burgundy, Charles duke of, 268
    John duke of, 97, 265–7
    Philip duke of, 15, 263, 267–8
Burley, Sir Simon, 234
Burnell, Robert, 193–4
Bury St Edmunds (Suffolk), 32, 36

Cade, Jack, his revolt (1450), 15, 232–3, 236, 238, 243, 246
Cadwallader, 130
Calais, 11, 184, 248, 259, 268
Cambridge, university of, 91
Campsey Ash (Suffolk), 77
Canterbury, cathedral, 31, 152, 157–8
    Gervase of, chronicler, 158
    Michael of, mason, 162, 168
Canterbury Tales, 140–4
Capgrave, John, 146–7
Cassy, Sir John, 212–13
Castile, disputed succession in, 260, 263
Castle Combe (Wiltshire), 49, 52
castles, 6, 36–7, 121, 251–2
Catesby, William, 215–16
Caus (Shropshire), 32, 50
chamber, royal, 195–6
chancery, royal, 190–4, 212
Charles IV, king of France (1322–28), 257–8
Charles V, king of France (1364–80), 11, 263–4
Charles VI, king of France (1380–1422), 15, 163, 245, 264–7
Charles VII, king of France (1422–61), 15, 267–8
Charles VIII, king of France (1483–98), 268–9
Chaucer, Geoffrey, 14, 86–7, 96, 122, 128–9, 138–45, 150–1
Chauliac, Guy de, surgeon, 97

Cheapside (London), 33
Cheyne, Roger, esquire, 117–18
Chichele, Henry, archbishop of
    Canterbury, 114–15
children, inheritance by, 66–75, 77–80
    legitimacy of, 68–74, 78, 80
    provision for, 73–4
civil war, causes of, 229–47
    effects of, 245–6
Clarence, George duke of, 15, 86
    Lionel duke of, 89, 232, 260–3
Clement V, pope, 3
Clement VI, pope, 97
Clerk, Roger, of Wandelsworth, 89
climate, 22
Clopton (Suffolk), 78
cloth, production and export of, 51–2
Cloud of Unknowing, 132–3
Clynn, John, 4
coal, 53–4
coinage, 48–9
Colchester (Essex), 49, 51
Collyweston (Northamptonshire), 56
Columbus, Christopher, 16
commercialisation, 47
'community of the realm', 244–7
Commynes, Philippe de, 229
Constantinople, 1, 2
Corfe (Dorset), 56
Corneybury (Hertfordshire), 49
Cornwall, Richard earl of, 237
Coronation Chair (Westminster abbey),
    161, 253–4
Coterel gang, 222, 224
council and counsellors, royal, 196–8, 227,
    233
court and household, royal, 187–90
Courtrai, battle of (1302), 256
courts of law, 206–24
Coventry (Warwickshire), 51
Craven (Yorkshire), 54
Crecy, battle of (1346), 11, 259
crime, criminal law, 206–24
crofts, 25
Cromwell, Ralph Lord, 195
Crophill, John, 96
Cropley park (Suffolk), 29

David, prince of Wales, 251
David II, king of Scotland (1329–71), 11,
    254–5, 257, 259–60, 264
Dean, forest of, 51, 54
death, memorials of, 111–19
Decorated style, of art, 161–2
de la Mare, Peter, 11, 202

Despenser, Hugh the elder and younger,
    11, 237, 241
    Thomas, earl of Gloucester, 234
de Vere, Robert, earl of Oxford, 7, 262
devotional literature, 132–4, 145–8
Dialogue of the Exchequer, 194
diet, 84–91, 98
disease, 99, and see Black Death
Domesday Book (1086), 22, 42, 47
drama, medieval, 147
dream-poetry, 134–7
dress, 87
Dunsthorpe (Lincolnshire), 39
Dunwich (Suffolk), 22
Durham, cathedral, 6, 207–8
    city, 32, 51

East Anglian style, of art, 161–2
East Witton (Yorkshire), 23
economic resources, 41–57
Edmund, earl of Lancaster, 9
Edward, St ('the Confessor', king of
    England 1042–66), 7, 154, 163
Edward I (1272–1307), 2, 3, 6–7, 8, 10, 90,
    92, 96, 161–2, 183, 186, 198, 200–1,
    208, 234, 242–3, 251–2, 269–70
    descendants of, 61
    Margaret of France, wife of, 86, 189
Edward II (1307–27), 7, 8, 10–11, 13, 86,
    181, 183, 185–7, 195, 232, 234, 237,
    241, 244–5, 251–4, 257
    descendants of, 61
    Isabella of France, wife of, 11, 187–8,
    239, 246, 257
Edward III (1327–77), 6, 7, 8, 11–12, 28,
    82, 90, 92, 99, 164, 182–7, 190, 198,
    234, 242, 245, 254–63, 267, 270
    Isabella, his daughter, 174
    Philippa of Hainault, wife of, 176
Edward IV (1461–83), 6, 15–16, 87, 99,
    109, 185, 187, 198, 205, 209, 232, 241
    Elizabeth, wife of, see Woodville
Edward V (1483), 7, 16, 183, 185, 189, 242
Edward, the Black Prince, 11–12, 259–60,
    263
Edward, prince of Wales, 15
Eleanor Crosses, 162, 187
Ellis, Conan fitz, heirs of, 59
Ely (Cambridgeshire), 37, 47
    cathedral, 125
embroidery, 155, 164–5
employment, 46, 50–1, 57
enfeoffment-to-use ('use'), 66–7, 78–9, 81,
    212
entail, 77–8, 81

Epping (Essex), 28
Ermine Street, 34
estate administration, 37–8, 46
Etaples, treaty of (1492), 268
Everingham, Adam, of Laxton, 93
Evesham, battle of (1265), 10, 245
exchequer, royal, 194–5, 201
eyres, 214–16

fairs, 47, 50
    St Ives fair, 49
family, ideas of, 58–60, 80–1, 118–19
Fastolf, Sir John, 111
Fauconberg, Thomas, 246
Feldon area (Warwickshire), 24, 26
Ferrers, Robert, earl of Derby, 239–41
    William de, 241
festivals, 108–9
feudalism, feudal lordship, 2, 3, 17, 32, 42,
    57, 79–80, 208
    'Bastard Feudalism', 4, 217–22
field-systems, 25–7
fishing, 52–3
Flammanck, Ralph, 234
Flanders, 256–7
Fleta, 200
Flynt, Matthew, 'toothdrawer', 96
Folville gang, 222, 224
forests, royal, 28–30
Fortescue, Sir John, 184, 186, 205, 209
Forz, William de, 239
Fountains (Yorkshire), abbey, 6, 38
    Fell, 30
Fowler, Richard, 116
France, English lands in, 9
    war with, 8, 11–14, 248–70
frankpledge, 207
Froissart, Jean, 86, 89
funerals, 113–16

Gaddesden, John of, physician, 92
Galenism, 82–3
Gascony, see Aquitaine
gavelkind, 75
Gaveston, Piers, 7, 10, 237
Gawain-poet, 129, 137–8, 145
gentry, 6
Gildeslowe, Thomas, 246
Glendower, Owen, 14, 254–5, 270
Gloucester, dukes of, 13, 99, 263, 268
    Candlestick, 152
goldsmiths, 165–6, 176
Gower, John, 12, 14, 126, 129, 150
Grandisson, John, bishop of Exeter,
    168–72

'Great Cause', 253
Great Schism (1378–1417), 2, 3
Great Yarmouth (Suffolk), 53
Grey, Reginald de, 89
     Reynold de, 94
Grosseteste, Robert, bishop of Lincoln, 236
Grover, family, 118–19
guilds, of artists and craftsmen, 167–8
Guthlac roll, 157

Hache, Roger atte, and Johanna his wife, 89
hagiography, 131–2, 146–7
Halidon Hill, battle of (1333), 254–5
Harcourt, Sir Robert, 219–21
Hartington (Derbyshire), 53
health, attitudes to, 82–3
heathland, 29–30
Hedon, Robert of, 65
Heith, John del, and Katherine his wife, 68
Hengham, Ralph, chief justice, 73, 215
Henry I (1100–35), 87
Henry II (1154–89), 9, 213, 216, 249–50
Henry III (1216–72), 7, 9–10, 78, 90, 181, 184, 230, 236–7, 242, 249–50
     Eleanor of Provence, wife of, 92, 187
Henry IV (1399–1413), 7, 13–14, 94, 183–7, 242, 245, 264–5
     Joan of Navarre, wife of, 153, 187, 189
Henry V (1413–22), 6, 8, 14–15, 92, 129, 139, 145, 183–4, 187, 190, 245, 265–7, 269–70
     Katherine de Valois, wife of, 187, 189, 267
Henry VI (1422–61), 7, 8, 15, 92, 97, 122, 183, 185–7, 198, 203–5, 209–10, 229, 231, 236, 241, 244, 267–70
     Margaret of Anjou, wife of, 15, 187–9, 219, 245
Henry VII (1485–1509), 6, 16, 183, 185, 187, 198, 209, 211, 242, 268–9
Henry VIII (1509–47), 2, 3, 13, 16, 184
Herstmonceaux castle (Sussex), 36
Hertford, 33
Highworth (Wiltshire), 47
Hilton, Walter, 147–8
Hoccleve, Thomas, 129, 139, 145, 150
Hockwold (Norfolk), 25, 45
Holbein, Hans, 164
Holland, Henry, duke of Exeter, 241
Hopton, John, 119, 224
House of Fame, 139–40
houses, 24–5, 33, 47
How Moor (Cambridgeshire), 31

Hugo, Master, artist, 167
Hundred Years War, 2, 8, 11–16, 205, 257–70
Hungerford, Walter Lord, 195
hunting, 28–9
Huntingdon, David earl of, his descendants, 60

industrial production, 50–2
inheritance, law and customs of, 63, 66–79
     of the throne, 183–5, 241–2
Innocent III, pope, 3
inns of court, 214–15
Ireland, English lands in, 184, 250–1, 260–3, 269–70
     duke of, 7
iron, 54
Isleham (Cambridgeshire), 36
Italian Renaissance, 1–2

Jacobus the Englishman, *see* Palmer
James I, king of Scotland (1406–37), 265
Jervaulx abbey (Yorkshire), 23
Jews, 107
Joan of Arc, 15, 267–8
John, king of England (1199–1216), 3, 7, 8–10, 83, 184, 200, 231, 239, 245, 263, 269
John II, king of France (1350–64), 11, 259–60
John of Gaunt, duke of Lancaster, 12, 89, 92, 94–5, 112, 234, 260, 263–4
     his wife Blanche, 148
justice, royal, 7, 206–24
justices of the peace, 208, 216–17

Kempe, Margery, 122, 150
Kenilworth, castle (Warwickshire), 36, 92
     Dictum of, 235
Kennett Heath (Cambridgeshire), 30
Kentford (Suffolk), 35
Kersey (Suffolk), 51
Kilkenny, 4
     statute of (1366), 263
kingship, in England, 6–8, 181–8, 204–5, 208–9, 234–9
Kingston-upon-Hull (Yorkshire), 32
kinship, 58–60
'knightly class', 6
Kymer, Gilbert, physician, 99

Labourers, Statute of (1351), 42, 221
Lacock cup, 164
Lacy, Edmund, bishop of Exeter, 122
Lancaster, Henry earl of, 239

Thomas earl of, 10–11, 187, 219, 234, 240–1
landholding, patterns of, 41
landscape, English, 21–40
Lanfranc, archbishop of Canterbury, 155
Langland, William, 83, 87, 134–6, 145, 215
Langley, Edmund of, 260
Langley, Thomas, bishop of Durham, 118
Langton, Walter, 195
languages, in medieval England, 14, 127–9
Lavenham (Suffolk), 49, 52
Laxton (Nottinghamshire), 25
lead, 55
Leech, John, physician, 93
legal profession, 212–15
legal system, 47–8, 206–24
Legendys of Hooly Wummen, 147, 149
Lidgate (Suffolk), 32
life expectancy, 5
Lincoln, cathedral, 6
Lisle, Brian de, 241
literature, medieval English, 127–51
Little Missenden (Buckinghamshire), 120
livery and maintenance, 206, 219–24
Llywelyn ap Gruffydd, prince of Wales, 184, 251–2
Lollardy, 12–13, 112, 117–18, 122–5, 145–6, 150, 234
London, population of, 32, 48, 246
     medical practice in, 92
     St Paul's cathedral, 162
Lorenzetti, Ambrogio, 170
Louis, Prince (Louis VIII of France, 1223–6), 9, 184–5, 231, 248–9
Louis IX, king of France (1226–70), 250–1
Love, Nicholas, 145–6
Lusignan, Guy and Geoffrey de, 231, 237
Luther, Martin, 2, 16, 104
Luttrell, Sir Geoffrey, 162
     Psalter, 160–2
Lydgate, John, 129, 142
Lyme Regis (Dorset), 49

Magna Carta (1215), 2, 9, 63, 186, 230, 235–6, 246
Maine, 9, 267–8
Malmesbury, William of, 154
Malory, Sir Thomas, 229
Mannings Heath (Sussex), 55
manuscript illustration, 155–6, 158–62
Margaret of Flanders, 260, 263
Margaret, 'Maid of Norway', queen of Scotland (1286–90), 253
markets, 47–50

Marlow (Buckinghamshire), St Peter's church, 121
marriage law and custom, 58–68, 79–80
Marshfield (Gloucestershire), 32
marshland, 31
Mary Tudor, queen of England (1553–58), 186
Massey, Sir Geoffrey, 111
meadowland, 30–1
medicine, practice of, 83–4, 87–99
Melchbourne (Bedfordshire), 23
merchants, 48
Merton, council of (1236), 69
Mevagissey (Cornwall), 53
middle ages, definition of, 1–3
Middleham jewel, 153–4
Middleton, Sir Gilbert, 222
Middleton (Suffolk), 78
Milemete, Walter de, 82–5
Mirfield, John of, 90, 93
Mirror of the Blessed Life of Jesus Christ, 145–6, 148
'Mirrors for Princes', 186
monasteries, 5, 37–8
    dissolution of, 16–17, 152
Mondeville, Henri de, surgeon, 93
Monmouth, Geoffrey of, 129
Montereau, 267
Montfort, Simon de, 10, 232, 236, 241, 246–7
Montpellier, Richard of, 96
moorland, 29–30
More, Thomas, 222
Mortimer family, 15
    Edmund, 14, 244
    Roger, 11, 202, 232, 239, 241
Moulton (Suffolk), 35
Mowbray, Ann, 115
Multon, Thomas, 99

nation-states, development of, 2–4, 57
Navestok, Edmund of, 68
Neville, Ann, 115
Neville's Cross, battle of (1346), 11, 259–60
New Radnor (Herefordshire), 32
Newton (Dorset), 32
Nigarellis, David de, 92
nobility, artistic patronage of, 154
    diet of, 86
    dress of, 87
    political behaviour of, 186–7, 209, 217–24, 239–42, 246–7
    religious practices of, 121–2
Norfolk, duke of, 222

Norman Conquest, 9, 21, 127–9, 248–9
Normandy, 9
    conquest of (1417–19), 14–15, 267
    loss of (1204), 2; (1449–50), 15, 268
Norwich, Julian of, 133–4

Oldcastle, Sir John, 234
Ordinances, of 1311, 230, 243
Orford (Suffolk), 32
    castle, 36
Orleans, Louis duke of, 265
    siege of (1429), 15, 267–8
Oxford, Provisions of (1258), 10, 197, 200, 230
    university of, 91–2

painting, mural, 153
Palmer, James ('Jacobus the Englishman'), 96
Palmieri, Matteo, 2
papacy, 2–3, 9
Paper Constitution (1244), 230
Paris, 15, 268–9
    Matthew, 157–8, 167
    treaty of (1259), 9, 250–1
parish churches, 24, 38–9, 116–21
parish priests, 119–20
parks, 28
parliament, English, 4, 6, 10, 198–204
    of 1258, 10
    of 1362, 14, 129
    of 1376, 11, 202, 244
    of 1385, 231
    of 1388, 13
Paston, family, 115, 224
    John, 114, 222
pasture, 45–6
patronage, artistic, 13–14, 152–4, 162, 166–76
    royal, 7, 237
Pearl, 136–7, 151
'peasants revolt' (1381), 12, 192, 217, 232–3, 243, 246, 263
Peatling Magna (Leicestershire), 232
Pecock, Reginald, 150
Pendock (Worcestershire), 24
Pepysian Sketchbook, 172–5
Percy, family, 187, 217, 241, 244
Perkins, William, 234
Perpendicular style, 38, 117, 162–6, 176
Perrers, Alice, 262
Petrarch, 2
Philip II 'Augustus', king of France (1180–1223), 9, 249–50

Philip IV, king of France (1285–1314), 3, 255–8
Philip VI, king of France (1328–50), 257–8
Piers Plowman, 83, 87, 134–6
pigs, 44
pilgrimage routes, 35, 122
plague, *see* Black Death
Poitiers, battle of (1356), 11, 259
political institutions, 181–206
    local and central, 203–4, 206–7, 246–7
Polperro (Cornwall), 53
Pontefract (Yorkshire), 13
population, level of, 4–5, 31–2, 39, 42–4
post-modernism, 104
Prick of Conscience, 151
Princes in the Tower, 16, 185
property, law and customs of, 65–81, 224
Puckeridge (Hertfordshire), 32
purgatory, 111
purveyance, 243

Quartermain, Richard, 117–18
Queenborough (Kent), castle, 7
Queen Mary Psalter, 161
queens of England, 187–8

rabbits, 30
Radford, Henry, 222
Radwell, Robert of, and Beatrice his widow, 73
Ramsey, William de, architect, 176
Ramsey Abbey censer, 165–6
Ravenserodd (Yorkshire), 22
Ravenspur (Humberside), 13, 16
rebellion, causes of, 229–47
Redcliffe (Bristol), 33
    St Mary's church, 39
Reformation, 2, 4, 103–4, 125–6
Regement of Princes, 145
relics, 121–2, 152
religious expression, 103–26
religious history, sources for, 110–11
religious orders, 5
Rellesford, Matthew, surgeon, 96
Remonstrances (1297), 230, 243
renaissance, twelfth-century, 156
retaining, 222–3
Revelations of Divine Love, 133–4
Rhuddlan, statute of (1284), 251–2
Richard I 'the Lionheart' (1189–99), 269
Richard II (1377–99), 7, 8, 12–14, 92–3, 118, 162–3, 182–6, 196, 231, 234, 237–8, 241, 244, 246, 262–5, 270

Anne of Bohemia, wife of, 113
Isabella of France, wife of, 264
Richard III (1483–5), 7, 16, 115, 185, 209, 219, 222, 242, 246
Rievaulx abbey (Yorkshire), 38
roads, 34–5
Robert II 'the Steward', king of Scotland (1371–90), 260, 264
Rolle, Richard, 150
Roman Empire, fall of, 2
romances, 130–2, 137–9, 147
Rome, 3
break with, 16
Romney Marsh (Kent), 31
Roper, John, tailor, 96
Rotheram, Thomas, archbishop of York, 194
Russell, John, 181
Rutherford, Matthew, 96

St Albans (Hertfordshire), 37
saints, 121–2, 146–9, and see hagiography
Salisbury, earl of, 267
sanctuary, 207–8
Scarborough (Yorkshire), 53
Scheere, Herman, artist, 164
Schorne, John, 122–5
Scotland, 269–70
war with, 8, 10–15, 247–58
sculpture, 164
Sculthorpe, Thomas of, and Agnes his widow, 70
seals, royal, 196–7
Sens, William of, 157–8
serfdom (villeinage), 17, 42, 47, 57, 63, 66–7, 73
sermons, 119
settlement, 22–7, 39
Shakespeare, William, 7
sheep, 30, 44
Shene, Thomas, 96
sheriffs, 207–9
Shrewsbury, battle of (1403), 92
Sicily, 9
Siena, Aldobrandino of, 90
Sir Gawain and the Green Knight, 137–8, 151
Sir Gowther, 131–2
Sir Orfeo, 130–1
Sizewell (Suffolk), 53
Skirlaw, Walter, bishop of Durham, 118
Sluys, battle of (1340), 11, 259
Somerset, duke of, 231
Southampton (Hampshire), 34
Spicer, John le, surgeon, 96
Sponne, William, 115

Stafford, family, 119
John, archbishop of Canterbury, 194
stained-glass, 175–6
standards of living, 22, 46–7, 49, 52, 57, 86–7
Stapledon, Walter, treasurer, 195
Star Chamber, 198, 212
stone quarrying, 55–6
Stonor family, 115
Stour valley (Essex), 44
Stoyle, family, 58
Stratford, John, archbishop of Canterbury, 183
Sudbury, Simon, archbishop of Canterbury, 194
Suffolk, duke of, 7, 234
Surrey, disafforestation of, 28
earl of, 7, 92
Sutton (Norfolk), 24

Tattershall castle, 217–18
taxation, 8, 10, 52, 200–1, 242–3
Taynton (Oxfordshire), 56
Tewkesbury, battle of (1471), 16
Thame (Oxfordshire), St Mary's church, 116
Thorpe, William, 122
tin, 54–5
Tintern abbey, 6
tofts, 24–5
tombs, 113–19
Touraine, 9
Tours, truce of (1444), 268
towns, 5, 31–4, 47–8, 90–1
Towton, battle of (1461), 15, 245
trade, 47–52, 57
transport, horse-drawn, 34, 44
water-borne, 35–6
Trevisa, John, 14, 229
Troilus and Criseyde, 140–1
Troponell, Thomas, 215
Troyes, treaty of (1420), 15, 266–7, 280
Tudor, dynasty, 2, 16–17
Owen, 189
Turks, Ottoman, 2
Tusser, Thomas, 21
Twynho, Ankarette, 222
Tyler, Wat, 12, 233
Tyngewick, Nicholas, physician, 93, 96

universities, 156
medicine at, 91–2
Upton, Stephen of, and Sybil his wife, 65
Urban VI, pope, 3
Usk, Adam, chronicler, 234

Valence, William and Aymer de, 231
Vesci, Eustace de, 232
villages, 22–4
villeinage, see serfdom
Visconti, Galeazzo, duke of Milan, 89

Wace, Robert, 129
Wakefield, battle of (1460), 15
Wales, conquest of, 10, 184, 250–1, 269–70
marches of, 246
prince of, 184
revolt in, 14, 254–5
Wallace, William, 253
Walsham-le-Willows (Suffolk), 24
Walworth, William, 12
Warbeck, Perkin, 231
wardrobe, royal, 195–6
wardship, 79–80
Warkworth castle, 217
Warrington (Lancashire), 113–14
Wars of the Roses, 2, 4, 7, 15–16, 268–9
Warwick, earls of, 13, 206–7, 226
Richard Neville ('the kingmaker'), 15–16, 187, 241
Wawe, William, 222
wealth, distribution of, 41, 56–7
weights and measures, 48
Westminster, 32
abbey, 9, 154–5, 158, 161
Edward of, and his mistress Katherine, 78
Painted Chamber at, 168, 193
palace of, 199
retable, 161
royal administration at, 190–6
St Stephen's chapel at, 162
statute of (1285), 77
Weyland, Thomas, chief justice, and his wife Margery, 66, 77–8
Whittington, Richard, 111
Whittlesford (Cambridgeshire), 24
William I 'the Conqueror' (1066–87), 14, 155, 249
William 'the Englishman', architect, 158
William the Lion, king of Scotland (1165–1214), 250
wills, 110–11
Wilton Diptych, 13–14, 162–3
Wimbish (Essex), 35
Winchelsea (Sussex), 22
Winchester (Hampshire), 33
'Winchester School' of art, 155–7
Windsor, castle, 11, 36
William de, 262

wine, import of, 86
Wisbech (Cambridgeshire), 31
Witney, Thomas of, architect, 176
women, status of, 58–63, 80–1, 107
woodland, 28–9, 54
Woodville, Elizabeth, wife of Edward IV,
    queen of England, 15, 109, 187, 197,
    207

wool, 44–5, 48, 51–2
Worcester, bishopric of, 46
Worsley, William, 167
Worstead (Norfolk), 51
Wyclif, John, 2, 12–13, 118, 234
Wykeham, William de, bishop of
    Winchester, 176
Wyncelowe, William, 92

Wynford, William, architect, 176

Yevele, Henry, artist, 167, 176
York,
    cathedral, 6
    Richard duke of, 15, 185, 231–2, 239,
        242, 244
    William of, surgeon, 93